# ARCHITECTURAL ACOUSTICS

# ARCHITECTURAL ACOUSTICS

**M. David Egan**

Consultant in Acoustics

Associate Professor, College of Architecture,
Clemson University

Lecturer (part-time), College of Architecture,
University of North Carolina at Charlotte

**McGraw-Hill, Inc.**
New York  St. Louis  San Francisco  Auckland  Bogotá
Caracas  Lisbon  London  Madrid  Mexico City  Milan
Montreal  New Delhi  San Juan  Singapore
Sydney  Tokyo  Toronto

**Notice**

Information contained in this work has been obtained by McGraw-Hill, Inc. from sources believed to be reliable. However, neither McGraw-Hill nor its authors guarantees the accuracy or completeness of any information published herein and neither McGraw-Hill nor its authors shall be responsible for any errors, omissions or damages arising out of use of this information. This work is published with the understanding that McGraw-Hill and its authors are supplying information but are not attempting to render engineering or other professional services. If such services are required, the assistance of an appropriate professional should be sought.

**Cover Photographs**

Front cover photo by Peter Vanderwarker shows interior of Boston Symphony Hall (McKim Mead & White, architects and Wallace C. Sabine, acoustical consultant). Back cover photo by Paul C. Beswick, AIA shows exterior of South Central Bell, Birmingham, Alabama (Giattina Fisher & Co., architects and M. David Egan, acoustical consultant). Inset photo on back cover by E. Alan McGee shows exterior of Georgia Power, Atlanta, Georgia (Heery Architects & Engineers, Inc. and M. David Egan, acoustical consultant).

1112131415 QWKQWK 0987654321

ISBN 0-07-019111-5

This book was set in Univers by Intergraphic Technology, Inc.
The editor was B. J. Clark;
the production supervisor was Denise L. Puryear;
the designer was Merrill Haber.
The art was drawn by Glen S. LeRoy, AIA, AICP.
Project supervision was done by The Total Book.

**Library of Congress Cataloging-in-Publication Data**

Egan, M. David
    Architectural acoustics.

    Includes index.
    1. Acoustical engineering.    2. Architectural
acoustics.    I. Title.
TA365.E33    1988        729'.29        87-14031
ISBN 0-07-019111-5

Jennie E. Brown
( 1887–1966 )

# About the Author

M. David Egan, P.E., is a consultant in acoustics and part-time professor at the College of Architecture, Clemson University. He has worked as a consultant in acoustics for Bolt Beranek and Newman (BBN) in Cambridge, Massachusetts, and has been principal consultant of his own firm in Anderson, South Carolina for over 15 years. His firm has consulted on over 400 building projects in the United States and abroad. A graduate of Lafayette College (B.S.) and the Massachusetts Institute of Technology (M.S.), where he studied acoustics under the late Professor Robert B. Newman, Professor Egan also has taught at Tulane University, Georgia Institute of Technology, University of North Carolina at Charlotte, and Washington University (St. Louis), and has lectured at numerous schools of design. He is the author of several books in the area of architectural technologies, including *Concepts in Architectural Acoustics* (McGraw-Hill, 1972), *Concepts in Thermal Comfort* (Prentice-Hall, 1975), *Concepts in Building Firesafety* (Wiley-Interscience, 1978 and Kajima Institute, Tokyo, 1981), and *Concepts in Architectural Lighting* (McGraw-Hill, 1983). In addition to consulting, teaching, and writing, Professor Egan is a fellow of the Acoustical Society of America (ASA), former director and two-term vice president of the National Council of Acoustical Consultants (NCAC), associate editor for NOISE/NEWS published by the Institute of Noise Control Engineering (INCE), and national awards coordinator for The Robert Bradford Newman Student Award Fund, Lincoln Center, Massachusetts.

# Contents

# Foreword

The need for practical working knowledge in the environmental sciences for those in the building professions will continue for the foreseeable future. Acoustics, like lighting and the thermal environment, is an environmental science that has become a recognized and respected discipline within the past half century. The fruits of these expanding bodies of scientific knowledge, i.e., practical engineering applications, are increasingly being taken seriously on a widespread basis by architects, engineers, and planners in the solutions of acoustical problems in and around buildings.

Although there are a few exceptions, adequate courses in acoustics have been notably lacking in schools of architecture and engineering. A number of us, including Professor M. David Egan, were fortunate in learning about acoustics at the Massachusetts Institute of Technology through the pioneering and inspirational teaching of the late Professor Robert B. Newman and his colleagues, Professors Leo Beranek and Richard Bolt. Some of their former students, like M. David Egan, have gone on to spread the word not only through design applications of their knowledge but also through lecturing and teaching efforts.

With his earlier book *Concepts in Architectural Acoustics* (McGraw-Hill, 1972), Professor Egan identified the pressing need for a textbook which would cut through to the core of the information needed to understand acoustics problems and to develop practical solutions. The book could hardly be called a textbook in the traditional sense, since the verbal descriptions were few and the major emphasis was on graphic displays of concepts as well as engineering data and problem-solving techniques. This unique approach, as he has found with his students at the Clemson University College of Architecture and elsewhere, appealed to most students of architecture and engineering (of all ages) who need comprehensive yet encapsulated treatments of the environmental sciences. *Concepts in Architectural Acoustics* became a widely used text not only in architectural schools but in the offices of practicing professionals as well. Indeed, many acoustical consultants recommend the book to clients when the need for a little more understanding of technical details exists.

In this new text, *Architectural Acoustics,* Professor Egan has retained all the desirable features of its predecessor and has updated the material with the experience gained this past decade, as well as added several new useful features such as checklists on design and problem areas in building acoustics. The clarity of the illustrations and format of tables of engineering data greatly enhance the usefulness of the book for reference. Like its predecessor, *Architectural Acoustics* emphasizes concepts and aids the designer/decisionmaker in judging the relative importance of acoustical considerations in the context of the overall building environmental system.

This book is an important contribution to the better understanding of building acoustics problems in a growing multidisciplinary design environment.

William J. Cavanaugh
*Fellow, Acoustical Society of America*
*Natick, Massachusetts*

# Preface

The goal of this book is to present in a highly illustrated format the principles of design for good hearing and freedom from noise in and around buildings. The over 540 illustrations are not merely supplements to the text as with nearly all traditional books. In this book, the illustrations are the core of the coverage of basic principles of sound and hearing, sound absorption and noise reduction, sound isolation and criteria for noise, control of HVAC systems noise and vibrations, auditorium acoustics design, and electronic sound systems.

The book is written for architects, interior designers, engineers, and all others concerned with the design and construction of buildings who need to know the basics of architectural acoustics, but who do not have the time needed to digest wordy presentations. The book is a successor to *Concepts in Architectural Acoustics* (McGraw-Hill, 1972) with the overwhelming majority of the illustrations, case histories, and example problem solutions either entirely new or substantially revised.

The late Professor Robert B. Newman was the author's mentor and teacher in graduate school. His course on architectural acoustics was the inspiration to become an acoustical consultant. The message of that course, offered by Professor Newman for nearly four decades at the MIT School of Architecture and Planning and at the Harvard University Graduate School of Design, was that designers who understand the basic principles of acoustics possess an important new tool for shaping the built environment. The intentions of this book, therefore, are similar. That is, to diffuse knowledge of acoustics and to promote its creative applications in design. Hopefully, not only better acoustical environments, but also better buildings should result.

The book also contains numerous checklists of design aids, data tables of sound absorption and sound isolation properties for a wide variety of modern building materials, case study examples, and step-by-step practical problem solutions. Extensive references are provided so that the interested reader can dig deeper. The appendix includes a metric system conversion table for common building acoustics terms and a summary of useful formulas.

M. David Egan, P.E., FASA
Anderson, South Carolina

# Acknowledgements

Thanks are due to many people who helped me during the preparation of this book.

Jeannie Egan edited the manuscript and text for the illustrations and reviewed the numerous drafts and proofs.

Gratitude is extended to Glen S. LeRoy, School of Architecture and Urban Design, University of Kansas, who prepared all the illustrations. Glen LeRoy's steadfast dedication to effective and innovative graphic communication techniques is deeply appreciated. Glen also prepared the illustrations for the author's books *Concepts in Thermal Comfort, Concepts in Building Firesafety,* and *Concepts in Architectural Lighting.*

It would be nearly impossible to name all the people who have influenced me in the fields of architecture and acoustical design, and thereby contributed to the preparation of this book, without inadvertently overlooking someone. Nevertheless, thanks are due to the following persons who provided reviews of portions of chapters in their area of special professional interest: James J. Abernethy, Eric Neil Angevine, Elliott H. Berger, John S. Bradley, Daniel R. Flynn, Ernest E. Jacks, John W. Kopec, Jerry G. Lilly, L. Gerald Marshall, James B. Moreland, Bynum Petty, Gregory C. Tocci, Keith W. Walker, Brian L. Williams, and Randolph E. Wright.

Special recognition should be given to the following colleagues who kindly provided in-depth reviews of one or more chapters. Their comments, criticisms, and suggestions were invaluable and are gratefully acknowledged.

Oliver L. Angevine, P.E., FASA
*Angevine Acoustical Consultants, Inc.*
*West Falls, New York*

Robert E. Apfel, Ph.D., FASA
*Department of Mechanical Engineering*
*Yale University*

Leo L. Beranek, Sc.D., FASA
*Founding Partner*
*Bolt Beranek and Newman Inc.*
*Winchester, Massachusetts*

Bruce Bassler, AIA
*Department of Architecture*
*Iowa State University*

Virginia Cartwright
*Department of Architecture*
*University of Oregon*

William J. Cavanaugh, FASA
*Cavanaugh Tocci Associates, Inc.*
*Sudbury, Massachusetts*

Parker W. Hirtle, FASA
*Bolt Beranek and Newman Inc.*
*Cambridge, Massachusetts*

Robert M. Hoover, FASA
*Hoover Keith & Bruce, Inc.*
*Houston, Texas*

J. Christopher Jaffe, D. Eng.
   (Hon.), FASA, FIOA
*Jaffe Acoustics, Inc.*
*Norwalk, Connecticut*

David H. Kaye
*Consultant in Acoustics*
*Boston, Massachusetts*

Bertram Y. Kinzey, Jr., AIA, FASA
*College of Architecture*
*University of Florida*

David L. Klepper, FASA, FAES
*Klepper Marshall King Associates,*
   *Ltd.*
*White Plains, New York*

Peter R. Lee, AIA
*College of Architecture*
*Clemson University*

Ronald Moulder
*Battelle Memorial Institute*
*Columbus, Ohio*

Chris Paulhus, P.E.
*Paulhus Consulting*
*Harvard, Massachusetts*

Richard J. Peppin, P.E.
*Norwegian Electronics*
*Rockville, Maryland*

Jack B. C. Purcell, FASA
*Purcell + Noppe + Associates, Inc.*
*Chatsworth, California*

J. David Quirt, Ph.D.
*National Research Council of Canada*
*Ottawa, Ontario, Canada*

H. Stanley Roller
*U.S. Gypsum Company*
*Chicago, Illinois*

Larry H. Royster, Ph.D., FASA
*Department of Mechanical*
   *Engineering*
*North Carolina State University*

Charles M. Salter, P.E.
*Charles M. Salter Associates, Inc.*
*San Francisco, California*

Theodore J. Schultz, Ph.D., FASA
*Theodore J. Schultz Associates*
*Boston, Massachusetts*

Ludwig W. Sepmeyer, P.E., FASA
*Consulting Engineer*
*Los Angeles, California*

Ted Uzzle, FAES
*Altec Lansing Corporation*
*Oklahoma City, Oklahoma*

David P. Walsh
*Wilson, Ihrig & Associates, Inc.*
*Oakland, California*

Ewart A. Wetherill, AIA, FASA
*Wilson, Ihrig & Associates, Inc.*
*Oakland, California*

# Introduction

Almost all acoustical situations can be described by three parts: source, path, and receiver. Sometimes the *source* (human speech, HVAC equipment) can be made louder or quieter. For example, strategic placement of reflecting surfaces near the speaker in lecture rooms, churches, and auditoriums can reinforce and evenly distribute sound to all listeners. The *path* (air, earth, building materials) can be made to transmit more or less sound. When required, double-wall and other complex constructions can be designed to interrupt the sound path, thereby providing satisfactory sound isolation and privacy. The *receiver* (usually humans, although sometimes animals or sensitive medical equipment) also can be affected. Usually building occupants will hear better, or be more comfortable, if distracting HVAC system noise can be controlled or if intruding environmental noise can be isolated or removed. In most situations, it is best to focus on all three parts. For example, concentrating only on the direct path for sound travel through common walls may at best result in costly overdesign or at worst, no solution at all!

Acoustical requirements always should be considered during the earliest stages of design. Even though corrections can be accomplished during the mid- and latter stages of design, it usually is very difficult to change shapes, room heights, and adjacencies within buildings when spatial relationships and budgets have been fixed. Similarly, deficiencies in completed spaces are often extremely difficult and costly to correct. For example, the addition of an electronic, sound-reinforcing system to an auditorium which is excessively reverberant may exaggerate deficiencies rather than improve listening conditions. This kind of acoustical surprise should not occur if designers understand the basic principles of acoustics. Successful designers provide the spatial relationships, cubic volumes, shapes, and the like so their buildings maintain design quality while best serving their intended purposes, whether it be for work, play, or rest.

Designers should not rely on oversimplified articles in trade magazines, misleading advertisements and incomplete technical data from manufacturers, or highly specialized texts written in technical jargon. The goal of this book, therefore, is to provide a comprehensive framework for the study of acoustics as well as a long-term resource for designers. The designer should be able to anticipate the acoustical problems inherent to most buildings, solve those of a routine nature, and determine when professional assistance is required. A reference source for information on qualified acoustical consultants is the biennial *Directory* of the National Council of Acoustical Consultants (NCAC). The Acoustical Society of America (ASA) also maintains a listing of persons and firms offering acoustical consulting services.

The designer who understands the essential elements of architectural acoustics will be able to best collaborate with acoustical consultants by asking the right questions, identifying alternative solutions, and implementing successful designs. The illustration below identifies essential elements of architectural acoustics and the corresponding chapters in the book.

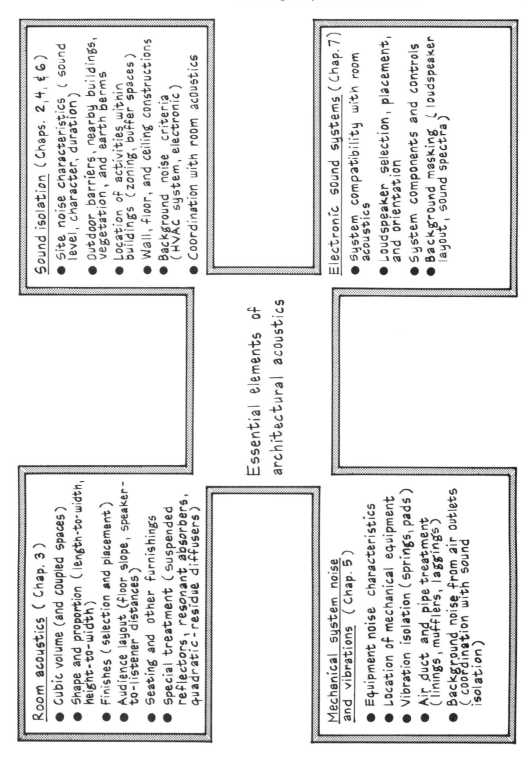

Essential elements of architectural acoustics

Sound isolation (Chaps. 2, 4, & 6)
- Site noise characteristics (sound level, character, duration)
- Outdoor barriers, nearby buildings, vegetation, and earth berms
- Location of activities within buildings (zoning, buffer spaces)
- Wall, floor, and ceiling constructions
- Background noise criteria (HVAC system, electronic)
- Coordination with room acoustics

Electronic sound systems (Chap. 7)
- System compatibility with room acoustics
- Loudspeaker selection, placement, and orientation
- System components and controls
- Background masking (loudspeaker layout, sound spectra)

Room acoustics (Chap. 3)
- Cubic volume (and coupled spaces)
- Shape and proportion (length-to-width, height-to-width)
- Finishes (selection and placement)
- Audience layout (floor slope, speaker-to-listener distances)
- Seating and other furnishings
- Special treatment (suspended reflectors, resonant absorbers, quadratic-residue diffusers)

Mechanical system noise and vibrations (Chap. 5)
- Equipment noise characteristics
- Location of mechanical equipment
- Vibration isolation (springs, pads)
- Air duct and pipe treatment (linings, mufflers, laggings)
- Background noise from air outlets (coordination with sound isolation)

# Chapter 1
# Basic Theory

# SOUND AND VIBRATION

*Sound* is a vibration in an elastic medium such as air, water, most building materials, and the earth.* An elastic medium returns to its normal state after a force is removed. *Pressure* is a force per unit area. Sound energy progresses rapidly, producing extremely small changes in atmospheric pressure, and can travel great distances. However, each vibrating particle moves only an infinitesimal amount to either side of its normal position. It "bumps" adjacent particles and imparts most of its motion and energy to them. A full circuit by a displaced particle is called a *cycle* (see illustration below). The time required for one complete cycle is called the *period* and the number of complete cycles per second is the *frequency* of vibration. Consequently, the reciprocal of frequency is the period. Frequency is measured in cycles per second, the unit for which is called the hertz (abbreviated Hz).

## Vibration of Particle in Air

The back and forth motion of a complete cycle is shown below.

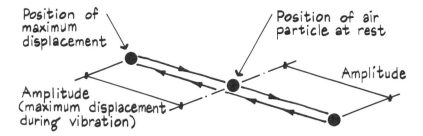

## Pure Tones

A *pure tone* is vibration produced at a single frequency. Shown below is the variation in pressure caused by striking a tuning fork, which produces an almost pure tone by vibrating adjacent air molecules. Symphonic music consists of numerous tones at different frequencies and pressures (e.g., a tone is composed of a fundamental frequency with multiples of the fundamental, called *harmonics*). To find the period corresponding to a frequency of vibration, use the following formula:

$$T_p = \frac{1}{f}$$

where   $T_p$ = period (s/cycle)
   $f$ = frequency (cycles/s or Hz)

---

*Noise is unwanted sound (e.g., annoying sound made by other people or very loud sound which may cause hearing loss).

For example, a frequency of 63 Hz has a period $T_p$ of $1/63 \simeq 0.02$ s/cycle (roughly 30 times longer than the period at 2000 Hz).

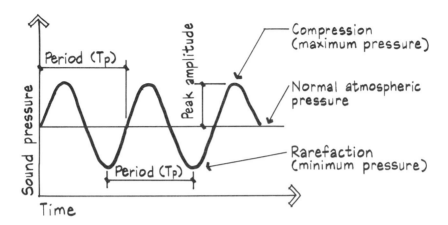

## Complex Sounds

The variation in pressure caused by speech, music, or noise is shown below. Most sounds in the everyday world are complex, consisting of a variety of pressures which vary with time. The threshold of hearing for humans is one-millionth of normal atmospheric pressure.

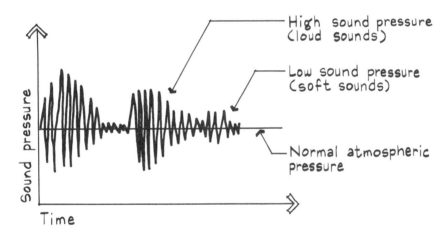

*Frequency* is the rate of repetition of a periodic event. Sound in air consists of a series of compressions and rarefactions due to air particles set into motion by a vibrating source. The frequency of a sound wave is determined by the number of times per second a given molecule of air vibrates about its neutral position. The greater the number of complete vibrations (called *cycles*), the higher the frequency. The unit of frequency is the hertz (Hz). *Pitch* is the subjective response of human hearing to frequency. Low frequencies generally are considered "boomy," and high frequencies "screechy" or "hissy."

Most sound sources, except for pure tones, contain energy over a wide range of frequencies. For measurement, analysis, and specification of sound, the frequency range is divided into sections (called *bands*). One common standard division is into 10 octave bands identified by their center frequencies: 31.5, 63, 125, 250, 500, 1000, 2000, 4000, 8000, and 16,000 Hz. An octave band in sound analysis, like an octave on the piano keyboard shown below, represents a frequency ratio of 2:1. Octave-band ranges of three other musical instruments are also shown below.

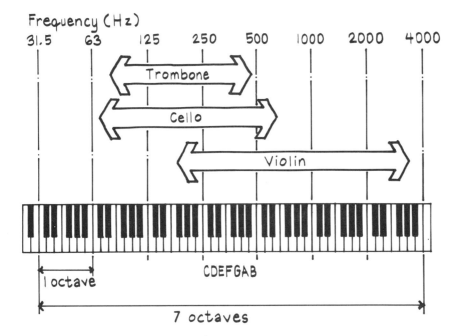

Further divisions of the frequency range (e.g., one-third or one-tenth octave bands) can be used for more detailed acoustical analyses. Sound level meters can measure energy within octave bands by using electronic filters to eliminate the energy in the frequency regions outside the band of interest. The sound level covering the entire frequency range of octave bands is referred to as the *overall* level.

## WAVELENGTH

As sound passes through air, the to-and-fro motion of the particles alternately pushes together and draws apart adjacent air particles, forming regions of rarefaction and compression. *Wavelength* is the distance a sound wave travels during one cycle of vibration. It also is the distance between adjacent regions where identical conditions of particle displacement occur, as shown below by the wire spring (called a "slinky" toy). When shaken at one end, the wave moves along the slinky, but the particles only move back and forth about their normal positions.

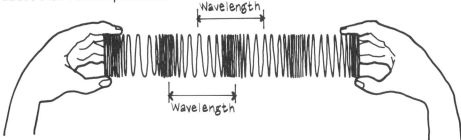

Sound waves in air also are analogous to the ripples (or waves) caused by a stone dropped into still water. The concentric ripples vividly show patterns of molecules transferring energy to adjacent molecules along the surface of the water. In air, however, sound spreads in all directions.

To find the wavelength of sound in air at a specific frequency, use the following formula:

$$\lambda = \frac{1130}{f}$$

where    $\lambda$ = wavelength (ft)
          $f$ = frequency (Hz)

Shown below is the wavelength in air from the to-and-fro motion of a vibrating tuning fork. The movement of the prongs alternately compresses and rarefies adjacent air particles. This cyclical motion causes a chain reaction between adjacent air particles so that the waves (but *not* the air particles) propagate away from the tuning fork. Remember sound travels, but the elastic medium only vibrates.

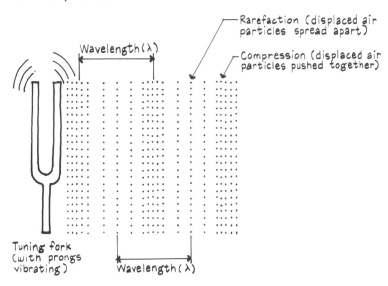

## SOUND SPECTRUM

Because most sounds are complex, fluctuating in pressure, level, and frequency content, the relationships between sound pressure level and frequency are required for meaningful analysis (data so plotted are called a *sound spectrum*). This requirement is similar to indoor climate control, where thermal comfort cannot be specified as a 70°F temperature alone because comfort also depends on relative humidity, air motion, and so on. Sound spectra are used to describe the magnitude of sound energy at many frequencies. The frequency scale given below is an *octave-band scale* because the ratio of successive frequencies is 2:1, the ratio for an octave in music. In acoustics, the extent or width of octave bands is geometric. For example, the octave band for a center frequency of 125 Hz contains sound energy from $125 \div \sqrt{2}$ Hz to $125 \times \sqrt{2}$ Hz.

The line graph at the right depicts the octave-band spectrum for a noise consisting of the sound energy measured within octave bands (see bar graph at left). The line graph is plotted at the respective center frequencies of the bands. Also shown on the graph is the sound level of a 512-Hz tuning fork. Note that the tuning fork produces sound energy at a single frequency only. A tuning fork will vibrate at the same frequency if struck lightly or forcefully, but the sound levels produced can differ greatly.

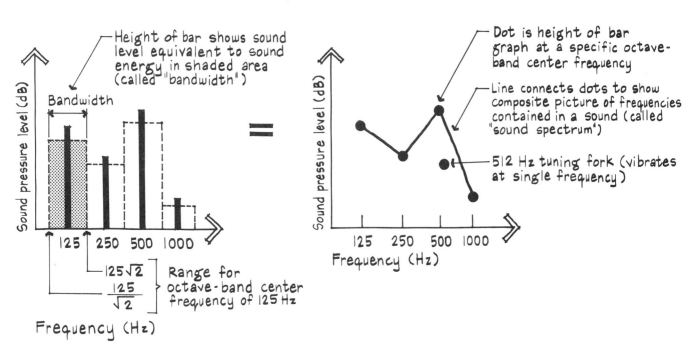

If a pianist uses both forearms to simultaneously strike as many piano keys as possible, the resulting noise will be *broadband* because the sound produced will be spread throughout a wide range of frequencies. A graph of this noise, therefore, would plot as a wide, flat spectrum.

## VELOCITY OF SOUND

Sound travels at a *velocity* that depends primarily on the elasticity and density of the medium. In air, at normal temperature and atmospheric pressure, the velocity of sound is approximately 1130 feet per second (ft/s), or almost 800 mi/h. This is extremely slow when compared to the velocity of light, which is about 186,000 mi/s, but much faster than even hurricane winds.

In building air distribution systems, the air velocity at registers, diffusers, and in ducts is so much slower than the velocity of sound that its effect can be neglected. For example, an extremely high air velocity of 2000 ft/min (about 33 ft/s) in a duct is less than 3 percent of the velocity of sound in air. Consequently, airborne sound travels with equal ease upstream and downstream within most air ducts!

However, sound may travel at a very fast 16,000 ft/s along steel pipes and duct walls as shown below. It is therefore important to block or isolate paths where sound energy can travel through building materials (called *structure-borne* sound) to sensitive areas great distances away where it may be regenerated as airborne sound.

In buildings, the effect of temperature on sound also is negligible. For example, a 20°F rise or drop in room air temperature is significant, but would cause only a 2 percent change in the velocity of sound in air.

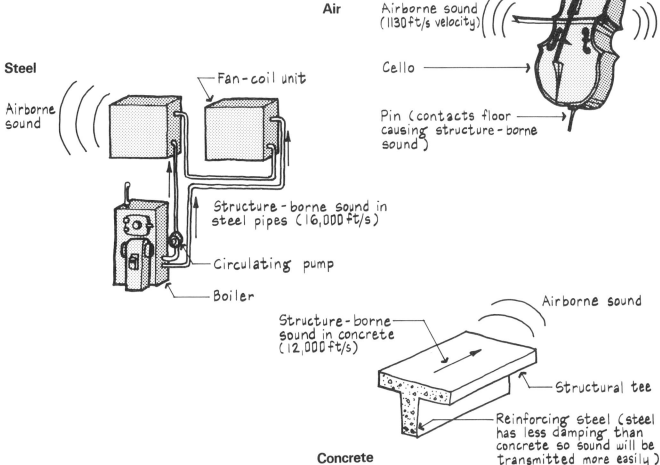

# FREQUENCY RANGES OF AUDIBLE SOUNDS

Hearing ranges for both young and older persons (> 20 years old) are shown below. A healthy young person is capable of hearing sound energy from about 20 to 20,000 Hz. Hearing sensitivity, especially the upper frequency limit, diminishes with increasing age even without adverse effects from diseases and noise—a condition called *presbycusis*. Long-term and repeated exposure to intense sounds and noises of everyday living can cause permanent hearing damage (called *sociocusis*), and short-term exposure can cause temporary loss. Consequently, the extent of the hearing sensitivity for an individual depends on many factors, including age, sex, ethnicity, previous exposure to high noise levels from the workplace, gunfire, power tools, rock music, etc. All other hearing losses (e.g., caused by mumps, drugs, accidents) are called *nosocusis*. An audiologist should be consulted if a ''ringing'' sensation occurs in ears after exposure to moderately loud noise or if sounds seem muffled or dull.

Also shown below are frequency ranges for human speech (divided into *consonants*, which contain most of the information for articulation, and *vowels*), piano music, stereo sounds, and acoustical laboratory tests (e.g., tests used to determine absorption and isolation properties of building materials). Human speech contains energy from about 125 to 8000 Hz. Women's vocal cords are generally thinner and shorter than men's, so the wavelengths produced are smaller. This is the reason the female frequency of vibration for speech is normally higher. Wavelengths in SI and English units are indicated by the scales at the top of the graph above the corresponding frequency.

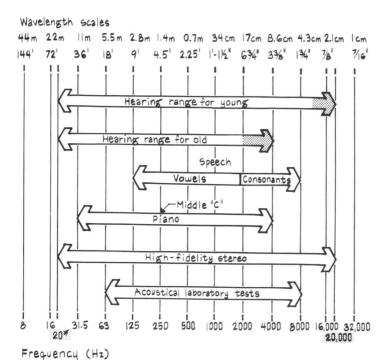

Frequency (Hz)

*Vibrations below 20 Hz are *not* audible, but can be felt.

## Reference

E. H. Berger et al. (eds.), *Noise and Hearing Conservation Manual*, American Industrial Hygiene Association, Akron, Ohio, 1986.

## SENSITIVITY OF HEARING

The graph below shows the tremendous range of sound levels in decibels (abbreviated dB)* and frequency in hertz over which healthy young persons can hear. Also shown on the graph is the frequency range for "conversational" speech, which occurs in the region where the ear is most sensitive. For comparison, the region where symphonic music occurs is indicated on the graph by the large shaded area extending at mid-frequencies from below 25 dB to over 100 dB (called *dynamic range*). The dynamic range for individual instruments can vary from 30 dB (woodwinds) to 50 dB (strings). The lowest level of musical sound energy that can be detected by the audience largely depends on the background noise in the music hall (see Chap. 4), and the upper level depends on the acoustical characteristics of the hall (see Chap. 3). Electronically amplified rock music in arenas and coliseums far exceeds the maximum sound levels for a large symphonic orchestra. Rock music, purposefully amplified to be at the threshold of feeling ("tingling" in the ear), is considered to be a significant cause of sociocusis.

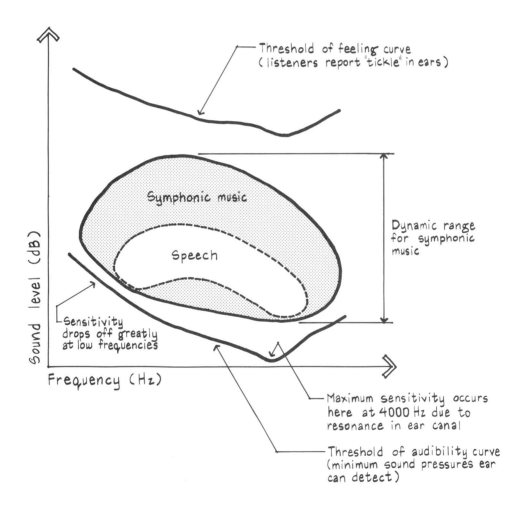

*Decibel* is the unit used to express the pressure (or intensity) level of sound energy. In this book, *sound level* is always measured in decibels by precision sound level meters at a specific frequency or weighting.

Sound waves from a point source outdoors with no obstructions (called *free-field* conditions) are virtually spherical and expand outward from the source as shown below. A point source has physical dimensions of size that are far less than the distance an observer is away from the source.

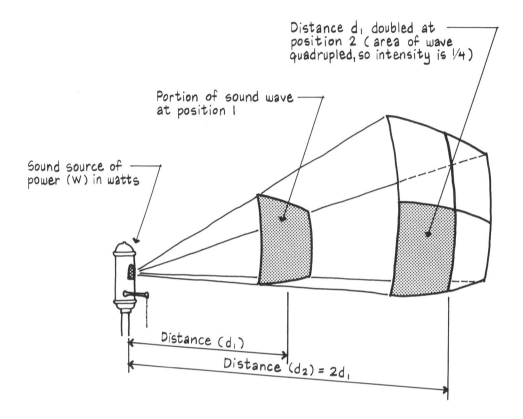

*Power* is a basic quantity of energy flow. Although both acoustical and electric energies are measured in watts, they are different forms of energy and cause different responses. For instance, 10 watts (abbreviated W) of electric energy at an incandesent lamp produces a very dim light, whereas 10 W of acoustical energy at a loudspeaker can produce an extremely loud sound. Peak power for musical instruments can range from 0.05 W for a clarinet to 25 W for a bass drum.

The intensity from a point source outdoors at a distance $d$ away is the sound power of the source divided by the total spherical area $4\pi d^2$ of the sound wave at the distance of interest. This relationship can be expressed as:

$$I = \frac{W}{4\pi d^2}$$

where      $I$ = sound intensity $(W/m^2)$
         $W$ = sound power (W)
         $d$ = distance from sound source (m)

If the distance is measured in feet, multiply the result by 10.76, because 1 m² equals 10.76 ft².

The *inverse-square law* for sound is:

$$\frac{I_1}{I_2} = \left(\frac{d_2}{d_1}\right)^2$$

where    $I$ = sound intensity $(W/m^2)$
$d$ = distance from sound source (ft or m)

**Note:**  To derive the inverse-square law, consider a wavefront at positions 1 and 2 as shown on the above illustration. At position 1, $W = I_1 4\pi d_1^2$, and at position 2, $W = I_2 4\pi d_2^2$. Since the energies are the same (because the source is the same), $I_1 4\pi d_1^2 = I_2 4\pi d_2^2$. Therefore, $I_1/I_2 = d_2^2/d_1^2$, which is the inverse-square law for sound.

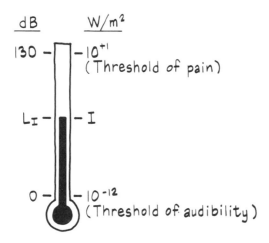

Ernst Weber and Gustav Fechner (nineteenth-century German scientists) discovered that nearly all human sensations are proportional to the logarithm of the intensity of the stimulus. In acoustics, the *bel* unit (named in honor of Alexander Graham Bell) was first used to relate the *intensity* of sound to an *intensity level* corresponding to the human hearing sensation. Sound intensity level in bels equals the logarithm of the intensity ratio $I/I_0$, where $I_0$ is the minimum sound intensity audible to the average human ear at 1000 Hz. *Decibels* (prefix deci- indicates that logarithm is to be multiplied by 10) can be found by the following formula:

$$L_I = 10 \log \frac{I}{I_0}$$

where  $L_I$ = sound intensity level (dB)
  $I$ = sound intensity (W/m²)
  $I_0$ = reference sound intensity, $10^{-12}$ (W/m²)

The illustration on the following page gives the decibel level of some familiar sounds. The human hearing range from the threshold of audibility at 0 dB to the threshold of pain at 130 dB represents a tremendous intensity ratio of 10 trillion (10,000,000,000,000) to 1. This is such a wide range of hearing sensitivity that it may be hard to imagine at first. For example, if a bathroom scale had a sensitivity range comparable to that of the human ear, it would have to be sensitive enough to weigh both a human hair and a 30-story building! Logarithms allow the huge range of human hearing sensitivity to be conveniently represented by smaller numbers.

It is difficult to measure sound intensity directly. However, sound intensity is proportional to the square of sound pressure, which can more easily be measured by sound level meters. In air under normal atmospheric conditions, sound intensity level and sound pressure level are nearly identical.

## COMMON SOUNDS IN DECIBELS

Some common, easily recognized sounds are listed below in order of increasing sound levels in decibels. The sound levels shown for occupied rooms are only example activity levels and do *not* represent criteria for design. Note also that thresholds vary among individuals.

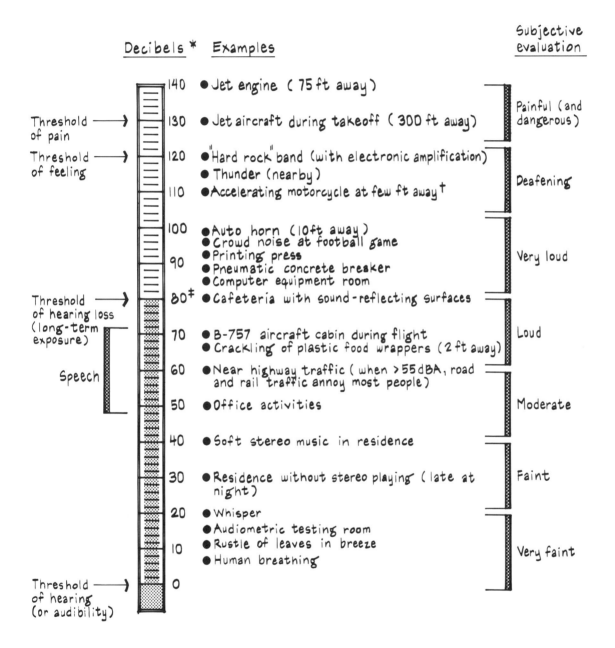

*dBA are weighted values measured by a sound level meter. See page 31 for details of electronic weighting networks which modify the sensitivity of meters.

†50 ft from a motorcycle can equal the noise level at less than 2000 ft from a jet aircraft.

‡Continuous exposure to sound energy above 80 dBA can be hazardous to health and can cause hearing loss for some persons.

## NOISE REDUCTION WITH DISTANCE

Outdoors in the open and away from obstructions, sound energy from *point sources* drops off by 6 dB for each doubling of the distance from the source. (According to the inverse-square law, the intensity ratio for a doubling of distance is $2^2 = 4$, and the corresponding decibel reduction is 10 log 4, or 6 dB.) Sound energy from *line sources* (e.g., stream of automobiles or railroad cars) drops off by 3 dB for each doubling of distance. This is because line sources consist of successive point sources which reinforce each other. Thus the spread of sound energy is cylindrical, *not* spherical. Cylindrical surface areas increase in proportion to the radius (distance), whereas spherical surface areas increase in proportion to the square of the radius. The graph below shows noise reduction due to distance for point and line sources. Additional reductions can be caused by large buildings, earth berms, trees and vegetation, and other environmental effects (see Chap. 4).

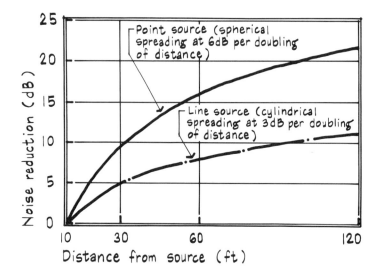

An *area source*, produced by several adjacent line sources (e.g., rows of cheering spectators at sports events) or large radiating surfaces of mechanical equipment, has little reduction of sound energy with distance close to the source. Within distances of $b/\pi$ to $c/\pi$, where $b$ is the short and $c$ the long dimension of an area source, sound energy drops off by 3 dB for each doubling of distance. Beyond distances of $c/\pi$, the drop-off will be 6 dB for each doubling of distance outdoors (cf., E. J. Rathe, "Note on Two Common Problems of Sound Propagation," *Journal of Sound and Vibration*, November 1969, pp. 472-479).

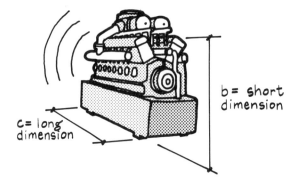

### Logarithm Basics

The first step to find the *logarithm* of a number is to express it as a digit from 1 to 9 multiplied by 10 to a power. A logarithm usually consists of two parts—the *characteristic*, which is the power of 10, and the *mantissa*, which is the decimal found in log tables (or from pocket calculators). In solving logarithms, remember that

$$10^5 = 100,000$$
$$10^4 = 10,000$$
$$10^3 = 1000$$
$$10^2 = 100$$
$$10^1 = 10$$
$$10^0 \equiv 1 \ (\equiv \text{means } equal\ to \text{ by definition})$$
$$10^{-1} = 0.1$$
$$10^{-2} = 0.01$$
$$10^{-3} = 0.001$$

and when the decimal point is shifted to the left by $n$ places, the number is to be multiplied by $10^n$; when the decimal is shifted to the right by $n$ places, the number is to be divided by $10^n$. This may seem complicated at first, but after reviewing a few examples it should become routine.

$$4,820,000.0 = 4.82 \times 10^6 \simeq \boxed{5 \times 10^6} \ (\simeq \text{means } approximately\ equal\ to)$$

Numbers ending in 0.5 and greater should be rounded up as shown by the example above. If less than 0.5, the decimal should be dropped.

$$0.0000258 = 2.58 \times 10^{-5} \simeq \boxed{3 \times 10^{-5}}$$

$$8,400,000,000.0 = 8.4 \times 10^9 \simeq \boxed{8 \times 10^9}$$

The following shortened logarithm table can be used to quickly find the mantissa of numbers from 1 to 9.

### A USEFUL LOG TABLE

| Number | Mantissa |
| --- | --- |
| 1 | 0 |
| 2 | 0.3 |
| 3 | 0.48 |
| 4 | 0.6 |
| 5 | 0.7 |
| 6 | 0.78 |
| 7 | 0.85 |
| 8 | 0.9 |
| 9 | 0.95 |

In almost all acoustical problems, it is not necessary to work with small fractions of decibels. Use either the log table above, or a four-place log table, and round the final answer to the nearest decibel. A pocket calculator that finds an entire logarithm in one step is very handy when working with decibels.

The following examples represent logs of very large and very small numbers. Remember, the first step is to arrange the number as a digit times 10 to a power.

$$\log (4{,}820{,}000.0) = \log (5 \times 10^6) = 6.7 = \boxed{6.7}$$

enter number
column to find

$$\log (0.0000258) = \log (3 \times 10^{-5}) = -\log \left(\frac{1}{3} \times 10^5\right)$$

$$= -\log (0.33 \times 10^5) = -\log (3 \times 10^4) = \boxed{-4.48}$$

$$\log (8{,}400{,}000{,}000.0) = \log (8 \times 10^9) = \boxed{9.9}$$

## Antilogarithms

The *antilogarithm* of a quantity, such as antilog $(x)$, is the number for which the quantity $x$ is the logarithm. For example,

$$\text{antilog } (6.7) = 5 \times 10^6 = \boxed{5 \times 10^6}$$

enter mantissa
column to find

$$\text{antilog } (-4.48) = -3 \times 10^4 = \frac{1}{3} \times 10^{-4} = 0.33 \times 10^{-4} = \boxed{3 \times 10^{-5}}$$

When the mantissa of a log falls between values in the log table on page 15, use the closest mantissa to find the corresponding number from 1 to 9.

## Properties of Logs

1. $\log xy = \log x + \log y$
2. $\log \frac{x}{y} = \log x - \log y$
3. $\log x^n = n \log x$
4. $\log 1 = 0$*

*This property is important in acoustical analysis because openings in building elements have no resistance to sound flow which then can be expressed as 0 dB of isolation.

**Powers of 10 Review**

Remember, the symbol $10^3$ is a shorthand notation for $10 \times 10 \times 10 = 1000$. Also, the product of two powers of the same number has an exponent equal to the sum of the exponents of the two powers:

$$10^2 \times 10^3 = (10 \times 10) \times (10 \times 10 \times 10) = \boxed{10^5}$$

or

$$10^2 \times 10^3 = 10^{(2+3)} = \boxed{10^5}$$

Additional examples follow:

$$10^7 \times 10^5 = 10^{(7+5)} = \boxed{10^{12}}$$

$$\frac{10^{-9}}{10^{-12}} = 10^{-9} \times 10^{+12} = 10^{(-9+12)} = \boxed{10^3}$$

When combining exponents, be careful of the signs. Dividing by a negative exponent such as $10^{-12}$ is equivalent to multiplying by its reciprocal, $10^{+12}$.

$$\frac{10^{-3}}{10^{-12}} = 10^{-3} \times 10^{+12} = 10^{(-3+12)} = \boxed{10^9}$$

You have now learned to handle powers of 10 and logarithms, which are fundamental relationships needed to describe how humans perceive sound and how building materials affect sound energy. Several examples are presented below and on the following pages.

**Examples**

1. The intensity $I$ of a rock music group is $8.93 \times 10^{-2}$ W/m². Find the corresponding sound intensity level $L_I$.

$$L_I = 10 \log \frac{I}{10^{-12}}$$

$$= 10 \log \frac{8.93 \times 10^{-2}}{10^{-12}} = 10 \log (8.93 \times 10^{10})$$

$$L_I = 10 \,(10.9509) = \boxed{110 \text{ dB}}$$

2. Loud speech, measured at 3 ft away, has a sound intensity level $L_I$ of 73 dB. Find the corresponding intensity $I$.

$$L_I = 10 \log \frac{I}{10^{-12}}$$

$$73 = 10 \log \frac{I}{10^{-12}}$$

Next, divide both sides of the equation by 10.

$$7.3 = \log \frac{I}{10^{-12}}$$

The above expression states that the log of a ratio $(I/10^{-12})$ is equal to 7.3. When the number for which the log is 7.3 (i.e., antilog) is found, set it equal to the ratio.

$$\text{antilog } (7.3) = 1.995 \times 10^7$$

└─from mantissa table or pocket calculator─┘

Therefore,

$$1.995 \times 10^7 = \frac{I}{10^{-12}}$$

and by cross multiplication

$$I = 1.995 \times 10^7 \times 10^{-12} = \boxed{1.995 \times 10^{-5} \text{ W/m}^2}$$

## EXAMPLE PROBLEM (INVERSE-SQUARE LAW)

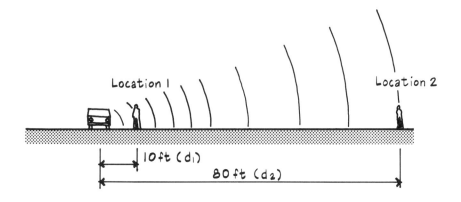

**1.** A car horn outdoors produces a sound intensity level $L_I$ of 90 dB at 10 ft away. To find the intensity $I_1$ at this first location, use

$$L_I = 10 \log \frac{I}{10^{-12}}$$

$$90 = 10 \log \frac{I_1}{10^{-12}}$$

$$9.0 = \log \frac{I_1}{10^{-12}}$$

$$\text{antilog } (9.0) = 1.0 \times 10^9$$

$$1.0 \times 10^9 = \frac{I_1}{10^{-12}}$$

$$I_1 = 1.0 \times 10^9 \times 10^{-12} = \boxed{10^{-3} \text{ W/m}^2} \text{ at 10 ft away}$$

**2.** If the sound intensity $I$ is known at a given distance in feet away from the source, sound power $W$ can be found by the following formula.

$$I = \frac{W}{4\pi d^2} \times 10.76$$

By cross multiplication

$$W = 4\pi d^2 \times \frac{1}{10.76} \times I$$

Since $I_1 = 10^{-3}$ W/m² at 10 ft away

$$W = 4 \times 3.14 \times 10^2 \times \frac{1}{10.76} \times 10^{-3} = \boxed{0.12 \text{ W}}$$

**3.** The intensity level $L_I$ at 80 ft away can be found by the inverse-square law. First, find the sound intensity $I_2$ at the location 80 ft away.

$$\frac{I_1}{I_2} = \left(\frac{d_2}{d_1}\right)^2$$

$$\frac{10^{-3}}{I_2} = \left(\frac{80}{10}\right)^2$$

$$\frac{10^{-3}}{I_2} = 64$$

$$64I_2 = 10^{-3}$$

$$I_2 = \frac{1}{64} \times 10^{-3} = \boxed{1.56 \times 10^{-5} \text{ W/m}^2} \text{ at 80 ft away}$$

Next, find $L_I$.

$$L_I = 10 \log \frac{I_2}{10^{-12}} = 10 \log \frac{1.56 \times 10^{-5}}{10^{-12}}$$

$$L_I = 10 \log (1.56 \times 10^7) = 10(7.1931) = \boxed{72 \text{ dB}} \text{ at 80 ft}$$

This means a listener moving from location 1 at 10 ft away to location 2 at 80 ft away would observe a change in intensity level of 18 dB (that is, 90 dB − 72 dB). This reduction would be judged by most listeners as "very much quieter" (see table on the following page). However, a car horn at 72 dB would still be considered "loud" by most people.

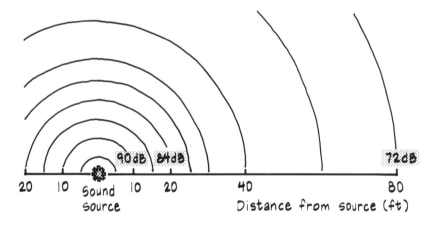

**Note:** From 10 to 80 ft away is three doublings of distance (i.e., 10 to 20 ft, 20 to 40 ft, and 40 to 80 ft). Therefore, three doublings × 6 dB/doubling = 18 dB reduction and $L_I$ = 90 − 18 = 72 dB at 80 ft away.

## CHANGES IN SOUND LEVEL

The table below is an approximation of human sensitivity to changes in sound level. Sound intensity is not perceived directly at the ear; rather it is transferred by the complex hearing mechanism to the brain where acoustical sensations can be interpreted as *loudness*. This makes hearing perception highly individualized. Sensitivity to noise also depends on frequency content, time of occurrence, duration of sound, and psychological factors such as emotion and expectations (cf., O. L. Angevine, "Individual Differences in the Annoyance of Noise," *Sound and Vibration*, November 1975). Nevertheless, the table is a reasonable guide to help explain increases or decreases in sound levels for many architectural acoustics situations.

| Change in Sound Level (dB) | Change in Apparent Loudness |
|:---:|:---|
| 1 | Imperceptible (except for *tones*) |
| 3 | Just barely perceptible |
| 6 | Clearly noticeable * |
| 10 | About twice (or half) as loud |
| 20 | About 4 times (or one-fourth) as loud |

* For example, distance to the point source outdoors is halved or doubled.

The change in intensity level (or *noise reduction*, abbreviated NR) can be found by:

$$NR = L_1 - L_2$$

and

$$NR = 10 \log \frac{I_1}{I_2}$$

where   NR = difference in sound levels between two conditions (dB)
   $I_1$ = sound intensity under one condition (W/m²)
   $I_2$ = sound intensity under another condition (W/m²)

**Note:** By substitution of the inverse-square law expression from page 11 into the above formula

$$NR = 10 \log \left(\frac{d_2}{d_1}\right)^2$$

and therefore, in terms of distance ratio $d_2/d_1$

$$NR = 20 \log \left(\frac{d_2}{d_1}\right)$$

for point sources outdoors, where $d$'s are the distances.

## EXAMPLE PROBLEM (MUSIC MAN)

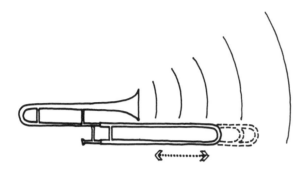

The measured sound intensity level $L_I$ of one trombone is 80 dB. To find the sound intensity level $L_I$ from 76 trombones, first find the intensity $I_1$ of one trombone.

$$L_I = 10 \log \frac{I_1}{I_0}$$

$$80 = 10 \log \frac{I_1}{10^{-12}}$$

$$8.0 = \log \frac{I_1}{10^{-12}}$$

$$1.0 \times 10^8 = \frac{I_1}{10^{-12}}$$

$$I_1 = 1.0 \times 10^8 \times 10^{-12}$$

$$I_1 = \boxed{10^{-4} \text{ W/m}^2} \text{ for one trombone}$$

To combine the intensities of 76 trombones, each producing 80 dB at a listener's position, find the intensity $I_2$ of 76 trombones. $I_2$ will be $76 \times I_1 = 76 \times 10^{-4}$ W/m².

$$L_I = 10 \log \frac{I_2}{I_0}$$

$$= 10 \log \frac{76 I_1}{10^{-12}} = 10 \log \frac{76 \times 10^{-4}}{10^{-12}}$$

$$= 10 \log (7.6 \times 10^9)$$

$$L_I = 10 (9.8808) = \boxed{99 \text{ dB}} \text{ for 76 trombones}$$

This is not as great an increase as might at first be expected. It would take 100,000 trombones to reach the threshold of pain at 130 dB (although the threshold of disgust might be reached at a much lower level). A composer is aware that a large number of instruments playing the same score may not produce a tremendous sound impression. Large numbers of instruments are used to achieve the desired *tonal texture* or blend in the overall sound from the individual instruments. For example, one solo violin by its location and frequency range may dominate portions of an orchestral performance.

# DECIBEL ADDITION

Because decibels are logarithmic values, they cannot be combined by normal algebraic addition. For example, when the decibel values of two sources differ by 0 to 1 dB, 3 dB should be added to the higher value to find the combined sound level. Therefore, the sound level of two violins, each playing at 60 dB, would be 60 + 3 = 63 dB, *not* 60 + 60 = 120 dB (which would be near the threshold of pain!). This is similar to lighting, where two 35-W fluorescent lamps are not twice as bright as one. The following table can be used to rapidly combine sound levels.

| When Two dB Values Differ by | Add the Following dB to the Higher Value |
|---|---|
| 0 or 1 | 3 |
| 2 or 3 | 2 |
| 4 to 8 | 1 |
| 9 or more | 0 |

When several decibel values are to be added, use the table to find the combined value by adding the decibels two at a time. For example, to find the combined sound level of 34 dB, 41 dB, 43 dB, and 58 dB, add as follows:

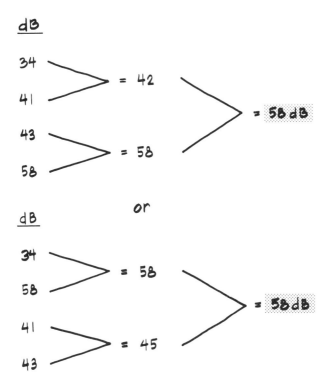

Notice that 43 + 58 = 58 dB and 34 + 58 = 58 dB because the higher sound level (by > 9 dB) swamps out the lower sound level.

To find the combined sound level of 82 dB, 101 dB, 106 dB, 102 dB, 90 dB, and 78 dB, add as follows:

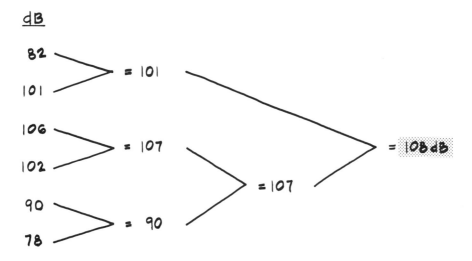

Using different orders of addition may give results that differ by 1 dB, which is normally not too significant. However, to achieve the greatest precision, combine decibels logarithmically. For example, using a pocket calculator, first compute $10^x$, where $x$ is the decibel value divided by 10, sum $10^x$ answers for all decibels to be combined, and then take 10 log of the sum. The simplified table method can be used to check your answer.

The table also can be used to subtract decibel values. For example, it is necessary to subtract decibel values to find the noise from a printer if the measured noise level in a computer room is 80 dB and the background noise level with the printer turned off is 73 dB. According to the table, because the two decibel values differ by 7, subtract 1 dB from the higher value. Therefore, the printer noise alone would be $80 - 1 = 79$ dB.

**Note:** If a number of equal decibel values are to be combined, add 10 log $n$ to the decibel value, where $n$ is the number of equal decibel values. For example, if $n = 76$ trombones at an $L_I$ of 80 dB each, then the total $L_I = 80 + 10$ log $76 = 80 + 10(1.8808) = 99$ dB for 76 trombones.

## HUMAN EAR

The sketch below is a general description of how the human ear functions. The ear can detect sounds over a wide range of loudness and frequency. In addition, it has the ability to detect individual sounds (e.g., familiar voice) from within a complex background of loud, unwanted sounds (in a noisy, crowded room, called *cocktail party effect*). However, perception of speech can be nearly impossible at noise levels above 80 dBA (cf., J. C. Webster, "Noise and Communication" in D. M. Jones and A. J. Chapman (eds.), *Noise and Society*, Wiley, New York, 1984).

Sound energy, which travels through the ear canal, first impinges on the *eardrum* membrane causing it to vibrate. Eardrum vibrations are then transmitted across the middle ear by the lever action of three small bones (called *hammer*, *anvil*, and *stirrup* due to their shapes). The motion of the eardrum over a large area is thereby converted into a more forceful motion over a smaller area of the stirrup which contacts the oval window of the snail-shaped *cochlea*. The middle ear cavity contains air at atmospheric pressure due to the eustachian tube which connects to the throat (this is why it helps to swallow

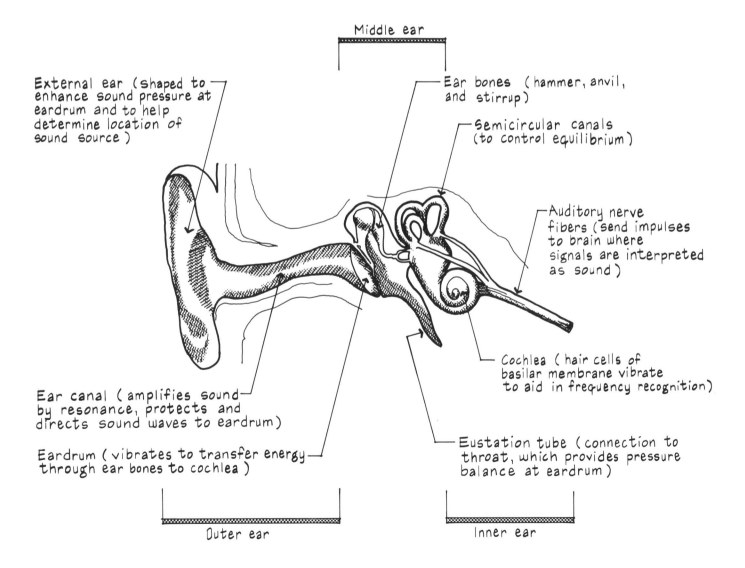

or yawn when experiencing sudden pressure changes such as rapid airplane descents). Vibrations of the stirrup are transmitted through fluid in the cochlea to hair cells where they are converted into electrical impulses. These impulses are transmitted by the auditory nerve fibers leading to the brain where they are interpreted as sound.

Long-term and repeated exposure to loud sounds can cause permanent damage to the inner ear (commonly called *nerve deafness*). When it is necessary to shout to be heard by normal-hearing persons less than 3 ft away, the noise may be hazardous to ears. In this situation, wear hearing-protection devices such as earplugs (which fit snugly into the ear canal), earmuffs (which fit over and around the ear), or both when noise levels exceed about 100 dBA.

**Reference**

L. L. Langley et al., *Dynamic Anatomy & Physiology*, McGraw-Hill, New York, 1974, pp. 330-345.

## NOISE EXPOSURE LIMITS

In 1971, the U.S. Department of Labor established the Occupational Safety and Health Administration (OSHA) and adopted regulations to protect against hearing loss caused by exposure to noise in the workplace. The permissible daily upper limit of noise exposure in A-weighted decibels (abbreviated dBA) for continuous noise is shown on the graph below for 1983 rules and regulations. Single-number decibels in dBA units are measured by sound level meters with internal electronic networks that tend to discriminate with frequency like the human ear does at low sound levels. Note that amplified rock music at 120 dBA and higher would exceed even the shortest permissible noise exposure. Exposure to *impulsive* noise such as gunfire or *impact* noise from heavy machinery should not exceed 140 dBA *peak* sound level.

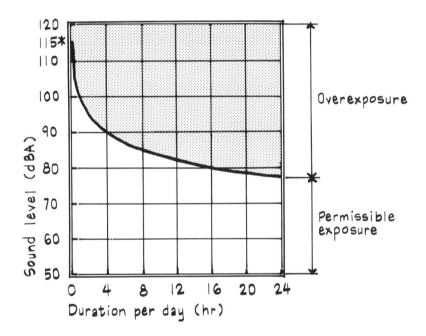

*Upper limit (*not* design value) for exposure to continuous noise in the workplace without hearing testing program or use of hearing-protection devices.

Although exposure limits are given in dBA, only octave-band (or narrower) analysis of noise will give a more complete picture of how severe the problems are at specific frequencies. This kind of detailed information (called *frequency analysis*) is also needed to determine the corrective measures because solutions for high-frequency noise problems may differ considerably from those for low-frequency. Corrective measures can involve reducing noise levels at the *source* (e.g., by redesign of noisy equipment or industrial processes), interrupting the *path* (see Chaps. 2 and 4 for principles of noise control by absorption and isolation), protecting the *receiver* (by using individual hearing-protection devices), or combinations of all these measures. An effective hearing conservation program normally consists of five phases: (1) education (to inform about harmful effects of noise), (2) sound surveys (to determine daily noise exposure of workers and identify the sources of noise), (3) engineering and administrative controls (to reduce noise levels and, if necessary, to reduce workers' exposure to noise), (4) use of hearing-protection devices, and (5) audiometric testing (to examine hearing at regular intervals). According to OSHA, hearing conservation measures are mandatory when workers are exposed to sound levels of 85 dBA or more for 8 h per day. For the basics of hearing conservation programs, see L. H. Royster, J. D. Royster, and E. H. Berger, "Guidelines for Developing an Effective Hearing Conservation Program," *Sound and Vibration*, May 1982, pp. 22-25.

## LOUDNESS PERCEPTION

The curves on the graph below (called *equal loudness contours*) show conditions of sound level and frequency which listeners perceive as being equally loud. Because variations occur from individual to individual, the curves represent averages for many test subjects. The number on the curves is the loudness level, called the *phon*. Therefore, sounds which produce an equal sensation of loudness will have the same phon value. Note that an increase in sound level at low frequencies is usually perceived as being much louder than an equivalent increase at high frequencies.

High-frequency sounds (> 2000 Hz) are generally more annoying than middle- or low-frequency sounds because human hearing is less sensitive to low-frequency sounds. However, any noise which is abrupt, intermittent, or fluctuates widely can be extremely annoying. It also is hard to disregard sound that contains information such as speech or music.

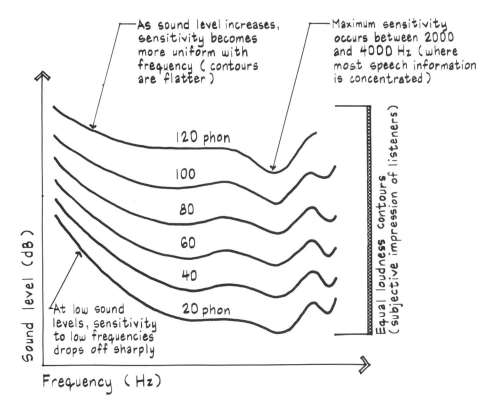

### References

D. W. Robinson and L. S. Whittle, "The Loudness of Octave-Bands of Noise," *Acustica*, vol. 14, 1964.

S. S. Stevens and H. Davis, *Hearing*, Wiley, New York, 1938.

Sound level meters contain microphones which transform sound pressure variations in air into corresponding electric signals. The signals are then amplified internally and measured by electronic filters, which reject all signals outside the selected frequency band, or by electronic weighting networks, with the results in decibels displayed on a digital readout or range indicator.

The weighting networks tend to represent the frequency characteristics of human hearing by modifying the sensitivity of the meter in patterns similar to specific equal loudness contours on page 29. The standard weighting networks are identified as A to E, and the resultant decibel values are abbreviated dBA, dBB, etc. The primary difference between the standard weightings is that the A weighting tends to considerably neglect low-frequency sound energy; the B weighting moderately; and the C weighting hardly at all. Some meters also have a flat response, which has no frequency discrimination. The single-number result for a flat response is called the *overall decibel level*.

For detailed analysis of sound energy, sound level meters with narrowband "frequency analysis" filters should be used (e.g., octave band for most sources, one-third octave band or narrower for more detailed analyses). Frequency analysis of sound (graphic plot of level vs. frequency) is extremely important because human response to sound and noise control by absorption (see Chap. 2) and isolation (see Chap. 4) are frequency dependent.

Although weighting networks do not provide direct information on the frequency content of measured sound energy, they can be used to determine if the sound energy is primarily above or below 1000 Hz. For example, if the dBC reading exceeds the dBA reading by 20 decibels or more, the measured sound energy is primarily low frequency. If the difference is 10 decibels or less, the measured sound energy is primarily mid- and high frequency.

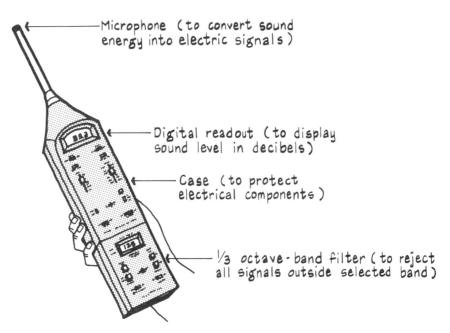

Microphone (to convert sound energy into electric signals)

Digital readout (to display sound level in decibels)

Case (to protect electrical components)

1/3 octave-band filter (to reject all signals outside selected band)

**Reference**

G. M. Hynes, "How To Select a Low-Priced Sound Level Meter," *Sound and Vibration*, May 1983.

## A-WEIGHTED SOUND LEVELS

*A-weighted* sound levels (in decibels, abbreviated dBA) largely ignore low-frequency sound energy just as our ears do. Nevertheless, single-number decibel values in dBA often cannot totally represent human perception of noise and the effects of noise on human comfort. For example, the graph of noise levels for a residential whirlpool tub shows two widely varying sound spectra which have identical single-number dBA values (curves 1 and 2 shown below). However, the noises represented by the spectra would be perceived by listeners as sounding vastly different: low-frequency noise caused by "gurgling" turbulence from water jets and "humming" pump noise (curve 1), and high-frequency noise caused by "splashing" impact from the water stream filling the tub (curve 2). Single-number sound levels, therefore, should be used with caution because human hearing perception does not respond to sound in a simple, decibel-averaged manner. In addition to sound level, an individual's sensitivity to sound varies with frequency content, duration, and psychological factors.

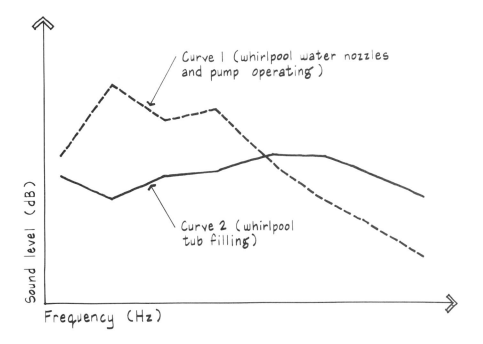

In spite of these limitations, the dBA can be used to predict community response to many kinds of environmental noise, including vehicular transportation noise. Therefore, noise ordinances and regulations use the dBA unit as a measure to specify limits on noise. Shown below is the frequency discrimination in dB for A weighting. Note that the curve connecting the plotted "weighting dBs" is similar to the shape of equal loudness contours at low sound levels.

| A Weighting (dB) | | | | | | | |
|---|---|---|---|---|---|---|---|
| 63 Hz | 125 Hz | 250 Hz | 500 Hz | 1000 Hz | 2000 Hz | 4000 Hz | 8000 Hz |
| −25 | −15 | −8 | −3 | 0 | +1 | +1 | −1 |

An example computation for sound level in dBA from sound levels in octave bands at 125 to 4000 Hz follows:

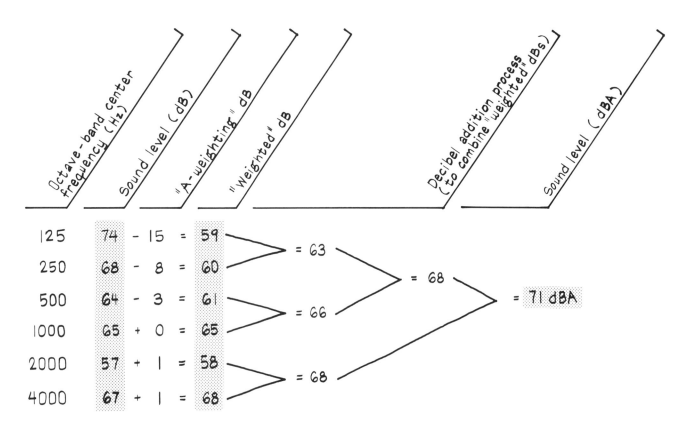

## SOUND SPECTRA FOR COMMON NOISES

The graph below shows sound spectra (plotted on a standard grid typically used by acoustical consultants) for three common household appliances. The vacuum cleaner noise is broadband because it consists of a complex mixture of sound generally spread throughout a wide range of the audible spectrum. The mixture may include "whining" noise from the suction air intake, "whistling" noise from the corrugated hose, and "screeching" impeller noise. The electric shaver and hair dryer are complex sounds which have identical single-number sound levels (in dBA). However, they would not sound the same to a listener because their sound energy and frequency characteristics differ widely. The shaver noise is "whining" and the hair dryer "hushing." Remember the *equal loudness contours* show that individuals are most sensitive to high-frequency sounds such as whining, hissing, or whistling noises.

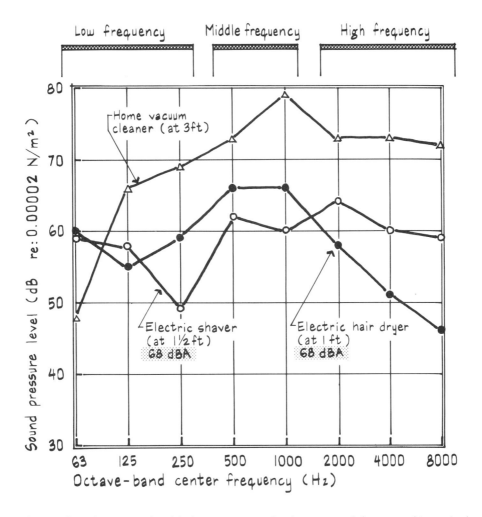

**Note:** Sound pressure level $L_p$ is more conveniently measured than sound intensity level $L_I$. For most architectural acoustics situations, they can be considered equivalent. The reference value for $L_p$ in this book is 0.00002 N/m² (newtons per square meter), the minimum sound pressure at 1000 Hz audible to young persons with normal hearing. Decibel values are meaningless without a reference value!

# NOISE LEVEL DATA

The table presents noise data at octave-band center frequencies for familiar residential, outdoor, transportation, and building activity noise sources. Intermittent or peak noises may exceed the data given in the table by 5 dB or

| Example Source | Sound Pressure Level (dB) | | | | | | | | dBA |
|---|---|---|---|---|---|---|---|---|---|
| | 63 Hz | 125 Hz | 250 Hz | 500 Hz | 1000 Hz | 2000 Hz | 4000 Hz | 8000 Hz | |
| **Home** | | | | | | | | | |
| Alarm clock at 4 to 9 ft (ringing) | .. | 46 | 48 | 55 | 62 | 62 | 70 | 80 | 80 |
| Electric shaver at 1 ½ ft | 59 | 58 | 49 | 62 | 60 | 64 | 60 | 59 | 68 |
| Vacuum cleaner at 3 ft | 48 | 66 | 69 | 73 | 79 | 73 | 73 | 72 | 81 |
| Garbage disposal at 2 ft | 64 | 83 | 69 | 56 | 55 | 50 | 50 | 49 | 69 |
| Clothes washer at 2 to 3 ft (wash cycle) | 59 | 65 | 59 | 59 | 58 | 54 | 50 | 46 | 62 |
| Toilet (refilling tank) | 50 | 55 | 53 | 54 | 57 | 56 | 57 | 52 | 63 |
| Whirlpool, six nozzles (filling tub) | 68 | 65 | 68 | 69 | 71 | 71 | 68 | 65 | 74 |
| Window air-conditioning unit | 64 | 64 | 65 | 56 | 53 | 48 | 44 | 37 | 59 |
| Telephone at 4 to 13 ft (ringing) | .. | 41 | 44 | 56 | 68 | 73 | 69 | 83 | 83 |
| TV at 10 ft | 49 | 62 | 64 | 67 | 70 | 68 | 63 | 39 | 74 |
| Stereo (teenager listening level) | 60 | 72 | 83 | 82 | 82 | 80 | 75 | 60 | 86 |
| Stereo (adult listening level) | 56 | 66 | 75 | 72 | 70 | 66 | 64 | 48 | 75 |
| Violin at 5 ft (fortissimo) | .. | .. | 91 | 91 | 87 | 83 | 79 | 66 | 92 |
| Normal conversational speech at 3 ft | .. | 57 | 62 | 63 | 57 | 48 | 40 | .. | 63 |
| **Outdoors** | | | | | | | | | |
| Birds at 10 ft | .. | .. | .. | .. | .. | 50 | 52 | 54 | 57 |
| Cicadas | .. | .. | .. | .. | 35 | 51 | 54 | 48 | 57 |
| Large dog at 50 ft (barking) | .. | 50 | 58 | 68 | 70 | 64 | 52 | 48 | 72 |
| Lawn mower at 5 ft | 85 | 87 | 86 | 84 | 81 | 74 | 70 | 72 | 86 |
| Pistol shot at 250 ft (peak impulse levels) | .. | .. | .. | 83 | 91 | 99 | 102 | 106 | 106 |
| Surf at 10 to 15 ft (moderate seas) | 71 | 72 | 70 | 71 | 67 | 64 | 58 | 54 | 78 |
| Wind in trees (10 mi/h) | .. | .. | .. | 33 | 35 | 37 | 37 | 35 | 43 |
| **Transportation** | | | | | | | | | |
| Large trucks at 50 ft (55 mi/h) | 83 | 85 | 83 | 85 | 81 | 76 | 72 | 65 | 86 |
| Passenger cars at 50 ft (55 mi/h) | 72 | 70 | 67 | 66 | 67 | 66 | 59 | 54 | 71 |
| Motorcycle at 50 ft (full throttle, without baffle) | 95 | 95 | 91 | 91 | 91 | 87 | 87 | 85 | 95 |
| Snowmobile at 50 ft | 65 | 82 | 84 | 75 | 78 | 77 | 79 | 69 | 85 |
| Train at 100 ft (pulling hard) | 95 | 102 | 94 | 90 | 86 | 87 | 83 | 79 | 94 |
| Train siren at 50 ft | 88 | 90 | 110 | 110 | 107 | 100 | 91 | 78 | 109 |
| Car horn at 15 ft | .. | .. | .. | 92 | 95 | 90 | 80 | 60 | 97 |
| Commercial turbofan airplane at 1 mile (from takeoff flight path) | 77 | 82 | 82 | 78 | 70 | 56 | .. | .. | 79 |
| Military helicopter at 500 ft (single engine, medium size) | 92 | 89 | 83 | 81 | 76 | 72 | 62 | 51 | 80 |
| **Interiors** | | | | | | | | | |
| Amplified rock music performance (large arena) | 116 | 117 | 119 | 116 | 118 | 115 | 109 | 102 | 121 |
| Audiovisual room | 85 | 89 | 92 | 90 | 89 | 87 | 85 | 80 | 94 |
| Auditorium (applause) | 60 | 68 | 75 | 79 | 85 | 84 | 75 | 65 | 88 |
| Classroom | 60 | 66 | 72 | 77 | 74 | 68 | 60 | 50 | 78 |
| Computer equipment room | 78 | 75 | 73 | 78 | 80 | 78 | 74 | 70 | 84 |
| Dog kennel | .. | .. | 90 | 104 | 106 | 101 | 89 | 79 | 108 |
| Gymnasium | 72 | 78 | 84 | 89 | 86 | 80 | 72 | 64 | 90 |
| Kitchen | 86 | 85 | 79 | 78 | 77 | 72 | 65 | 57 | 81 |
| Laboratory | 65 | 70 | 73 | 75 | 72 | 69 | 65 | 61 | 77 |
| Library | 60 | 63 | 66 | 67 | 64 | 58 | 50 | 40 | 68 |
| Mechanical equipment room | 87 | 86 | 85 | 84 | 83 | 82 | 80 | 78 | 88 |
| Music practice room | 90 | 94 | 96 | 96 | 96 | 91 | 91 | 90 | 100 |
| Racquetball court | 82 | 85 | 80 | 85 | 83 | 75 | 68 | 62 | 86 |
| Reception and lobby area | 60 | 66 | 72 | 77 | 74 | 68 | 60 | 50 | 78 |
| Teleconference | 65 | 74 | 78 | 80 | 79 | 75 | 68 | 60 | 83 |

more, depending on the source or environment. For many practical problems, however, the data can be considered to be typical source levels at the given distance and condition, or average general activity levels for interiors. The data can be used for design purposes if proper consideration is given to especially loud equipment or sources which may exceed it, unusual site conditions, and any other conditions that deviate from normal. For example, it is prudent to measure transportation noise at proposed building sites near highways, airports, etc., so design data will represent existing noise sources and reflect specific site features. Note also that many modern aircraft, trucks, and office equipment are not as loud as examples in the table.

**Note:** Sources for noise level data include *Journal of the Acoustical Society of America, Sound and Vibration, Noise Control Engineering Journal,* and technical publications of the U.S. Environmental Protection Agency and National Bureau of Standards (U.S.).

# DECIBEL SCALES FOR SOUND INTENSITY, PRESSURE, AND POWER

Sound pressure level $L_p$ may be considered equivalent to sound intensity level $L_I$ in most architectural acoustics situations. These levels in decibel units are affected by the environment in which the sound is measured. Sound power level $L_W$, on the other hand, is a more fundamental measure of a source of sound. It expresses the amount of energy or power that is radiated by a given source, regardless of the space into which the source is placed. Thus $L_W$, unlike $L_I$ and $L_p$, is independent of the acoustical characteristics of the space in which the sound is heard. $L_W$ is somewhat analogous to the lumen rating of lamps in lighting, and $L_I$ and $L_p$ to the footcandle level or illuminance in a room (cf., M. D. Egan, *Concepts in Architectural Lighting*, McGraw-Hill, New York, 1983). The table below summarizes various characteristics of sound intensity, sound pressure, and sound power levels. Refer to Appendix C for a method to convert $L_W$ to $L_p$.

|  | Sound Intensity Level | Sound Pressure Level | Sound Power Level |
|---|---|---|---|
| Symbol | $L_I$ | $L_p$ | $L_W$ |
| Express as | $10\ \log \dfrac{I}{I_0}$ | $20\ \log \dfrac{p}{p_0}$ | $10\ \log \dfrac{W}{W_0}$ |
| Units | $L_I$ *measured in* dB<br>$I$ *measured in* W/m² | $L_p$ *measured in* dB<br>$p$ *measured in* N/m²<br>(or pascal, Pa) | $L_W$ *measured in* dB<br>$W$ *measured in* Watt |
| Reference value* | $I_0 = 10^{-12}$ W/m² | $p_0 = 2 \times 10^{-5}$ N/m² | $W_0 = 10^{-12}$ W<br>(1pW) |
| At reference value | $L_I = 0$ dB | $L_p = 0$ dB | $L_W = 0$ dB |
| Pain threshold value | $I = 10$ W/m² | $p = 63$ N/m² |  |
| At pain threshold value | $L_I = 130$ dB | $L_p = 130$ dB |  |

*Usually taken as the lowest audible value for young persons with good hearing.

# Chapter 2
## Sound Absorption

## SOUND-ABSORBING TREATMENT

When sound impinges on the boundary surfaces of a room, part of its energy is absorbed and transmitted, and part is reflected back into the room. Sound levels in a room can be reduced by effective use of sound-absorbing treatment, such as fibrous ceiling boards, curtains, and carpets.

In the room with no acoustical treatment shown below, office workers hear direct sound energy from the computer equipment as well as reflected sound energy from the ceiling, floor, and walls. The computer operators, on the other hand, primarily hear direct sound from the nearest sound source, the computer. If sound-absorbing materials are added to the room, the office workers will hear considerably less sound because the reflected sound is reduced in their part of the room. The sound level near the computer equipment, however, is due mainly to direct sound and remains unchanged.

**Room with No Acoustical Treatment**

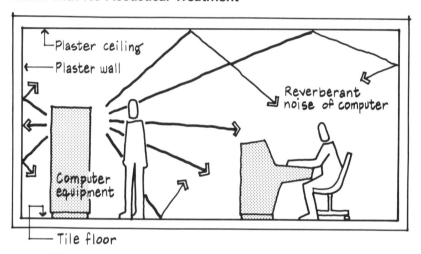

**Room with Sound-Absorbing Treatment**

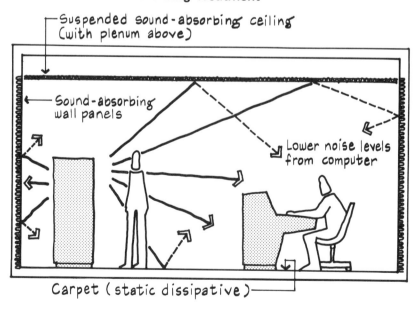

# NOISE REDUCTION OUTDOORS AND WITHIN ENCLOSURES

### Free Field

*Free-field* conditions occur when sound waves are free from the influence of reflective surfaces (e.g., open areas outdoors, anechoic rooms*). Under free-field conditions, sound energy from *point sources* (e.g., warning siren, truck exhaust) spreads spherically and drops off 6 dB for each doubling of distance from the source. *Line sources* of vehicular traffic consist of successive point sources which reinforce each other. Sound energy from line sources spreads cylindrically, *not* spherically, and drops off only 3 dB for each doubling of distance.

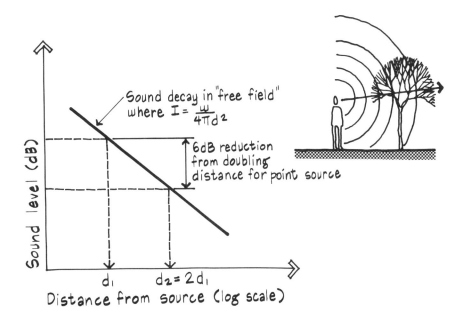

Sound decay in "free field" where $I = \frac{W}{4\pi d^2}$

6 dB reduction from doubling distance for point source

Sound level (dB)

$d_1$    $d_2 = 2d_1$

Distance from source (log scale)

### Reverberant Field

Indoors, sound energy drops off under free-field conditions only near the source (usually < 5 ft for small rooms). Because room surfaces reflect sound, there will be little further noise reduction with distance away from the source (called *reverberant field*). The more absorption in a room, the less the buildup of sound energy in the reverberant field. As shown on the graph below, the reverberant buildup of sound is lower for situation 2 than for situation 1 due to a greater amount of absorption.

---

*Anechoic rooms* have sound-absorbing wedges ( ≥ 2 ft deep) on all six enclosing surfaces to simulate the free field. These extremely "dead" rooms allow indoor study of and research on direct sound without room reflection effects.

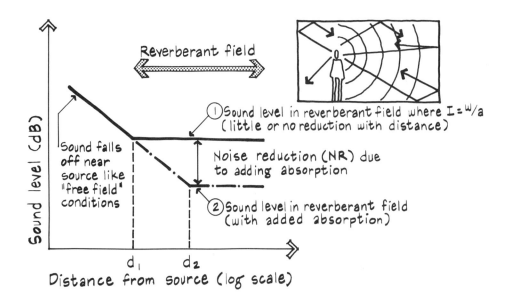

**Note:** Beyond distance $d \simeq \sqrt{a/6\pi}$ from the source, the sound level is relatively constant and depends primarily on the total room absorption $a$, where $a$ is measured in sabins.

# EFFECT OF ADDING SOUND-ABSORBING TREATMENT TO ROOMS

The addition of sound absorption to the ceiling of a small room (< 500 ft²) can reduce the reverberant sound levels by 10 dB as shown below for an example noise source. However, close to the source, the reduction will be only about 3 dB. If the ceiling and all four walls are treated with sound-absorbing material, the sound level in the reverberant field drops an additional 6 dB, but the sound levels near the source (in the free field) are *not* affected. Note that no reduction is achieved from further sound-absorbing treatment. Also, in this example the room initially was completely enclosed by sound-reflecting surfaces and had few furnishings to absorb sound energy. Thus a reduction of 6 to 8 dB in reverberant noise is more likely the upper limit for furnished spaces of comparable size.

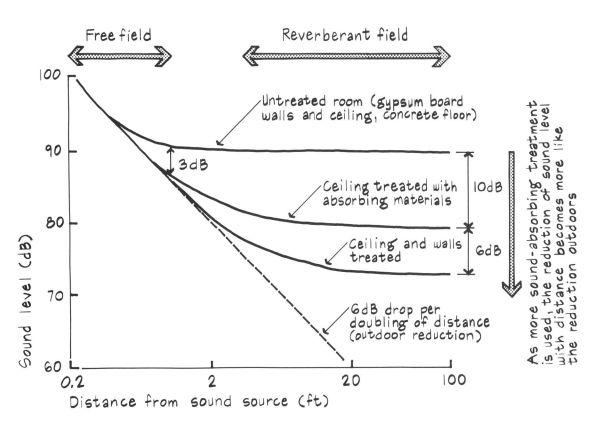

# SOUND ABSORPTION COEFFICIENT

The effectiveness of a sound-absorbing material can be expressed by its *absorption coefficient* α. This coefficient describes the fraction of the incident sound energy that a material absorbs. Theoretically, it can vary from 0 (*no sound energy absorbed*) to 1.0 (perfect absorption with *all* incident sound energy absorbed). Coefficients are derived from laboratory tests or estimated from measurements in finished rooms. In the laboratory test, sound energy from all directions is incident on the sample being tested (called *random incidence*).

| | % reflected | % absorbed and transmitted | Sound absorption coefficient (α) |
|---|---|---|---|
| Open window * (1 ft × 1 ft) | 0 | 100 | 1.0 |
| 1½" thick glass fiber | 20 | 80 | 0.80 |
| 4" thick brick | 98 | 2 | 0.02 |

*1 ft² of perfect absorption is equivalent to 1 sabin.

The total room absorption (i.e., the sum of all room surface areas times their respective sound absorption coefficients) for a space can be found by:

$$a = \Sigma \, S\alpha$$

where  $a$ = total room absorption (sabins)
  $S$ = surface area (ft²)
  $\alpha$ = sound absorption coefficient at given frequency (decimal percent)

**Note:** To find metric sabins, divide *a* by 10.76.

Absorption coefficients for building materials normally vary from about 0.01 to 0.99. However, acoustical testing laboratories sometimes report coefficients which exceed perfect absorption of 1.0. This apparent impossibility can occur because of peculiarities of testing methods (e.g., effects from size of test specimen or exposed edges of test samples) and diffraction of sound energy.

Materials with medium to high sound absorption coefficients (usually > 0.50) are referred to as *sound-absorbing*; those with low coefficients (usually < 0.20) are *sound-reflecting*. The effect of a difference in coefficients between two materials at a given frequency is shown by the following table.

| Difference in Coefficient | Effect for Most Situations |
| --- | --- |
| < 0.10 | Little (usually *not* noticeable) |
| 0.10 to 0.40 | Noticeable |
| > 0.40 | Considerable |

Exceptions to the difference in absorption coefficient $\alpha$ given in the table are rooms used for hearing research, testing of sound-absorbing materials, and the like. For example, reverberation rooms used to measure "random incidence" $\alpha$'s must have highly reflective surfaces ($<< 0.20$). Even very small differences in $\alpha$ for the enclosing surfaces are therefore extremely important.

**Note:** Sound absorption coefficients for normal incidence $\alpha_n$ (i.e., sound waves perpendicular to the surface of the absorber) can be measured using a closed tube, called an *impedance tube*. With the sample to be tested placed at one end of the tube, pure tones can be generated and measured within the tube to determine the absorption efficiency of the sample. For materials with low absorption coefficients, $\alpha_n \simeq \alpha/2$; for materials with very high coefficients, $\alpha_n \simeq \alpha$. Details of the test are given by ASTM C 384.

# REVERBERATION ROOMS

*Reverberation rooms* are fairly large (usually $> 10,000$ ft³), and all interior boundary surfaces are highly sound reflecting ($\alpha < 0.05$ at 125 to 4000 Hz). Walls normally are painted concrete block, metal panels, or concrete. To provide isolation from exterior noises, enclosing constructions usually consist of double or triple layers (e.g., double walls, floated floors) and must be completely isolated from the rest of the building. That is, a room is constructed within a room!

Reverberation rooms can be used to measure the absorption efficiency of building materials (under provisions of ASTM test method C 423), sound power levels of noise-producing equipment (ANSI S1.21, ASHRAE 36), and can be the source or receiving room for sound transmission loss TL tests (ASTM E 90) and impact noise tests (ASTM E 492).

To measure sound absorption, a large sample of the material (72 ft²) is placed in the reverberation room. The time it takes a test sound signal to decay by 60 dB (roughly to inaudibility) after the source of sound is stopped is measured first with the sample in the room and again with the room empty. The difference in decay time defines the efficiency of the absorbing material. For example, the shorter the decay time, the more efficient the sound-absorbing material being tested.

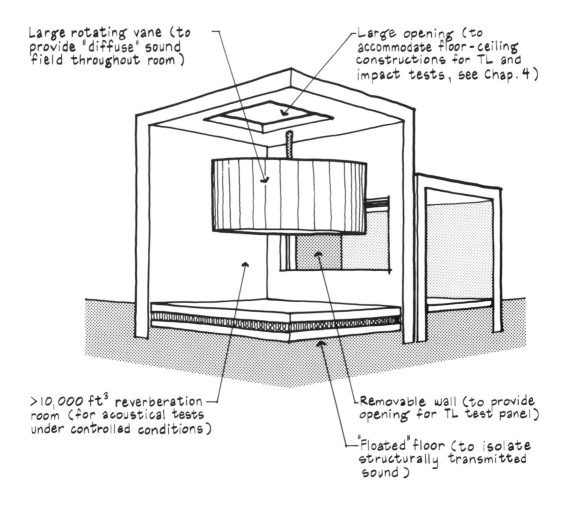

Large rotating vane (to provide "diffuse" sound field throughout room)

Large opening (to accommodate floor-ceiling constructions for TL and impact tests, see Chap. 4)

\>10,000 ft³ reverberation room (for acoustical tests under controlled conditions)

Removable wall (to provide opening for TL test panel)

"Floated" floor (to isolate structurally transmitted sound)

The sketch above depicts an example reverberation room which has a rotating vane to help achieve a *diffuse* reverberant sound field during test measurements by constantly changing the orientation of the surfaces enclosing the sound waves. The goal is to achieve diffusion over as wide a frequency range as possible. In addition, panels can be removed to provide openings between adjacent test rooms for evaluating the sound isolation effectiveness of wall and ceiling systems. The two adjacent rooms must be completely isolated from each other and from the rest of the building.

**Test References**

"Standard Test Method for Sound Absorption and Sound Absorption Coefficients by the Reverberation Room Method," ASTM C 423.

"Standard Method for Laboratory Measurement of Airborne Sound Transmission Loss of Building Partitions," ASTM E 90.

"Standard Method of Laboratory Measurement of Impact Sound Transmission Through Floor-Ceiling Assemblies Using the Tapping Machine," ASTM E 492.

Sound absorption by porous sound absorbers (identified on drawings by a "ribbon candy" symbol) is predominately the indirect conversion of sound energy into thermal energy. The impinging sound wave has its energy reduced largely due to frictional flow resistance from the walls of mazelike interconnected pores. The amount of absorption that can be achieved is determined by the physical properties of thickness, density, and porosity for most porous materials, and fiber diameter and orientation for fibrous materials. Manufacturers try to optimize these properties to achieve high sound absorption efficiencies. Fibrous sound absorbers (such as glass fiber or mineral fiber) are sometimes referred to as *fuzz*.

As shown by the curves below, thickness has a significant effect on the efficiency of a porous sound absorber. It is also essential that the internal structure of a porous material has interconnected pores. For example, plastic and elastomeric foams which have closed, nonconnected pores provide little sound absorption although they may be effective thermal insulators.

A simple test to determine if a porous material can be an effective sound absorber is to blow through it. If the material is thick and passes air under moderate pressure, it should be a good absorber.

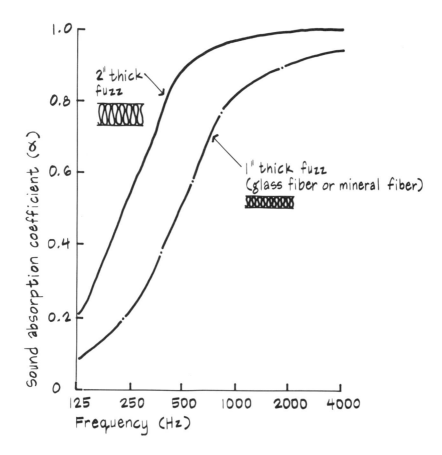

**Note:** Porous sound absorbers are extremely poor sound isolators! Due to their soft, lightweight, interconnected structure, sound energy easily passes from one side of the material to the other. See Chap. 4 for a discussion of the principles of sound isolation.

# RELATIVE EFFICIENCY OF SOUND ABSORBERS

The basic types of sound absorbers are porous materials, vibrating (or resonant) panels, and volume resonators (called *Helmholtz resonators*). Porous sound absorbers (thick materials or thin materials with airspace behind) should be placed at location of maximum compression for impinging sound waves (e.g., $\lambda/4$ distance from backup wall surface). Combinations of porous materials and vibrating panels or volume resonators can provide the uniform, or "flat," sound absorption with frequency required in recording or radio/TV studios.

**Thin Porous Materials** (Convert sound energy into heat by friction)

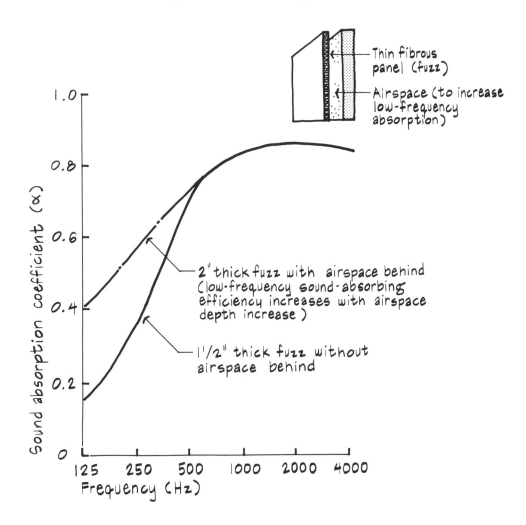

Thin fibrous panel (fuzz)

Airspace (to increase low-frequency absorption)

2" thick fuzz with airspace behind (low-frequency sound-absorbing efficiency increases with airspace depth increase)

1½" thick fuzz without airspace behind

## Thick Porous Materials

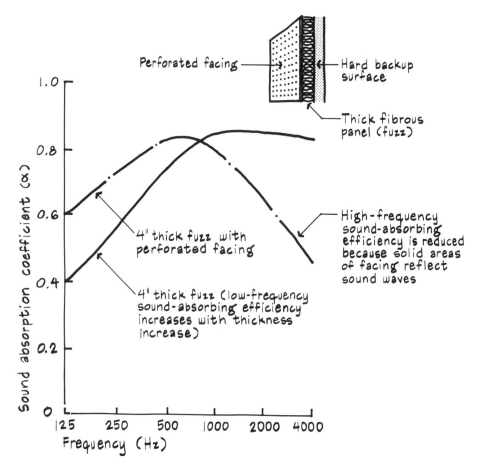

Perforated facing — Hard backup surface

Thick fibrous panel (fuzz)

4" thick fuzz with perforated facing

4" thick fuzz (low-frequency sound-absorbing efficiency increases with thickness increase)

High-frequency sound-absorbing efficiency is reduced because solid areas of facing reflect sound waves

Sound absorption coefficient ($\alpha$)

Frequency (Hz)

## Vibrating Panels* (Convert sound energy into vibrational energy which is dissipated by internal damping and radiation)

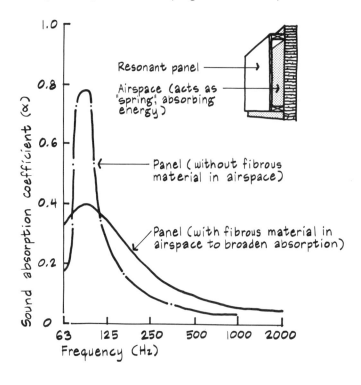

Resonant panel

Airspace (acts as "spring", absorbing energy)

Panel (without fibrous material in airspace)

Panel (with fibrous material in airspace to broaden absorption)

Sound absorption coefficient ($\alpha$)

Frequency (Hz)

**Volume Resonators*** (Reduce sound energy by friction at opening and by interreflections within cavity)

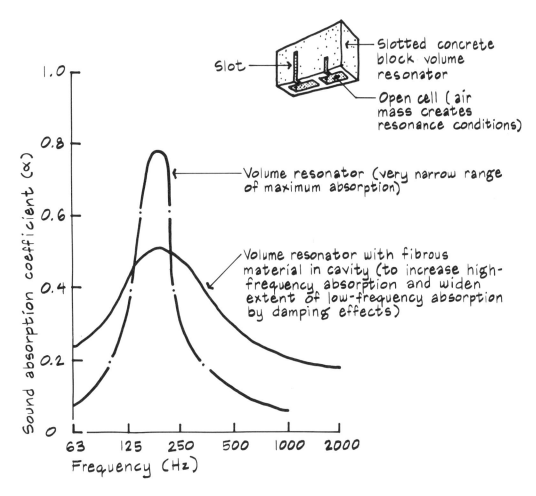

Slot

Slotted concrete block volume resonator

Open cell (air mass creates resonance conditions)

Volume resonator (very narrow range of maximum absorption)

Volume resonator with fibrous material in cavity (to increase high-frequency absorption and widen extent of low-frequency absorption by damping effects)

*These specialized types of sound absorption can be used to supplement porous materials or to absorb specific low-frequency sound energy (e.g., 120-Hz "hum" from electrical equipment).

# NOISE REDUCTION COEFFICIENT

The *noise reduction coefficient* NRC is the arithmetic average, rounded off to the nearest multiple of 0.05, of the sound absorption coefficients $\alpha$'s at 250, 500, 1000, and 2000 Hz for a specific material and mounting condition. The $\alpha$'s at 125 Hz and 4000 Hz, although measured during the ASTM C 423 test, are *not* used to calculate the NRC. Therefore, the NRC is intended as a single-number rating of sound-absorbing efficiency at mid-frequencies. It is *not*, as its name implies, the difference in sound levels between two conditions or between rooms (see also Chap. 4). The NRC can be found by:

$$NRC = \frac{\alpha_{250} + \alpha_{500} + \alpha_{1000} + \alpha_{2000}}{4}$$

where   NRC = noise reduction coefficient (decimal percent)
         $\alpha$ = sound absorption coefficient (decimal percent)

Be careful when selecting a product based on its NRC alone. Because the NRC is an average number over a limited frequency range, two materials may have identical NRCs but very different absorption characteristics. In addition, because the NRC does not include the $\alpha$'s at 125 Hz and 4000 Hz, it should not be used to evaluate materials for rooms where music or speech perception is important (e.g., music practice rooms, courtrooms). As shown by the two curves at the top of the graph below, fibrous acoustical board panels have far greater absorption at 125 Hz than shredded-wood formboard. Although the $\alpha$'s differ by more than 0.50 at 125 Hz, the NRCs differ by only 0.15. Where low-frequency absorption may not be an important factor (e.g., lobbies, small offices), the NRC can be an adequate rating to compare materials.

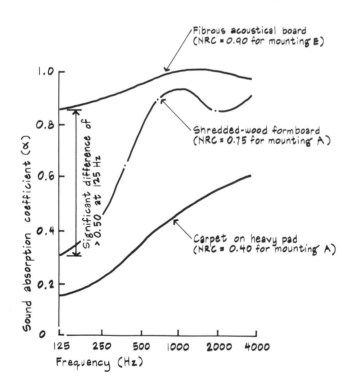

## EXAMPLE PROBLEM (NRC COMPUTATION)

Find the NRC for a carpet with the following sound absorption coefficients: 0.20 at 250 Hz, 0.35 at 500 Hz, 0.45 at 1000 Hz, and 0.55 at 2000 Hz.

$$NRC = \frac{0.20 + 0.35 + 0.45 + 0.55}{4} = \frac{1.55}{4} = 0.39$$

This answer must be rounded off to the nearest 0.05 increment. Therefore, the NRC for this carpet will be 0.40.

# SOUND ABSORPTION DATA FOR COMMON BUILDING MATERIALS AND FURNISHINGS

| Material | \multicolumn{6}{Sound Absorption Coefficient} | NRC |
|---|---|---|---|---|---|---|---|
| | 125 Hz | 250 Hz | 500 Hz | 1000 Hz | 2000 Hz | 4000 Hz | Number* |
| **Walls**[1-3, 9, 12] | | | | | | | |
| **Sound-Reflecting:** | | | | | | | |
| 1. Brick, unglazed | 0.02 | 0.02 | 0.03 | 0.04 | 0.05 | 0.07 | 0.05 |
| 2. Brick, unglazed and painted | 0.01 | 0.01 | 0.02 | 0.02 | 0.02 | 0.03 | 0.00 |
| 3. Concrete, rough | 0.01 | 0.02 | 0.04 | 0.06 | 0.08 | 0.10 | 0.05 |
| 4. Concrete block, painted | 0.10 | 0.05 | 0.06 | 0.07 | 0.09 | 0.08 | 0.05 |
| 5. Glass, heavy (large panes) | 0.18 | 0.06 | 0.04 | 0.03 | 0.02 | 0.02 | 0.05 |
| 6. Glass, ordinary window | 0.35 | 0.25 | 0.18 | 0.12 | 0.07 | 0.04 | 0.15 |
| 7. Gypsum board, 1/2 in thick (nailed to 2 × 4s, 16 in oc) | 0.29 | 0.10 | 0.05 | 0.04 | 0.07 | 0.09 | 0.05 |
| 8. Gypsum board, 1 layer, 5/8 in thick (screwed to 1 × 3s, 16 in oc with airspaces filled with fibrous insulation) | 0.55 | 0.14 | 0.08 | 0.04 | 0.12 | 0.11 | 0.10 |
| 9. Construction no. 8 with 2 layers of 5/8-in-thick gypsum board | 0.28 | 0.12 | 0.10 | 0.07 | 0.13 | 0.09 | 0.10 |
| 10. Marble or glazed tile | 0.01 | 0.01 | 0.01 | 0.01 | 0.02 | 0.02 | 0.00 |
| 11. Plaster on brick | 0.01 | 0.02 | 0.02 | 0.03 | 0.04 | 0.05 | 0.05 |
| 12. Plaster on concrete block (or 1 in thick on lath) | 0.12 | 0.09 | 0.07 | 0.05 | 0.05 | 0.04 | 0.05 |
| 13. Plaster on lath | 0.14 | 0.10 | 0.06 | 0.05 | 0.04 | 0.03 | 0.05 |
| 14. Plywood, 3/8-in paneling | 0.28 | 0.22 | 0.17 | 0.09 | 0.10 | 0.11 | 0.15 |
| 15. Steel | 0.05 | 0.10 | 0.10 | 0.10 | 0.07 | 0.02 | 0.10 |
| 16. Venetian blinds, metal | 0.06 | 0.05 | 0.07 | 0.15 | 0.13 | 0.17 | 0.10 |
| 17. Wood, 1/4-in paneling, with airspace behind | 0.42 | 0.21 | 0.10 | 0.08 | 0.06 | 0.06 | 0.10 |
| 18. Wood, 1-in paneling with airspace behind | 0.19 | 0.14 | 0.09 | 0.06 | 0.06 | 0.05 | 0.10 |
| **Sound-Absorbing:** | | | | | | | |
| 19. Concrete block, coarse | 0.36 | 0.44 | 0.31 | 0.29 | 0.39 | 0.25 | 0.35 |
| 20. Lightweight drapery, 10 oz/yd², flat on wall (Note: Sound-reflecting at most frequencies.) | 0.03 | 0.04 | 0.11 | 0.17 | 0.24 | 0.35 | 0.15 |
| 21. Mediumweight drapery, 14 oz/yd², draped to half area (i.e., 2 ft of drapery to 1 ft of wall) | 0.07 | 0.31 | 0.49 | 0.75 | 0.70 | 0.60 | 0.55 |
| 22. Heavyweight drapery, 18 oz/yd², draped to half area | 0.14 | 0.35 | 0.55 | 0.72 | 0.70 | 0.65 | 0.60 |
| 23. Fiberglass fabric curtain, 8 1/2 oz/yd², draped to half area (Note: The deeper the airspace behind the drapery (up to 12 in), the greater the low-frequency absorption.) | 0.09 | 0.32 | 0.68 | 0.83 | 0.39 | 0.76 | 0.55 |
| 24. Shredded-wood fiberboard, 2 in thick on concrete (mtg. A) | 0.15 | 0.26 | 0.62 | 0.94 | 0.64 | 0.92 | 0.60 |
| 25. Thick, fibrous material behind open facing | 0.60 | 0.75 | 0.82 | 0.80 | 0.60 | 0.38 | 0.75 |
| 26. Carpet, heavy, on 5/8-in perforated mineral fiberboard with airspace behind | 0.37 | 0.41 | 0.63 | 0.85 | 0.96 | 0.92 | 0.70 |
| 27. Wood, 1/2-in paneling, perforated 3/16-in-diameter holes, 11% open area, with 2 1/2-in glass fiber in airspace behind | 0.40 | 0.90 | 0.80 | 0.50 | 0.40 | 0.30 | 0.65 |
| **Floors**[9, 11] | | | | | | | |
| **Sound-Reflecting:** | | | | | | | |
| 28. Concrete or terrazzo | 0.01 | 0.01 | 0.02 | 0.02 | 0.02 | 0.02 | 0.00 |
| 29. Linoleum, rubber, or asphalt tile on concrete | 0.02 | 0.03 | 0.03 | 0.03 | 0.03 | 0.02 | 0.05 |
| 30. Marble or glazed tile | 0.01 | 0.01 | 0.01 | 0.01 | 0.02 | 0.02 | 0.00 |
| 31. Wood | 0.15 | 0.11 | 0.10 | 0.07 | 0.06 | 0.07 | 0.10 |
| 32. Wood parquet on concrete | 0.04 | 0.04 | 0.07 | 0.06 | 0.06 | 0.07 | 0.05 |
| **Sound-Absorbing:** | | | | | | | |
| 33. Carpet, heavy, on concrete | 0.02 | 0.06 | 0.14 | 0.37 | 0.60 | 0.65 | 0.30 |
| 34. Carpet, heavy, on foam rubber | 0.08 | 0.24 | 0.57 | 0.69 | 0.71 | 0.73 | 0.55 |
| 35. Carpet, heavy, with impermeable latex backing on foam rubber | 0.08 | 0.27 | 0.39 | 0.34 | 0.48 | 0.63 | 0.35 |
| 36. Indoor-outdoor carpet | 0.01 | 0.05 | 0.10 | 0.20 | 0.45 | 0.65 | 0.20 |
| **Ceilings**[6, 8-10] † | | | | | | | |
| **Sound-Reflecting:** | | | | | | | |
| 37. Concrete | 0.01 | 0.01 | 0.02 | 0.02 | 0.02 | 0.02 | 0.00 |
| 38. Gypsum board, 1/2 in thick | 0.29 | 0.10 | 0.05 | 0.04 | 0.07 | 0.09 | 0.05 |
| 39. Gypsum board, 1/2 in thick, in suspension system | 0.15 | 0.10 | 0.05 | 0.04 | 0.07 | 0.09 | 0.05 |
| 40. Plaster on lath | 0.14 | 0.10 | 0.06 | 0.05 | 0.04 | 0.03 | 0.05 |
| 41. Plywood, 3/8 in thick | 0.28 | 0.22 | 0.17 | 0.09 | 0.10 | 0.11 | 0.15 |
| **Sound-Absorbing:** | | | | | | | |
| 42. Acoustical board, 3/4 in thick, in suspension system (mtg. E) | 0.76 | 0.93 | 0.83 | 0.99 | 0.99 | 0.94 | 0.95 |
| 43. Shredded-wood fiberboard, 2 in thick on lay-in grid (mtg. E) | 0.59 | 0.51 | 0.53 | 0.73 | 0.88 | 0.74 | 0.65 |

| Material | Sound Absorption Coefficient | | | | | | NRC Number* |
|---|---|---|---|---|---|---|---|
| | 125 Hz | 250 Hz | 500 Hz | 1000 Hz | 2000 Hz | 4000 Hz | |
| 44. Thin, porous sound-absorbing material, 3/4 in thick (mtg. B) | 0.10 | 0.60 | 0.80 | 0.82 | 0.78 | 0.60 | 0.75 |
| 45. Thick, porous sound-absorbing material, 2 in thick (mtg. B), or thin material with airspace behind (mtg. D) | 0.38 | 0.60 | 0.78 | 0.80 | 0.78 | 0.70 | 0.75 |
| 46. Sprayed cellulose fibers, 1 in thick on concrete (mtg. A) | 0.08 | 0.29 | 0.75 | 0.98 | 0.93 | 0.76 | 0.75 |
| 47. Glass-fiber roof fabric, 12 oz/yd² | 0.65 | 0.71 | 0.82 | 0.86 | 0.76 | 0.62 | 0.80 |
| 48. Glass-fiber roof fabric, 37 1/2 oz/yd² (Note: Sound-reflecting at most frequencies.) | 0.38 | 0.23 | 0.17 | 0.15 | 0.09 | 0.06 | 0.15 |
| 49. Polyurethane foam, 1 in thick, open cell, reticulated | 0.07 | 0.11 | 0.20 | 0.32 | 0.60 | 0.85 | 0.30 |
| 50. Parallel glass-fiberboard panels, 1 in thick by 18 in deep, spaced 18 in apart, suspended 12 in below ceiling | 0.07 | 0.20 | 0.40 | 0.52 | 0.60 | 0.67 | 0.45 |
| 51. Parallel glass-fiberboard panels, 1 in thick by 18 in deep, spaced 6 1/2 in apart, suspended 12 in below ceiling | 0.10 | 0.29 | 0.62 | 1.12 | 1.33 | 1.38 | 0.85 |
| **Seats and Audience**[1, 5, 7, 9] ‡ | | | | | | | |
| 52. Fabric well-upholstered seats, with perforated seat pans, unoccupied | 0.19 | 0.37 | 0.56 | 0.67 | 0.61 | 0.59 | |
| 53. Leather-covered upholstered seats, unoccupied§ | 0.44 | 0.54 | 0.60 | 0.62 | 0.58 | 0.50 | |
| 54. Audience, seated in upholstered seats§ | 0.39 | 0.57 | 0.80 | 0.94 | 0.92 | 0.87 | |
| 55. Congregation, seated in wooden pews | 0.57 | 0.61 | 0.75 | 0.86 | 0.91 | 0.86 | |
| 56. Chair, metal or wood seat, unoccupied | 0.15 | 0.19 | 0.22 | 0.39 | 0.38 | 0.30 | |
| 57. Students, informally dressed, seated in tablet-arm chairs | 0.30 | 0.41 | 0.49 | 0.84 | 0.87 | 0.84 | |
| **Openings**[9] ¶ | | | | | | | |
| 58. Deep balcony, with upholstered seats | | | 0.50–1.00 | | | | |
| 59. Diffusers or grilles, mechanical system | | | 0.15–0.50 | | | | |
| 60. Stage | | | 0.25–0.75 | | | | |
| **Miscellaneous**[3, 9, 11] | | | | | | | |
| 61. Gravel, loose and moist, 4 in thick | 0.25 | 0.60 | 0.65 | 0.70 | 0.75 | 0.80 | 0.70 |
| 62. Grass, marion bluegrass, 2 in high | 0.11 | 0.26 | 0.60 | 0.69 | 0.92 | 0.99 | 0.60 |
| 63. Snow, freshly fallen, 4 in thick | 0.45 | 0.75 | 0.90 | 0.95 | 0.95 | 0.95 | 0.90 |
| 64. Soil, rough | 0.15 | 0.25 | 0.40 | 0.55 | 0.60 | 0.60 | 0.45 |
| 65. Trees, balsam firs, 20 ft² ground area per tree, 8 ft high | 0.03 | 0.06 | 0.11 | 0.17 | 0.27 | 0.31 | 0.15 |
| 66. Water surface (swimming pool) | 0.01 | 0.01 | 0.01 | 0.02 | 0.02 | 0.03 | 0.00 |

*NRC (noise reduction coefficient) is a single-number rating of the sound absorption coefficients of a material. It is an average that only includes the coefficients in the 250 to 2000 Hz frequency range and therefore should be used with caution. See page 50 for a discussion of the NRC rating method.

†Refer to manufacturer's catalogs for absorption data which should be from up-to-date tests by independent acoustical laboratories according to current ASTM procedures.

‡Coefficients are per square foot of seating floor area or per unit. Where the audience is randomly spaced (e.g., courtroom, cafeteria), mid-frequency absorption can be estimated at about 5 sabins per person. To be precise, coefficients per person should be stated in relation to spacing pattern.

§The floor area occupied by the audience must be calculated to include an *edge effect* at aisles. For an aisle bounded on both sides by audience, include a strip 3 ft wide; for an aisle bounded on only one side by audience, include a strip 1 1/2 ft wide. No edge effect is used when the seating abuts walls or balcony fronts (because the edge is shielded). The coefficients are also valid for orchestra and choral areas at 5 to 8 ft² per person. Orchestra areas include people, instruments, music racks, etc. No edge effects are used around musicians.

¶Coefficients for openings depend on absorption and cubic volume of opposite side.

## Test Reference

"Standard Test Method for Sound Absorption and Sound Absorption Coefficients by the Reverberation Room Method," ASTM C 423. Available from American Society for Testing and Materials (ASTM), 1916 Race Street, Philadelphia, PA 19103.

## Sources

1. L. L. Beranek, "Audience and Chair Absorption in Large Halls," *Journal of the Acoustical Society of America*, January 1969.

2. A. N. Burd et al., "Data for the Acoustic Design of Studios," British Broadcasting Corporation, BBC Engineering Monograph no. 64, November 1966.

3. E. J. Evans and E. N. Bazley, "Sound Absorbing Materials," H. M. Stationery Office, London, 1964.

4. R. A. Hedeen, *Compendium of Materials for Noise Control*, National Institute for Occupational Safety and Health (NIOSH), Publication no. 80-116, Cincinnati, Ohio, May 1980. (Contains sound absorption data on hundreds of commercially available materials.)

5. H. F. Kingsbury and W. J. Wallace, "Acoustic Absorption Characteristics of People," *Sound and Vibration*, December 1968.

6. T. Mariner, "Control of Noise by Sound-Absorbent Materials," *Noise Control*, July 1957.

7. J. E. Moore and R. West, "In Search of an Instant Audience," *Journal of the Acoustical Society of America*, December 1970.

8. R. Moulder and J. Merrill, "Acoustical Properties of Glass Fiber Roof Fabrics," *Sound and Vibration*, October 1983.

9. "Performance Data, Architectural Acoustical Materials," Acoustical and Insulating Materials Association (AIMA). (This bulletin was published annually from 1941 to 1974.)

10. W. E. Purcell, "Materials for Noise and Vibration Control," *Sound and Vibration*, July 1982.

11. W. Siekman, "Outdoor Acoustical Treatment: Grass and Trees," *Journal of the Acoustical Society of America*, October 1969.

12. "Sound Conditioning with Carpet," The Carpet and Rug Institute, Dalton, Ga., 1970.

**Note:** For flame spread ratings of finish materials, refer to current edition of "Building Materials," available from Underwriters' Laboratories (UL), 333 Pfingsten Road, Northbrook, IL 60062.

# LABORATORY TEST MOUNTINGS

Laboratory tests to determine sound absorption efficiency should be conducted according to the current ASTM C 423 procedures. The types of mounting shown below are intended to represent typical installation methods for sound-absorbing materials used in buildings. Mountings A, B, D, and E apply to most prefabricated products, F to sound-absorbing mechanical air-duct linings, and C is used for specialized applications. Numerical suffix indicates distance in millimeters that the test specimen is from test room surface (e.g., E-400 is mounting depth of 400 mm or 15 3/4 in).

When data is reported, the mounting method used during the test always should be indicated along with the sound absorption coefficients. Without identifying the mounting method, sound absorption data will be meaningless. For example, a product having an advertised sound absorption coefficient of 0.80

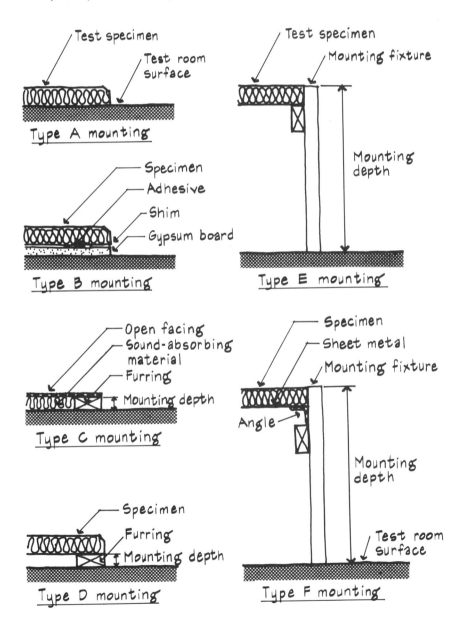

was used in a finished space; however, a sound absorption coefficient of only 0.40 was achieved because the actual installation (mounting A) did not duplicate the laboratory test, which had a deep airspace behind the sound-absorbing material (mounting E).

Samples to be evaluated by the ASTM C 423 laboratory test are installed on the floor of the reverberation room as depicted above. Therefore, the illustrations for mountings A through F appear to be upside down for ceiling applications.

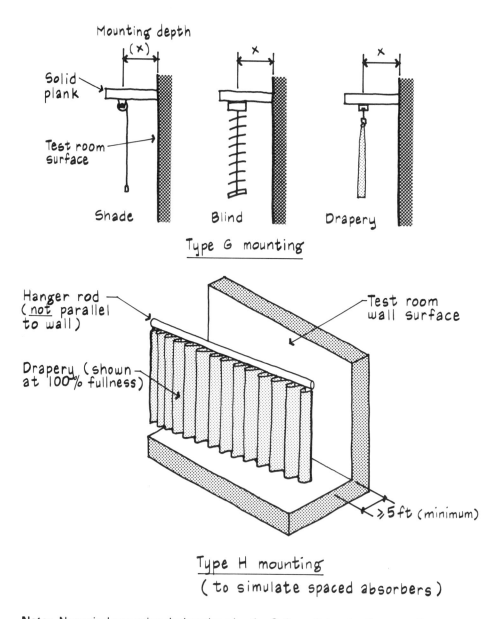

**Note:** Numerical mounting designations by the Ceilings & Interior Systems Construction Association (CISCA) correspond to the ASTM mountings as follows: 1 is B, 2 is D, 4 is A, 5 is C, 6 is F, and 7 is E.

**References**

"Practice for Mounting Test Specimens During Sound Absorption Tests," ASTM E 795.

"Standard Test Method for Sound Absorption and Sound Absorption Coefficients by the Reverberation Room Method," ASTM C 423.

# PREFABRICATED SOUND-ABSORBING MATERIALS

Generic examples of the numerous commercially available prefabricated sound-absorbing materials are shown below. Most sound-absorbing tiles and panels are not sufficiently durable for wall application. For walls, use fibrous materials with protective *open facings* (e.g., perforated or expanded metal, perforated hardboard, metal slats), fabric-covered panels, or shredded-wood formboard.

Use membrane-faced or ceramic tile materials for humid environments such as swimming pools, locker rooms, and kitchens. (Sound energy readily passes through membranes with a thickness of less than 1 mil.)

Observe manufacturer's recommendations for the cleaning and painting of porous sound-absorbing materials. Lightly *tint* or stain, rather than paint, sound-absorbing materials, because painting can seriously diminish the sound-absorbing efficiency by clogging the openings. For many situations, spray applications can achieve a thinner coating than brushes or rollers. (The out-of-print AIMA booklet "How to Clean and Maintain Acoustical Tile Ceilings" presents useful guidelines.) When in doubt, a painted specimen can be tested according to the provisions of ASTM C 643 to determine effects of paint (or compare painted to unpainted specimens following ASTM E 1050 procedures for determining absorption using an impedance tube).

**Regular Perforated Tile***

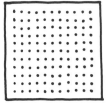

**Textured and/or Patterned Tile or Panel**

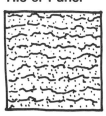

**Fissured Tile or Panel**

**Slotted Tile or Panel**

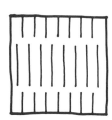

**Random Perforated Tile***

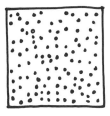

**Membrane-Faced or Ceramic Tile Materials**

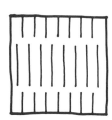

**Shredded-Wood Formboard**

**Smooth Spray-On Material**†
(Mineral or Cellulose Fibers)

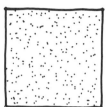

**Glass-Fiber Blankets and Boards**

**Rough Spray-On Material**†

*Openings provide about 15 percent open area to allow painting without bridging over the holes. Avoid using oil and rubber-base paints which may clog pores. Materials with large perforations normally can be painted without serious reduction of sound-absorbing efficiency.

†Use spray-on materials at 1 to 3 in thickness on hard backup surface or apply to open lath, which can provide increased absorption at low frequencies due to resonant-panel effects.

The efficiency of a sound-absorbing material can be affected by its distribution and location in a room. For example, 25 panels of sound-absorbing material, each 2 ft by 2 ft, will absorb more sound energy per panel when spaced in a "checkerboard" pattern on a 200-ft² plaster ceiling than a uniform coverage of the same material.

This increase in efficiency (called the *area effect*) is due to the diffraction of sound energy around the perimeters of the spaced sound-absorbing panels and to the additional absorption provided by the exposed panel edges. The efficiency of sound-absorbing panels increases as the ratio of perimeter to surface area increases. The 25 spaced absorbers have a ratio of perimeter to surface area 5 times the ratio for the 25 uniform-coverage absorbers. Sound energy reflected from the hard-surfaced plaster adjacent to the absorbent edges in the checkerboard configuration tends to spill over onto the absorbing panels. Therefore, the spaced absorbing material absorbs more sound energy than would be accounted for by its area. This kind of surface treatment also can be used to achieve a diffuse sound field, which is desired in music practice rooms. Note that the total absorption contributed by spaced absorbers in this example will only be slightly less than the absorption provided by coverage of the entire 200-ft² ceiling.

**Checkerboard Pattern**          **Uniform Coverage**

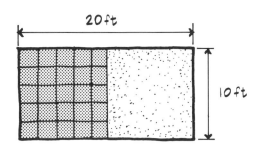

**Reference**

T. W. Bartel, "Effect of Absorber Geometry on Apparent Absorption Coefficients as Measured in a Reverberation Chamber," *Journal of the Acoustical Society of America*, April 1981.

# SUSPENDED SOUND-ABSORBING PANELS AND UNITS

Sound-absorbing materials are commercially available for installation in a *spaced* regular pattern. When these units (or panels) are installed with all edges and sides exposed, they can provide extremely high absorption per square foot of material because at least six surfaces will be exposed to sound waves. Absorption data for spaced units are normally presented in terms of sabins per unit at the recommended spacings. Note that the total absorption from suspended units is limited by the quantity that can be installed at the recommended spacings. For example, suspended units tend to shield each other when their density (expressed as ratio of exposed surface area of absorbers to area of ceiling) exceeds 0.5.

Examples of parallel, honeycomb, and egg-crate layout patterns of suspended, sound-absorbing panels are shown below. Suspended spaced absorbers can be used where a uniform or continuous application of conventional sound-absorbing materials is *not* feasible (e.g., industrial plants with extremely high ceilings).

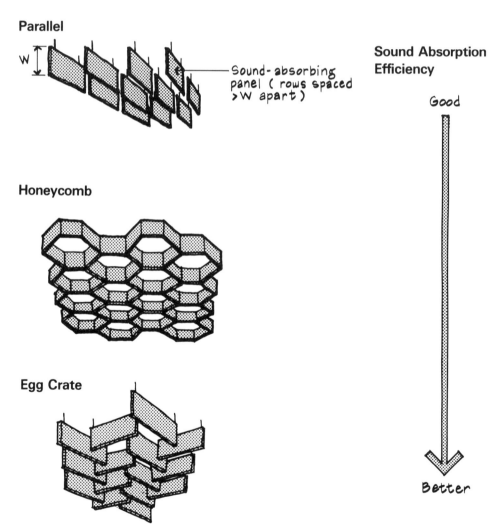

**Parallel**

W

Sound-absorbing panel (rows spaced >W apart)

**Sound Absorption Efficiency**

Good

**Honeycomb**

**Egg Crate**

Better

**Note:** Suspended flat-panel and spaced sound-absorbing units (e.g., prisms, cones, tetrahedrons) should be well braced to prevent motion from air circulation in rooms.

# APPLICATIONS FOR SOUND-ABSORBING MATERIALS

### Reverberation Control

Sound-absorbing materials can be used to control reverberation so speech will not be garbled. The larger the room volume, the longer the reverberation time because sound waves will encounter room surfaces less often than in small rooms. Each doubling of the total amount of absorption in a room reduces the reverberation time by one-half. Sound absorption can make the sound seem to come directly from the actual source rather than from everywhere in the room. For example, in recreational facilities, it is important that instructions and warnings be identified with the actual source location.

### Noise Reduction in Rooms

When correctly used, sound-absorbing materials can be effective in controlling noise buildup within a room. However, they have a limited application for noise control and are not the panacea for all noise problems. For example, each doubling of the total amount of absorption in a room reduces the noise level by only 3 dB. Thus, as with other aspects of sound behavior, the law of diminishing returns can quickly limit the effectiveness of this approach to noise control. In large open-plan rooms, sound-absorbing materials can contribute to speech privacy by causing sound energy to decrease with distance according to the inverse-square law (see Chap. 6).

### Echo Control

Sound-absorbing materials can be used to control echoes (usually simultaneously with controlling reverberation). *Echoes* are long-delayed, distinct reflections of sufficient sound level to be clearly heard above the general reverberation as a repetition of the original sound. *Flutter echo*, which can be heard as a ''rattle'' or ''clicking'' from a hand clap, may be present in small rooms (or narrow spaces with parallel walls). It also can be effectively controlled with sound-absorbing materials. Control measures for *creep echo* (useless sound reflections concentrated near and along smooth concave surfaces) are presented in Chap. 3.

Until the pioneering work of Wallace Clement Sabine, beginning in 1895 at age 27, criteria for good listening conditions in rooms were largely nonexistent. Professor Sabine was asked to improve the atrocious listening conditions for speech in the new lecture hall in the Fogg Art Museum, Harvard University, Cambridge, Massachusetts (Richard Morris Hunt, architect; see plan and section drawings below). Sound in the hall would persist for about 5 1/2 s due to the multiple reflections from the hard-surfaced plaster finish materials in the hall. Because most English-speaking persons can complete 15 syllables in 5 1/2 s, words were almost impossible to understand nearly everywhere in the hall.

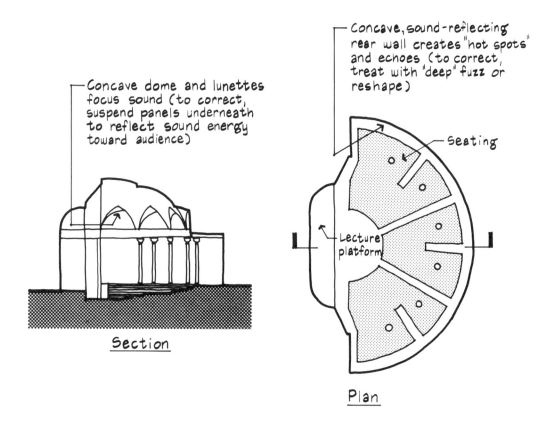

Concave dome and lunettes focus sound (to correct, suspend panels underneath to reflect sound energy toward audience)

Concave, sound-reflecting rear wall creates "hot spots" and echoes (to correct, treat with "deep" fuzz or reshape)

Seating

Lecture platform

Section

Plan

Sabine recognized that the problem of the persistence of reflected sound energy was due to the size of the room* and its furnishings, including the occupants. He called this persistence the "duration of audibility of residual sound." Repeated tests were conducted in the hall using organ pipes as noise sources. The organ pipes had an initial sound level in the hall of about 60 dB above a young listener's threshold of audibility at a frequency of 512 Hz.

*The size of a room affects the average length of reflections, called the *mean free path*. The mean free path is approximately equal to $4V/S$, where $V$ is room volume in cubic feet and $S$ is surface area in square feet.

Sabine used his disciplined sense of hearing to judge when the sound from the organ pipes ceased to be audible. The time it took the sound to decay the estimated 60 dB (or to one-millionth, 1/1,000,000) of its initial sound level was measured by chronograph and defined by Sabine to be what is now called the *reverberation time*. Sabine was able to conduct his tests only at night (between midnight and 5 a.m.) when it was relatively quiet—after the streetcars stopped running and before the milkmen started rattling their carts over the cobblestones.

With the help of two student laboratory assistants, seat cushions were borrowed from nearby Sanders Theater. These 3-in-thick cushions were made of porous, sound-absorbing hair-fiber material covered with canvas and light damask cloth. The more cushions brought in, the greater the total room absorption and the lower the reverberation time. Sabine found that he could lower the reverberation time to about 1 s when nearly 550 cushions, each about 1 m long, covered the platform, bench seats, aisles, and rear wall to the ceiling. Consequently, the first unit of sound absorption was a meter length of a seat cushion from the Sanders Theater!

The results of Sabine's work made it possible to plan reverberation time in advance of construction. For the first time, desired reverberation time in rooms, at least at 512 Hz, could be the result of design, *not* luck or faithful reproduction. The equation which Sabine defined and proved empirically is:

$$T = 0.05 \frac{V}{a}$$

where $T$ = reverberation time, or time required for sound to decay 60 dB after the source has stopped (s)
$V$ = room volume (ft$^3$)
$a$ = total ft$^2$ of room absorption (sabins, so named to honor W. C. Sabine)

The above formula (often referred to as the *Sabine formula*) is generally used by testing laboratories to compute absorption coefficients and is appropriate for use in most architectural work. It is reasonably accurate when sound field conditions are diffuse (e.g., sound absorption uniformly distributed) and room dimensions do not vary widely (e.g., compact rooms without one extremely long dimension, rooms without deep side pockets, or transepts in a church). It should not be used for recording studios or anechoic chambers, which have extremely high ratios of absorption to room volume. In these cases the *Eyring formula* should be used (see Appendix A).

### References

L. L. Beranek, "The Notebooks of Wallace C. Sabine," *Journal of the Acoustical Society of America*, March 1977.

L. L. Beranek and J. W. Kopec, "Wallace C. Sabine, Acoustical Consultant," *Journal of the Acoustical Society of America*, January 1981.

W. D. Orcutt, *Wallace Clement Sabine, A Biography*, Plimpton, Norwood, Mass., 1933 (no longer in print, but should be available in most university libraries).

W. C. Sabine, *Collected Papers on Acoustics*, Dover, New York, 1964 (reprint of 1922 Harvard University Press publication).

# OPTIMUM REVERBERATION TIME

The preferred ranges of reverberation time at mid-frequency (average of reverberation at 500 and 1000 Hz) for a variety of activities are given on the bar graph below. The ranges, based on the experience of normal-hearing listeners in completed spaces, are extended by dashed sections at the ends of the bars to indicate the extreme limits of acceptability. Satisfactory listening conditions can be achieved in auditoriums which have different reverberation times within the preferred range, provided other important acoustical needs are fulfilled. In general, large rooms should be nearer the upper end of the reverberation time ranges than smaller rooms of the same type (see Chap. 3). For example, liturgical organ music is composed for church- or cathedral-sized rooms; chamber music is intended for small rooms.

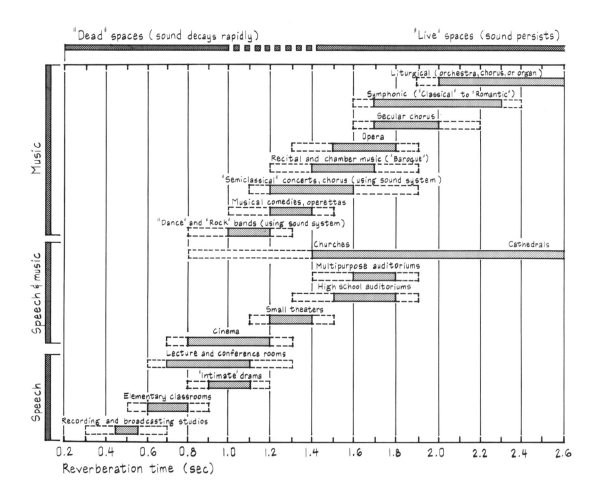

**Note:** Long reverberation times degrade speech perception of hearing-impaired persons far more than normal-hearing persons. For hearing-impaired and elderly listeners, reverberation times should be well below most of the values in the graph (e.g., < 0.5 s for satisfactory speech perception).

**Reference**

R. B. Newman, "Acoustics" in J. H. Callender (ed.), *Time-Saver Standards for Architectural Design Data*, McGraw-Hill, New York, 1974, p. 696.

## EXAMPLE PROBLEM (REVERBERATION TIME)

A classroom 60 ft long by 35 ft wide by 15 ft high has sound absorption coefficients α's of 0.30 for walls, 0.04 for ceiling, and 0.10 for floor. All α's are at 500 Hz.

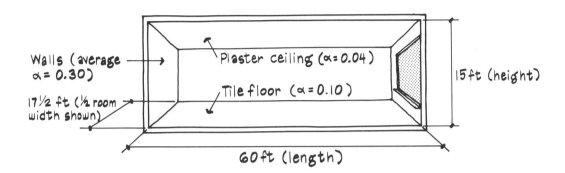

Find the reverberation time $T$ at 500 Hz in this space with no occupants and no sound-absorbing treatment.

**1.** Compute the room volume $V$.

$$V = 60 \times 35 \times 15 = \boxed{31,500 \text{ ft}^3}$$

**2.** Compute the surface areas $S$.

Ceiling  $S = 60 \times 35 = 2100 \text{ ft}^2$
Walls    $S = 2 \times 35 \times 15 = 1050 \text{ ft}^2$
         $S = 2 \times 60 \times 15 = 1800 \text{ ft}^2$
Floor    $S = 60 \times 35 = 2100 \text{ ft}^2$

**3.** Compute the total room absorption $a$ using $a = \Sigma S\alpha$.

|         | $S$    | $\alpha$    | $a$ (sabins) |
|---------|--------|-------------|--------------|
| Ceiling | 2100 × | 0.04 =      | 84           |
| Walls   | 2850 × | 0.30 =      | 855          |
| Floor   | 2100 × | 0.10 =      | 210          |
|         |        | Total $a$ = | 1149 sabins  |

**Note:** Include air absorption in total for large rooms at frequencies greater than 1000 Hz (see Chap. 3).

**4.** Compute the reverberation time $T$ using $T = 0.05 \dfrac{V}{a}$.

$$T = 0.05 \frac{V}{a} = \frac{0.05 \times 31{,}500}{1149} = \frac{1575}{1149} = \boxed{1.37 \text{ s}} \text{ at 500 Hz}$$

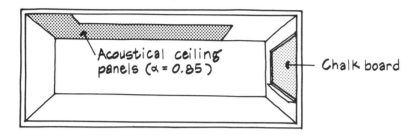

Acoustical ceiling panels ($\alpha = 0.85$)  —— Chalk board

Find the reverberation time $T$ if 50 percent of the ceiling surface (along the perimeter of the room) is treated with acoustical panels at $\alpha$ of 0.85. The central area remains sound-reflecting to help distribute sound energy from lectern end toward rear of the room.

**1.** Compute the total room absorption $a$ using $a = \Sigma\, S\alpha$.

|  | $S$ | $\alpha$ | $a$ (**sabins**) |
|---|---|---|---|
| Bare ceiling | $1050 \times 0.04 =$ | | 42 |
| Treated ceiling | $1050 \times 0.85 =$ | | 892 |
| Walls | $2850 \times 0.30 =$ | | 855 |
| Floor | $2100 \times 0.10 =$ | | 210 |
| | | Total $a =$ | 1999 sabins |

**2.** Compute new reverberation time $T$.

$$T = 0.05 \frac{V}{a} = \frac{0.05 \times 31{,}500}{1999} = \frac{1575}{1999} = \boxed{0.79 \text{ s}} \text{ at 500 Hz}$$

The reverberation time is reduced to below 1 s with 50 percent ceiling treatment for unoccupied conditions. This represents a reduction of $\frac{1.37 - 0.79}{1.37} \times 100 = 42$ percent, which is a "clearly noticeable" change. Absorption provided by teachers and students will further reduce reverberation depending on the number of occupants, their distribution throughout the room, and the clothing worn.

## HOW TO COMPUTE SURFACE AREAS

To find total absorption in a room, first compute the surface areas of ceiling, walls, and floor and then multiply by their respective sound absorption coefficients. Next, add absorption from occupants and furnishings. A wide variety of surface shapes, along with corresponding formulas to find area, are shown below. Areas of irregular shapes can be found by subdividing the surface into smaller areas of equal widths. The more divisions by parallel lines, the greater the accuracy. For alternate methods to compute areas of irregular shapes, see p. 667 in J. N. Boaz (ed.), *Architectural Graphic Standards*, Wiley, New York, 1970.

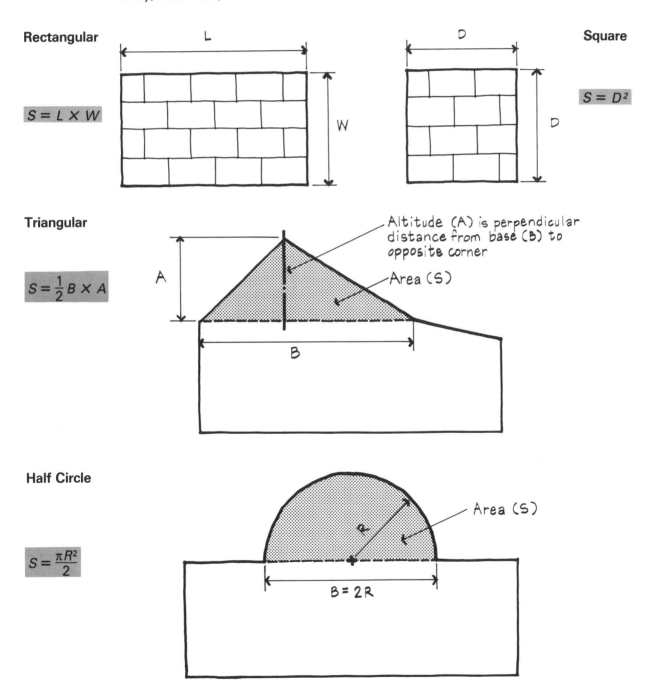

**Rectangular**

$$S = L \times W$$

L

W

**Square**

$$S = D^2$$

D

D

**Triangular**

$$S = \frac{1}{2}B \times A$$

A

B

Altitude (A) is perpendicular distance from base (B) to opposite corner

Area (S)

**Half Circle**

$$S = \frac{\pi R^2}{2}$$

Area (S)

R

$$B = 2R$$

## Half Parabola

$$S = \frac{4}{3} H \times B$$

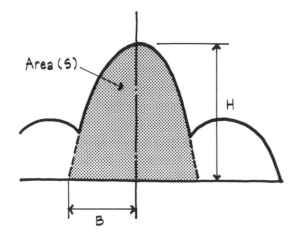

## Irregular

$S = B \times \Sigma$ (length of parallels, counting first and last at 1/2 length)

Divide by equally spaced parallel lines (B)

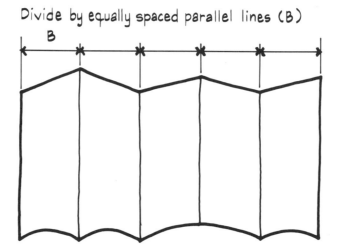

**Note:** For a review of trigonometry, see pp. 144-145 in M. D. Egan, *Concepts in Architectural Lighting*, McGraw-Hill, 1983. A comprehensive self-study review of mathematics for architecture is presented by M. Salvadori, *Mathematics in Architecture*, Prentice-Hall, Englewood Cliffs, N.J., 1968.

## ROOM NOISE REDUCTION

The buildup of sound levels in a room is due to the repeated reflections of sound from its enclosing surfaces. This buildup is affected by the size of the room and the amount of absorption within the room. The difference in decibels in reverberant noise levels, or *noise reduction*, under two conditions of room absorption can be found as follows:

$$NR = 10 \log \frac{a_2}{a_1}$$

where   NR = room noise reduction (dB)
      $a_2$ = total room absorption after treatment (sabins)
      $a_1$ = total room absorption before treatment (sabins)

The chart below also can be used to determine the reduction of reverberant noise level within a room due to changing the total room absorption. For example, if the total amount of absorption in a space can be increased from 700 to 2100 sabins, the reduction in reverberant noise level NR will be about 5 dB. (See dot on chart scale at absorption ratio of $a_2/a_1 = 2100/700 = 3$.) Since absorption efficiencies vary with frequency, the NR should be calculated at all frequencies for which sound absorption coefficients are known.

Reduction in reverberant noise level (dB)

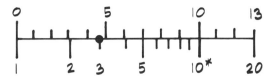

Ratio of total room absorptions ($a_2/a_1$)

*Practical upper limit of improvement for most situations.

The NR is the reduction in *reverberant* noise level. This does not affect the noise level very near the source of sound in a room. Also, as indicated on the chart, a reduction in reverberant noise level of 10 dB (an increase in absorption of greater than 10 times the initial value before treatment) is the practical upper limit for most remedial situations.

# EXAMPLE PROBLEM (ROOM NOISE REDUCTION)

A small room 10 ft by 10 ft by 10 ft has all walls and floor finished in exposed concrete. The ceiling is completely covered with sound-absorbing spray-on material. Sound absorption coefficients $\alpha$'s are 0.02 for concrete and 0.70 for spray-on material, both at 500 Hz.

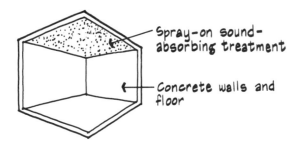

Spray-on sound-absorbing treatment

Concrete walls and floor

Find the noise reduction NR in this room if sound-absorbing panels are added to two adjacent walls. The sound absorption coefficient $\alpha$ is 0.85 for panels at 500 Hz.

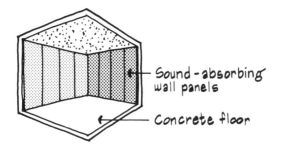

Sound-absorbing wall panels

Concrete floor

1. Compute the surface areas $S$.

$$S = 5 \times 10 \times 10 = \boxed{500 \text{ ft}^2} \text{ of concrete}$$
$$S = 10 \times 10 = \boxed{100 \text{ ft}^2} \text{ of spray-on material}$$

2. Compute the total room absorption $a_1$ with spray-on material on the ceiling.

$$a_1 = \Sigma S\alpha = (500 \times 0.02) + (100 \times 0.70) = 10 + 70 = \boxed{80 \text{ sabins}}$$

3. Compute the total room absorption $a_2$ with sound-absorbing panels covering two walls and spray-on material on ceiling.

$$a_2 = \Sigma S\alpha = (300 \times 0.02) + (200 \times 0.85) + (100 \times 0.70)$$
$$= 6 + 170 + 70 = \boxed{246 \text{ sabins}}$$

4. Compute the noise reduction NR.

$$NR = 10 \log \frac{a_2}{a_1} = 10 \log \frac{246}{80} = 10 \log (3.075 \times 10^0)$$
$$= 10(0.4878) = \boxed{5 \text{ dB}}$$

This would be a "noticeable" improvement. (See the table Changes in Sound Level, p. 21, in Chap. 1.) With no treatment, the total absorption in the room would only be 600 × 0.02 = 12 sabins. Therefore, treating the ceiling alone provides

$$NR = 10 \log \frac{80}{12} = 10 \log 6.67 = 10(0.8241) = \boxed{8 \text{ dB}}$$

which is a "significant" reduction. However, initial conditions of all hard surfaces in unfurnished rooms rarely occur.

Find the noise reduction NR if all four wall surfaces are treated with fabric-covered panels and the floor is carpeted. The sound absorption coefficient $\alpha$ of the carpet is 0.50 at 500 Hz.

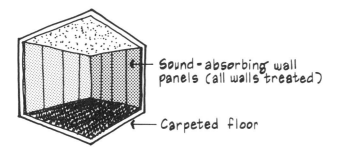

Sound-absorbing wall panels (all walls treated)

Carpeted floor

**1.** Compute the total room absorption $a_3$ with sound-absorbing panels on all walls, spray-on material on ceiling, and carpet on floor.

$$a_3 = \Sigma S\alpha = (400 \times 0.85) + (100 \times 0.70) + (100 \times 0.50)$$
$$= 340 + 70 + 50 = \boxed{460 \text{ sabins}}$$

**2.** Compute the noise reduction NR for these improvements compared to room conditions of spray-on ceiling treatment alone.

$$NR = 10 \log \frac{a_3}{a_1} = 10 \log \frac{460}{80} = 10 \log (5.75 \times 10^0)$$
$$= 10(0.7597) = \boxed{8 \text{ dB}}$$

The results from both parts of the problem are summarized below.

| Surfaces Treated (in addition to ceiling) | Room NR (at 500 Hz) |
|---|---|
| Two walls | 5 dB |
| Four walls and floor | 8 dB |

**Note:** The NRs given in the above table would not be as great at low frequencies because sound absorption coefficients usually are smaller at low frequencies than at mid- or high frequencies.

# NOISE REDUCTION FOR HIGH-NOISE ENVIRONMENTS

### Low Ceiling, Machines Widely Spaced

In the example shown below, machines are widely spaced so that installing efficient sound-absorbing treatment on the ceiling and upper walls can reduce reverberant noise levels throughout the room. However, the sound-absorbing treatment will be of little benefit to the individual equipment operators in the *free field* because the direct sound energy will reach the operator before it reaches the sound-absorbing materials.

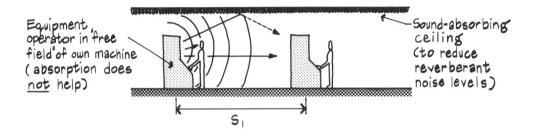

Equipment operator in "free field" of own machine (absorption does not help)

Sound-absorbing ceiling (to reduce reverberant noise levels)

$S_1$

### High Ceiling, Machines Closely Spaced

In the example of closely spaced machines in a room with a high ceiling, room surface treatment can be effective if reverberant noise levels are higher than the free-field noise of some machines. A reduction in reverberation will help make machine noise more directional (by reducing the reflected sound), allowing workers to be more responsive to their own machines. However, operators of closely spaced machines may be in the free field of several machines, which would be unaffected by ceiling and upper-wall treatment.

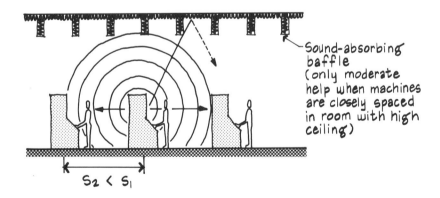

Sound-absorbing baffle (only moderate help when machines are closely spaced in room with high ceiling)

$S_2 < S_1$

### Enclosure To Contain Machine Noise

The sound-isolating enclosure shown below can be designed to provide noise reduction near the source so individual operators can be close to their machines without experiencing high noise levels. Enclosures can be designed with operable viewing panels to allow rapid access when needed (see Chap. 4 for sound-isolation principles, materials, and constructions).

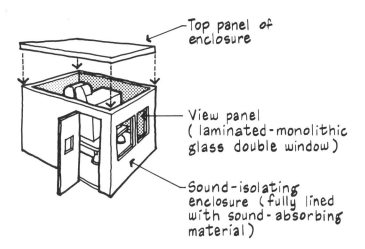

Top panel of enclosure

View panel (laminated-monolithic glass double window)

Sound-isolating enclosure (fully lined with sound-absorbing material)

**Note:** Where noisy machines are located close to walls, sound-absorbing wall treatment may provide useful noise reduction.

### References

P. D. Emerson et al., *Manual of Textile Industry Noise Control*, Center for Acoustical Studies, North Carolina State University, 1978 (contains over 20 case studies).

P. Jensen et al., *Industrial Noise Control Manual*, U.S. Department of Health, Education, and Welfare, December 1978 (contains over 60 case studies on a wide variety of industries).

R. B. Newman and W. J. Cavanaugh, "Design for Hearing," *Progressive Architecture*, May 1959.

W. G. Orr, *Handbook for Industrial Noise Control*, National Aeronautics and Space Administration, NASA SP-5108, 1981.

# TRANSONDENT FACINGS

Sound-transparent facings (called *transondent*) may range from 5 to 50 percent or more open area, depending on absorption requirements. Facings tend to reduce the effectiveness of sound-absorbing materials by reflecting high-frequency sound waves. In general, the lower the percentage of open area in the facing, the less absorption of high-frequency sound energy. Sizes of holes, number of holes per unit area, and dimensions of solid area between openings also affect the reduction in absorption. Transondent facings such as perforated sheet metal, expanded metal, or punched and pressed metal can be used alone in front of sound-absorbing materials, or in combination with wood slats or other large-scale protective elements.

Examples of open metal materials and a table of perforation sizes and spacings for facing materials are shown below.

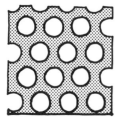
1/4" staggered holes at 3/8" o.c. (40% open)

1/4" staggered holes at 5/16" o.c. (58% open)

17/64" staggered holes at 5/16" o.c. (65% open)

**Note:** When painting open facings, use rollers, *not* sprayers, to reduce the likelihood that the openings will become blocked. Be careful also to avoid using facings with very tiny holes which may easily become clogged with paint.

### Perforation Sizes and Spacings

| Hole Diameter (in) | Spacing (in oc) |
|---|---|
| 3/16 | 0.50* |
| 5/32 | 0.40 |
| 1/8 | 0.30† |
| 3/32 | 0.22† |
| 1/16 | 0.15 |
| 1/32 | 0.08 |

*Do not exceed this spacing for hardboard material (e.g., pegboard).

† Most suitable for wall materials. Holes are small enough to discourage jabbing with sharp objects and large enough so facing can be carefully painted without becoming clogged.

### Reference

W. R. Farrell, "Sound Absorption for Walls," *Architectural & Engineering News*, October 1965.

## PERFORATED FACINGS

Perforated facings can be used to protect and conceal porous sound-absorbing materials or, if highly transparent to sound waves, to conceal sound-reflecting or diffusing surfaces. When used over a solid backup surface without *fuzz* (fibrous materials) in the cavity, perforated facings can act as multiple volume resonators to selectively absorb sound with the individual holes sharing a common volume. Partitioned (or subdivided) cavities can provide wider absorption near the resonant frequency.

As shown by the graph below, the thinner the facing, the more efficient the absorption of sound energy at mid- and high frequencies. The higher the percentage of open area (from numerous, closely spaced perforations to reduce size of solid areas), the more efficient the absorption of sound energy at high frequencies. Sound transparency increases as the size of the holes and number of holes per unit area increases, and as the distance between holes decreases.

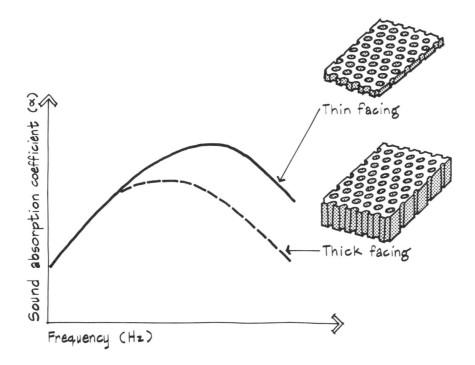

The critical frequency $f_c$ for circular perforations, above which sound absorption efficiency drops off rapidly, can be found as follows:

$$f_c \simeq \frac{40P}{D}$$

where    $f_c$ = critical frequency (Hz)
           $P$ = open area (%)
           $D$ = hole diameter (in)

For example, 25 percent open perforated facing with 1/4-in-diameter holes will have a critical frequency of

$$f_c \simeq \frac{40 \times 25}{0.25} = \boxed{4000 \text{ Hz}}$$

Precise analysis should also take into account the thickness of the facing and depth of the airspace behind the facing (cf., P. V. Brüel, *Sound Insulation and Room Acoustics*, Chapman & Hall, London, 1951, pp. 114-123).

**Reference**

T. J. Schultz, *Acoustical Uses for Perforated Metals*, Industrial Perforators Association, Milwaukee, Wis., 1986, pp. 14-20.

## PROTECTIVE FACINGS FOR WALL ABSORPTION

When absorption of high-frequency sound energy is *not* critical, the open area of protective facings need only be greater than about 10 percent to control reverberation or noise buildup within rooms. As a consequence, a wide variety of textures and forms can be used to satisfy this requirement. When absorption is used to control echoes, however, protective facings should have a higher percentage of open area from numerous, closely spaced openings. To conceal the sound-absorbing material behind most facings, tint the material black by spraying with nonbridging water-base paint or use a dark sound-transparent protective cover (e.g., burlap or open-weave fabric).

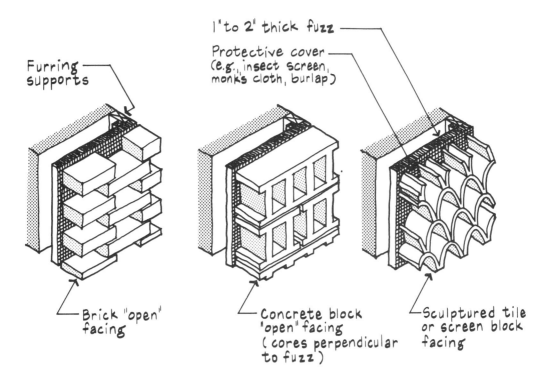

### Reference

R. B. Newman and W. J. Cavanaugh, "Acoustics" in J. H. Callender (ed.), *Time-Saver Standards for Architectural Design Data*, McGraw-Hill, New York, 1966, p. 622.

# RESONANT PANELS

*Resonant panels* are sound-absorbing panels which are designed to provide low-frequency absorption ( $\leq 250$ Hz). Example applications for resonant panels are music practice rooms, radio/TV studios, and the like. Resonant panels absorb energy from sound waves by vibrating at a frequency determined by the geometry and damping characteristics of the panel.

To decrease the resonant frequency, use wide spacings between supports ( > 2 ft), thin panel materials (e.g., plywood, hardboard), and "deep" airspace behind panels. To increase the resonant frequency, use close spacings between supports, thick panel materials (or perforated, thin panel materials with sound-absorbing material located close behind the panel), and shallow or narrow airspace behind panels.

It is prudent to test unique resonant panel designs in reverberation rooms to evaluate their performance. The resonant frequency $f_r$ can be estimated by:

$$f_r = \frac{170}{\sqrt{wd}}$$

where   $f_r$ = resonant frequency (Hz)
$w$ = surface weight of panel (lb/ft$^2$)
$d$ = depth of airspace behind panel (in)

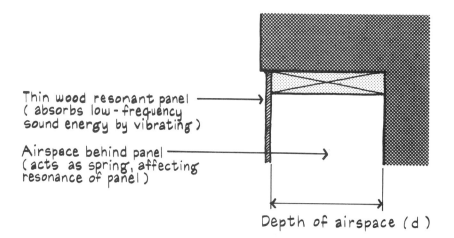

Thin wood resonant panel
( absorbs low-frequency
sound energy by vibrating )

Airspace behind panel
( acts as spring, affecting
resonance of panel )

Depth of airspace (d)

## Reference

V. O. Knudsen and C. M. Harris, *Acoustical Designing in Architecture*, Wiley, New York, 1950, p. 120 (paperback reprint is available from the Acoustical Society of America, 500 Sunnyside Blvd., Woodbury, NY 11797).

# SUGGESTED SOUND-ABSORBING TREATMENT FOR ROOMS

Although the NRC rating method has the limitations presented earlier in this chapter, it can be an adequate index to evaluate sound-absorbing materials for use in treating the noncritical spaces listed below. The last two groups in the table represent many of the spaces where the NRC by itself does *not* provide sufficient information. Therefore, special study may be required to determine the specific absorption needs. For example, absorption for ceilings in open-plan offices, where sound can reflect over partial-height barriers, destroying speech privacy, should be evaluated *only* by *noise isolation class prime* NIC' ratings (see Chap. 6), although a minimum NRC is given.

| Type of Space | Preferred NRC Range | Ceiling Treatment | Wall Treatment |
| --- | --- | --- | --- |
| Private offices, large offices, small conference rooms, hospitals, laboratory work spaces, libraries, retail shops and stores | 0.65 to 0.75 | Full | None required |
| Lobbies, corridors, gymnasiums | 0.65 to 0.75 | Full | Yes |
| Secondary and college classrooms, large meeting rooms | 0.65 to 0.75 | Partial | Yes |
| Kitchens, cafeterias, laundries, restaurants | > 0.75 | Full | Usually none required |
| Computer equipment rooms, school and industrial shops, machinery spaces | > 0.75 | Full | Yes |
| Auditoriums, theaters, radio/TV studios, music practice rooms, audiovisual facilities, churches, courtrooms, chapels, mechanical equipment rooms, open-plan schools, language laboratories, factories | (These spaces in particular require special study to determine the appropriate type, amount, and location of sound-absorbing treatment.) | | |
| Open offices | > 0.80 | Full | Yes (see Chap. 6) |

# CHECKLIST FOR EFFECTIVE ABSORPTION OF SOUND

1. Apply sound-absorbing materials on surfaces that may contribute to excessive reverberation, produce annoying echoes, or focus sound energy. In auditoriums and similar facilities, use sound-absorbing materials to control echoes and reverberation. Excessive reverberation can seriously interfere with listening conditions, especially for hearing-impaired and older persons. A doubling of the existing absorption in a room will reduce the reverberation by one-half.

2. Do *not* use sound-absorbing materials on surfaces which should provide useful sound reflections (e.g., above lecterns in auditoriums). Sound-reflecting surfaces must have sound absorption coefficients well below 0.20 and be properly shaped and oriented (see Chap. 3).

3. Use sound-absorbing ceilings to control the buildup of noise within rooms, unless the floor is carpeted and the room is filled with heavy draperies and other sound-absorbing furnishings. Sound-absorbing materials are commercially available that have a factory-applied surface finish which is reasonably durable for ceiling applications as well as satisfying appearance, light reflectance, and other architectural and fire safety requirements.

4. Place absorption on the walls of very high rooms, small rooms, or long and narrow rooms, where flutter echo may occur. In very large rooms with low ceilings, wall absorption is rarely beneficial unless needed to prevent flanking of sound energy around partial-height barriers in open plans. Sound-absorbing wall panels that have a fabric finish and hardened edges to maintain their shape are commercially available.

5. Be sure the mounting method used is best suited for the amount of absorption desired. The actual method of mounting is important because it will affect absorption efficiency. For example, sound-absorbing materials directly attached with mechanical fasteners (mounting A) are poor absorbers of low-frequency sound. However, when attached to furring supports (mounting D), they will provide more absorption at low frequencies; and when used in suspended ceiling systems (mounting E), they can provide considerable low-frequency absorption. To achieve maximum absorption from special sound-absorbing materials and units, such as suspended baffles and spaced absorbers, install them at the spacings recommended by manufacturers.

6. Do *not* overestimate the noise control benefits from sound absorption. Remember, it takes a doubling of the existing absorption to achieve only 3 dB of noise reduction! It requires an enormous increase in existing absorption to achieve 6 dB of noise reduction. Consequently, in most situations, 3 to 6 dB is the practical limit of noise reduction benefits from adding sound absorption to rooms.

# Chapter 3
## ROOM ACOUSTICS

# ANCIENT THEATERS

Open-air Greek and Roman theaters (constructed about 2000 years ago) most often had good listening conditions for drama and instrumental recitals by small groups. The Greek theaters usually were located on steep hillsides in quiet rural locations. Successful sites had few gusty winds (which cause noise when they blow past trees, buildings, and audience). Seating layouts were semicircular so the audience would be close to the stage, thus reducing sound energy loss by distance (see Chap. 1 for inverse-square law). The tiers were constructed with a steep rise ($> 20°$) to provide good sight lines, permit reflected sound energy from the orchestra floor, and reduce attenuation caused by the seated audience. The unoccupied seats (with backs or risers sloped backward by about 10°) and the heads of the audience also scattered sound to adjacent areas (cf., R. S. Shankland, "Acoustics of Greek Theatres," *Physics Today,* October 1973). In addition, actors wore masks which exaggerated their expressions and reinforced their voices since conical-shaped megaphones were built into the mouths of the masks. However, onstage whispers were not audible throughout the audience area. Some characteristic design features of ancient theaters are shown below.

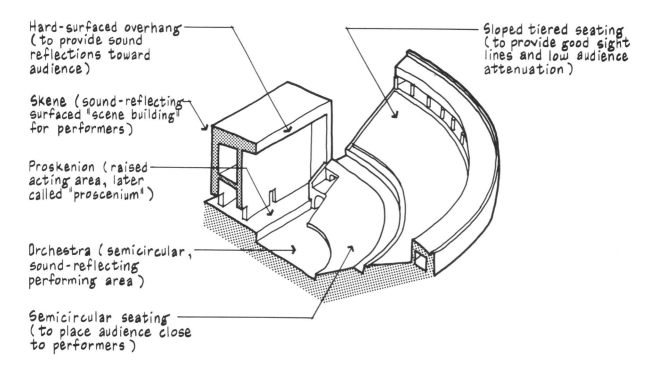

Hard-surfaced overhang (to provide sound reflections toward audience)

Skene (sound-reflecting surfaced "scene building" for performers)

Proskenion (raised acting area, later called "proscenium")

Orchestra (semicircular, sound-reflecting performing area)

Semicircular seating (to place audience close to performers)

Sloped tiered seating (to provide good sight lines and low audience attenuation)

Modern open-air theaters should be designed to achieve low noise intrusion (see Chap. 4) and satisfactory distribution of sound. However, an enclosure is required to achieve the reverberation and fullness of tone needed for modern symphonic music and opera (especially since the nineteenth century).

**Note:** For comprehensive studies of the development of the ancient theater, see M. Bieber, *The History of Greek and Roman Theater*, Princeton University Press, Princeton, N.J., 1961, and G. C. Izenour, *Theater Design*, McGraw-Hill, New York, 1977.

## DIRECTIVITY CONTOURS FOR SPEECH

The polar coordinate graph below plots contours of sound levels for speech. The shapes of the contours show the directional characteristics of speech at low frequencies (≤ 500 Hz to represent *vowels*, which contribute to the tone of an individual's speech) and at high frequencies (≥ 4000 Hz to represent *consonants*, which strongly influence intelligibility of sibilants). 0° is the direction the speaker is facing, 180° the direction behind the speaker. Sound levels at low frequencies are diminished very little at the sides (90° orientation) and moderately at the rear (8 dB lower). However, sound levels at high frequencies are diminished by about 6 dB at the sides and 20 dB (about one-fourth as loud) at the rear. When speakers turn their backs to the audience, consonants can become completely inaudible!

**Speech Contours** (500 and 4000 Hz)

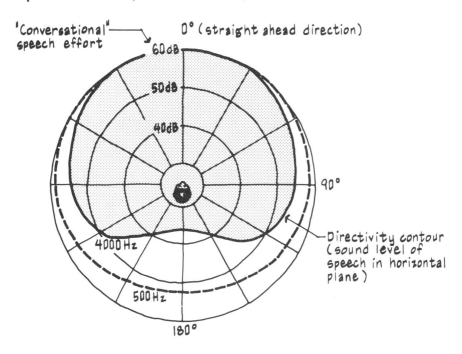

**Auditorium Plan with Speech Contour Overlay**

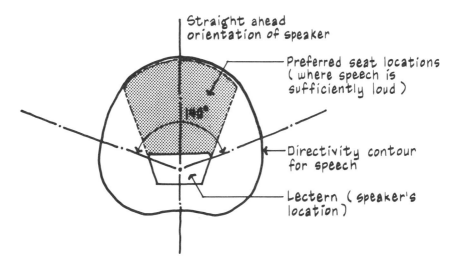

Sound level outdoors falls off with *distance* (as sound spreads outward it loses energy according to the inverse-square law) and from *audience attenuation* (as sound grazes the seated audience it is scattered and absorbed). When steeply sloped seating is used, the sound level outdoors falls off primarily with distance. An overhead sound-reflecting panel or ceiling, as shown by the illustration at the bottom of the page, can provide reflected sound to reinforce the direct sound. For example, installing a hard, sound-reflecting enclosure outdoors near the sound source can greatly improve listening conditions by reflecting sound energy toward the audience and by shielding the audience from noise sources located behind the enclosure.

### Level Seating Outdoors

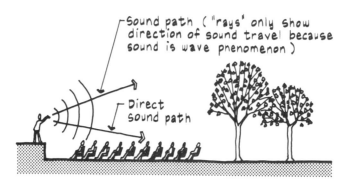

### Steeply Sloped Seating Outdoors

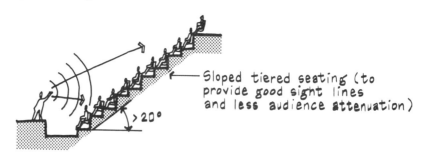

### Level Seating Indoors

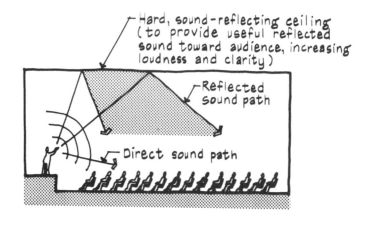

## SIGHT LINE BASICS

Unobstructed *sight lines* (i.e., straight lines drawn from eyes of seated occupants to stage area) from all seats to the front of the forestage allow full view of performers and unobstructed propagation of the direct sound. Sight lines are normally drawn to converge at a point on stage called the *arrival point of sight* APS. Audiences should be able to hear and to see clearly and comfortably to fully perceive the intended effects of performances. Laterally staggered seating layouts can achieve satisfactory *every-other-row* vision for back-to-back seat dimension *B* of 40 in for continental seating and 36 in for radial and parallel aisle seating. Nonstaggered seating layouts cannot achieve satisfactory conditions for every-other-row vision (cf., G. C. Izenour, *Theater Design*, McGraw-Hill, New York, 1977, p. 26). Shown below are sight lines for every-row and every-other-row seating layouts, and average seating dimensions.

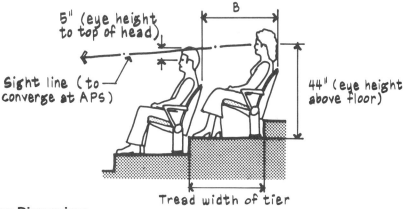

**Average Seating Dimensions**

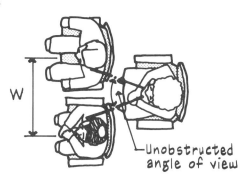

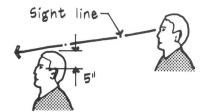

**Every-Row Vision**

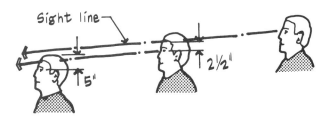

**Every-Other-Row Vision**

**Note:** To achieve liveness within a reasonable room volume, the back-to-back seat dimension *B* and center-to-center seat dimension *W* should be as small as possible consistent with the requirements for comfort and life safety.

For proscenium theaters, *lateral sight lines* (shown in plan view below) normally should be within a preferred "view angle" of 30°. View angle is measured from the perpendicular at the end of the proscenium opening. In multipurpose auditoriums, the proscenium line may vary from full width for ballet and symphonic orchestra (often located downstage to provide orchestra enclosure of shallow depth) to smaller widths for drama and music performance by soloists or small ensembles.

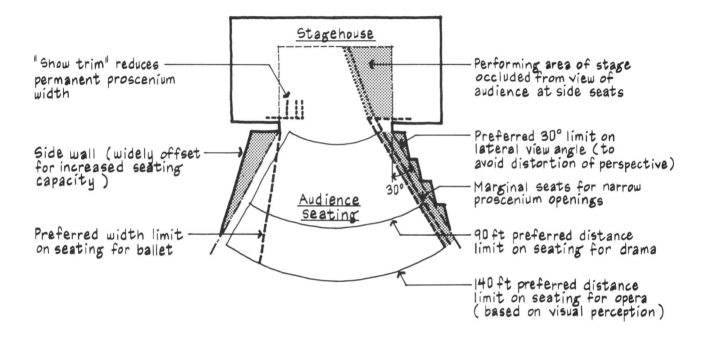

**Plan View**

Floor and balcony slopes should be designed so seated audience will have unobstructed view of entire performing area, performers, and scenery. For example, the *vertical sight lines* shown below illustrate acceptable viewing conditions and preferred layout of seating in the front of auditorium where an unin-

**Detail at Stage**

terrupted view of entire stage floor is essential for ballet. Balconies should not have excessive floor slope ( > 26°), and the top balcony should not be more than 65 ft above the stage to avoid vertigo. A balcony view of the first few rows of main floor seating also may be desirable to achieve a sense of congregation with audience below and the proscenium arch should not obstruct the view of bottom 7 ft of the backstage wall.

**Section View**

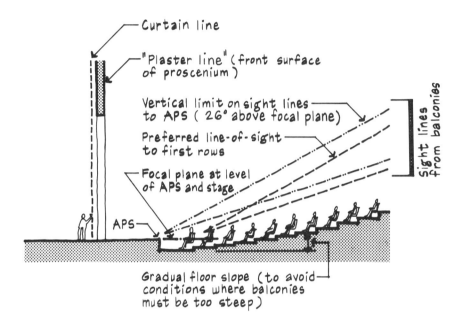

## References

J. R. Hyde and J. von Szeliski, ''Acoustics and Theater Design,'' 12th International Congress on Acoustics, *Proceedings of the Vancouver Symposium on Acoustics and Theatre Planning for the Performing Arts*, August 1986, pp. 55-60.

J. Mielziner, *Theatre Check List*, Wesleyan University Press, Middletown, Conn., 1969.

# CHECKLIST FOR LECTURE ROOMS

When auditoriums are used primarily for speech (e.g., theaters, conference rooms, classrooms), the design goal should be high intelligibility of spoken words throughout the room. To achieve high *signal-to-noise ratios* ($>$ 15 dB), rooms should be shaped to direct sound from the speaker's location toward the audience, designed to avoid echoes and "hot" (or "bright") spots, and planned to have low background noise levels. Important acoustical parameters affecting the perception of speech in lecture rooms are summarized by the list below.

1. To help achieve satisfactory loudness, provide compact room shape with relatively low room volume. Volume per seat ratio should be 80 to 150 ft$^3$ per person.

2. Reverberation times should be less than 1.2 s from 250 to 4000 Hz for theaters and less than 0.8 s for classrooms. Long reverberation times reduce the intelligibility of speech the same way noise masks speech signals (see Chap. 6). Select sound-absorbing finishes so absorption will be constant within the frequency range for speech. It is preferable to place absorption on side walls rather than on ceilings. In small rooms, use sound-absorbing panels with airspace behind to prevent "boominess" at low frequencies.

3. Distance between speaker and the rear of the audience area should be short so that loudness will be sufficient throughout the room and the audience will have ability to see the person talking. For drama, it is difficult to see expressions of performers beyond 40 ft, gestures beyond 65 ft, and large body movements beyond 100 ft. For fan-shaped rooms, seating should be within 140° angle measured at the location of the speaker (see auditorium plan on page 83).

4. Ceiling or overhead sound-reflecting surfaces should provide short-delayed sound reflections directly to the audience (i.e., path differences between direct and reflected sound should be less than 34 ft).

5. Seating should be sloped greater than 7° to provide good sight lines and reduce audience attenuation. (Without electronic speech reinforcement, 1000 seats is about the upper limit for drama using a proscenium stage; 700 seats using an open or thrust stage; and 400 seats using an arena stage.)

6. Background noise levels from the mechanical system should not exceed 34 dBA or noise criterion NC-25. Enclosing constructions should reduce intruding noise to below this preferred criterion to avoid interference with desired sounds and prevent distractions (see Chap. 4). Even lower limits should be considered where rooms are to be used by young children, older adults, or hearing-impaired persons.

7. When seating capacity exceeds about 500, provide a sound-reinforcing system to augment the natural sound from source to listener (see Chap. 7). Smaller lecture rooms, courtrooms, conference rooms, and the like may also require a sound-reinforcing system to assist weak-voiced speakers and to project recorded material evenly. (Be careful because electronically reproduced sound may sound "harsh" and unnatural when played in rooms with extremely low reverberation times.)

REFLECTION, DIFFUSION, AND DIFFRACTION

### Reflection ($x > 4\lambda$)

*Reflection* is the return of a sound wave from a surface. If the surface dimension $x$ is larger than about 2 to 4 times the wavelength $\lambda$ of the impinging sound wave, the angle of incidence $\angle i$ will equal the angle of reflection $\angle r$. For example, 1000 Hz corresponds to a wavelength of 1.1 ft; therefore, a surface dimension (length or width) of about $4\lambda = 4 \times 1.1 \cong 4\ 1/2$ ft will reflect sound energy wavelengths of 1000 Hz and above. When an array of suspended panels is used to direct reflected sound energy toward the audience, the individual panels should be of varying sizes to prevent creating a "rasping" sound.

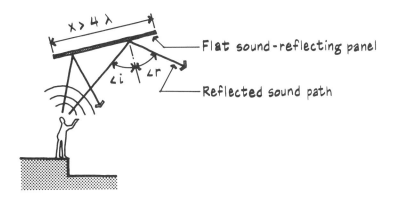

### Diffusion ($x = \lambda$)

*Diffusion* is the scattering or random redistribution of a sound wave from a surface. It occurs when the surface depths of hard-surfaced materials are comparable to the wavelengths of the sound. Diffusion does not "break up" or absorb sound—sound is not fragile or brittle! However, the direction of the incident sound wave is changed as it strikes a sound-diffusing material. Diffusion is an extremely important characteristic of rooms used for musical performances. When satisfactory diffusion has been achieved, listeners will have the sensation of sound coming from all directions at equal levels.

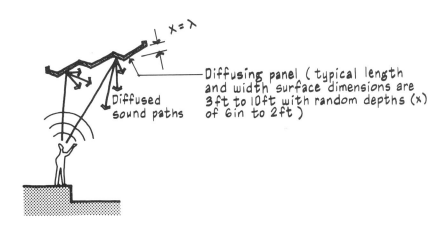

## Diffraction $(x < \lambda)$

*Diffraction* is the bending or "flowing" of a sound wave around an object or through an opening. For example, a truck located behind a building can be heard because the sound waves bend around the corners. In auditoriums, because impinging sound waves will readily diffract around panels that are smaller than their wavelength, suspended panels must be carefully designed to be large enough (length and width) to effectively reflect the desired wavelengths of sound.

A single frequency can be emphasized (called *diffraction grating effect*) when an array of small overhead panels are of equal length and width or vertical projecting slats on walls are of equal depth and spacing. This phenomenon must be avoided because it can impart an odd tonal distortion to music due to cancellation effects.

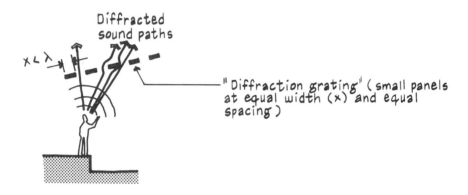

### Reference

R. W. Leonard, L. P. Delsasso, and V. O. Knudsen, "Diffraction of Sound by an Array of Rectangular Reflective Panels," *Journal of the Acoustical Society of America*, December 1964.

## WAVELENGTH AND FREQUENCY FOR SOUND IN AIR

The scale below shows the relationship of wavelength and frequency for sound in air under normal conditions of temperature and atmospheric pressure. For example, below 1500 Hz many musical instruments are *omnidirectional* (i.e., they radiate sound energy in all directions). From the scale, at 1500 Hz the wavelength of sound is 0.75 ft, or 9 in, and $4 \lambda = 4 \times 9 = 36$ in. Therefore, panel dimensions greater than 3 ft will be required to reflect sound energy at 1500 Hz (and higher).

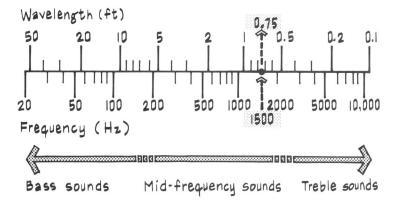

Most musical instruments do not, however, radiate sound in all directions at the same sound level. The directional characteristics of example wind instrument (trombone) and string instrument (cello) are shown below. The shaded portion between sound rays on the illustrations indicate where the sound level is within 3 dB of its maximum level. Note that sound from a trombone is directed primarily toward the front at high frequencies and to the ceiling at low frequencies. For a comprehensive presentation of the complex directional characteristics of musical instruments, see J. Meyer, *Acoustics and the Performance of Music,* Verlag Das Musikinstrument, Frankfurt, F.R.G., 1978.

Sound toward ceiling
(or overhead panels
of orchestra shell)

**Cello at 500 Hz**

Sound toward ceiling

**Trombone at 650 Hz**

Sound reflected toward audience
(if not obstructed by other musicians)

**Cello at > 2000 Hz**

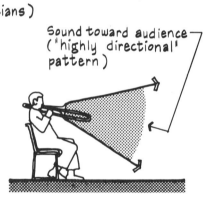

Sound toward audience
("highly directional"
pattern)

**Trombone at > 2000 Hz**

Shown below in order of increasing effectiveness for distributing sound are concave, flat, and convex sound-reflecting surfaces. The shading on the illustrations indicates the distribution pattern of reflected sound energy from equivalent lengths of reflector.

## Concave Reflector

Concave sound-reflecting surfaces (such as barrel-vaulted ceilings in churches and curved rear walls in auditoriums) can focus sound, causing hot spots and echoes in the audience seating area. Because concave surfaces focus sound, they also are poor distributors of sound energy and therefore should be avoided where sound-reflecting surfaces are desired (e.g., near stage, lectern, or other source locations in rooms).

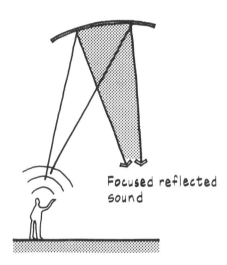

Focused reflected sound

## Flat Reflector

Flat, hard-surfaced building elements, if large enough and oriented properly, can effectively distribute reflected sound. The reflector shown below is tilted slightly to project sound energy toward the rear of an auditorium.

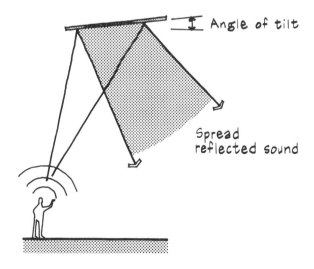

Angle of tilt

Spread reflected sound

## Convex Reflector

Convex, hard-surfaced building elements, if large enough, can be most effective as sound-distributing forms. The reflected sound energy from convex surfaces diverges, enhancing diffusion, which is highly desirable for music listening. In addition, reflected sound from convex surfaces is more evenly distributed across a wide range of frequencies.

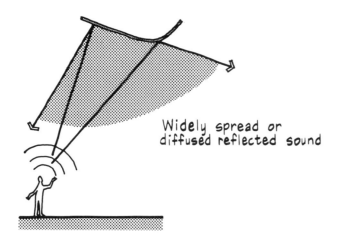

Widely spread or diffused reflected sound

# RAY DIAGRAMS

Ray-diagram analyses can be used to study the effect of room shape on the distribution of sound and to identify surfaces which may produce echoes. A ray diagram is an acoustical analogy to the *specular* reflection of light where the angle of incidence $\angle i$ of an impinging sound wave equals the angle of reflection $\angle r$, with angles measured from the perpendicular to the surface. That is, sound waves are reflected from surfaces in the same way a billiard ball, without spin, rebounds from a cushion. Because of this, small mirrors or silvered paper can be used with architectural drawings (or small-scale models) in a darkened room to reflect light from a point source. The patterns of reflected light demonstrate, during the design process, the effect of room shape on the distribution of sound.

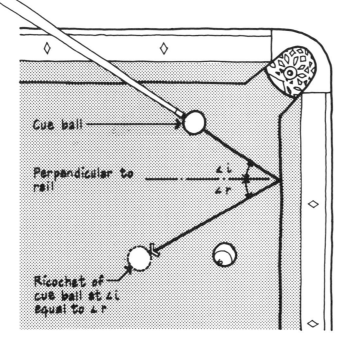

**Billiard Table**

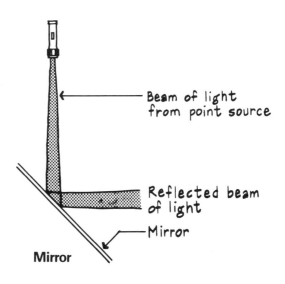

**Mirror**

Some limitations of ray-diagram studies are as follows:

1. Sound reflects in the manner indicated by ray diagrams only when surface dimensions are large relative to the wavelength λ of sound being evaluated ($> 4\,\lambda$).
2. Normally, the source of speech or music will not radiate from a fixed position. Optimum room shape therefore depends on a careful balance of the best sound distribution from several source positions to the listening area.
3. A detailed evaluation of diffusion of sound by room surfaces is not possible with ray diagrams. Therefore, scale models which allow frequency-scaled acoustical studies are often used in design, particularly in rooms where music perception is important (cf., V. O. Knudsen, "Model Testing of Auditoriums," *Journal of the Acoustical Society of America*, February 1970, pp. 401-407).

In spite of these limitations, ray diagrams can be an important design tool in establishing optimum room shape. The table below is a design guide that can be used with ray-diagram analyses to evaluate general listening conditions. The difference in length between the reflected sound path and the direct sound path at any listening position is directly related to the time difference which the ear detects. For example, if a reflected sound wave is heard 1/17 s or later after it was first heard as a direct sound, the reflected sound wave can be perceived as a discrete *echo*. A familiar example of this situation would be the echoes from cliffs in mountain regions, where reflected sounds are heard as distinct repetitions of the direct (or original) sound. The sound path difference in feet from a sound delayed by 1/17 s (about 0.06 s) can be found as follows:

$$\text{Distance} = \text{velocity} \times \text{time} = 1130 \times 0.06 = \boxed{68 \text{ ft}}$$

| Sound Path Difference (ft) | Time Delay Gap (ms) | Listening Conditions |
|---|---|---|
| < 23 | < 20 | Excellent for speech and music |
| 23 to 34 | 20 to 30 | Good for speech, fair for music |
| 34 to 50 | 30 to 45 | Marginal (*blurred*) |
| 50 to 68 | 45 to 60 | Unsatisfactory |
| > 68 | > 60 | Poor (*echo* if strong enough) |

**References**

L. L. Beranek and T. J. Schultz, "Some Recent Experiences in the Design and Testing of Concert Halls with Suspended Panel Arrays," *Acustica*, vol. 15, 1965.

V. O. Knudsen, "Architectural Acoustics," *Scientific American*, November 1963.

R. L. McKay, *Notes on Architectural Acoustics*, Stipes Publishing, Champaign, Ill., 1964.

**Note:** For an overview of acoustical modeling fundamentals, see R. G. Cann, "Principles of Acoustical Scale Modeling," *Sound & Video Contractor*, July 1985, pp. 30-35. Small-scale models at 1:20 and 1:50 scale ratios are useful for the study of initial design alternates, while larger scale ratios of 1:10 are best for detailed analyses of complex sound fields in concert halls.

## RAY-DIAGRAM GRAPHICS

An inexpensive protractor to measure angles, a pencil, scale, and paper are all the equipment required for ray-diagram calculations. Shown below is an auditorium section with sound path differences calculated to front and middle-rear audience locations from a typical source location.

Path difference = reflected path − direct path

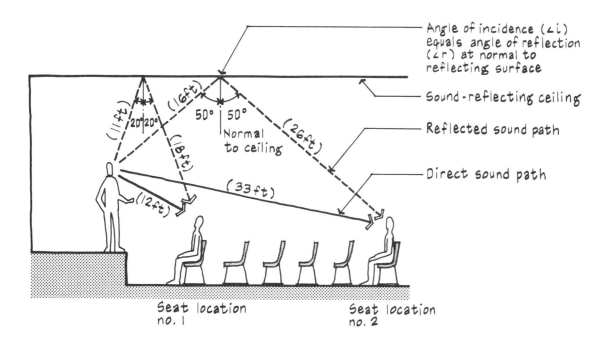

Example Ray-Diagram Measurements (Distances are shown in parentheses on above drawing)

*Front location no. 1:*

Path difference = (11 + 18) − (12) = 17 ft

Excellent for speech and music because path difference is less than 23 ft.

*Middle location no. 2:*

Path difference = (16 + 26) − (33) = 9 ft

Excellent for speech and music because path difference is less than 23 ft.

## SOUND PATHS IN AUDITORIUMS

The *initial-time-delay gap* is the time interval between the arrival of the direct sound and the first reflected sound of sufficient loudness. It should be less than about 30 ms (path difference < 34 ft) for good listening conditions because sounds within this time interval can coalesce as one impression in a listener's brain.

Early-arriving reflected sound energy is important for clarity and definition of music. "Early" sound is usually defined as the direct and reflected sound arriving within the first 80 ms. *Clarity* can be defined as the ratio of early sound energy to late or reverberant sound energy. Auditoriums with narrow shapes support direct and early-reflected sound because the initial-time-delay gaps will be short. In the design of auditoriums, ray diagrams can be used to determine initial-time-delay gaps. The initial-time-delay gap also strongly influences a listener's perception of the size of an auditorium (called *intimacy*).

The listener in the auditorium shown below will hear the direct sound first and then, after the initial-time-delay gap, reflections from the walls (path 1 on the drawing), ceiling (path 2), stage enclosure (path 3), and so on. These arrival times and sound levels are indicated by the bars on the sound level vs. time graph shown below.

### Sound Paths from Stage in Auditorium

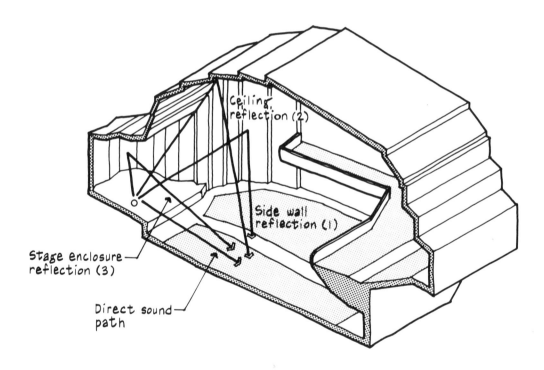

## Sound Level vs. Time Graph for Auditorium

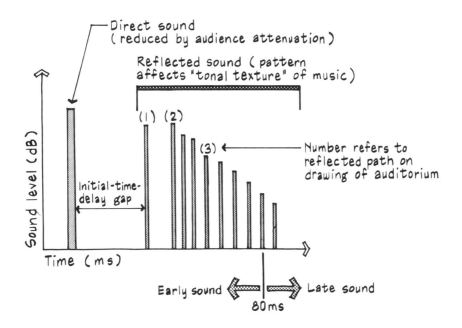

Direct sound (reduced by audience attenuation)

Reflected sound (pattern affects "tonal texture" of music)

(1) (2)

(3)

Number refers to reflected path on drawing of auditorium

Sound level (dB)

Initial-time-delay gap

Time (ms)

Early sound ⟷ Late sound

80ms

## References

L. L. Beranek, *Music, Acoustics and Architecture*, Wiley, New York, 1962, p. 27.

H. Kuttruff, *Room Acoustics*, 2d edition, Applied Science Publishers, Barking, England, 1979, pp. 180-192.

## CEILINGS

The preferred ceiling shape and height depend on the intended use of the room. For example, ray-diagram analysis indicates that the hard, sound-reflecting flat ceiling shown below provides useful sound reflections which cover the entire seating area in a lecture room. Useful sound reflections for speech are those which come from the same direction as the source and are delayed by less than 30 ms. However, by carefully reorienting the ceiling, as shown by the lower illustration, the extent of useful ceiling reflections can be increased so that the middle-rear seats actually receive reflections from both ceiling planes.

The average ceiling height $H$ in auditoriums with upholstered seats and absorptive rear walls is approximately related to the mid-frequency reverberation time $T$ as follows:

$$H \simeq 20T$$

where  $H =$ ceiling height (ft)
$\phantom{where } T =$ mid-frequency reverberation time (s)

**Flat Ceiling**

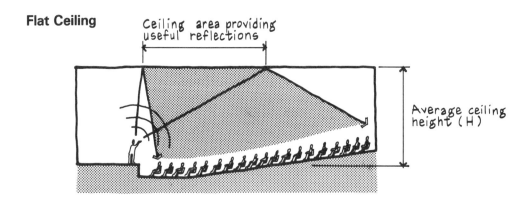

**Sloped Ceiling**

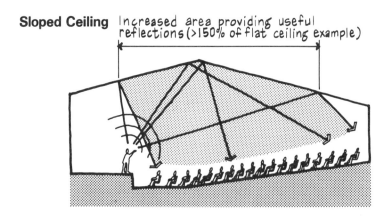

For concert halls, where long reverberation is a design goal, high ceilings are preferred and all walls should be sound-reflecting. In addition, ceilings that are diffusing can improve audibility of lateral sound by diminishing the strength of ceiling reflections [cf., A. H. Marshall, "Acoustical Determinants for the Architectural Design of Concert Halls," *Architectural Science Review* (Australia), September 1968, p. 86].

## ECHOES

An *echo* is the distinct repetition of the original sound and is sufficiently loud to be clearly heard above the general reverberation and background noise in a space. To determine if echoes are present in completed spaces, sharply clap your hands or slap two books together. Listen for any strong repetition of the original clap. Note the direction and strength of any echoes and how long it takes any "fluttering" or "ringing" to drop off to inaudibility. For speech signals, echoes can be perceived when the time intervals between the direct and reflected sounds are greater than 60 ms (about 1/17 s). In auditoriums, sound-reflecting flat or concave rear walls and high or vaulted ceilings are potential echo producers. The following pages show design techniques which can be used to prevent echoes. The graph below shows the amount in decibels an echo is above or below the direct speech for time delays (ms) in rooms with a reverberation time of about 1 s at mid-frequencies. An echo that falls in the shaded area on the upper right of the graph will be annoying to most listeners (> 50 percent disturbed).

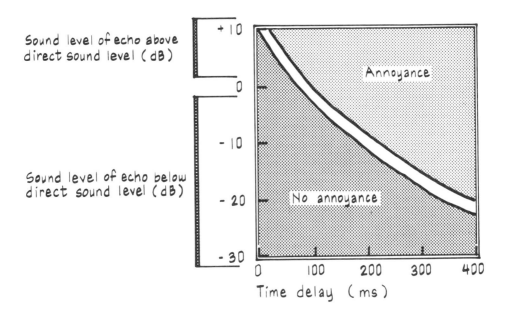

**References**

R. H. Bolt and P. E. Doak, "A Tentative Criterion for the Short-Term Transient Response of Auditoriums," *Journal of the Acoustical Society of America*, April 1950.

M. B. Gardner, "Historical Background of the Haas and/or Precedence Effect," *Journal of the Acoustical Society of America*, June 1968.

H. Haas, "The Influence of a Single Echo on the Audibility of Speech," *Journal of the Audio Engineering Society*, March 1972 (English translation by K. P. R. Ehrenberg).

# ECHO CONTROL PRINCIPLES

Potential echo-producing surfaces should be treated with efficient sound-absorbing materials (see Chap. 2) or shaped as shown below. The front portion of the ceiling is lowered to reduce the delayed reflections from overhead and reoriented to provide useful reflections toward the rear of the auditorium.

**Potential Echo-Producing Surfaces**

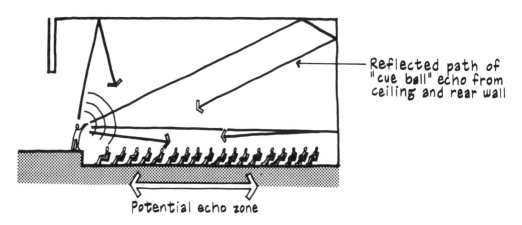

Reflected path of "cue ball" echo from ceiling and rear wall

Potential echo zone

**Revised Ceiling Profile** (To prevent echoes and distribute sound evenly)

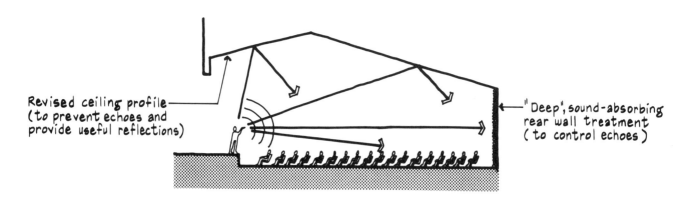

Revised ceiling profile (to prevent echoes and provide useful reflections)

"Deep", sound-absorbing rear wall treatment (to control echoes)

## Sound-Absorbing Wall Treatments

"Deep" treatment can be provided by either thick sound-absorbing materials or thin sound-absorbing materials installed with an airspace behind as shown below.

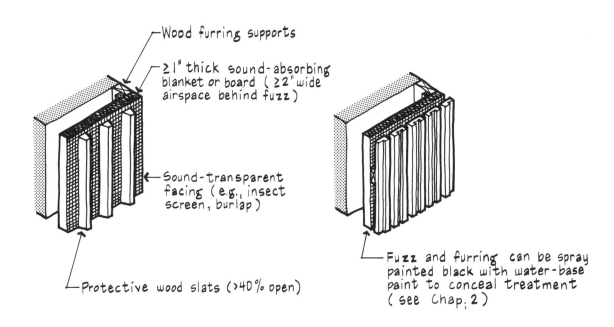

Wood furring supports

≥1" thick sound-absorbing blanket or board ( ≥2" wide airspace behind fuzz )

Sound-transparent facing ( e.g., insect screen, burlap )

Protective wood slats (>40% open)

Fuzz and furring can be spray painted black with water-base paint to conceal treatment ( see Chap. 2 )

# REAR-WALL ECHO CONTROL TREATMENT

   A flat, sound-reflecting rear wall can produce echoes or unwanted, long-delayed reflections in medium to large auditoriums. Three solutions to control "slap" echoes (i.e., sharp return of sound) from a rear wall are shown below.

   Perforated facings, which are highly transparent to sound waves, can be used to conceal sound-absorbing treatment (e.g., dome at Rotunda, University of Virginia) or sound-diffusing treatment (e.g., curved surfaces over stage at Orpheum Theatre, Vancouver, B.C., Canada).

**Echo-Producing Rear Wall**
(Echo at ceiling-wall
reentrant angle)

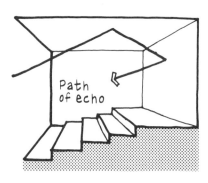

Path of echo

**Sound-Absorbing Treatment**
(Extend deep treatment
from seated head level)

"Deep" sound-absorbing treatment such as glass-fiber blanket (or board) supported by furring

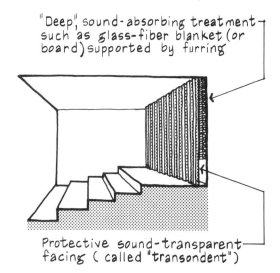

Protective sound-transparent facing (called "transondent")

**Surface Modulations or "Rumples"**
(Use cylinders with different radii for optimum diffusion)

Large-scale irregularities or modulations at cylinder diameter > ½ λ (to provide diffusion)

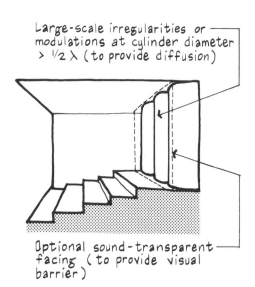

Optional sound-transparent facing (to provide visual barrier)

**Splayed Wall**
(To produce useful short-delayed reflections)

Splayed surface (to direct sound downward)

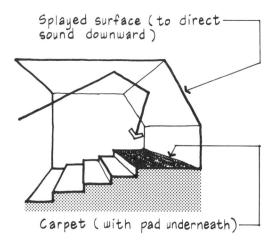

Carpet (with pad underneath)

**Reference**

L. L. Doelle, *Environmental Acoustics,* McGraw-Hill, New York, 1972, pp. 58-61.

## SIDE WALLS

Ray-diagram analyses are useful in the horizontal plane to study sound energy reflected from the side walls. These *lateral reflections* help create a favorable auditory spatial impression (or *intimacy*), which is essential for the satisfactory perception of music performances. Early sound reflections from side walls can add strength to the direct sound.

The *initial-time-delay gap* ITDG can be found by subtracting the direct sound path $D$ from the reflected sound path $R$. Both paths are measured to a listener seated near the centerline of the hall, halfway between the conductor and the first balcony face (or rear wall). ITDG in milliseconds equals the path difference $(R - D)$ in feet times 0.9. For concert halls, ITDG should be less than 20 ms.

Wide fan shapes and semicircular floor plans usually do not provide strong, early lateral reflections because the side walls will be located too far apart. Unless overhead sound reflectors can be used to help overcome the absence of lateral sound reflected from walls, music will sound distant and lack *fullness of tone*. The "reverse" fan shape (rooms with decreasing width toward rear) can provide strongest lateral reflections and spatial impression for music.

**Fan Shape** (For lecture room)

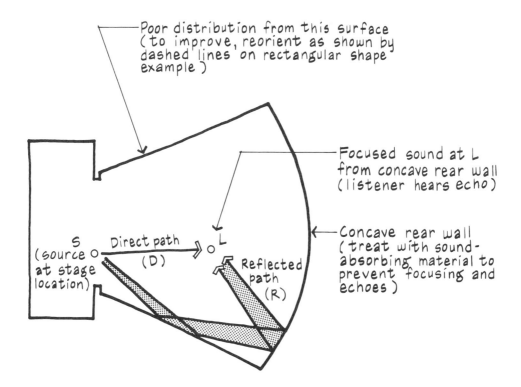

Poor distribution from this surface (to improve, reorient as shown by dashed lines on rectangular shape example)

Focused sound at L from concave rear wall (listener hears echo)

Concave rear wall (treat with sound-absorbing material to prevent focusing and echoes)

S (source at stage location)

Direct path (D)

L

Reflected path (R)

**Rectangular Shape** (Dashed lines indicate preferred orientations for a lecture room)

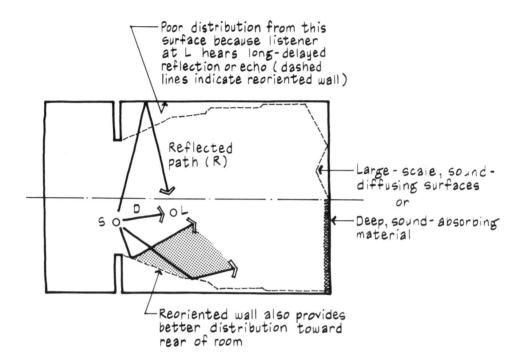

Poor distribution from this surface because listener at L hears long-delayed reflection or echo (dashed lines indicate reoriented wall)

Reflected path (R)

Large-scale, sound-diffusing surfaces

or

Deep, sound-absorbing material

S ○ D ↘ ○ L

Reoriented wall also provides better distribution toward rear of room

**Stepped Shape** (Alternate elements of side walls are parallel to provide lateral reflections toward audience for music hall)

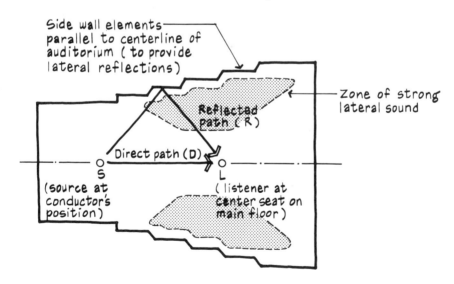

Side wall elements parallel to centerline of auditorium (to provide lateral reflections)

Zone of strong lateral sound

Reflected path (R)

Direct path (D)

○ S (source at conductor's position)

○ L (listener at center seat on main floor)

**Reverse Fan Shape** (Side walls at rear reflect sound toward audience for definition of music)

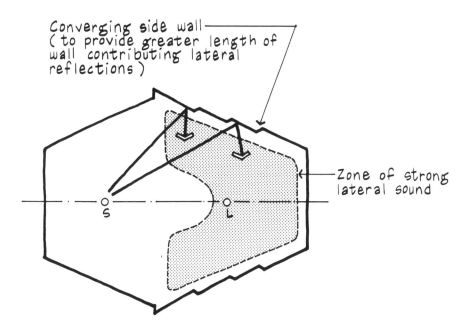

Converging side wall
(to provide greater length of wall contributing lateral reflections)

Zone of strong lateral sound

### References

Y. Ando, *Concert Hall Acoustics,* Springer-Verlag, Berlin, 1985.

L. Cremer and H. A. Müller, *Principles and Applications of Room Acoustics,* vol. 1, Applied Science Publishers, Barking, England, 1978, pp. 127-134 (English translation by T. J. Schultz).

M. Forsyth, *Auditoria,* Van Nostrand Reinhold, New York, 1987 (Contains over 40 case studies of modern concert halls and theaters).

R. B. Newman, "Acoustics" in J. H. Callender (ed.), *Time-Saver Standards for Architectural Design Data,* McGraw-Hill, New York, 1974, p. 719.

# PATTERNS OF REVERBERANT DECAY

Examples of sound decay in large and small rooms are shown below. A noise source (e.g., broadband noise from a loudspeaker, a bursting fully inflated balloon, or the "blast" of a blank fired from a starter's revolver) can be used to determine the time it takes the sound to fall off, or decay, by 60 dB. The starter's revolver has directional characteristics and a sound spectrum similar to speech.

Because the noise source is abruptly stopped or impulsive, its decay can be recorded and displayed on a graph of sound level vs. time. This graphical information can provide the designer with a greater understanding of the acoustical quality of rooms. For example, spikes on the decay curves shown below indicate echoes. Double-sloped decay curves could indicate room resonances or reverberance from coupled spaces such as large stagehouses or transepts.

## Reverberant Decay of Sound in Large Room

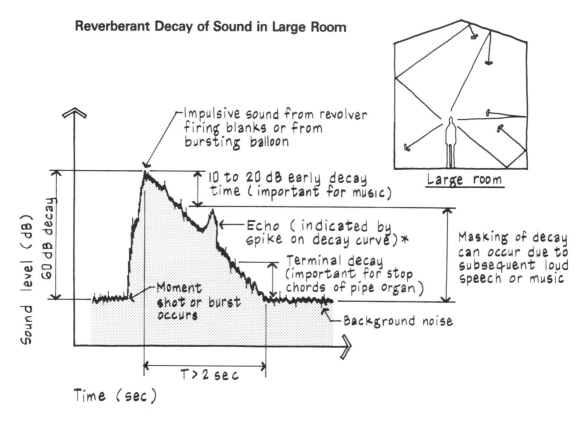

*Echo may be due to rear wall or other remote sound-reflecting surface.

### Reverberant Decay of Sound in Small Room

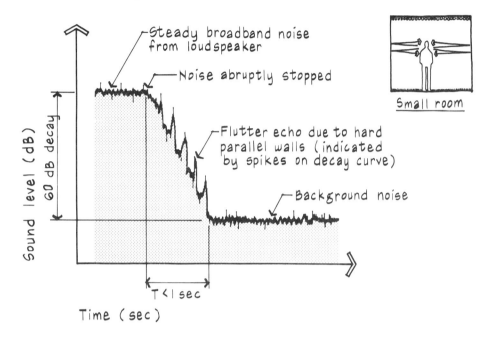

An articulation index AI, a measure of speech intelligibility, can be derived from laboratory analysis of electronically recorded reverberation (cf., J. P. A. Lochner and J. F. Burger, "The Influence of Reflections on Auditorium Acoustics," *Journal of Sound and Vibration,* October 1964, pp. 426-454). The AI for symphonic music should be 0.4 to 0.5; for organ music, less than 0.2; and for drama, greater than 0.7 (i.e., very high intelligibility conditions).

### References

L. L. Beranek (ed.), *Noise Reduction,* McGraw-Hill, New York, 1960, pp. 155-159.

H. Kuttruff, *Room Acoustics,* Applied Science Publishers, Barking, England, 1973, p. 191.

M. J. R. Lamothe and J. S. Bradley, "Acoustical Characteristics of Guns as Impulse Sources," *Canadian Acoustics,* April 1985, pp. 16-24.

## ARTICULATION INDEX

The *articulation index* AI is a subjective measure of speech intelligibility. It can be calculated from the scores of a group of experienced listeners with normal hearing who write sentences, words, or syllables read to them from selected lists. The graph below relates AI to the percentage intelligibility of clearly spoken sentences or words that skilled listeners hear correctly. For example, if a speaker calls out 100 words and a listener correctly hears 90, the AI would be greater than 0.7, which indicates "very good" intelligibility conditions. Sample lists, which can be used to establish AIs in a room, are presented in Appendix D.

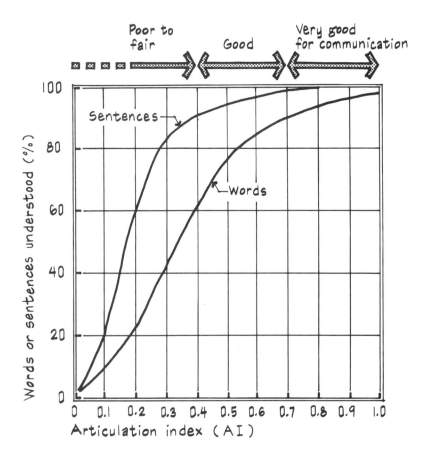

The plan view of the lecture room shown below has superimposed on it a plot of seat locations having equal AIs in decimal percent (called *AI contours*). The contours shown indicate "very good" speech listening conditions (AI > 0.70) near the source located at the left end of the stage platform. Note also that the AI drops off with distance from the source. Reshaping of the ceiling and control of echoes off the rear wall could raise the AI at these remote locations.

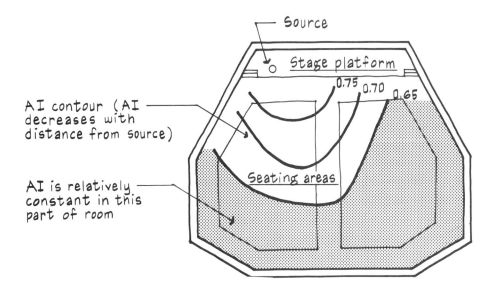

**Equal AI Contours in Lecture Room**

An objective evaluation test method, called the rapid speech transmission index (RASTI), has been developed to electronically measure speech intelligibility in rooms. The method uses a modulated test signal spectrum to simulate speech at 500 Hz and 2000 Hz. For details of the method, see T. Houtgast and H. J. M. Steeneken, "A Review of the MTF Concept in Room Acoustics and its Use for Estimating Speech Intelligibility in Auditoria," *Journal of the Acoustical Society of America,* March 1985.

**Note:** For communication requirements (e.g., speech, drama, musical comedy) high AIs are essential for optimum listening conditions. Conversely, to achieve satisfactory speech privacy, a low AI is desired. An AI of 0.05 to 0.15, or 4 to 14 percent of the words heard correctly, usually indicates satisfactory speech privacy conditions (see Chap. 6).

**Reference**

L. L. Beranek, *Acoustic Measurements*, Wiley, New York, 1949, pp. 625-632.

# FLUTTER ECHO

Flutter echo is usually caused by the repetitive interreflection of sound energy between opposing parallel or concave sound-reflecting surfaces. Flutter is normally heard as a high-frequency ringing or buzzing. It can be prevented by reshaping to avoid parallel surfaces, providing deep sound-absorbing treatment, or breaking up smooth surfaces with splayed or "scalloped" elements. A 1:10 splay (or > 5° tilt) of one of the parallel walls will normally prevent flutter echo in small rooms.

### Flutter Echoes

In small rooms flutter can be most noticeable at specific locations of noise source and listener.

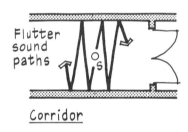

Corridor

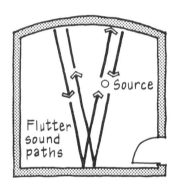

Small room with concave wall

### Pitched-Roof Flutter Echo

The echo phenomenon shown below (called *pitched-roof flutter*) can occur in rooms with nonparallel walls.

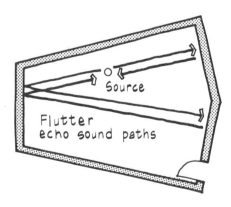

Audible *resonance* is the emphasis of sound energy at particular frequencies. It can occur in small rooms entirely finished with sound-reflecting materials when the dimensional ratios are whole numbers (e.g., cube). This phenomenon is sometimes referred to as the "bathroom tenor" effect. Consequently, preferred ratios of room dimensions may be recommended to prevent resonance (or "boominess") by achieving even distribution of low-frequency sound energy (cf., M. Rettinger, *Acoustic Design and Noise Control*, Chemical Publishing, New York, 1973, pp. 376-379). However, because most rooms contain absorptive materials such as carpets, curtains, and furnishings, the provision of preferred dimensional ratios usually is unimportant.

### Sound-Absorbing Surfaces Opposite Sound-Reflecting Surfaces

In the small music practice rooms shown in plan view below, the amount of sound which will reflect between hard, sound-reflecting surfaces will be minimized by installing sound-absorbing materials on adjacent walls or at two opposite corners. Effective treatment finishes can be provided by sound-absorbing panels furred out from the backup wall or heavy fabric curtains hung 100 percent *full* (i.e., 2 ft of curtain to 1 ft of surface width). To enhance low-frequency absorption, be sure there is a deep airspace between the sound-absorbing treatment and the backup surface.

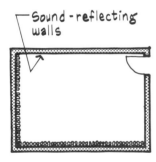

Sound-reflecting walls

**Adjacent-Wall Treatment**

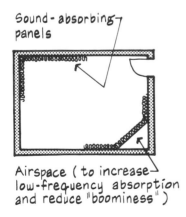

Sound-absorbing panels

Airspace (to increase low-frequency absorption and reduce "boominess")

**Corner Treatment**

**Nonparallel-Wall Surfaces** (In the example below, sound-absorbing ceiling or fully carpeted floor normally will be required if walls are hard-surfaced)

**Sound-Diffusing Wall Modulations** (Large-scale cylindrical, triangular, or other surface irregularities can be used to provide diffusion)

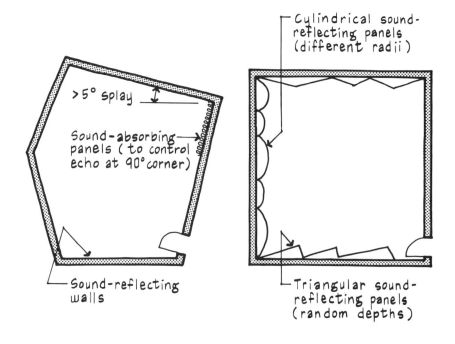

References

C. A. Andree, "The Effect of Position on the Absorption of Materials for the Case of a Cubical Room," *Journal of the Acoustical Society of America*, April 1932.

M. R. Schroeder, "Toward Better Acoustics for Concert Halls," *Physics Today*, October 1980.

## CONCAVE SURFACES

Concave wall and ceiling surfaces usually require treatment to prevent annoying sound reflections which reduce intelligibility of direct sound. Concave shapes (circle, ellipse, parabola) cause reflected sound to converge at a focal point. For example, sound energy may be concentrated in certain areas (called *focusing*) or reflected along smooth concave surfaces (called *creep* echo, or the "whispering gallery effect" because low voice levels can be heard at considerable distances away).

Shown below are problem situations and corresponding corrective measures. Note that focusing can be more noticeable for low-frequency sound energy because most finish materials are less absorptive at low frequencies.

| Problem | Solution |
|---|---|
| Focused sound | *Surface undulations*: Large-scale, random-sized surface undulations can provide diffusion to minimize focusing of reflected sound energy (e.g., convex brick surfaces at M.I.T. Chapel, Cambridge, Mass., Eero Saarinen, architect). |

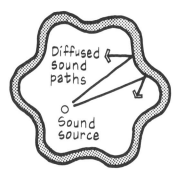

| Problem | Solution |
|---|---|
| Creep | *Sound-absorbing treatment*: Acoustically transparent material (e.g., spaced wood slats or open metal grille) conceals actual enclosure, which can be treated with deep sound-absorbing material to reduce reflected sound energy and creep echoes. |

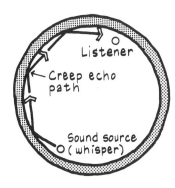

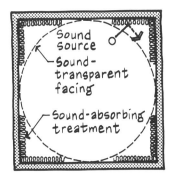

An example of the whispering gallery effect occurs in the Union Terminal Building, Cincinnati, Ohio (see sketch below). Sound energy is reflected along the domed ceiling surface allowing persons at opposite ends of the rotunda (> 180 ft apart) to easily converse at whisper voice levels; however, persons only a few feet away from the speakers cannot hear the conversation! Other examples where similar effects occur include the dome of St. Paul's Cathedral, London, England, and the old Senate Chamber at the U.S. Capitol, Washington, D.C.

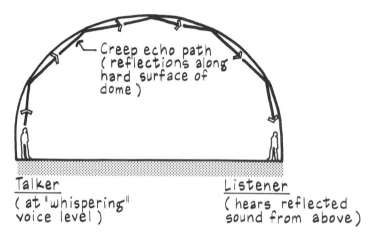

**Creep Echo from Dome**

**Note:** Domed planetariums can be designed to avoid focusing by using a sound-transparent liner on which the sky images are projected. The plenum above the perforated liner can be treated with either deep sound absorption or sound-diffusing elements.

Shown below are examples of poor distribution of sound in domed auditoriums. In the auditorium shown at the left, the extent of seating affected by focusing will be far greater than indicated because source locations on the stage will vary.

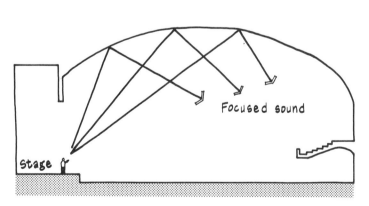

**Auditorium** (Focused reflections from concave-shaped ceiling)

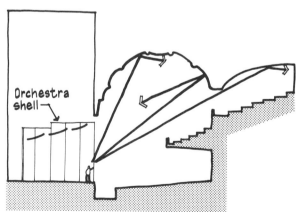

**Motion Picture Theater** (Useless reflections from dome)

## SOUND REFLECTORS

An effective sound reflector has a hard surface, such as thick plaster, double-layered gypsum board, sealed wood, or acrylic plastic, and is significantly larger than the wavelength of sound it is designed to reflect. For example, at a frequency of 500 Hz, the wavelength of sound is about 2 ft. Consequently, an 8-ft-diameter panel (i.e., dimension about 4 times the wavelength) should be used to reflect sound energy greater than 500 Hz. However, sound energy less than 500 Hz can bend around the panel, enhancing reverberance at low frequencies.

The sound-reflecting pulpit canopy shown below can provide useful reinforcement of the direct sound as well as prevent long-delayed reflections and potential echo conditions from the high ceiling. In the church example shown below, the organ and console are located within the sanctuary, not in a gallery or other deep recess. For guidelines on space requirements and preferred placement of pipe organs, see H. Klotz, *The Organ Handbook*, Concordia Publishing, St. Louis, Mo., 1969, pp. 102-116.

### Section View of Church

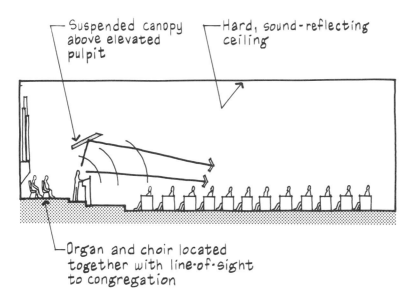

Suspended canopy above elevated pulpit

Hard, sound-reflecting ceiling

Organ and choir located together with line-of-sight to congregation

**Note:** In churches, an interior of thin wood paneling applied to furring can be an unintended, effective vibrating panel sound absorber (see Chap. 2). The absorption by the panel action can reduce low-frequency reverberation considerably, giving an unpleasant "shrill" characteristic to music. If wood is desired, vibrating-panel effects can be avoided by adhering the wood directly to a rigid backup wall or by using closely spaced furring supports (< 1 ft apart).

**Pulpit Canopy Details**

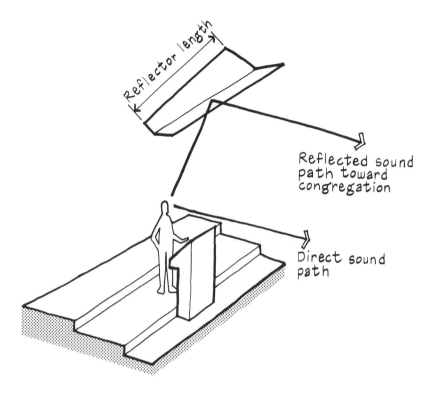

Reflector length

Reflected sound path toward congregation

Direct sound path

**References**

W. J. Cavanaugh, "Acoustics in Church Design," *Liturgical Arts*, May 1959.

B. G. Watters et al., "Reflectivity of Panel Arrays in Concert Halls," *Sound*, May-June 1963.

# CHECKLIST FOR WORSHIP SPACES

In *spaces for worship* there is the need for acoustical properties to support both intelligible speech and sufficient reverberance for music. It may be possible to satisfy both needs by providing a long reverberation time for music (about 2 s at mid-frequencies) and an electronic, sound-reinforcing system for speech articulation. In some churches, the most important part of the service may be either speech or music, which will determine the optimum reverberance. For example, if organ music is the most important, a long reverberation time (>2 s) will be required for enhancement of tone and blending. (It should be noted, however, that many organ builders seem to emphasize reverberance to the exclusion of other equally important acoustical properties for music, such as even distribution of sound energy, sufficient lateral reflections, and tonal balance.) Reverberance can also help the congregation avoid the feeling of "singing alone" during hymns or sung responses or "speaking alone" during prayer or responsive readings. The volume, finishes, and shape of a worship space will affect the articulation of speech and quality of music.

Listed below are guidelines to help designers achieve conditions for good hearing in worship spaces.

1. Music is best supported in churches with relatively narrow plans (providing short initial-time-delay gaps) and high *room volume.* Wide plans, which wrap the congregational seating around the pulpit/choir area, do not provide sufficient lateral sound. Its absence contributes to an impression of distant sound, lacking fullness of tone. For planning purposes, volume per seat ratio should be 180 to 300 ft³ per person for churches where speech is the most important part of the service; 200 to 400 ft³ per person for churches where music is the most important part. Avoid deeply recessed seating areas which shield listeners from reverberant sound.

2. *Pulpit* or *lectern* should be elevated and located close to the walls. In spaces with especially high ceilings, use a pulpit canopy (with upward tilt) to enhance the direct sound and to prevent long-delayed reflections from the ceiling.

3. Avoid domes, barrel vaults, and other concave *shapes* which focus sound energy. To mitigate focusing effects, concave ceilings can be "flattened" in the

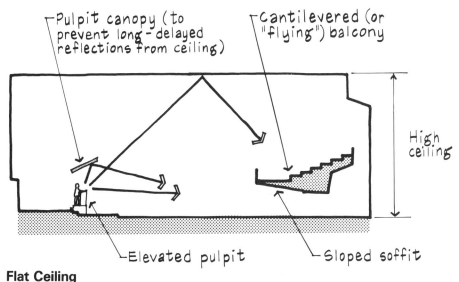

**Flat Ceiling**

center or treated with sound-diffusing elements such as unequal facets. If the focal point is far above the seating ($>$ 1/2 floor-to-ceiling height), reflected sound will be weaker than it would be if the ceiling were flat.

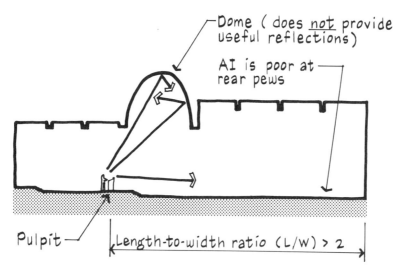

**Domed Ceiling**

4. Lay out *seating* to achieve good sight lines and minimum pew-to-pulpit distances to enhance speech perception. Pew cushions and carpeting used only in the seating areas can provide constant sound absorption, so reverberance does not vary greatly with the number of occupants present. Where carpet is used primarily to control footfall impact and shuffling noises, use carpet having low pile weight and low pile height, installed without a pad underneath. Loop pile will be more sound reflective than cut pile of the same weight. Do *not* use carpet in the chancel or choir areas, or in pew areas if active participation of congregation is desired.

5. Wall and ceiling surfaces generally should be sound-reflecting (concrete, thick plaster, or double layer of thick gypsum board or thick wood supported by closely spaced studs) with large-scale irregularities, splays, or bumps such as deep coffers to contribute to desired *reverberance, diffusion,* and *lateral reflections* (to surround listeners with sound). In general, avoid materials which selectively absorb sound energy at low frequencies (e.g., single layer of thin wood or gypsum board). For example, adding a second layer of 5/8-in-thick gypsum board to 5/8-in-thick gypsum board supported by 1 x 3 wood furring with fibrous insulation fill between furring can reduce absorption at 125 Hz by one-half (absorption coefficient reduced from 0.55 to 0.28).

6. *Underbalconies* may need special treatment such as sloped soffits and depths restricted to less than the opening heights. Shape balcony faces and rear walls with large splays or convex elements to avoid long-delayed reflections and echoes (or carefully treat with limited amount of sound-absorbing finishes).

7. Locate *choir, organ,* and *organ console* close together ($<$ 40 ft apart) to achieve balance between organ tone and choral music. Surround both with sound-reflecting surfaces shaped to blend and project sound toward the congregation. Ceiling height above the choir should not be too low ($<$ 20 ft). The choir must clearly hear the organ for proper support and rhythmic guidance. If the organist is also the choir director, orient the organ console so the choir can see the hands of the organist. Avoid using carpet and pew cushions in the choir areas because the absence of sound-absorbing materials at these critical locations have an overwhelming influence on loudness and pattern of

early sound energy distribution. Choir areas should be somewhat elevated with direct line of sight to the congregation (*not* located in deep recesses).

8. *Organ pipes* should be located in the open where they will be acoustically connected or coupled to the sanctuary (*not* in deep recess or transept) with direct line of sight to the congregtion. Provide space (> 1.5-ft clearance) at sides and rear of organ to allow servicing. Organs can have freestanding pipes or pipes in a wood panel casework (to blend sound and help develop harmonics). All ranks of the organ must be clearly heard. If the organ is to be visually hidden, place pipes in a shallow recess (> 125 ft$^3$ for each stop or set of pipes) finished in hard, sound-reflecting materials. Use sound-transparent grille with framing members less than 2 in wide and deep, with spacing between to provide more than 75 percent unobstructed open area.

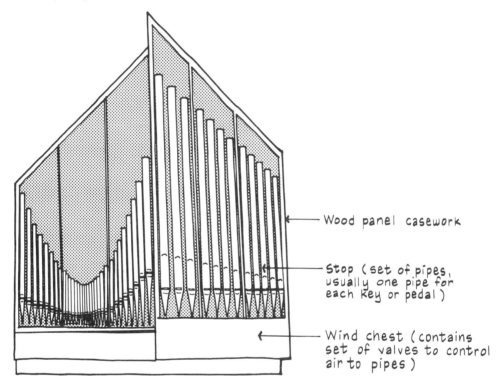

— Wood panel casework

— Stop (set of pipes, usually one pipe for each key or pedal)

— Wind chest (contains set of valves to control air to pipes)

**Chest of Organ Pipes**

9. To prevent interference with meditation, prayer, and appreciation of worship services, *background noise levels* from the mechanical system should not exceed noise criterion NC-25 for large spaces, or NC-30 for smaller spaces. Enclosing constructions must reduce intruding noise to levels below these criteria (see Chap. 4). In small sanctuaries, be careful to control the noise produced by air outlets and return grilles because occupants will be seated closer to these terminal devices than they would be in large spaces. Isolate noise and vibrations of the organ blower (see Chap. 5).

10. To achieve intelligible speech in reverberant spaces, use the highly directional, *central electronic sound-reinforcing system* to concentrate amplified speech over the congregational seating area and allow the sound to come from the direction of the pulpit location. As an alternative to the preferred central system, use a *distributed system* such as a dense array of cone loudspeakers located overhead or a *pew-back system* with signal-delay features (see Chap. 7). In churches with flexible seating, overhead distributed systems can be designed

to switch off loudspeakers located above the unoccupied areas (see illustration below).

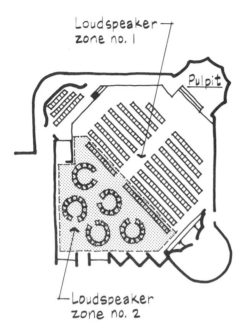

**Zones for Overhead Distributed System**

**Note:** To respond to the special needs of hearing-impaired persons, consider installing an *assistive listening system* (e.g., magnetic induction loop, FM radio, infrared) which allows the individual listener to control the sound level through a headset or connection to personal hearing aid. For a comprehensive review of these basic systems, along with a directory of manufacturers, see R. Brook, "Sound Systems for the Hearing Impaired," *Theatre Design & Technology*, Summer 1983, pp. 22-25.

**References**

D. Fitzroy, "The Sounds of St. Mary's," *Journal of the Acoustical Society of America*, August 1973.

D. Ingram et al., "Acoustics in Worship Spaces," American Guild of Organists (pamphlet available from AGO, 815 Second Ave., New York, NY 10017).

B. Y. Kinzey and H. M. Sharp, *Environmental Technologies in Architecture*, Prentice-Hall, Englewood Cliffs, N.J., 1963, pp. 367-372.

H. G. Klais, *Reflections on the Organ Stoplist*, Praestant Press, Delaware, Ohio, 1975, p. 124. (English translation by H. D. Blanchard. Contains formulas and tables which can be used as guide to allocate space for pipe organs.)

D. L. Klepper, "Church Acoustics," *Sound & Video Contractor*, January 1985.

D. L. Klepper, "Sound Systems in Reverberant Rooms for Worship," *Journal of the Audio Engineering Society*, August 1970.

D. Lubman and E. A. Wetherill (eds.), *Acoustics of Worship Spaces*, Acoustical Society of America, New York, 1985. (Contains technical data for numerous case studies of chapels, churches, temples, and synagogues.)

A. R. Rienstra, "Acoustical and Organ Design for Church Auditoriums," *Journal of the Acoustical Society of America*, July 1957, p. 787.

# AIR ABSORPTION

As sound waves pass through air, energy is absorbed. This phenomenon is called *molecular relaxation* because the air molecules absorb energy when they bump each other. The amount of absorption is insignificant at frequencies below 2000 Hz and above 10,000 Hz. However, the effect of air absorption should be included when calculating the total room absorption of large spaces and when sound propagates over great distances outdoors (see page 266n).

The curves below show air absorption $a_{air}$ in sabins *per 1000 ft$^3$*, so be careful to divide the room volume by 1000 before multiplying by the $a_{air}$ coefficient from the graph. When estimating air absorption for large spaces, use an $a_{air}$ of 8 per 1000 ft$^3$ at 4000 Hz. If thermal conditions are to be precisely controlled by the HVAC system, use $a_{air}$ at the anticipated air temperature and relative humidity conditions.

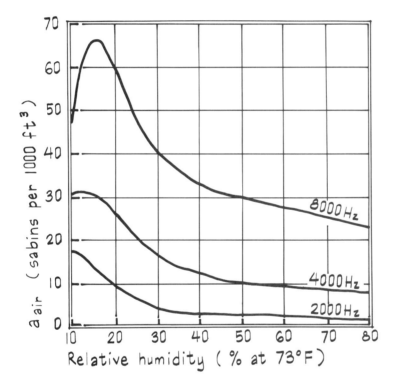

**Note:** Air absorption is the reason thunder "cracks" when heard up close, but "rumbles" when heard from a distance—the high frequencies are attenuated by the air! It is also why jet aircraft "rumble" when far overhead, yet "screech" at high frequencies when nearby at airports.

## Reference

C. M. Harris, "Absorption of Sound in Air versus Humidity and Temperature," *Journal of the Acoustical Society of America*, July 1966.

# CHECKLIST FOR MULTIPURPOSE AUDITORIUMS

The list below presents important acoustical parameters affecting the design of multipurpose school auditoriums (e.g., middle and high schools, colleges) with seating capacities in the range of 1000 to 2000.

1. **Site:** Select a quiet exposure far away from highways, flight paths, or noisy industries.

2. **Space Use:** Multipurpose uses include lectures, dramas, instrumental recitals, and symphonic music. Consequently, a full-frequency-response sound-reinforcing system will be required (see Chap. 7).

3. **Interior Location:** Use corridors, storage rooms, and other "buffer" spaces to isolate the auditorium from noise. Avoid locations adjacent to music rehearsal rooms, mechanical equipment rooms (e.g., do *not* locate HVAC equipment under the stage), carpentry shops, and other noisy spaces. Enclosing constructions should be based on the principles presented by Chap. 4. For example, all doors to the auditorium should be solid, heavy, and gasketed around their entire perimeters to be airtight when closed. Treat corridors and lobbies with generous amounts of sound-absorbing materials to control noise buildup. Dead spaces tend to induce occupants to speak at lower voice levels.

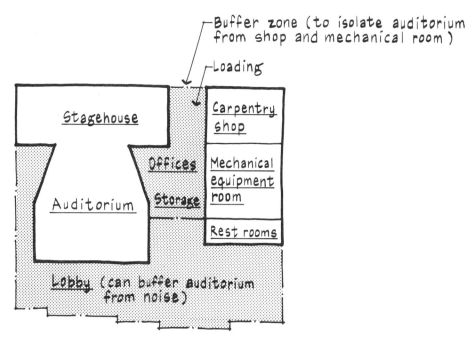

**Layout Using Buffer Spaces**

4. **Volume:** Volume per seat ratio should be 200 to 240 ft³ per person, which can be achieved with a room volume less than 500,000 ft³. The preliminary shape can be based on visual or seating considerations alone. However, to emphasize lateral reflections, plans that are rectangular, roughly square, or only slightly fanned are preferred. Arrange seating to provide the audience with good sight lines (e.g., moderately sloped seating layouts at >7°) and to minimize the distance to the performing area.

5. **Reverberation:** Use the Sabine equation to determine the reverberation times at 125, 500, and 4000 Hz. This is the formula generally used by acoustical testing laboratories. Published absorption data on most building materials are intended for use in this formula. Be sure to include air absorption, which may be significant at high frequencies in large spaces. The reverberation time $T$ should be 1.4 to 1.9 s at mid-frequencies (i.e., average of reverberation at 500 and 1000 Hz), $1.3T$ at 125 Hz, and $0.8T$ at 4000 Hz. At high frequencies, too much reverberation usually means "harsh" or "rasping" listening conditions. At low frequencies, too much reverberation usually sounds "boomy," whereas too little sounds "shrill." The following general guidelines can be used to select finish materials and furnishings.

*Ceiling:* Use sound-reflecting materials such as concrete, thick wood, or thick gypsum board. However, if required for control of reverberation, the perimeter along both sides and rear can be sound-absorbing (about one-third to one-half of the ceiling area covered in a horseshoe pattern) or use a checkerboard pattern consisting of alternate areas of sound-absorbing and reflecting materials.

*Side Walls:* Use sound-reflecting and diffusing surfaces with as many irregularities as possible (e.g., sunken panels, splays, and undulations). For variable sound absorption, hang large amounts of fabric curtains or banners along the rear portion of side walls or in cubic volume above suspended sound-reflecting panels.

*Rear Wall:* Use diffusing surface with large-scale irregularities or, if this is not possible, treat with carefully placed deep sound-absorbing finish to control echoes.

*Floor:* Carpet all aisles, except in front of the stage, to aid in footfall impact noise control. Do not use carpet in seating areas.

*Seating:* Use fabric-upholstered seats (never leatherette, thin metal, or plastic). Absorptive seating will help provide "stable" reverberation conditions, so the reverberation will be nearly the same when the auditorium is full as when it is partially occupied. Use seating that does not selectively absorb sound at low frequencies. Continental seating layouts have greater spacing between rows than conventional seating with center aisles. However, continental seating in large auditoriums can present a vast uninterrupted sea of absorptive people to performers on stage.

6. **Ray Diagrams:** Use ray-diagram analyses to properly orient the ceiling and side walls, especially near the proscenium. Ceiling and wall surfaces should provide useful sound reflections (i.e., early reflections with < 28 ft path difference from direct sound) and diffusion. Avoid vaults, domes, and other concave surface shapes.

7. **Background Noise:** Background noise should be low so it will not cover up or mask performances (see Chap. 4). The HVAC system should be designed so its noise will not exceed the preferred noise criteria. Control air velocities at room registers and grilles, and use internal sound-absorbing duct linings and/or mufflers to prevent duct-borne noise transmission in both the supply and return air-distribution systems (see Chap. 5).

8. **Stage Enclosure and Orchestra Pit:** Shape to provide good distribution of strong early reflections and diffusion. The reverberation time of the stagehouse should be approximately equal to that of the auditorium. Reverberation will be longer when surfaces surrounding the stage are shaped to interreflect or scatter sound rather than to reflect sound toward the absorptive audience.

The orchestra pit, sized at about 14 to 16 ft$^2$ per musician, should have a removable sound-absorbing curtain (or panels) along its rear wall to allow the conductor to control loudness in the pit.

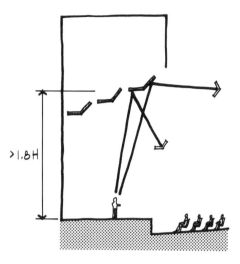

**Low Shell** (Side panels > 50 ft apart)

**Preferred High Shell** (Stage ceiling > 30 ft high, side walls < 50 ft apart, and shell < 30 ft deep)

9. **Balcony:** Use balconies to reduce the distance to the farthest row of seats and/or to increase seating capacity. Keep the overhang shallow (i.e., depth less than twice the opening height), slope the soffit, and treat the face with sound-diffusing elements (or sound-absorbing material) to prevent echoes.

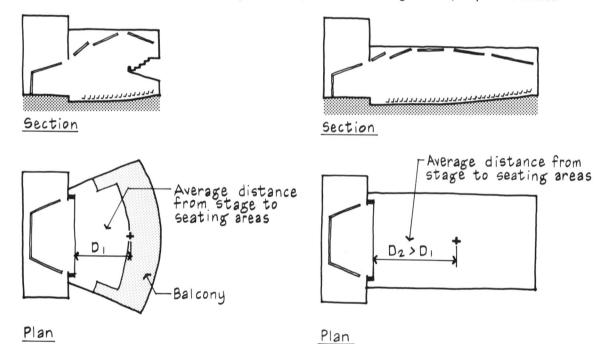

Section

Section

Average distance from stage to seating areas

Average distance from stage to seating areas

Balcony

Plan

Plan

**Auditorium with Balcony**

**Auditorium without Balcony**

10. **Sound-Reinforcing System:** Provide a central space just above and slightly in front of the proscenium opening to accommodate a cluster of loudspeakers (see Chap. 7). Be sure the audience has line of sight to the high-frequency horns of the cluster. Locate the control console for the sound system at a central location in the audience seating area. A far less effective alternative location is the rear of auditorium in a separate room which can be opened to allow the operator to attempt to hear the sound being controlled.

# HOW TO COMPUTE CUBIC VOLUME

Because reverberation time is directly proportional to the size of a room, it is extremely important that cubic volume be correctly computed. For example, if cubic volume is *x* percent in error, predicted reverberation time would be a corresponding *x* percent in error. For most situations, a change of 10 percent or more in reverberation can be detected by listeners. Volume of rooms that are cubic or rectangular solid in shape can be readily computed by multiplying length times width times height. Shown below are volume formulas for several regular and irregular shaped rooms. In many designs, it is best to subdivide room volume into smaller volumes, such as in an auditorium: main hall, orchestra pit, underbalcony, abovebalcony, and so on. The resulting total should be far more accurate than an estimate based on average overall dimensions of length, width, and height.

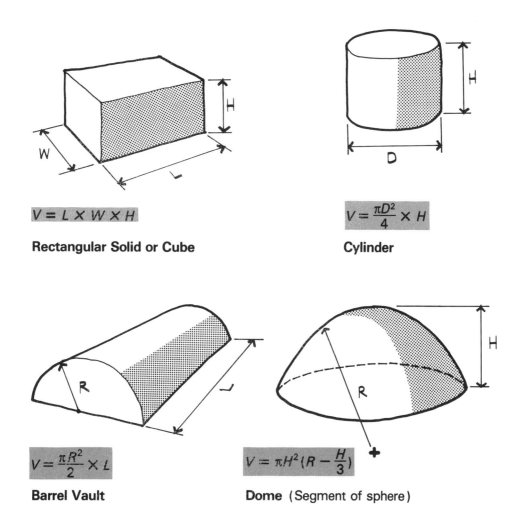

$$V = L \times W \times H$$

**Rectangular Solid or Cube**

$$V = \frac{\pi D^2}{4} \times H$$

**Cylinder**

$$V = \frac{\pi R^2}{2} \times L$$

**Barrel Vault**

$$V = \pi H^2 \left(R - \frac{H}{3}\right)$$

**Dome** (Segment of sphere)

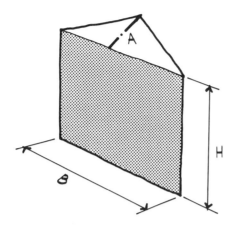

$$V = \frac{B \times A}{2} \times H$$

**Prism**

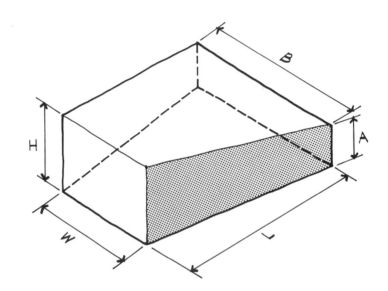

$$V = \frac{L}{6}(2HW + 2AB + HB + WA)$$

**Irregular**

## EXAMPLE PROBLEM (VOLUME COMPUTATION)

A classroom/small theater is described by the plan and section drawings below. Find the total cubic volume *V* in this room.

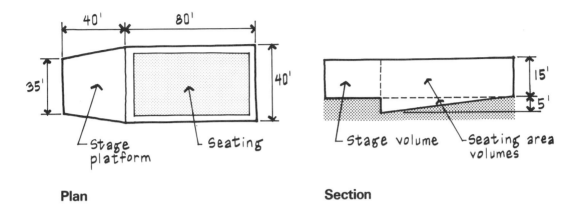

**Plan**                                      **Section**

**1.** Subdivide the room into three volumes: irregular, rectangular solid, and prism.

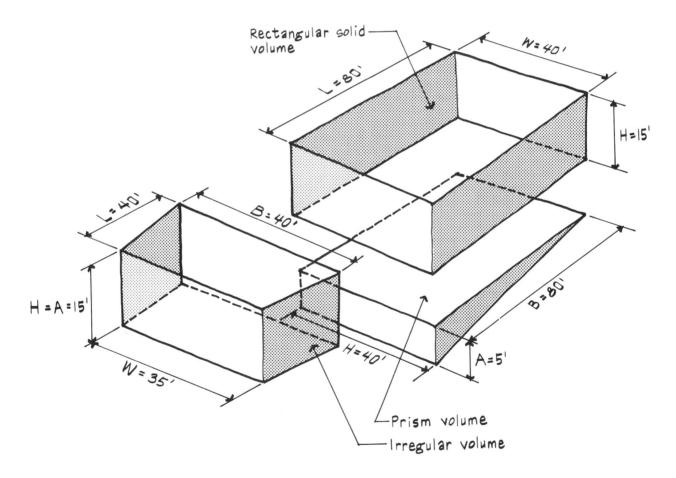

**2.** Compute cubic volume for each volume using formulas from preceding pages.
Total cubic volume is sum of three subvolumes.

Total volume $V = V_{irregular} + V_{rectangular\ solid} + V_{prism}$

$$V_{irregular} = \frac{L}{6}(2HW + 2AB + HB + WA)$$

$$= \frac{40}{6}[(2 \times 15 \times 35) +$$
$$(2 \times 15 \times 40) +$$
$$(15 \times 40) +$$
$$(35 \times 15)]$$

$$= \frac{40}{6}(3375) \qquad\qquad\qquad = 22{,}500$$

$$V_{rectangular\ solid} = L \times W \times H$$

$$= 80 \times 40 \times 15 \qquad\qquad = 48{,}000$$

$$V_{prism} = \frac{B \times A}{2} \times H$$

$$= \frac{80 \times 5}{2} \times 40 \qquad\qquad = \underline{\ 8{,}000}$$

Total $V = \boxed{78{,}500\ ft^3}$

# EXAMPLE PROBLEM (REVERBERATION TIMES)

The reverberation time in a 250,000-ft$^3$ high school auditorium is calculated below for full and one-half occupancy conditions. An auditorium of this type, which serves many functions, must be designed with a compromise reverberation time. For example, a short reverberation time is desirable for speech activities and a long reverberation time is needed for instrumental music, chorus, and organ music. Consequently, a mid-frequency reverberation time of 1.8 s at 500 Hz is selected from the chart on page 64. This reverberation time will be appropriate for music activities, where blending is needed, and will not be too long for speech activities, especially if a properly designed sound-reinforcing system is used (see Chap. 7).

For guidelines on how to select reverberation times at low and high frequencies, see page 125. In this example school auditorium, the reverberation time at 125 Hz should be about $1.3T = 1.3 \times 1.8 = 2.3$ s. If the preferred reverberation times from the table below can be achieved, the bass ratio therefore will be approximately 1.3. This ratio of low- to mid-frequency reverberation times is a very important characteristic of rooms where music is to be performed (see page 155).

To find the required total absorption $a$, use the Sabine formula rearranged so:

$$a = \frac{0.05V}{T}$$

$$= \frac{0.05 \times 250,000}{1.8} = 6944 \text{ sabins at 500 Hz}$$

|  | 125 Hz | 500 Hz | 4000 Hz |
|---|---|---|---|
| Preferred reverberation time (s) | 2.3 | 1.8 | 1.4 |
| Required total absorption from Sabine formula (sabins) | 5435 | 6944 | 8929 |

Using the required absorption totals in the above table as a goal, calculate absorption $a$ in sabins for all surfaces by multiplying given surface area in ft$^2$ times the respective sound absorption coefficient $\alpha$. The table on the following page shows the step-by-step computation process at sound frequencies of 125, 500, and 4000 Hz.

| Material | Area (ft²) | 125 Hz | | 500 Hz | | 4000 Hz | |
|---|---|---|---|---|---|---|---|
| | | α | sabins | α | sabins | α | sabins |
| **Fully Occupied** | | | | | | | |
| Ceiling: | | | | | | | |
|   Gypsum board (in suspension system) | 8150 | 0.15 | 1223 | 0.05 | 408 | 0.09 | 734 |
| Side walls: | | | | | | | |
|   Plaster on concrete block | 5700 | 0.12 | 684 | 0.07 | 399 | 0.04 | 228 |
| Rear wall: | | | | | | | |
|   Thick fibrous blanket behind open facing | 1500 | 0.60 | 900 | 0.82 | 1230 | 0.38 | 570 |
| Aisles: | | | | | | | |
|   Carpet on foam rubber | 1600 | 0.08 | 128 | 0.57 | 912 | 0.73 | 1168 |
|   Wood | 250 | 0.15 | 38 | 0.10 | 25 | 0.07 | 18 |
| Orchestra pit and apron: | | | | | | | |
|   Wood | 950 | 0.15 | 143 | 0.10 | 95 | 0.07 | 67 |
| Proscenium opening: | | | | | | | |
|   (Moderately furnished stage) | 1100 | 0.40 | 440 | 0.50 | 550 | 0.60 | 660 |
| Air: | | | | | | | |
|   (Coefficient per 1000 ft³) | .. | .. | .. | .. | .. | 8 | 2000 |
| Audience: | | | | | | | |
|   Seated in upholstered seats (includes edge effect) | 4500 | 0.39 | 1755 | 0.80 | 3600 | 0.87 | 3915 |
| Total absorption (sabins) | | | 5311 | | 7219 | | 9360 |
| **One-Half Occupied** | | | | | | | |
| Total absorption in auditorium less audience absorption from "fully occupied" computation | | | 3556 | | 3619 | | 5445 |
| Seats: | | | | | | | |
|   Fabric, well-upholstered seats | 2000 | 0.19 | 380 | 0.56 | 1120 | 0.59 | 1180 |
| Audience: | | | | | | | |
|   Includes edge effect | 2500 | 0.39 | 975 | 0.80 | 2000 | 0.87 | 2175 |
| Total absorption (sabins) | | | 4911 | | 6739 | | 8800 |

Finally, use the absorption totals (highlighted above) in the Sabine formula: $T = 0.05V/a = (0.05 \times 250,000)/a = 12,500/a$ to find the reverberation times summarized below.

| Conditions | Reverberation Time (s) | | |
|---|---|---|---|
| | 125 Hz | 500 Hz | 4000 Hz |
| Fully occupied | 2.4 | 1.7 | 1.3 |
| One-half occupied | 2.5 | 1.9 | 1.4 |

Since the anticipated normal use condition will be between one-half and full occupancy, the above computations show that the auditorium satisfactorily meets reverberation time criteria.

# OPTIMUM REVERBERATION TIME

The graph below presents optimum reverberation times at mid-frequencies (average of reverberation at 500 and 1000 Hz) for auditoriums with volumes of 10,000 to 1,000,000 ft³. A deviation of as much as 10 percent from optimum reverberation generally will be satisfactory if other important attributes of room acoustics have been successfully achieved. For music perception, reverberation adds to the *fullness of tone*, blended sound, and richness of bass frequencies.

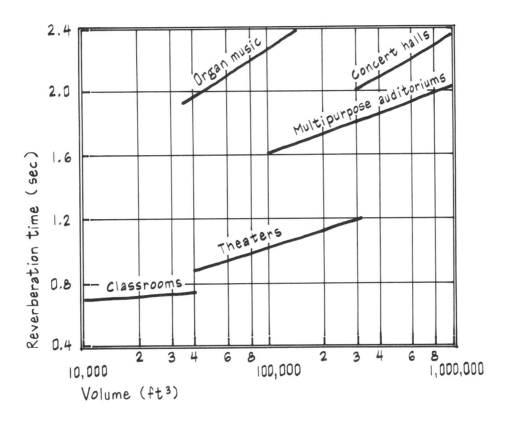

## References

L. L. Beranek, *Acoustics*, McGraw-Hill, New York, 1954, p. 425.

L. L. Beranek, *Music, Acoustics and Architecture*, Wiley, New York, 1962, pp. 488-489.

J. S. Bradley, "Uniform Derivation of Optimum Conditions for Speech in Rooms," Building Research Note No. 239, National Research Council of Canada, November 1985.

L. Cremer and H. A. Müller, *Principles and Applications of Room Acoustics*, vol. 1, Applied Science Publishers, Barking, England, 1978, pp. 610-627.

V. O. Knudsen and C. M. Harris, *Acoustical Designing in Architecture*, Wiley, New York, 1950, pp. 375 and 394.

## VARIABLE SOUND ABSORBERS

When the reverberation time must be varied to satisfy the requirements of different activities in a room, the sound-absorbing treatment can be designed to be adjustable. For most situations, listeners can detect a change in reverberation greater than or equal to 0.1 s. Surfaces or furnishings can be designed to expose either sound-absorbing materials (see column at left) or sound-reflecting materials (see column at right). In rooms for music, be careful to avoid placing absorption near the sources of sound where it can adversely affect early sound energy.

### Retractable Sound-Absorbing Curtains

Curtains can be adjusted to vary the amount of absorption and, when stored in a recess, to expose a sound-reflecting backup surface. For music perception needs, curtains should be stored in a high transmission loss enclosure so they will contribute almost no absorption.

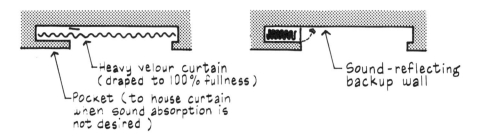

Heavy velour curtain (draped to 100% fullness)

Pocket (to house curtain when sound absorption is not desired)

Sound-reflecting backup wall

**Note:** A visually opaque, sound-transparent screen (called *transondent*) can be placed in front of curtains to allow changes in curtain extension without affecting appearance. This prevents the adjustment of the curtains for visual, not acoustical, reasons. Be careful where music perception is important because the deep airspace behind the sound-transparent screen could absorb too much low-frequency sound energy by acting as a volume resonator.

### Sliding Facings

Two panels of perforated material can be used to vary absorption by sliding one panel in front of the other. The holes are lined up for maximum absorption and are staggered (or offset) for maximum reflection. The latter alignment blocks the path to the sound-absorbing treatment installed behind the panels.

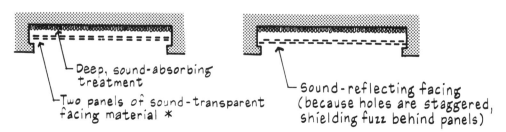

Deep, sound-absorbing treatment

Two panels of sound-transparent facing material *

Sound-reflecting facing (because holes are staggered, shielding fuzz behind panels)

*Holes lined up to provide maximum absorption.

## Hinged Panels

Sound-absorbing material installed on back of sound-reflecting panel can be swung into position to vary conditions from hard to soft.

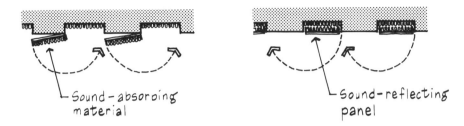

## Rotatable Elements

The details shown below are similar to the rotatable prism elements at l'Espace de Projection, IRCAM, Paris, France ( V. M. A. Peutz, acoustical consultant) which have three sides: reflecting, absorbing, and diffusing.

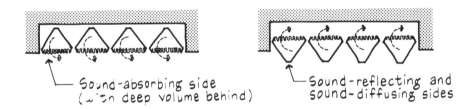

**Note:** Variable absorption also can be used to adjust the reverberation during orchestra rehearsals in music halls so rehearsal conditions match performing conditions, when the audience is present.

## VARIABLE VOLUME EXAMPLES

Shown below and on the facing page are examples of auditoriums where the cubic volume can be varied to match reverberance and patterns of reflected sound energy to the intended functions. The reverberation times needed for intimate drama ($< 1$ s) and symphonic music ($> 1.8$ s) require radical changes in volume with corresponding changes in seating capacities. In the following examples, seating capacities vary from more than 3000 at the top to less than 1000 at the bottom. Below are depicted variable volume configurations at Jesse Jones Hall, Houston, Texas (CRS Sirrine, architects and BBN, acoustical consultants) and on page 137, variations at Edwin Thomas

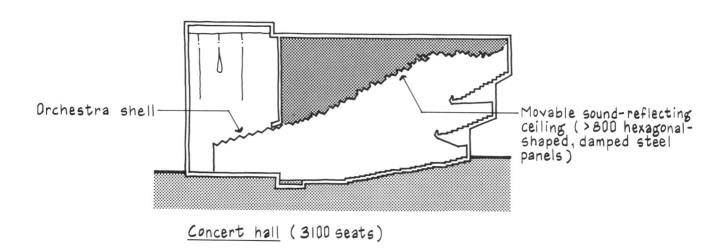

Orchestra shell

Movable sound-reflecting ceiling ($>800$ hexagonal-shaped, damped steel panels)

Concert hall (3100 seats)

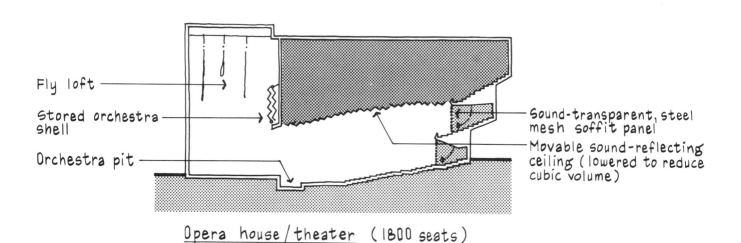

Fly loft

Stored orchestra shell

Orchestra pit

Sound-transparent, steel mesh soffit panel

Movable sound-reflecting ceiling (lowered to reduce cubic volume)

Opera house/theater (1800 seats)

**Jones Hall**

Hall, University of Akron, Akron, Ohio (CRS Sirrine, architects and V. O. Knudsen, acoustical consultant). In practice, there is the almost irresistible economic temptation for owners to use the largest seating capacity for all functions.

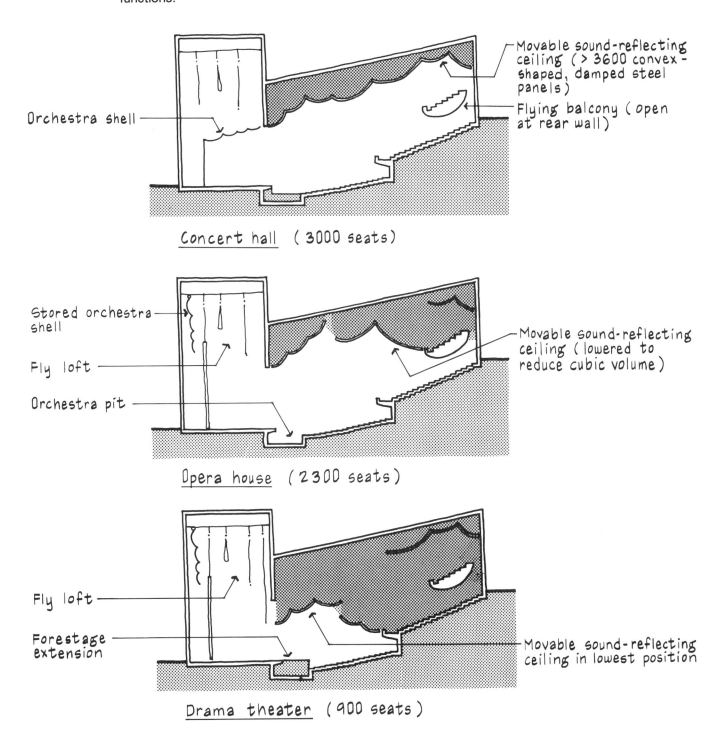

Orchestra shell

Movable sound-reflecting ceiling ( > 3600 convex-shaped, damped steel panels)

Flying balcony (open at rear wall)

Concert hall ( 3000 seats )

Stored orchestra shell

Fly loft

Orchestra pit

Movable sound-reflecting ceiling (lowered to reduce cubic volume)

Opera house ( 2300 seats )

Fly loft

Forestage extension

Movable sound-reflecting ceiling in lowest position

Drama theater ( 900 seats )

**Thomas Hall**

## BASIC THEATER STAGES

The basic theater stages are the *proscenium* stage (where the performing area is largely in a coupled stagehouse viewed through a "picture frame" opening), the *open*, or *thrust*, stage (where the performing area extends into the audience area), and the *arena* stage (where the performing area is entirely surrounded by audience). In the open and arena stages, sound-reflecting walls and ceiling (or suspended panels) are extremely important to help compensate for the directivity of high-frequency speech signals. Because the human voice is more directional at high frequencies than at low frequencies, considerably less high-frequency sound energy (10 to 20 dB lower) is radiated behind the performer than in front of the performer. In addition, this portion of the frequency range strongly influences speech intelligibility.

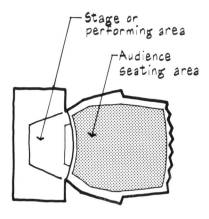

**Proscenium**

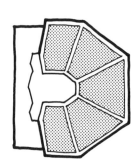

**Open or Thrust**

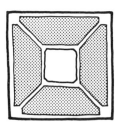

**Arena**

**Note:** For preliminary estimates of stage areas, use an area based on 15 to 20 ft² per musician for stages for orchestra alone. Add 800 ft² for chorus.

## STAGE ENCLOSURES FOR ORCHESTRA

Panels constructed of thick plywood, damped sheet metal, or heavy gypsum board can be used on stages to surround (or enclose) the sources of sound. These sound-reflecting and diffusing panels (called a *stage enclosure*, or *orchestra shell*) can help distribute balanced and blended sound uniformly throughout the listening area by connecting (or "coupling") a portion of the stagehouse cubic volume to the volume within the main hall. Stage enclosures (< 2 percent open) increase *loudness* by preventing sound energy from being absorbed by scenery in the fly loft and wings. The *fly loft* is the volume above the stage where scenery is "flown" out of sight when not in use. Therefore, this portion of the stagehouse normally is highly sound absorptive. When not needed to support music performances, enclosures should be designed to be dismantled and stored compactly without interfering with other stage functions.

The surfaces surrounding an orchestra should also contain small-scale irregularities to blend and reflect the high-frequency sound energy from the various instruments. The enclosure can contribute to good music-listening conditions onstage (i.e., provide *balance* between various sections of the orchestra), where it is essential that musicians and chorus members clearly hear themselves and each other to perform as a coordinated group (called *ensemble*). Note that the specific arrangement of musicians depends on the number of musicians and style of music to be performed. It is prudent to design enclosure panels so they can be adjusted ("tuned") while the orchestra performs in rehearsal.

### Plan of Stage Enclosure

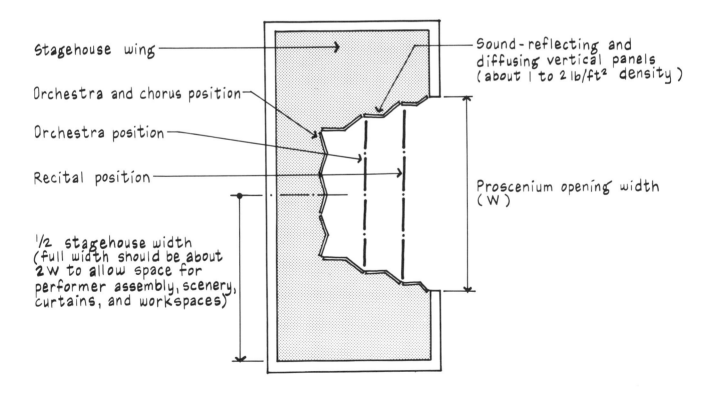

Stagehouse wing

Orchestra and chorus position

Orchestra position

Recital position

½ stagehouse width
(full width should be about
2W to allow space for
performer assembly, scenery,
curtains, and workspaces)

Sound-reflecting and diffusing vertical panels (about 1 to 2 lb/ft² density)

Proscenium opening width (W)

## Stagehouse Section

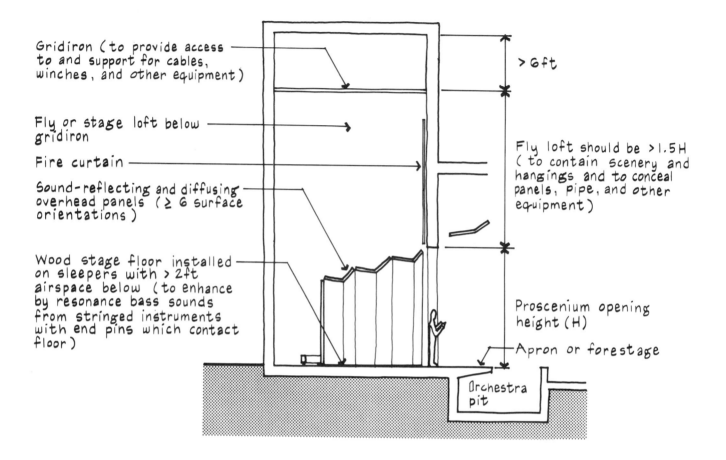

Gridiron (to provide access to and support for cables, winches, and other equipment)

Fly or stage loft below gridiron

Fire curtain

Sound-reflecting and diffusing overhead panels ($\geq$ 6 surface orientations)

Wood stage floor installed on sleepers with > 2ft airspace below (to enhance by resonance bass sounds from stringed instruments with end pins which contact floor)

> 6ft

Fly loft should be >1.5H (to contain scenery and hangings and to conceal panels, pipe, and other equipment)

Proscenium opening height (H)

Apron or forestage

Orchestra pit

**Note:** The fixed height of the proscenium opening $H$ usually varies from 20 to 35 ft (and higher for opera). The fixed width of the proscenium opening $W$ varies from 30 to 80 ft, depending on the type of theatrical or orchestral production.

## FORESTAGE CANOPIES

Sound-reflecting panels, suspended in front of the proscenium, reflect sound energy from the stage to the audience and decrease the initial-time-delay gap. These panels, called *forestage canopies*, extend the orchestra shell into the auditorium. This extension can enhance the direct sound needed for *intimacy* and can also reflect sound energy from the orchestra pit back toward the pit. The openings between the panels allow sound energy to flow into the upper volume so it can contribute to the low-frequency reverberance in the main auditorium below (needed for *warmth*).

**Forestage Canopy** (To extend contained shell)

**Coupled Stagehouse** (With open articulating shell to allow flow of low-frequency sound energy)

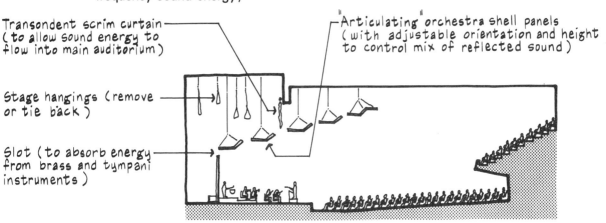

The reverberation time of stagehouses should be approximately equal to or less than that of the main auditorium, unless the stagehouse is to be used as a "coupled" reverberant chamber. To achieve a reverberant stagehouse for an articulating shell, do *not* specify unpainted concrete block or install sound-absorbing materials on the walls of the stagehouse, and keep the fly loft free of materials which absorb sound. The side walls of articulating shells should be 5 to 10 percent open; the overhead panels should be 15 to 50 percent open, depending on the height of the panels.

## References

C. Jaffe, "Design Considerations for a Demountable Concert Enclosure," *Journal of the Audio Engineering Society*, April 1974.

T. J. Schultz, "Acoustics of the Concert Hall," *IEEE Spectrum*, June 1965.

# ORCHESTRA PITS

*Orchestra pits* should be designed so music can be blended and balanced with sound from the stage. The section below shows the elements of a traditional orchestra pit located between the proscenium stage and the audience. Guidelines which give square feet per musician can be misleading in sizing orchestra pits because risers require extra space and the elbow room a musician requires varies from instrument to instrument (e.g., musicians playing cellos or trombones require more space than those playing clarinets). Nevertheless, for preliminary planning purposes, provide more than 16 ft² per musician. Also shown below are pit layouts which use movable reflectors to accommodate more than 100 musicians and less than 40 musicians.

## Orchestra Pit Details

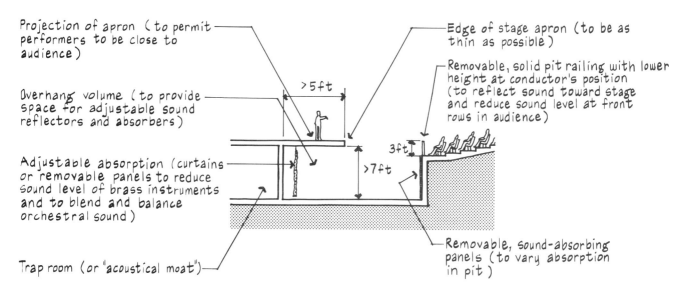

Projection of apron (to permit performers to be close to audience)

Overhang volume (to provide space for adjustable sound reflectors and absorbers)

Adjustable absorption (curtains or removable panels to reduce sound level of brass instruments and to blend and balance orchestral sound)

Trap room (or "acoustical moat")

Edge of stage apron (to be as thin as possible)

Removable, solid pit railing with lower height at conductor's position (to reflect sound toward stage and reduce sound level at front rows in audience)

Removable, sound-absorbing panels (to vary absorption in pit)

>5ft

3ft

>7ft

## Orchestra Pit Layouts

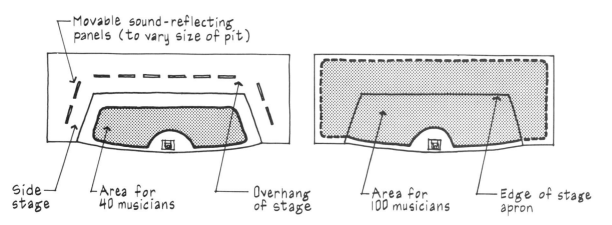

Movable sound-reflecting panels (to vary size of pit)

Side stage

Area for 40 musicians

Overhang of stage

Area for 100 musicians

Edge of stage apron

### References

E. L. Harkness, "Performer Tuning of Stage Acoustics," *Applied Acoustics*, vol. 17, 1984, pp. 92-96.

R. Johnson, "Orchestra Pits," *Theatre Design & Technology*, Fall 1979, pp. 8-20.

Balconies can be used in large auditoriums to reduce the distance to the rear seats and to increase seating capacity (e.g., narrow halls with shallow balconies can achieve optimum intimacy). The basic elements of a balcony are shown below. To prevent echoes or long-delayed reflections off the balcony face, apply deep sound-absorbing finish, tilt or slope the surface facing the stage so sound will be reflected toward nearby audience, or use diffusing shapes, such as convex elements, to scatter sound.

### Basic Elements

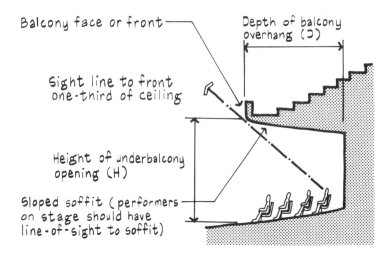

**Note:** For good sight lines, the highest seat in the balcony should not exceed a 26° angle to horizontal at stage floor (e.g., drawn from curtain line or bottom of motion picture screen).

### Examples of Poor Balconies

Persons seated deep under a balcony (or transept in a church) cannot receive useful reflected sound from the ceiling and are shielded from the reverberant sound. The listening conditions are therefore very poor because sound will be weak and dull. The example balcony designs shown below should be avoided because they shield the audience in the rear seats from most reflected sound.

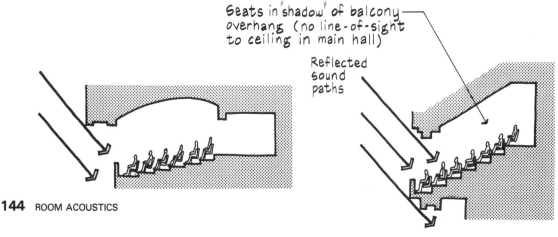

# BALCONY DESIGN EXAMPLES

### Concert Hall and Opera House

In a concert hall, the depth $D$ of the underbalcony should not exceed the height $H$ of the opening. This restriction on the depth helps reverberant sound energy reach listeners seated in the rear rows. In an opera house, $D$ should not exceed $1.5H$. The balcony soffit should be sloped to reflect sound toward the heads of the listeners seated underneath and to better connect, or couple, the underbalcony volume with the volume of the main hall. When the vertical separation $H$ between side balconies is sufficient, the balcony soffits can be designed to provide useful lateral reflections to the audience at the center of the main level seating area.

In halls with a *central* sound-reinforcing system, be sure the audience in the last row has line of sight to the cluster. If this cannot be achieved, use underbalcony loudspeakers with signal-delay features (see Chap. 7).

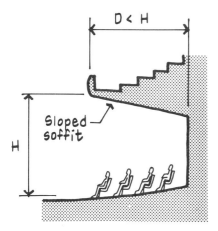

### Motion Picture Theater

*Direct* reinforced sound from loudspeakers located behind the screen allows deeper balcony overhang. Therefore, in motion picture theaters and similar facilities, $D$ should not exceed $3H$, although $2H$ is still the preferred limit in theaters where other functions occur.

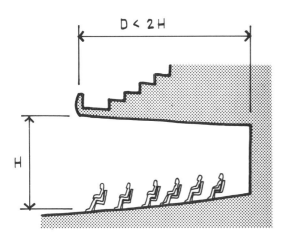

### Flying Balcony

The cantilevered balcony (or *flying balcony*) is open at the rear, allowing reverberant sound energy to surround the audience seated underneath. *D* can be longer than the conventional balcony of the same *H* because reverberant energy will be greater at the rear rows. An early example is the flying balcony completed in 1889 in the auditorium-theater in the Auditorium Building, Chicago. Unfortunately, the elliptical ceiling in this 4237-seat reverberant auditorium (Adler and Sullivan, architects) did not evenly distribute reflected sound energy, but focused sound into the central seating area causing hot spots and interference.

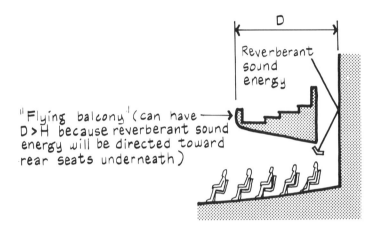

# EVALUATION GUIDE FOR MUSIC PERFORMANCE SPACES

## How To Use Evaluation Guide

The scales on the evaluation guide can be used by listeners to record their subjective impressions of spaces for music performance (e.g., concert halls, churches, recital halls). Place a checkmark in the section of the scale which best represents your individual judgment of the specific attribute or condition. The primary purpose of the evaluation guide is to encourage users to become familiar with important acoustical properties of rooms where music is performed. The guide is *not* intended to be used to rank the best or worst spaces because there always will be a wide range of individual judgments, even among experienced listeners and performers. Recognize also that it is extremely difficult to separate judgment of a hall from either judgment of the quality of a particular musical performance, or from longstanding personal musical preferences.

## Subjective Judgments of Music Performances

Subjective impressions can be recorded for the following conditions (see evaluation guide on page 149):

*Clarity* (listen to beginnings of musical notes and observe degree to which individual notes are distinct or stand apart)

*Reverberance* (listen to persistence of sound at mid-frequencies)

*Warmth* (listen for strength or liveness of bass compared to mid- and treble frequencies)

*Intimacy* (listen to determine if music sounds as though played in a small room regardless of actual size)

*Loudness* (listen for direct sound and reverberant sound; evaluate during louder passages for comfort conditions and weaker passages for audibility)

*Diffusion* (listen for envelopment of terminal sounds or feeling of immersion in sound; compare conditions with eyes open and closed)

*Balance* (listen for relative strength and quality of various sections of orchestra, and between orchestra and soloist or chorus)

Sounds which interfere with perception of music performances may also be observed. The most common are the following:

*Background noise* (sounds other than music or from audience, heard during times solo instrumentalists play faintest notes, or when hall is empty)

*Echoes* (notice direction and strength of any long-delayed, discrete sound reflections)

Use a separate evaluation sheet for each seat where performance is to be evaluated. Absence of "dead spots," that is, locations where music is very weak, and minimum variations in listening conditions throughout space indicate good *uniformity*. Remember, there are no absolute or "correct" answers. Subjective impressions by individuals are the only evaluations that really matter.

## Overall Impression

The box at the bottom of the guide should be used to record your overall impression of the musical performance at a given seat location. It is suggested that traditional academic ratings be used: A (for best ever, a most memorable listening experience) to F (for one of the worst, a truly bad listening experience), with C for average experience. Always keep in mind that this guide is intended to be used to develop an understanding of specific music performance conditions and, by careful observation, how they may be affected by architecture.

### References

M. Barron, "Subjective Survey of British Concert Halls," *Proceedings Institute of Acoustics*, vol. 7, February 1985, pp. 41-46.

L. L. Beranek, *Music, Acoustics and Architecture*, Wiley, New York, 1962, pp. 471-480. (The pioneering, comprehensive rating system based on detailed study and analysis of 54 concert halls and opera houses.)

J. S. Bradley, "Experience with New Auditorium Acoustic Measurements," *Journal of the Acoustical Society of America*, June 1983, pp. 2051-2058. (Presents data from measurements in Canadian halls where several acoustical properties have been evaluated.)

P. H. Heringa, "Comparison of the Quality for Music of Different Halls," 11th International Congress on Acoustics, Paris, vol. 7, July 1983, pp. 101-104.

T. J. Schultz, "Concert Hall Tour of North America," Bolt Beranek and Newman Reverberation Time Data Report, BBN Labs., Cambridge, Mass., 1980.

# EVALUATION GUIDE

(Place mark on section of scale which best represents your impression of listening condition. Use separate sheet for each seat where performance is to be evaluated.)

CLEAR SOUND ⌊___|___|___|___|___⌋ BLURRED SOUND
(varies from clear or distinct to blurred or muddy)

LIVE REVERBERANCE ⌊___|___|___|___|___⌋ DEAD REVERBERANCE
(liveness or persistence of mid-frequency sounds)

WARM BASS ⌊___|___|___|___|___⌋ COLD BASS
(relative liveness of bass or longer duration of reverberance at bass compared to mid- and treble frequencies)

INTIMATE SOUND ⌊___|___|___|___|___⌋ REMOTE SOUND
(auditory impression of apparent closeness of orchestra)

SATISFACTORY
LOUDNESS

UNSATISFACTORY
LOUDNESS (too weak
or too loud)

⌊___|___|___|___|___⌋

(indicate early or direct sound (symbol *D*) and reverberant sound (*R*) on scale)

RICH DIFFUSION
(expansive sound) ⌊___|___|___|___|___⌋

POOR DIFFUSION
(constricted sound)

(envelopment of sound which surrounds listener from many directions)

GOOD BALANCE ⌊___|___|___|___|___⌋ POOR BALANCE
(observe between musicians and soloist or chorus, among sections of orchestra)

SATISFACTORY
BACKGROUND NOISE
(very quiet)

UNSATISFACTORY
BACKGROUND NOISE
(very noisy)

⌊___|___|___|___|___⌋

(from HVAC system, or intruding noise from ancillary spaces or outdoors)

ECHOES ⌊_____⌋ No ⌊_____⌋ Yes Direction: _____
(long-delayed reflections that are clearly heard)

Music Performance Space: _____ Date: _____
Seating Capacity: _____ Cubic Volume: _____ ft³
Orchestra/Conductor: _____ Composer/Work: _____
Seat Location: _____ Seat No.: _____
(Use space at right to sketch floor plan, or cut and paste seating layout from program booklet.)

OVERALL IMPRESSION

(Refer to instructions on preceding pages.)

## EVALUATION GUIDE (EXAMPLE APPLICATION)

(Place mark on section of scale which best represents your impression of listening condition. Use separate sheet for each seat where performance is to be evaluated.)

CLEAR SOUND ⊢——✓——⊢——⊢——⊢——⊣ BLURRED SOUND
(varies from clear or distinct to blurred or muddy)

LIVE REVERBERANCE ⊢——✓——⊢——⊢——⊢——⊣ DEAD REVERBERANCE
(liveness or persistence of mid-frequency sounds)

WARM BASS ⊢——✓——⊢——⊢——⊢——⊣ COLD BASS
(relative liveness of bass or longer duration of reverberance at bass compared to mid- and treble frequencies)

INTIMATE SOUND ⊢——✓——⊢——⊢——⊢——⊣ REMOTE SOUND
(auditory impression of apparent closeness of orchestra)

SATISFACTORY LOUDNESS ⊢——R——D——⊢——⊢——⊣ UNSATISFACTORY LOUDNESS (too weak or too loud)
(indicate early or direct sound (symbol D) and reverberant sound (R) on scale)

RICH DIFFUSION (expansive sound) ⊢——✓——⊢——⊢——⊢——⊣ POOR DIFFUSION (constricted sound)
(envelopment of sound which surrounds listener from many directions)

GOOD BALANCE ⊢——✓——⊢——⊢——⊢——⊣ POOR BALANCE
(observe between musicians and soloist or chorus, among sections of orchestra)

SATISFACTORY BACKGROUND NOISE (very quiet) ⊢——✓——⊢——⊢——⊢——⊣ UNSATISFACTORY BACKGROUND NOISE (very noisy)
(from HVAC system, or intruding noise from ancillary spaces or outdoors)

ECHOES ⊢——✓——⊣ No ⊢————⊣ Yes Direction: _____
(long-delayed reflections that are clearly heard)

Music Performance Space: **Gallifrey Music Hall** Date: **13 Feb 95**
Seating Capacity: **2,000** Cubic Volume: **625,000** ft³
Orchestra/Conductor: **Dr. Whom** Composer/Work: **Shostakovich Symphony No.10**
Seat Location: **Main level near side wall** Seat No.: **K9**
(Use space at right to sketch floor plan, or cut and paste seating layout from program booklet.)

**B+** OVERALL IMPRESSION
(Refer to instructions on preceding pages.)

Seat K9 — seating — Stage

# MUSIC CONDITIONS AFFECTED BY ROOM ACOUSTICS DESIGN

The table below presents music listening conditions along with room acoustics properties which influence the corresponding subjective judgments of music performance. If a hall is to be successful, its design must satisfy all these requirements.

| Subjective Music Conditions | Acoustical Properties of Room |
|---|---|
| Clarity and intimacy | 1. Initial-time-delay gap ($< 20$ ms)<br>2. Shape and proportion (e.g., length-to-width ratio $< 2$, or use suspended sound-reflecting panels)<br>3. Avoidance of deep underbalconies |
| Reverberance (or "liveness") | 1. Volume ($300$ ft$^3$/person for rectangular halls, $450$ ft$^3$/person for surround halls) to provide sufficient reverberance ($1.6$ to $2.4$ s at mid-frequencies)<br>2. Shape and proportion<br>3. Furnishings and finishes (sound-reflecting walls and ceiling)<br>4. Audience capacity and seat spacing ($< 9$ ft$^2$/person including aisles) |
| Warmth | 1. Relationship of absorption at low frequencies to mid-frequencies (bass ratio $> 1.2$)<br>2. Thick, heavy enclosing surfaces<br>3. Width of room (height-to-width ratio $> 0.7$)<br>4. Size and shape of sound-reflecting side walls<br>5. Coupled spaces (stagehouses, understage moats) |
| Loudness | 1. Volume (and other reverberance properties listed above)<br>2. Distribution of sound-absorbing finishes<br>3. Stage enclosure and sound-reflecting surfaces at front end of room |
| Diffusion | 1. Large-scale wall and ceiling surface irregularities, quadratic-residue diffusers<br>2. Shape and proportion (e.g., narrow widths, large height-to-width ratios)<br>3. Finishes and furnishings |
| Balance and onstage hearing | 1. Size of stage enclosure (and use of risers for musicians)<br>2. Shape of sound-reflecting panels near orchestra (stage enclosure design)<br>3. Distribution of sound-absorbing finishes (and audience seating in surround hall)<br>4. Adjustability of overhead sound-reflecting panels |

After Wallace Clement Sabine completed his pioneering work to improve the listening conditions in the 436-seat lecture room of the Fogg Art Museum at Harvard University, he continued his studies testing a wide variety of rooms and measuring the sound absorption properties of numerous common building materials. Because of this work on room acoustics, in 1898 Sabine was asked to serve as acoustical consultant on the new Boston Symphony Hall (McKim, Mead, and White, architects). It was to be the first hall designed using scientifically derived principles of room acoustics.

Sabine favored the rectangular "shoebox" shape of the Boston Music Hall, the Leipzig Neues Gewandhaus, and other successful nineteenth-century European halls. In addition to recommending the proportion of length to width, he attempted to achieve a long reverberation time for music ($> 2$ s for the fully-occupied hall). He also recommended splaying the sides of the stage (to better project sound toward the audience), narrowing the stage width (to provide intimacy for orchestra performance), coffering the ceiling and constructing deep side-wall niches and pilasters (to diffuse sound throughout the hall), and controlling ventilation system noise. Nearly a century after its completion in 1900, Boston Symphony Hall is still rated as one of the outstanding concert halls in the world.

Shown below are plan and section views of three traditional *rectangular* halls: Boston Symphony Hall (see photo of interior on cover of book), Leipzig Neues Gewandhaus, and Vienna Grosser Musikvereinssaal.

**Symphony Hall, Boston, Massachusetts** (Completed 1900, seating capacity 2631-persons)

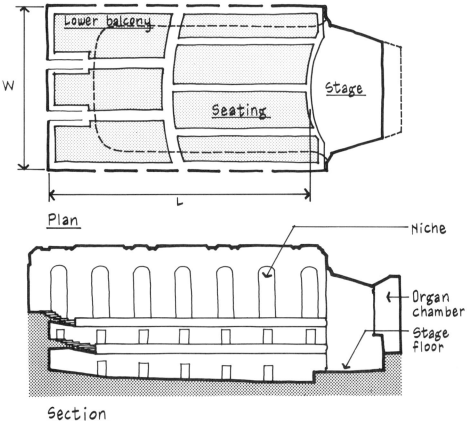

*Lincoln Russell*

**Stage of Boston Symphony Hall**

**Neues Gewandhaus, Leipzig, German Democratic Republic** (Completed 1886, seating capacity 1560-persons, destroyed during World War II)

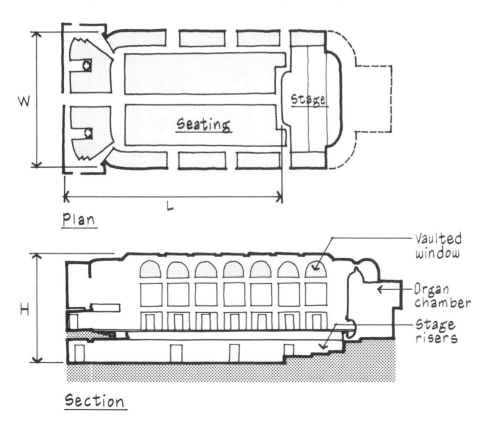

**Grosser Musikvereinssaal, Vienna, Austria** (Completed 1870, seating capacity 1680-persons)

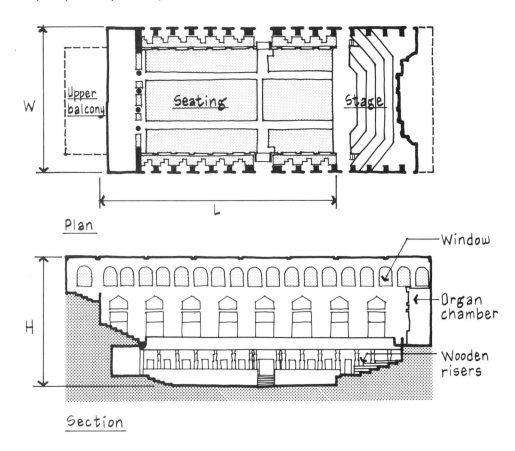

Plan

Section

The table below compares important characteristics of the three halls: height to width ratio $H/W$, length to width ratio $L/W$, ratio of volume (ft³) to audience areas (ft²), and reverberation time $T$ at mid-frequencies (500/1000 Hz).

| | H/W | L/W | Volume to Seating Area Ratio | T (s) |
|---|---|---|---|---|
| Boston | 0.8 | 1.7 | 40 | 1.8 |
| Leipzig | 0.7 | 1.7 | 34 | 1.6 |
| Vienna | 0.9 | 1.6 | 44 | 2.1 |
| Modern criteria | > 0.7 | < 2 | > 45 | 1.6 to 2.4 |

### References

L. L. Beranek, *Music, Acoustics and Architecture*, Wiley, New York, 1962 (case histories 3, 20, and 35).

L. L. Beranek, "Wallace Clement Sabine and Acoustics," *Physics Today*, February 1985.

W. J. Cavanaugh, "Preserving the Acoustics of Mechanics Hall," *Technology & Conservation*, Fall 1980.

## CHECKLIST FOR CONCERT HALLS

When auditoriums are used primarily for music performances, the design goal is to achieve throughout the hall: satisfactory level of sound or *loudness*, referred to as *dynamic range* by musicians; definition of music perception, i.e., *clarity*, *reverberance*, and *intimacy*; and appropriate *tonal balance* and *texture*. The list below summarizes important acoustical properties of rooms needed to achieve satisfactory music perception.

1. *Reverberation time* at mid-frequencies (i.e., average of reverberation at 500 and 1000 Hz) when hall is occupied should be 1.6 to 2.4 s for opera, symphonic, organ, and choral music. An empty hall should have longer reverberation times. See page 64 for preferred ranges of mid-frequency reverberation times for a wide variety of activities. Music in rooms with appropriate reverberation times sounds full-toned, live, and blended. In rooms with too much reverberance, music sounds "muddy" and indistinct.

2. For music performances, the *bass ratio,* a measure of the low-frequency responsiveness of a room, should be greater than 1.2. The bass ratio is the reverberation time at low frequencies (i.e., average of reverberation at 125 and 250 Hz) divided by the mid-frequency reverberation time. For example, if the mid-frequency reverberation time is 2 s and the low-frequency reverberation time is 2.4 s, the bass ratio will be $(2.4 \div 2) = 1.2$. Higher values of bass ratio, indicating fullness of bass tone or "warmth," may be acceptable in especially large halls. Reverberation times should increase about 10 percent per octave below 500 Hz to allow fundamental frequencies of musical instruments to persist sufficiently and to avoid masking from low-frequency background noise. Avoid thin (e.g., $< 3/4$-in-thick wood) or lightweight materials (not attached to a rigid backup surface), which absorb low-frequency sound energy by panel action. When coupled to the hall, a reverberant volume under the stage platform can be used to enhance low-frequency reverberation for the audience near the stage (see example below).

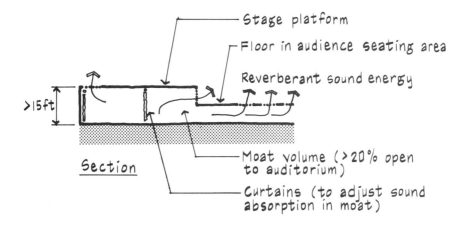

**Acoustical Moat**

3. *Intimacy* can be achieved by providing an initial-time-delay gap ITDG of less than 20 ms for reflected sound energy. For symphonic music, *rectangular* halls should have length-to-width ratio *L/W* of less than 2 to produce strong lateral reflections. Listeners prefer conditions under which sounds are different in each ear. An important goal, therefore, is to achieve strong lateral reflections

from the side walls. Ray-diagram analyses should be used to assure ITDGs from side walls are less than 23 ft (i.e., 20 ms × 1/1000 × 1130 ft/s). In wide halls, the first reflection will be from the ceiling, producing similar sounds in both ears. The ratio of early lateral sound energy to total early energy increases as the height-to-width ratio $H/W$ of the hall increases (i.e., less wide halls). Several highly regarded traditional *rectangular* concert halls in Europe have $H/W$ ratios greater than 0.7. Ray-diagram analyses also can be used to design suspended sound reflectors (convex or flat panel elements sloped about 45° to the horizontal) so early reflected lateral sound will be provided. Area of suspended panel arrays typically should be 40 to 50 percent of the stage area. To aim sound to desired locations, individual panels should be adjustable in height and orientation. This feature also allows "tuning" of the hall.

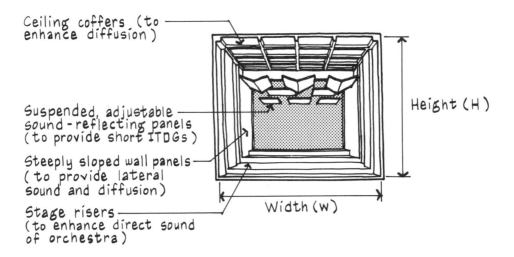

**Suspended Sound-Reflecting Panels**

4. *Loudness* is determined by cubic volume, sound absorption, and shape of front end of hall. It contributes to the definition of music. For *rectangular* concert halls, volume per seat ratio should be 300 ft³ per person; for *surround*

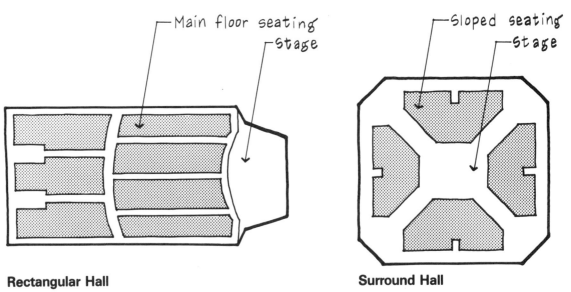

**Rectangular Hall**                    **Surround Hall**

halls, 450 ft³ per person.* Loudness can be measured by placing a standard fan sound source onstage. For concert and opera halls, mid-frequency sound levels (from a standard reference source: ILG blower driven by a 1/4-hp electric motor) should be 52 to 58 dB. For music perception during performances, peak levels often are 90 dBA or more at fortissimo playing (very loud), depending on dynamic range of instruments and passage being performed. However, preferred listening levels are normally less than 80 dBA.

5. Audience absorption can be a significant factor in concert hall design. Limit *seating density* to 6.5 to 9 ft² per person because the more the audience is spread out, the more sound it absorbs. Halls with fewer than 2000 seats can be designed to provide optimum *intimacy* and *loudness* for symphonic music.

6. Halls should have *diffusing* surfaces, such as deep coffers, carved decorations, large-scale pilasters, or projecting piers at $1/4 \lambda$ (i.e., > 6 1/2 in deep for 500 Hz and above) on side walls, balcony faces, ceilings (e.g., exposed beams, boxed-in air ducts), and stage walls, so that listeners perceive reflected sound from many directions. Even uniform coffers can enhance diffusion because the angle of incidence for sound waves from the stage will differ from front to rear coffers. It is especially important that musicians hear each other to play well. Sound-diffusing surfaces near musicians can provide useful early interreflection of sound energy. Avoid flat surfaces, which can cause "harsh" or "glaring" listening conditions for music. The *quadratic-residue diffuser* was invented in the 1970s by Dr. Manfred Schroeder to provide controlled diffusion in concert halls (cf., M. R. Schroeder, *Number Theory in Science and Communication*, Springer-Verlag, Berlin, 1986). These diffusers, constructed to have wells of varying depths, have found wide application in recording studios, where they are called *Schroeder boxes*. A prime number (i.e., no whole number larger than 1 goes into it evenly) divided into each of the squares of the series of all numbers less than the prime number yields a remainder (or residue) sequence. This sequence can be used to establish proportion for varying depths in a diffuser. The table below shows how residues are determined for the prime number 11. For example, 5 squared is 25, the prime number 11 goes into 25 twice ($2 \times 11 = 22$), and the remainder is 3 ($25 - 22$).

| Number $n$: | 1 | 2 | 3 | 4 | 5 | 6 | 7 | 8 | 9 | 10 |
|---|---|---|---|---|---|---|---|---|---|---|
| Number squared $n^2$: | 1 | 4 | 9 | 16 | 25 | 36 | 49 | 64 | 81 | 100 |
| Remainder sequence ($n^2$ divided by prime number): | 1 | 4 | 9 | 5 | 3 | 3 | 5 | 9 | 4 | 1 |

Example sound-diffusing shapes are shown below. Quadratic-residue diffusers QRDs for the prime number 7 are used at Segerstrom Concert Hall, Costa Mesa, Calif. (QRDs designed by J. R. Hyde, acoustical consultant).

**Folded-Panel Surface**

Depth > 1/4 λ — Sloped sound-reflecting panel (varying depths)

---

*Audience absorption is *not* directly related to the number of occupants. It is proportional to the total floor area of seating, including part of the floor area of the aisles (see definition of the *edge effect* in Chap. 2). The ratio of volume (ft³) to audience area (ft²), including orchestra seating, should be more than 45 for concert halls.

**Convex Modulations**

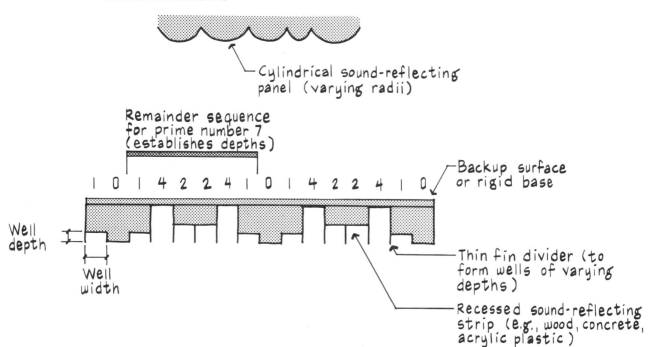

Cylindrical sound-reflecting panel (varying radii)

Remainder sequence for prime number 7 (establishes depths)

1 0 1 4 2 2 4 1 0 1 4 2 2 4 1 0

Backup surface or rigid base

Well depth

Well width

Thin fin divider (to form wells of varying depths)

Recessed sound-reflecting strip (e.g., wood, concrete, acrylic plastic)

**"Quadratic-Residue" Diffuser** (Prime no. 7)

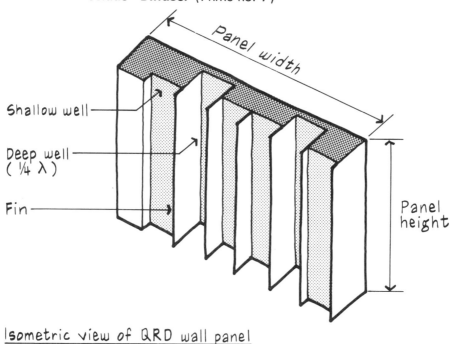

Panel width

Shallow well

Deep well ( ¼ λ )

Fin

Panel height

Isometric view of QRD wall panel

**7.** Sound-reflecting surfaces near the stage and orchestra should contribute to satisfactory *tonal texture* (i.e., subjective impression due to change or sequence of signal delays and levels of the sound reflections). These critical surfaces should be shaped so sound energy will reflect back toward the stage, providing performers with the essential sensation of responsiveness of the hall. Tonal texture is strongly affected by the acoustical properties of the hall, the composition and placement of the orchestra members, and the program selection and style of the conductor.

8. Avoid *echo*-producing surfaces onstage and in the hall. Discrete, flutter, creep, and other echo phenomena must be avoided. Nevertheless, some sound energy should return from the rear of *rectangular* halls to the stage so that the performers can gauge the responsiveness of the hall to their efforts. The balance between these conflicting goals is very delicate and requires careful tuning.

9. *Background noise levels* must be near the threshold of audibility (NC-15 or RC-15 for concert halls) to achieve high signal-to-noise ratios for good listening conditions and to allow musicians to produce the greatest possible audible dynamic ranges. (See Chap. 4 for preferred noise criteria NC levels for a variety of listening spaces. Do not exceed NC-20 for most auditoriums.) Lobbies and circulation corridors, when carefully designed, can act as buffers to noise.

10. Other important factors affecting the acoustical success of concert halls include psychological aspects of design such as: *color* (e.g., most orchestra conductors prefer white and gold interiors to blue interiors); *use of wood* (most musicians believe wood is essential in concert halls even though other materials reflect sound equally well!); *seating arrangement* (provide good sight lines and comfortable seats); *reference* of listeners to other halls (which establishes personal norms); *ancillary spaces* (e.g., "dead" foyers or lobbies, which tend to create the impression of solemnity when entering a more reverberant environment, instead of "live" foyers or lobbies, which tend to create the impression of dryness by contrast); *amenities* such as spacious "green" rooms to enhance morale of performers; etc.

**Note:** A special orchestral composition called "Catacoustical Measures," by T. J. Schultz and D. Pinkham, can be used to help evaluate listening conditions by measuring reverberance during pauses in both empty and occupied concert halls. This composition was scored by D. Pinkham to have musical interest while at the same time producing the entire frequency range of an orchestra with even distribution of frequencies from individual instruments (cf., T. J. Schultz, "Problems in the Measurement of Reverberation Time," *Journal of the Audio Engineering Society*, October 1963, pp. 313-315). The composition can also be used to facilitate the tuning process.

## References

Y. Ando, "Calculation of Subjective Preference at Each Seat in a Concert Hall," *Journal of the Acoustical Society of America,* September 1983.

L. L. Beranek, "Acoustics and the Concert Hall," *Journal of the Acoustical Society of America,* June 1975.

M. Forsyth, *Buildings for Music,* Cambridge University Press, Cambridge, England, 1985. (Also available from MIT Press, Cambridge, Mass.)

C. Jaffe, "Acoustics of Concert Halls," *Architectural Record,* March 1979, pp. 106-108.

V. L. Jordan, *Acoustical Design of Concert Halls and Theatres,* Applied Science Publishers, Barking, England, 1980.

R. Mackenzie (ed.), *Auditorium Acoustics,* Applied Science Publishers, Barking, England, 1975.

R. B. Newman et al., "Adjustable Acoustics for the Multiple-Use Auditorium" in G. C. Izenour, *Theater Design,* McGraw-Hill, New York, 1977, pp. 479-493.

R. S. Shankland, "Acoustical Designing for Performers," *Journal of the Acoustical Society of America,* January 1979.

# CASE STUDY 1: WOODRUFF CENTER, EMORY UNIVERSITY

**Woodruff Health Sciences Center Administration Building**
Emory University
Atlanta, Georgia

The section view of the Woodruff building at Emory University shows the classrooms and auditorium below the plaza level and the medical school administration offices above. The auditorium was designed to accommodate 500 people on two levels, primarily for lectures, convocations, and related speech activities. The balcony soffit was sloped to increase the size of the opening to the audience seated underneath ($D < 2H$), and to provide line of sight to the central loudspeaker cluster for persons in the last row (see Chap. 7). The sound-reflecting oak ceiling panels were oriented to evenly distribute sound energy throughout the auditorium. Concave balcony face and rear walls were finished with glass fiberboard covered with Belgian linen (i.e., deep absorption to prevent echoes and control reverberation). The ceiling above the suspended panels was covered with glass fiberboard to further control reverberance. Mid-frequency reverberation time is 0.8 s. Heavy enclosing concrete constructions and duct treatment reduce mechanical equipment noise to noise criteria NC-25 (see Chaps. 4 and 5).

*Architect*: Heery Architects & Engineers, Inc. (Atlanta, Georgia)
*Acoustical Consultant*: Office of M. David Egan (Anderson, South Carolina)

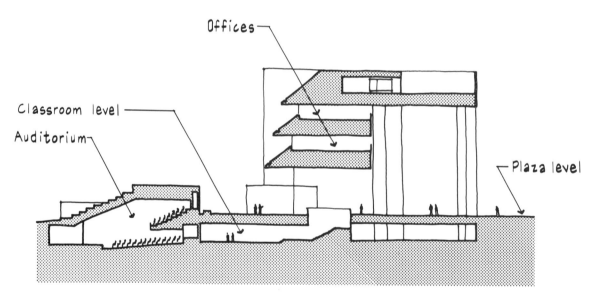

**Building Section**

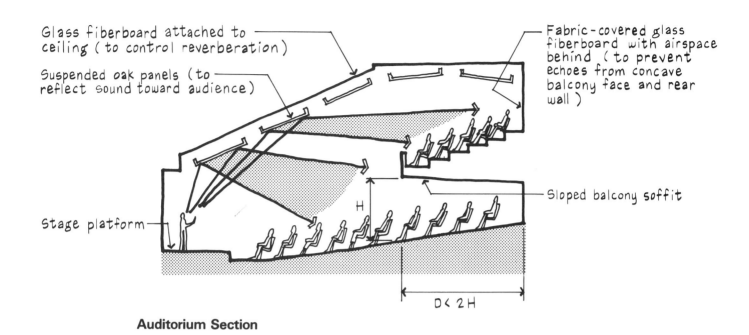

Glass fiberboard attached to ceiling (to control reverberation)

Suspended oak panels (to reflect sound toward audience)

Fabric-covered glass fiberboard with airspace behind (to prevent echoes from concave balcony face and rear wall)

Stage platform

Sloped balcony soffit

H

D < 2H

**Auditorium Section**

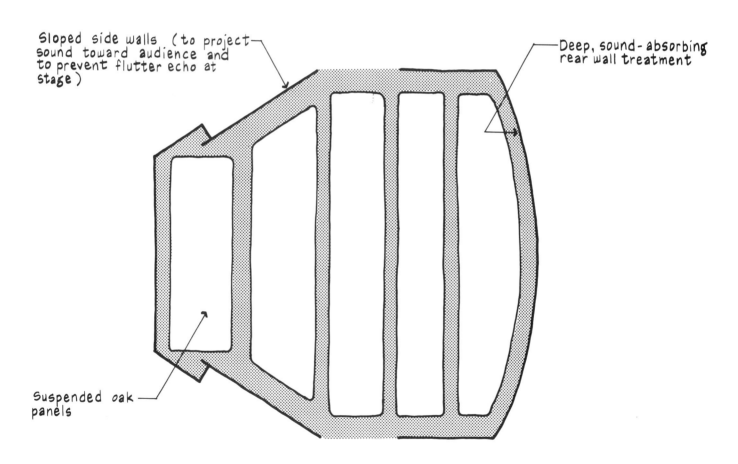

Sloped side walls (to project sound toward audience and to prevent flutter echo at stage)

Deep, sound-absorbing rear wall treatment

Suspended oak panels

**Auditorium Reflected-Ceiling Plan**

**Administration Building and Exterior of Auditorium Wing from Plaza Level**

**Auditorium from Balcony**

**Reference**

R. Yee, "Woodruff Medical Administration Building," *Contract Interiors*, October 1977, pp. 74-77.

# CASE STUDY 2: BOETTCHER CONCERT HALL

### Boettcher Concert Hall
Denver, Colorado

Boettcher Concert Hall, completed in 1978, is a 360° *surround* music hall designed to place the audience of 2750 close to the performers. More than 80 percent of audience is less than 65 ft from performers. Audience seating is organized into several "terrace block" balconies rather than a single circular amphitheater pattern. This increases the area of reflective surfaces near the audience. Balcony faces are thick plaster shaped in convex ribbon patterns (to diffuse sound), balconies are steeply sloped (to reduce audience attenuation), and seats have sound-reflecting high wood backs (to increase intimacy). This 1,315,000-ft³ hall has an overhead canopy (panel array) consisting of 106 adjustable, suspended, sound-reflecting circular-convex 1/2-in-thick acrylic plastic saucers (to improve onstage listening conditions and reflect sound to audience seated near stage). Mid-frequency reverberation time is 2 s and volume-to-audience-area ratio is 51 (to provide sufficient liveness at mid-frequencies and warmth at low frequencies).

*Architect:* Hardy, Holzman, Pfeiffer Associates (New York, New York)
*Acoustical Consultant:* Jaffe Acoustics, Inc. (Norwalk, Connecticut)
*Sound System Designer:* David H. Kaye (Boston, Massachusetts)

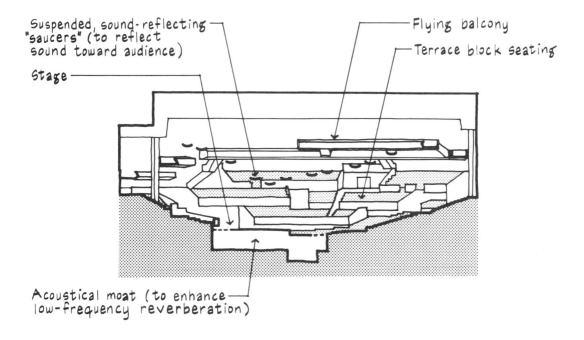

**Hall Section**

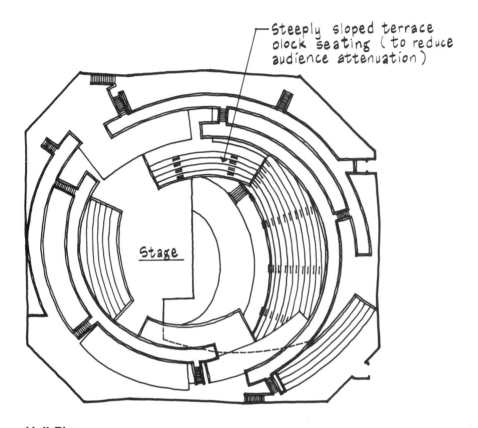

Steeply sloped terrace block seating (to reduce audience attenuation)

Stage

**Hall Plan**

**Hall from Upper-Level Balcony**

**References**

C. Jaffe, "360-degree Symphony Halls and Music Pavilions," Audio Engineering Society, New York, Preprint No. 1092, November 1975.

R. H. Talaske et al., *Halls for Music Performance,* American Institute of Physics, New York, 1982, pp. 16-17.

# CASE STUDY 3: DUNHAM AUDITORIUM, BREVARD COLLEGE

Dunham Auditorium
Brevard College
Brevard, North Carolina

The 500-seat auditorium, originally completed in 1957, had an extremely short mid-frequency reverberation time for music ($< 0.6$ s), poor diffusion, and poor coupling from stage to audience. To increase reverberance, the original sound-absorbing ceiling was removed, opening the entire auditorium to the attic volume above. In addition, the proscenium walls were removed to further increase the total effective cubic volume of the room by more than 40 percent. Windows along the side walls were filled in with masonry (to improve sound isolation from outdoor noise) and finished with large-scale gypsum board "bumps" (to provide diffusion and enhance lateral sound). The renovated auditorium reopened in 1981 with significant improvements in room acoustics, which greatly enhanced conditions for performance and perception of music. Mid-frequency reverberation time now is 1.4 s and improved volume-to-audience-area ratio is 44 (to increase liveness and warmth). Length-to-width ratio $L/W$ is 1.5.

*Architect:* Daniels-Worley, Architects (Brevard, North Carolina)
*Acoustical Consultant:* Office of M. David Egan (Anderson, South Carolina)

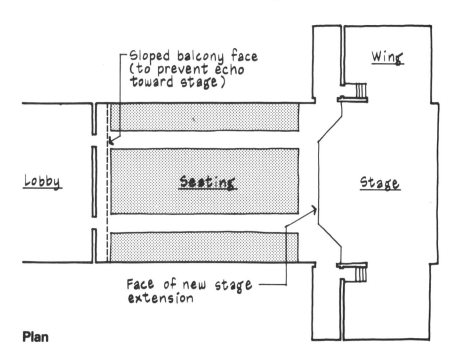

**Plan**

**View toward Stage (before renovation)**

**View toward Rear Wall (before renovation)**

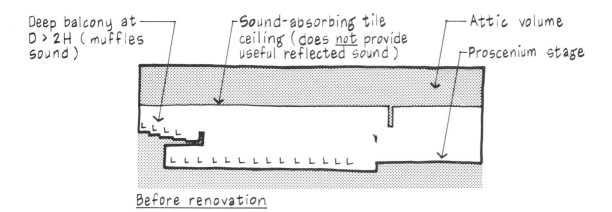

Deep balcony at D > 2H (muffles sound)

Sound-absorbing tile ceiling (does *not* provide useful reflected sound)

Attic volume

Proscenium stage

Before renovation

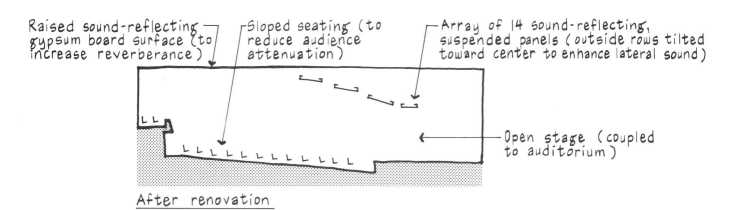

Raised sound-reflecting gypsum board surface (to increase reverberance)

Sloped seating (to reduce audience attenuation)

Array of 14 sound-reflecting, suspended panels (outside rows tilted toward center to enhance lateral sound)

Open stage (coupled to auditorium)

After renovation

**Sections**

R. B. Strong

**View toward Stage** (after renovation)

**View toward Rear Wall** (after renovation)

R. B. Strong

# CASE STUDY 4: STUDIO B, TODD-AO FILMS

**Studio B, Todd-AO Films**
Hollywood, California

    The film production studio shown below contains electronic control equipment for mixing and editing of prerecorded sound tracks. Loudspeakers are located behind a large perforated projection screen and "surround" loudspeakers are located on the side and rear walls. The walls are treated with thick glass fiberboard and mineral fiber behind a *transondent* protective facing of wood slats (see also Chap. 2). Three thicknesses of sound-absorbing material were randomly distributed on the walls to help achieve a relatively "dead" space with the desired reverberation times of 0.5 s at 125 Hz, 0.4 s at 500 Hz, and 0.4 s at 2000 Hz.

*Acoustical Consultant:* Charles M. Salter Associates, Inc. (San Francisco, California)

**Studio from Control Room**

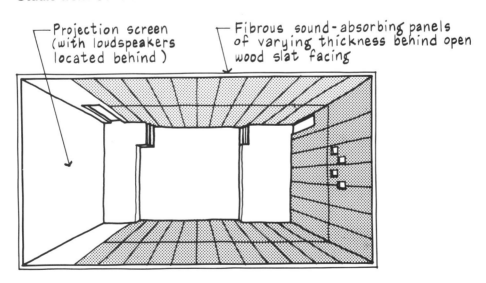

**Bird's-Eye View Perspective**

# CHECKLIST FOR ROOM ACOUSTICS DESIGN

1. The level of the background noise (e.g., HVAC, intruding environmental sources) must be sufficiently low to avoid interfering with the intended activities (see Chaps. 4 and 5).

2. Sound energy must be evenly distributed throughout the listening space.

3. Avoid echoes and any focusing effects. In small rooms for conferences or music practice, with relatively little sound absorption, avoid parallel surfaces and shapes which might emphasize certain frequencies (e.g., ratio of any two of the length, width, and height dimensions should not be a whole number).

4. The desired sounds must be sufficiently loud. Shape room surfaces to provide useful sound reflections toward the audience. If size of auditorium and its use require an electronic sound-reinforcing system, carefully integrate the system with the room acoustics design (see Chap. 7).

5. Provide the proper reverberation time characteristics. The reverberation time must be long enough to properly blend sounds, and yet short enough so there will be sufficient separation of successive sounds necessary for intelligibility. In rooms for both speech and music, there is a natural conflict. A long reverberation time is desirable for music so that successive notes blend together, giving richness in bass frequencies. However, for speech the reverberation time should be short so that the persistence of one syllable does not blur or mask subsequent syllables.

6. Provide short enough initial-time-delay gaps for the early sound reflections in concert halls and similar spaces. Initial-time-delay gaps should be less than 30 ms (i.e., a sound path difference < 34 ft) to provide useful reinforcement of direct speech sounds.

# Chapter 4
# Sound Isolation

A doorbell, as shown at the right on the facing page, can be used to demonstrate the basic principles of sound isolation. With no isolation, the doorbell produces 70 dB at a few inches away. When the doorbell is surrounded by a 3/4-in-thick enclosure of low-density, porous glass fiberboard (called *fuzz*), the transmitted noise is reduced by only 3 dB. Porous sound absorbers are very poor isolators because air molecules can readily pass through them. By themselves they act as sponges; they absorb sound but do *not* prevent its transmission!

When the doorbell is surrounded by a 1/2-in-thick plywood enclosure with an airtight seal around its edges, the noise is reduced by 28 dB (from 78 dB within the enclosure to 50 dB outside). This is a tremendous change in noise level and would be perceived by most observers as about one-fourth as loud. The plywood enclosure is an effective barrier because it is solid, has sufficient *mass,* and is sealed *airtight* around the edges. The seal is essential because even a very small opening can noticeably increase the transmitted sound.

When the doorbell is surrounded by a 1/2-in-thick plywood enclosure fully lined with 3/4-in-thick fuzz, the noise is reduced by 29 dB. However, the noise outside is further reduced to 43 dB because the sound-absorbing lining reduces the buildup of reflected sound energy within the enclosure by 6 dB.

The illustrations on the left show the effect that nearby reflective surfaces have on noise. A noise source close to a reflective wall surface can be 3 dB higher than in the open. When in a corner where two reflective wall and floor surfaces surround the source, the noise can be 6 dB or more higher. Both of these increases could be reduced by sound-absorbing surface treatment. As shown by the doorbell enclosure without a sound-absorbing lining, the buildup in a reverberant room can be 8 dB or more. Therefore, the most effective sound-isolating enclosures are heavy, airtight, and have sound-absorbing linings.

## Sound-Reflecting Surfaces

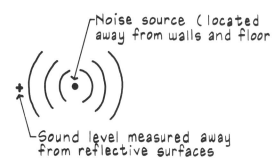

Noise source (located away from walls and floor

Sound level measured away from reflective surfaces

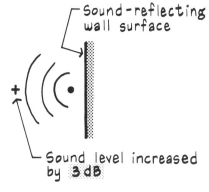

Sound-reflecting wall surface

Sound level increased by **3 dB**

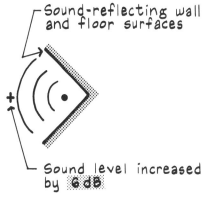

Sound-reflecting wall and floor surfaces

Sound level increased by **6 dB**

## Enclosures for Noise Isolation

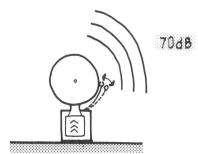

70 dB

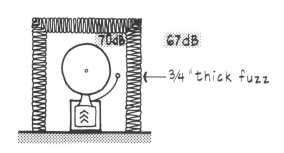

**70 dB**  **67 dB**

3/4" thick fuzz

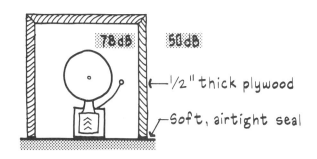

**78 dB**  **50 dB**

1/2" thick plywood

Soft, airtight seal

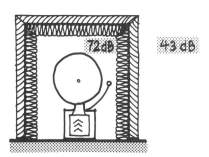

**72 dB**  43 dB

## VIBRATION OF BUILDING ELEMENTS

Sound waves impinging on building elements, such as walls, floor, or ceiling, produce back-and-forth motion. The magnitude of this motion or vibration depends on the weight (or mass) of the building element—the greater the weight, the greater the resistance to motion and the less sound energy transmitted.

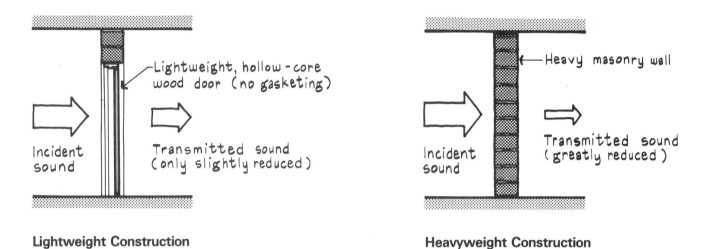

**Lightweight Construction**

**Heavyweight Construction**

In addition to weight, other factors affect wall motion. For example, certain *natural frequencies* (also called "favorite frequencies") for bending waves can exist, depending on the stiffness of the construction. When these waves are excited by impinging sound energy, the resistance to sound transmission is greatly reduced (a phenomenon called the *coincidence effect*).

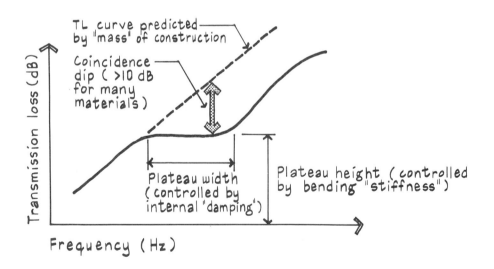

**TL Curve for Single-Layer Wall**

*Transmission loss* (abbreviated TL and measured in decibels) is a measure of how much sound energy is reduced in transmission through materials. The more massive a material, the higher its TL. However, due to coincidence effects, the TL at some frequencies will be far less than would be predicted by only considering the mass of a material. This effect is shown on the above graph of TL versus frequency.

Transmission loss can be expressed as follows:

$$TL = L_1 - L_2$$

where   TL = sound transmission loss (dB)
        $L_1$ = sound level in laboratory source room (dB)
        $L_2$ = sound level in laboratory receiving room (dB)

and

$$TL = 10 \log \frac{1}{\tau}$$

where   TL = sound transmission loss (dB)
        $\tau$ = sound transmission coefficient (no units)

$\tau$ is the ratio of the sound energy transmitted by a material to the incident sound energy.

## EXAMPLE PROBLEMS (TRANSMISSION LOSS)

1. Find the TL of a material that has a sound transmission coefficient $\tau$ of $6.0 \times 10^{-4}$.

$$TL = 10 \log \frac{1}{\tau}$$

$$= 10 \log \frac{1}{6 \times 10^{-4}}$$

$$= 10 \log (0.167 \times 10^4)$$

$$= 10 \log (1.67 \times 10^3)$$

$$TL = 10 (3.2227) = \boxed{32 \text{ dB}}$$

2. The TL of a heavy concrete block wall construction is 40 dB. Find the $\tau$ for this wall.

$$TL = 10 \log \frac{1}{\tau}$$

$$40 = 10 \log \frac{1}{\tau}$$

$$4 = \log \frac{1}{\tau}$$

$$\frac{1}{\tau} = 1 \times 10^4$$

$\tau = \boxed{10^{-4}}$ or 0.0001 of incident sound energy is transmitted.

3. An open casement window has a TL of 0 dB. Find the $\tau$ for this opening.

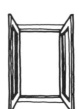

$$TL = 10 \log \frac{1}{\tau}$$

$$0 = 10 \log \frac{1}{\tau}$$

Because log 1 = 0

$$\frac{1}{\tau} = 1$$

$\tau = \boxed{1}$ for an opening (all incident sound energy is transmitted!)

# MASS LAW

According to the *mass law* for homogeneous building materials, such as glass, wood, and concrete, the TL and sound transmission class rating (abbreviated STC) increase by about 5 for each doubling of surface weight (in pounds per square foot). STC is a single-number rating of TL performance for a construction element tested over a standard frequency range. The higher the STC, the more efficient the construction is for reducing sound transmission. (See pages 199-201 for further details on the STC rating method.)

STC data for a variety of building constructions listed below have considerable scatter about the theoretical mass law curve. Nevertheless, the trend clearly indicates that heavier materials provide better sound isolation. This is the fundamental principle of sound isolation for architectural acoustics.

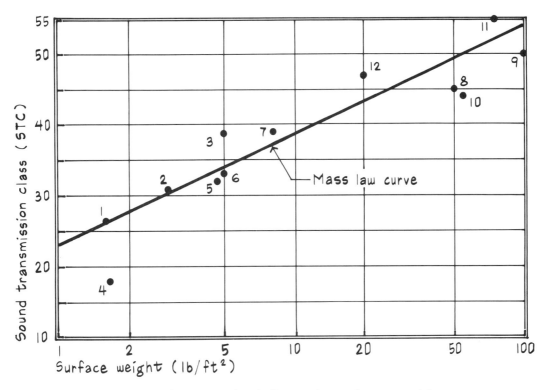

**Building Constructions** (number indicates data point on graph)

*Glass:*

    **1.** 1/8-in-thick monolithic float glass

    **2.** 1/4-in-thick monolithic float glass

    **3.** 1/4- + 1/8-in-thick double-layer glass window with 2-in airspace between panes

*Doors:*

    **4.** 1 3/4-in-thick hollow-core wood door, no gasketing

    **5.** 1 3/4-in-thick solid-core wood door, with gaskets and drop seal

*Walls:*

6. 2 by 4 wood studs with 1/2-in-thick gypsum board layer on both sides
7. 2 by 4 staggered wood studs with 1/2-in-thick gypsum board layer on both sides
8. 4 1/2-in-thick brick
9. Two wythes of 4 1/2-in-thick brick separated by 2-in airspace with metal ties between layers

*Floors/Ceilings:*

10. 4-in-thick reinforced concrete slab
11. 6-in-thick reinforced concrete slab
12. 18-in steel joists with 1 5/8-in-thick concrete on 5/8-in-thick plywood with carpet and pad on floor side, and 5/8-in-thick gypsum board attached to joists on ceiling side

## TL IMPROVEMENT FROM INCREASING WEIGHT

The table below gives the STC ratings for 3-in-thick dense concrete ( 12 lb/ft² per inch of thickness) and for three successive doubled thicknesses of 6 in, 12 in, and 24 in.

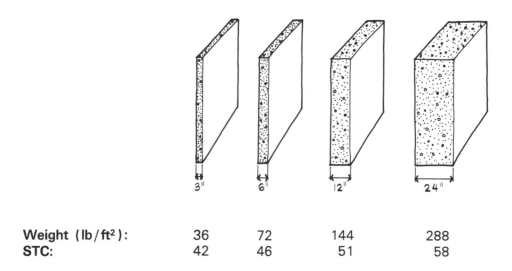

| | 3" | 6" | 12" | 24" |
|---|---|---|---|---|
| **Weight (lb/ft²):** | 36 | 72 | 144 | 288 |
| **STC:** | 42 | 46 | 51 | 58 |

*Mass law* follows the law of diminishing returns. As shown by the above data, the STC of a homogeneous construction increases about 5 for each doubling of weight. However, it is the initial doubling that provides the most practical improvement. Each successive doubling produces proportionally less STC (or TL) improvement per unit weight and a greater increase in cost per unit STC (or TL) increase. Consequently, complex constructions are required when it is necessary to achieve high STCs and TL improvements, especially at low frequencies. The graph below shows transmission loss performance for 3-in-thick and 12-in-thick concrete.

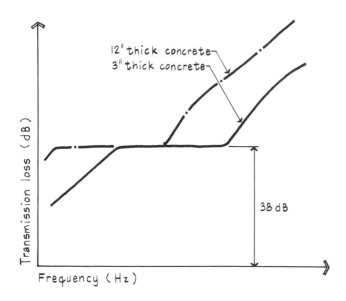

The sound isolation efficiency of materials depends on *stiffness* as well as mass. For example, the graph below shows TL performance for two plywood layers of equivalent total weight. According to the mass law, the TL performance should be the same. However, the grooved, less stiff layer has much higher TL performance, especially at mid- and high frequencies.

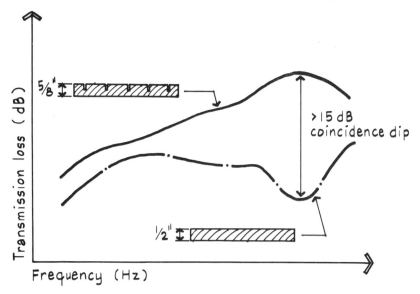

As shown by the above graph, the coincidence dip can be greater than 15 dB for stiff materials. This significant difference in TL is caused by the altered response to bending waves, which are excited by the impinging sound energy. Bending waves are similar to the wave motion in a rope shaken at one end. The exaggerated sketch below shows bending-wave coincidence for a wall.

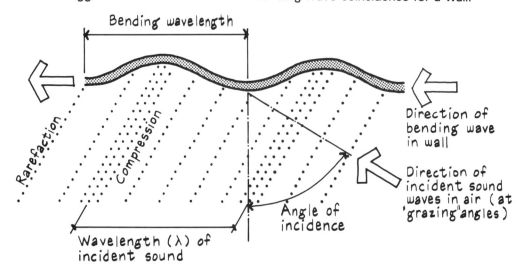

To achieve high TL performance, use double-wall constructions with wide separation between layers, light-gauge metal studs instead of wood studs, or metal channels to "resiliently" support gypsum board layers. These elements, if properly installed, can reduce the stiffness of a barrier. The ideal sound-isolating construction would be *heavy*, *limp*, and *airtight*!

## TL FOR SINGLE WALLS

The graph below shows transmission loss performance based on equal surface weight for several materials. The curve describing TL performance for most single (or homogeneous) walls consists of three basic parts: the low-frequency *mass*-controlled region at about 6 dB per octave slope; the plateau region of relatively constant TL which depends on bending *stiffness* and internal *damping* of the material; and the critical frequency (and mass-controlled) region above the plateau, usually at 10 dB per octave slope. Consequently, high-frequency hissing or whistling sounds can be isolated by a material which allows low-frequency rumbling sounds to be easily transmitted.

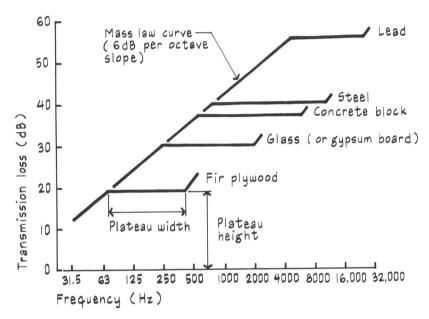

The stiffer a wall, the lower the plateau height, meaning the poorer the sound-isolating performance. Conversely, the limper a material, the higher the plateau height and the better the sound-isolating performance. As shown by the curves, lead has the highest plateau height and the best sound-isolating performance on an equivalent weight basis. The more *damping* a wall has (e.g., energy loss from internal friction), the narrower the plateau width, resulting in better sound-isolating performance. Notice that plywood and lead have far narrower plateau widths than steel. When plywood is struck, it "thuds" because of its internal damping. When steel is struck, it "rings" because it has far less internal damping. For example, sheet metal air-conditioning ducts are poor isolators of sound and, as a consequence, often must be enclosed by gypsum board when they pass through noisy areas (see Chap. 5).

The TL at 500 Hz of homogeneous materials can be estimated by the formula:

$$TL = 20 + 20 \log G$$

where  TL = transmission loss at 500 Hz (dB)
G = surface density (lb/ft²)

Surface densities for common building materials are: brick at 10 lb/ft² per inch of thickness, concrete block at 6 to 12 lb/ft² per inch, plywood at 3 lb/ft² per inch, and plaster at 9 lb/ft² per inch.

## SOUND LEAKS

Sound leaks, like water leaks, must be prevented because sound will travel through any size opening with little loss. As any homeowner knows, even the most expensive roofing system will leak when it is raining if there is only one tiny hole in it! For sound, the more effective a solid construction is as a sound isolator, the more serious the sound leak. For example, a 1-in$^2$ hole in a 100-ft$^2$ gypsum board partition can transmit as much sound energy as the rest of the partition, thereby destroying its sound-isolating effectiveness.

Consequently, when sound isolation is required, always seal cracks and open joints in partitions, avoid back-to-back electrical outlets, and eliminate all other potential sound leaks. The example partition shown at the left on the facing page has sound leaks along both the head and floor tracks. By caulking the perimeter of the gypsum board base layer on both sides, the TL can be increased by more than 20 dB.

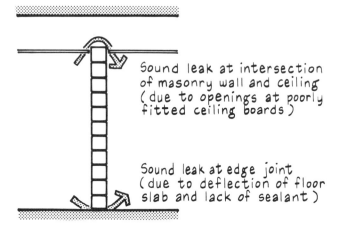

Sound leak at intersection of masonry wall and ceiling (due to openings at poorly fitted ceiling boards)

Sound leak at edge joint (due to deflection of floor slab and lack of sealant)

**Sound Leaks at Walls**

## Partition Leaks

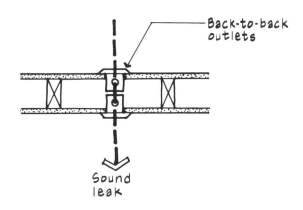

Two layers of gypsum board on steel studs

Sound leaks

Floor track or runner

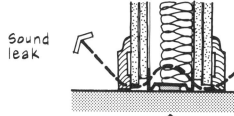

Sound leak

Caulking bead under floor track (does **not** block sound leak!)

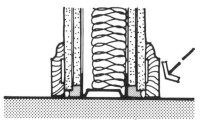

Caulked perimeter of base layer on both sides of partition (to prevent sound leaks)

## Electrical Outlet Leaks

Back-to-back outlets

Sound leak

Side-to-side outlets

Sound leak

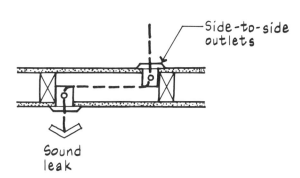

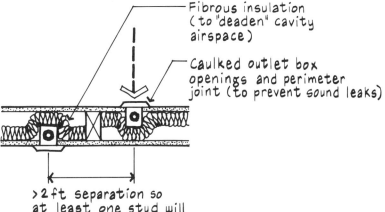

Fibrous insulation (to "deaden" cavity airspace)

Caulked outlet box openings and perimeter joint (to prevent sound leaks)

>2 ft separation so at least one stud will be between outlets

**Reference**

E. Ellwood, "The Anatomy of a Wall," *Sound and Vibration*, June 1972.

The graph below shows the loss in TL effectiveness for "leaky" doors. Openings such as louvers, gaps at thresholds, and the like have a TL of 0 dB. Therefore, these sound leaks can seriously reduce the TL of doors.

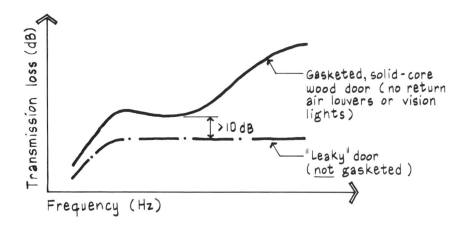

Example leaks in doors and corrective measures are presented below. When doors must provide high sound isolation, use solid-core wood (or fiber-filled hollow metal) doors which are gasketed around their entire perimeters in order to be airtight when closed, or use proprietary "acoustical" doors, which come from manufacturer complete with gasketing and stops.

| Sound Leak | Door | Corrective Measure |
|---|---|---|
| Louver | | Avoid. Route air through separate branch duct, or use muffler to corridor (see Chap. 5) |
| Vision panel at low TL | | Use at least 1/4-in-thick glass, laminated glass, or two separate panes of glass |
| Undercut threshold | | Use threshold gasket or effective drop seal |

## EFFECTS OF SOUND LEAKS ON TL

The graph below shows the reduction in TL caused by sound leaks such as unsealed open joints, openings in electrical boxes, and the like. For example, an opening only 0.01 percent of the wall surface area can reduce the TL from 50 to 39 dB (see dashed lines on graph). The higher the TL (or STC) of a construction, the more serious the sound leak. A leak of 1 percent in a gypsum board partition can reduce its TL by 15 dB (from 35 to 20 dB). However, in a heavy masonry construction with a significantly higher TL of 60 dB, the same 1 percent area of leak will cause a far greater reduction of 40 dB (from 60 to 20 dB). The plateau heights of the curves show the highest TLs that can be achieved at a percent sound leak no matter how effective the wall TL. For example, a total of 1 percent sound leak area would limit a wall TL to 20 dB.

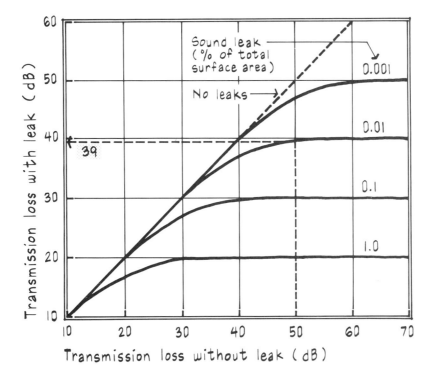

**Reference**

D. D. Reynolds, *Engineering Principles of Acoustics*, Allyn and Bacon, Boston, 1981, pp. 327-328.

The TL of a wall can be increased by separating the wall layers with an airspace to form a *double-wall* construction. For the wood stud constructions shown below, TL increases as the width of the cavity airspace increases. Further increases in TL can occur if sound-absorbing material is added to the airspace because absorption reduces the buildup of sound in the airspace. Shown below are example double-wall and double-stud constructions. The double-stud

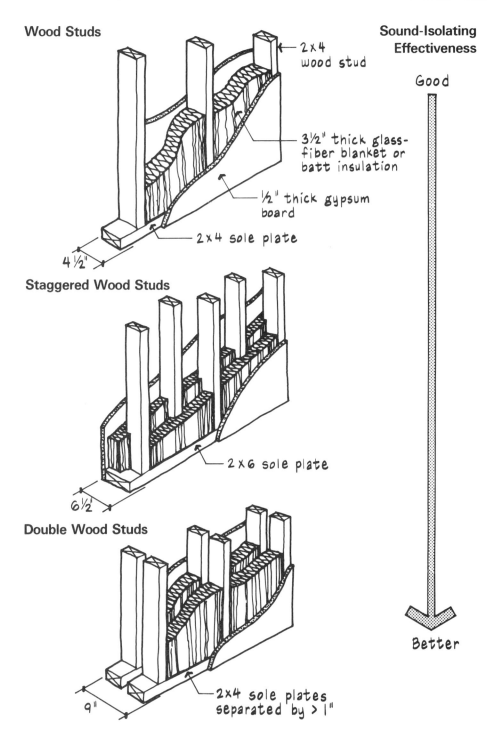

**Wood Studs**

2×4 wood stud

3½" thick glass-fiber blanket or batt insulation

½" thick gypsum board

2×4 sole plate

4½"

**Staggered Wood Studs**

2×6 sole plate

6½"

**Double Wood Studs**

2×4 sole plates separated by > 1"

9"

**Sound-Isolating Effectiveness**

Good

Better

construction breaks the direct sound transmission path through the studs from layer to opposite layer because there are two independent framing systems separated by 1 in or more. This construction technique widely separates both sides of the wall, so the full benefit of the cavity absorption can be achieved.

**Note:** TL performance of the double-wood-stud construction can be greatly improved when the weight of the gypsum board is doubled by adding a 1/2-in layer to both sides. Do *not* attach the additional layers to the inside of the wood stud framings because a small air gap between these two gypsum board inner layers (< 2-in separation) can be a significant short circuit through the wall acting as a ''bridge,'' which reduces TL by more than 10 dB at sound frequencies below 250 Hz.

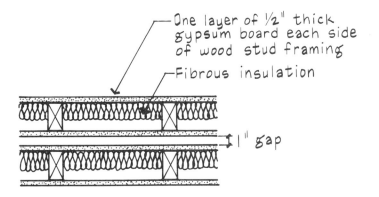

One layer of ½" thick gypsum board each side of wood stud framing

Fibrous insulation

1" gap

**Poor Low-Frequency Isolation**

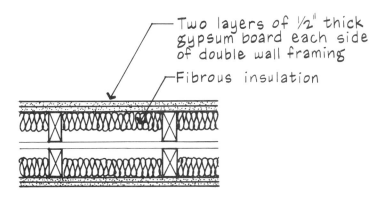

Two layers of ½" thick gypsum board each side of double wall framing

Fibrous insulation

**Better Sound Isolation**

When a "weaker" element, such as a window or door, is used in a construction, the composite TL for the combination is usually closer to the TL of the weaker element than to the "stronger." Composite TL can be found by:

$$\text{Composite TL} = 10 \log \frac{\Sigma S}{\Sigma \tau S}$$

where  TL = transmission loss (dB)

$S$ = surface area (ft$^2$)

$\tau$ = sound transmission coefficient (no units)

Combinations of brick with a TL of 50 dB and single glass with a TL of 20 dB are shown below. Because the sound isolation provided by the glass is so much lower than the sound isolation provided by the brick, only one-eighth glass (or 12 1/2 percent of wall surface area) will reduce the overall effectiveness of the composite construction to 29 dB!

| Wall | Composite TL (dB) |
|------|-------------------|
| *All Brick* | 50 |
| *One-Eighth Glass* | 29 |
| *One-Fourth Glass* | 26 |
| *One-Half Glass* | 23 |
| *All Glass* | 20 |

## EXAMPLE PROBLEMS (COMPOSITE TL)

1. A 12.5-ft² window with a TL of 20 dB is in a 100-ft² brick wall which has a TL of 50 dB. Find the composite TL of this window-wall construction. First, find the sound transmission coefficients for brick and glass.

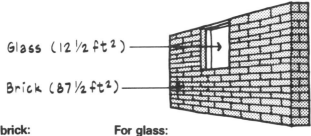

Glass (12 ½ ft²)

Brick (87 ½ ft²)

**For brick:**

$$TL = 10 \log \frac{1}{\tau}$$

$$50 = 10 \log \frac{1}{\tau}$$

$$5 = \log \frac{1}{\tau}$$

$$\frac{1}{\tau} = 10^5$$

$$\tau = \boxed{10^{-5}}$$

**For glass:**

$$TL = 10 \log \frac{1}{\tau}$$

$$20 = 10 \log \frac{1}{\tau}$$

$$2 = \log \frac{1}{\tau}$$

$$\frac{1}{\tau} = 10^2$$

$$\tau = \boxed{10^{-2}}$$

Next, find the composite TL.

$$\text{Composite TL} = 10 \log \frac{\Sigma S}{\Sigma \tau S}$$

$$= 10 \log \frac{100}{(10^{-5} \times 87.5) + (10^{-2} \times 12.5)}$$

$$= 10 \log \frac{100}{12.6 \times 10^{-2}} = 10 \log (8 \times 10^2)$$

$$\text{Composite TL} = 10 (2.9031) = \boxed{29 \text{ dB}}$$

2. A 3 by 7 ft louvered door which has a TL of 10 dB at 500 Hz is located in one wall of a conference room. The 18 ft long by 8 ft high wall with a TL of 45 dB at 500 Hz is staggered wood stud construction with two layers of gypsum board on both sides. Find the composite TL at 500 Hz for this wall-door construction.

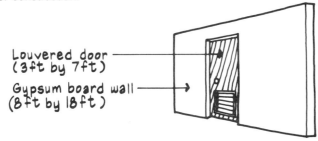

Louvered door
(3 ft by 7 ft)

Gypsum board wall
(8 ft by 18 ft)

First, find the sound transmission coefficients for the gypsum board wall construction and the louvered door.

**For wood stud wall:**

$$TL = 10 \log \frac{1}{\tau}$$

$$45 = 10 \log \frac{1}{\tau}$$

$$4.5 = \log \frac{1}{\tau}$$

$$\frac{1}{\tau} = 3.16 \times 10^4$$

$$\tau = 0.316 \times 10^{-4}$$

$$\tau = 3.16 \times 10^{-5}$$

**For louvered door:**

$$TL = 10 \log \frac{1}{\tau}$$

$$10 = 10 \log \frac{1}{\tau}$$

$$1 = \log \frac{1}{\tau}$$

$$\frac{1}{\tau} = 1 \times 10^1$$

$$\tau = 10^{-1}$$

Next, find the composite TL.

$$\text{Composite TL} = 10 \log \frac{\Sigma S}{\Sigma \tau S}$$

$$= 10 \log \frac{8 \times 18}{(3.16 \times 10^{-5} \times 123) + (10^{-1} \times 21)}$$

$$= 10 \log \frac{144}{2.1039} = 10 \log (6.84 \times 10^1)$$

$$\text{Composite TL} = 10 \ (1.8351) = 18 \ dB \text{ at 500 Hz}$$

## TL CHART FOR COMPOSITE CONSTRUCTIONS

The graph below can be used to find the composite TL. To solve the first example in the preceding example problems, first find the percentage of the weaker component (glass at 12.5 ft²): 12.5 ÷ 100 = 12.5 percent. Next, subtract the TL of the weaker component (glass) from the TL of the stronger component (brick): 50 − 20 = 30 dB. Enter the bottom scale at 30 dB to find the intersection with the 12.5 percent curve. Then read across to the vertical scale at the left to find the correction number to be subtracted from the higher TL value. (See dashed lines on graph.) Therefore, the composite TL will be 50 − 21 = 29 dB. By combining TLs two at a time, the graph also can be used to find the composite TL for multi-component constructions.

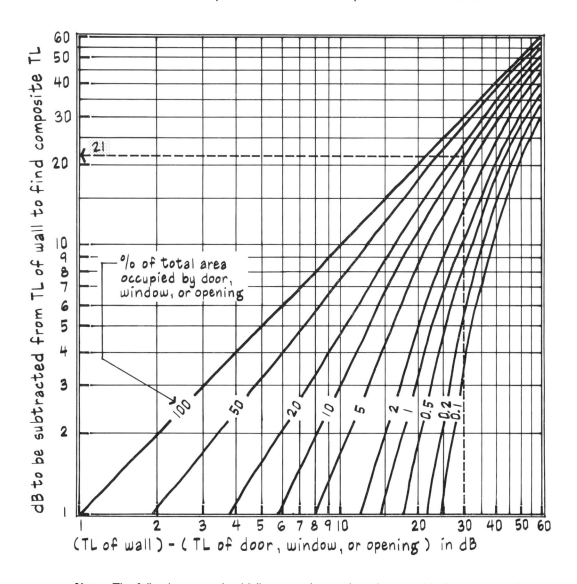

**Note:** The following general guidelines may be used to plan sound-isolating composite constructions. If the percentage of a weaker element is less than 25 percent, the TL of the weaker element should *not* be more than 5 dB lower than the TL of the stronger element; if 25 to 50 percent, the TL should *not* be more than 2 dB lower; and if greater than 50 percent, the TL of the weaker element will be the composite TL.

The *noise reduction* NR between rooms is the arithmetical difference in sound levels $L$'s in the rooms. That is, the NR is the noise in the source room at a sound level of $L_1$ less the noise transmitted into the receiving room at a reduced sound level of $L_2$.

$$NR = L_1 - L_2$$

where   NR = noise reduction (dB)
        $L_1$ = sound level in source room (dB)
        $L_2$ = sound level in receiving room (dB)

The NR at a given frequency is independent of the noise level in the source room. For example, if the NR is 40 dB and $L_1$ is 96 dB, $L_2$ will be $96 - 40 = 56$ dB. If $L_1$ is lowered to 62 dB in this example, $L_2$ will be $62 - 40 = 22$ dB.

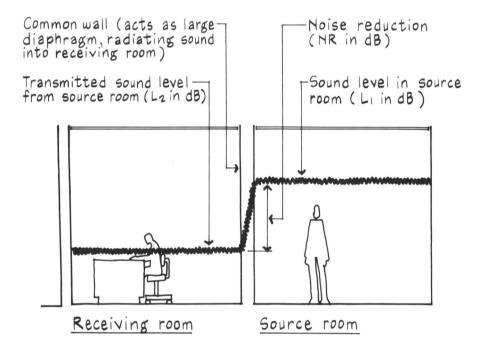

The NR is dependent on the three basic factors listed below.

1. *Area of wall transmitting sound* ($S$ in ft²). The size of the common barrier is important because it will be the source of sound in the receiving room. When a sound wave strikes the front side of a wall, its energy causes the wall to vibrate. This vibration sets into oscillation the air particles along the back (or opposite) side of the wall. These vibrating air particles then radiate sound into the receiving room.

2. *Absorption in receiving room* ($a_2$ in sabins). The noise buildup is greater in reverberant rooms than in "dead," or highly absorptive, rooms.

**3.** *Transmission loss of common wall* (TL in dB). TL is a physical property determined by standard laboratory tests. However, in buildings the TL of a barrier varies with edge support conditions, barrier size, and the quality of construction. Sound leaks and flanking paths also can ruin any TL prediction. For walls, TLs may range between 20 dB for lightweight partitions to 60 dB (or more) for heavy, well-sealed constructions.

The above three factors can be related to NR by the following formula:

$$NR = TL + 10 \log \frac{a_2}{S}$$

where   TL = sound transmission loss of common barrier (dB)
$a_2$ = absorption in receiving room (sabins)
$S$ = surface area of common barrier (ft$^2$)

The term $10 \log (a_2/S)$ may range between about +6 dB and −6 dB. If the barrier size in square feet coincidentally equals the sabins in the receiving room (the situation in many small enclosed office spaces with sound-absorbing ceilings), $10 \log (a_2/S)$ will equal 0 because 10 log 1 equals 0. In this situation NR will equal TL. However, for most situations, the NR will be higher or lower than the TL of the barrier, as shown by the graphs on the following page. If the common wall is constructed of two or more materials (e.g., base construction with window or door), the composite TL should be substituted for TL in the above formula.

The TL performance of a given wall construction varies with its design and where it is installed. In the examples below, the sound level $L_1$ is the same in both source rooms and, as shown by the floor plan illustrations and TL curves, the common partitions are identical. Although the $L_1$'s are equal, the $L_2$'s and NRs are not! This is because the noise reduction is greater when sound energy is transmitted into a large, highly sound-absorbent (*dead*) receiving room than when transmitted into a small, reverberant (*live*) receiving room. The transmitted sound does not build up in a dead room as much as in a live room.

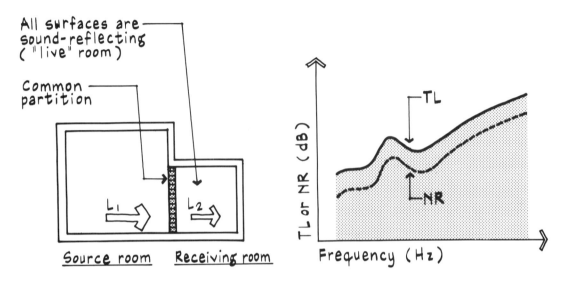

**Small, Reverberant Receiving Room**

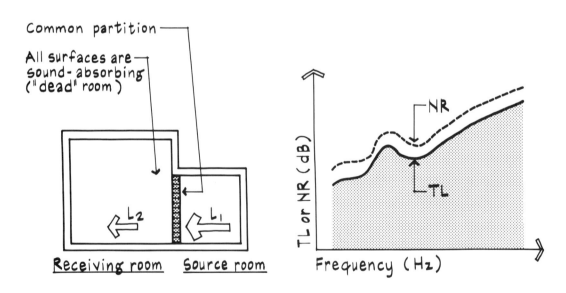

**Large, Absorbent Receiving Room**

## EXAMPLE PROBLEMS (NOISE REDUCTION)

1. In an apartment building, two adjacent living rooms have a party wall constructed of 4-in-thick brick which has a TL of 40 dB at 500 Hz. The surface area $S$ of the wall is 200 ft², and both rooms have 300 sabins of absorption $a_2$ at 500 Hz. Find the sound level $L_2$ in room 2 if the sound level $L_1$ in room 1 is 74 dB.

First, find the noise reduction NR between the rooms.

$$NR = TL + 10 \log \frac{a_2}{S}$$

$$= 40 + 10 \log \frac{300}{200} = 40 + 10 \log 1.5$$

$$NR = 40 + 10 \,(0.1761) = 41.8 \text{ dB}$$

Next, find the sound level $L_2$.

$$NR = L_1 - L_2$$

and therefore

$$L_2 = L_1 - NR$$

$$L_2 = 74 - 41.8 = 32.2 \simeq \boxed{32 \text{ dB}} \text{ at 500 Hz in room 2}$$

2. The common partition between a private office and a mechanical equipment room has a surface area of 100 ft² and a TL of 35 dB. The office has 200 sabins of absorption. Find the sound level $L_2$ in the office if the sound level $L_1$ in the mechanical equipment room is 98 dB.

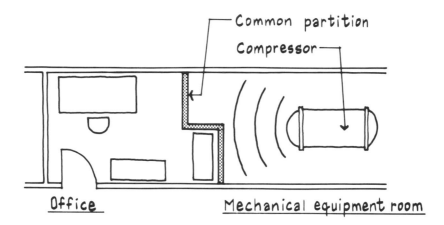

First, find the noise reduction NR between the rooms.

$$NR = TL + 10 \log \frac{a_2}{S}$$

$$= 35 + 10 \log \frac{200}{100} = 35 + 10 \log 2$$

$$NR = 35 + 10 \,(0.3010) = \boxed{38 \text{ dB}}$$

Next, find the sound level $L_2$ in the office.

$$NR = L_1 - L_2$$

and therefore

$$L_2 = L_1 - NR$$

$L_2 = 98 - 38 =$ ▢60 dB▢ which would be perceived as noisy by most listeners

3. Find the TL for the 90-ft² common partition between the two adjoining dormitory rooms shown below. Ceiling height in the rooms is 9 ft. Sound absorption coefficients α's are 0.04 for gypsum board walls and ceiling, and 0.69 for the carpeted floor. Absorption of the bed is 15 sabins. Noise level in the receiving room should not exceed 22 dB. Likely noise level from a stereo in the source room is 82 dB.

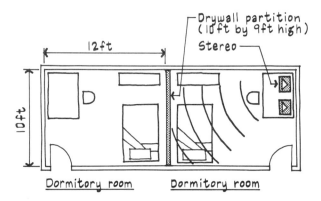

First, find the absorption in the receiving room using the formula $a = \Sigma S\alpha$.

| Surface | area (ft²) | α | a |
|---|---|---|---|
| Walls | 2(12 × 9) = 216 | | |
| | 2(10 × 9) = 180 | | |
| Ceiling | 10 × 12 = 120 | | |
| | 516 × 0.04 = | | 21 |
| Floor | 10 × 12 = 120 × 0.69 = | | 83 |
| Bed | | | 15 |
| | | $a_2 =$ | 119 sabins |

Next, find the required NR.

$$NR = L_1 - L_2$$
$$NR = 82 - 22 = \boxed{60 \text{ dB}}$$

Finally, find the required TL.

$$TL = NR - 10 \log \frac{a_2}{S}$$

$$= 60 - 10 \log \frac{119}{90}$$

$$= 60 - 10 \log (1.3) = 60 - 10 (0.1139)$$

$$TL = 60 - 1 = \boxed{59 \text{ dB}}$$

# LABORATORY TESTS FOR TL

The TL test panel (or "specimen") shown below fills an opening between two completely separated (no common footings, connecting ties, or the like) reverberation rooms constructed of thick, massive walls. The walls will transmit far less sound energy than the test panel and, therefore, virtually all the sound energy transmitted between the rooms will be through the panel being tested. This is necessary so TL data from different laboratories can be compared.

The difference between sound levels in the source room $L_1$ and receiving room $L_2$ is the *transmission loss* TL in decibels of the test specimen. The sound *transmission coefficient* $\tau$ is the ratio of radiated sound power $W_2$ to incident sound power $W_1$, where $W$ is measured in watts. For example, a TL of 40 dB would mean 1/10,000 of the incident sound power was radiated into the receiving room.

Note that the TL will be about 6 dB higher when incident sound waves are perpendicular to surfaces than when at "field" incidence (the usual situation in rooms where sound impinges from all directions). When sound waves from highway traffic or from aircraft are parallel to building facades, TL performance may be significantly lower than TL measured in laboratories.

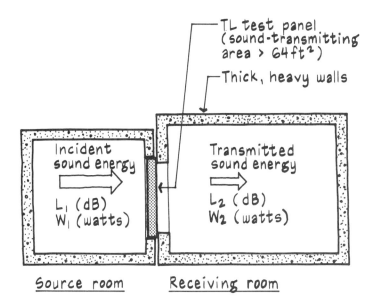

## References

"Laboratory Measurement of Airborne Sound Transmission Loss of Building Partitions," ASTM E 90.

"Field and Laboratory Measurements of Airborne and Impact Sound Transmission," ISO Recommendation R 140.

R. E. Jones, "Effects of Flanking and Test Environment on Lab-Field Correlations of Airborne Sound Insulation." *Journal of the Acoustical Society of America,* May 1975.

In addition to sound leaks through openings in common barriers, sound energy can bypass constructions through indirect paths (called *flanking*). Example flanking paths, which can seriously degrade the TL of common barriers, are: open ceiling plenums and attics, continuous side walls and floors, air duct and pipe penetrations, joist and crawl spaces, and many others. Some of the potential flanking paths in wood frame gypsum wallboard constructions (called *drywall*) are shown by the section illustration below. To achieve the full sound isolation potential of common barriers, flanking paths must be prevented by careful design of all connections, penetrations, and adjacent framing systems.

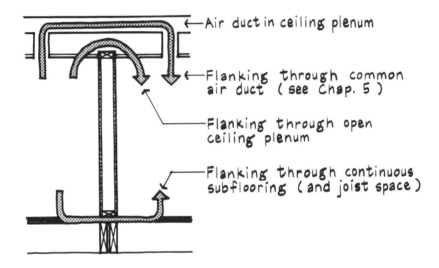

**Example Flanking in Drywall Construction**

Intersecting continuous glazed walls can become flanking paths which seriously reduce the sound isolation between rooms (see plan view below at left). For example, using fibrous-filled aluminum mullions instead of cementitious grout-filled mullions at the intersection of a window wall and an STC-45 drywall common barrier can reduce the STC by 5. Hollow mullions can reduce the STC by 10, and continuous glazing without mullions by 15.

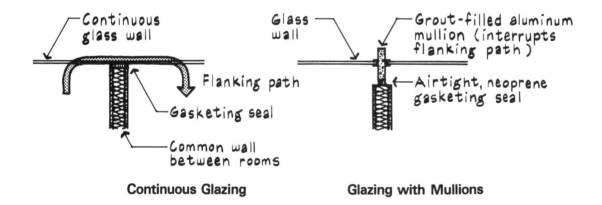

**Continuous Glazing**    **Glazing with Mullions**

# STC RATING SYSTEM

Until the early 1960s, the "nine-frequency average" was used to establish a TL rating for building constructions. The nine-frequency average TL proved to be an undesirable rating system because it implied that good sound isolation at one frequency could overcome or cover up poor isolation at another.

The modern *sound transmission class* STC system rates the entire TL curve at speech frequencies from 125 to 4000 Hz, using a standard contour as the reference. (The method does not, however, evaluate performance at low frequencies below 125 Hz where music and mechanical equipment noise levels often may be high.) The STC of a construction is the TL value at 500 Hz that the standard contour intersects at its final rating position.

The rating positions for example constructions A and B, which have nearly identical average TLs, are shown on the graph below. The STC rating for construction B is 9 below the rating for construction A, reflecting the significant sound-isolation weakness (coincidence dip) at 1000 Hz.

| Construction | Average TL (dB) | STC |
|---|---|---|
| A | 40 | 42 |
| B | 41 | 33 |

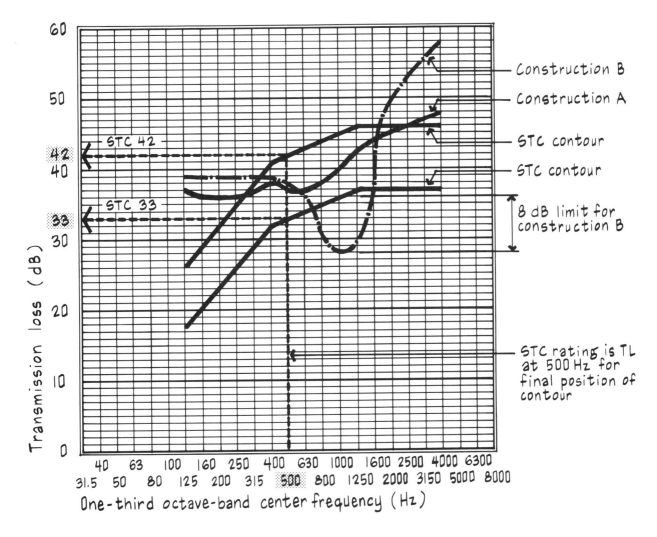

The STC contour and standard grid shown below can be reproduced on a transparent overlay, which then can be used to determine STC ratings according to the ASTM procedure outlined on the following page. The STC contour is similar in shape to the TL curve for 9-in-thick brick. This heavy construction has proven successful as an isolator of speech signals in apartments in Western Europe, where sound control codes have existed for many years. Again, special precautions must be taken where mechanical equipment noise or amplified music must be isolated because the STC method does not evaluate TL performance below 125 Hz.*

* The U.S. Gypsum Co. has developed a modified STC rating called the MTC rating, with the M representing music, machine, and mechanical equipment noise sources. Their technical publications provide both STC and MTC ratings for numerous drywall constructions. MTC ratings follow STC rating procedures, but do *not* permit deviations below the STC contour at 125 and 160 Hz. However, if there are surpluses at 125 and 160 Hz, the lesser of 4 or one-third of the surplus sum is added to the STC rating.

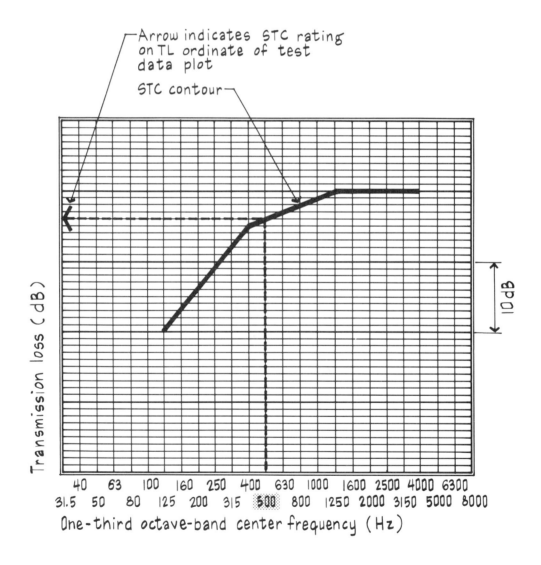

# STC RATING CRITERIA

The *sound transmission class* STC is a single-number rating of the airborne sound transmission loss TL performance of a construction measured at standard one-third octave band frequencies. The higher the STC rating, the more efficient the construction will be in reducing sound transmission within the frequency range of the test.

The STC rating method procedures are specified in the American Society for Testing and Materials (ASTM) annual book of standards. The TL of a construction test specimen is measured at 16 one-third octave bands with center frequencies from 125 to 4000 Hz. To determine the STC of a given specimen, its measured TL values are plotted against frequency and compared to the reference STC contour. The STC rating can be graphically determined by using a transparent overlay on which the STC contour is reproduced, as shown on the preceding page. The STC contour is shifted vertically relative to the plotted curve of test data to as high a final position as possible according to the following limiting criteria:

1. The maximum deviation of the test curve below the contour at any single test frequency shall *not* exceed 8 dB.

2. The sum of the deviations below the contour at all 16 frequencies of the test curve shall *not* exceed 32 dB (an average deviation of 2 dB per frequency).

When the STC contour is adjusted to the highest position that meets the above criteria, the STC rating is read from the vertical scale as the TL value (with dB unit dropped) corresponding to the intersection of the STC contour and the 500-Hz ordinate. In the examples on page 199, the STC ratings reflect the significance of deficiencies such as the dip in the TL curve of construction B. The STC 33 rating for construction B is governed by the 8 dB deviation below the contour at 1000 Hz, although the total of all the deviations is far less than the 32 dB limiting criterion.

**Note:** TL data measured in the field according to provisions of ASTM E 336 is reported as *field sound transmission class,* abbreviated FSTC. Results from a simplified test method to determine the FSTC directly from single A-weighted sound level measurements on the source and receiving sides of building constructions agree with ASTM E 336 results in most situations. For a detailed description of this method, see W. Siekman et al., "A Simplified Field Sound Transmission Test," *Sound and Vibration,* October 1971.

**References**

"Laboratory Measurement of Airborne Sound Transmission Loss of Building Partitions," ASTM E 90.

"Test for Measurement of Airborne Sound Insulation in Buildings," ASTM E 336.

"Classification for Determination of Sound Transmission Class," ASTM E 413.

"Standard Practice for Determining a Single-Number Rating of Airborne Sound Isolation for Use in Multiunit Building Specifications," ASTM E 597.

T. J. Schultz, "A-Level Differences for Noise Control in Building Codes," *Noise Control Engineering Journal,* Autumn 1973.

Laboratory TL data generally reflect "idealized" conditions because manu-facturers test carefully crafted and installed specimens only from components which have passed very strict inspections. In addition, the test specimens are expertly installed by highly trained technicians to have soft edge-support condi-tions in the laboratory. Consequently, laboratory TL data often will be far higher than reasonably can be expected in typical buildings.

In design, it is important to eliminate potential sound leaks and flanking paths which further reduce the field performance of barriers installed in build-ings. Shown below are laboratory and field measurements for an example 6-in-thick masonry wall.

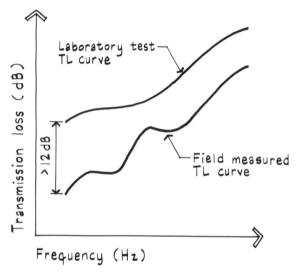

Poor workmanship also can cause sound leaks which seriously diminish sound-isolating performance. Construction should be closely supervised to en-sure that all sound leaks and flanking paths are isolated. However, even with close supervision, STCs for the identical construction component (wall, floor-ceiling can vary from the laboratory STC by more than 5 and by more than 15 if the construction is not carefully supervised.

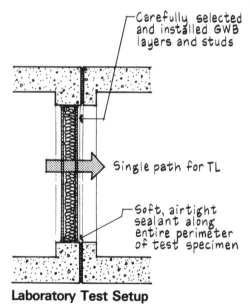

**Laboratory Test Setup**

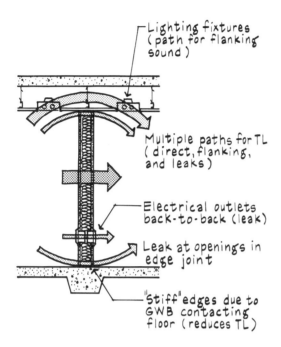

Lighting fixtures
(path for flanking sound)

Multiple paths for TL
(direct, flanking, and leaks)

Electrical outlets
back-to-back (leak)

Leak at openings in
edge joint

"Stiff" edges due to
GWB contacting
floor (reduces TL)

## Building Installation

### Reference

E. A. Wetherill, "Noise Control in Buildings," *Sound and Vibration,* July 1975.

**Note:** Where flanking paths cannot be isolated to establish the field sound transmission class FSTC of a building element, noise reduction data can be rated to yield a single number called the *noise isolation class* NIC. Because the NIC represents the sound-isolating performance of the field-tested situation only, NIC values may not apply to an identical construction in another building where room absorption and other factors may be different.

# TL DATA FOR COMMON BUILDING ELEMENTS*

| Building Construction | Transmission Loss (dB) | | | | | | STC Rating | IIC Rating† |
|---|---|---|---|---|---|---|---|---|
| | 125 Hz | 250 Hz | 500 Hz | 1000 Hz | 2000 Hz | 4000 Hz | | |
| **Walls**[2-6]‡ | | | | | | | | |
| *Monolithic:* | | | | | | | | |
| 1. 3/8-in plywood (1 lb/ft²) | 14 | 18 | 22 | 20 | 21 | 26 | 22 | |
| 2. 26-gauge sheet metal (1.5 lb/ft²) | 12 | 14 | 15 | 21 | 21 | 25 | 20 | |
| 3. 1/2-in gypsum board (2 lb/ft²) | 15 | 20 | 25 | 31 | 33 | 27 | 28 | |
| 4. 2 layers 1/2-in gypsum board, laminated with joint compound (4 lb/ft²) | 19 | 26 | 30 | 32 | 29 | 37 | 31 | |
| 5. 1/32-in sheet lead (2 lb/ft²) | 15 | 21 | 27 | 33 | 39 | 45 | 31 | |
| 6. Glass-fiber roof fabric (37.5 oz/yd²) | 6 | 9 | 11 | 16 | 20 | 25 | 16 | |
| *Interior:* | | | | | | | | |
| 7. 2 by 4 wood studs 16 in oc with 1/2-in gypsum board both sides (5 lb/ft²) | 17 | 31 | 33 | 40 | 38 | 36 | 33 | |
| 8. Construction no. 7 with 2-in glass-fiber insulation in cavity | 15 | 30 | 34 | 44 | 46 | 41 | 37 | |
| 9. 2 by 4 staggered wood studs 16 in oc each side with 1/2-in gypsum board both sides (8 lb/ft²) | 23 | 28 | 39 | 46 | 54 | 44 | 39 | |
| 10. Construction no. 9 with 2 1/4-in glass-fiber insulation in cavity | 29 | 38 | 45 | 52 | 58 | 50 | 48 | |
| 11. 2 by 4 wood studs 16 in oc with 5/8-in gypsum board both sides, one side screwed to resilient channels. 3-in glass-fiber insulation in cavity (7 lb/ft²) | 32 | 42 | 52 | 58 | 53 | 54 | 52 | |
| 12. Double row of 2 by 4 wood studs 16 in oc with 3/8-in gypsum board on both sides of construction. 9-in glass-fiber insulation in cavity (4 lb/ft²) | 31 | 44 | 55 | 62 | 67 | 65 | 54 | |
| 13. 6-in dense concrete block, 3 cells, painted (34 lb/ft²) | 37 | 36 | 42 | 49 | 55 | 58 | 45 | |
| 14. 8-in lightweight concrete block, 3 cells, painted (38 lb/ft²) | 34 | 40 | 44 | 49 | 59 | 64 | 49 | |
| 15. Construction no. 14 with expanded mineral loose fill in cells | 34 | 40 | 46 | 52 | 60 | 66 | 51 | |
| 16. 6-in lightweight concrete block with 1/2-in gypsum board supported by resilient metal channels on one side, other side painted (26 lb/ft²) | 35 | 42 | 50 | 64 | 67 | 65 | 53 | |
| 17. 2 1/2-in steel channel studs 24 in oc with 5/8-in gypsum board both sides (6 lb/ft²) | 22 | 27 | 43 | 47 | 37 | 46 | 39 | |
| 18. Construction no. 17 with 2-in glass-fiber insulation in cavity | 26 | 41 | 52 | 54 | 45 | 51 | 45 | |
| 19. 3 5/8-in steel channel studs 16 in oc with 1/2-in gypsum board both sides (5 lb/ft²) | 26 | 36 | 43 | 51 | 48 | 43 | 43 | |
| 20. Construction no. 19 with 3-in mineral-fiber insulation in cavity | 28 | 45 | 54 | 55 | 47 | 54 | 48 | |
| 21. 2 1/2-in steel channel studs 24 in oc with two layers 5/8-in gypsum board one side, one layer other side (8 lb/ft²) | 28 | 31 | 46 | 51 | 53 | 47 | 44 | |
| 22. Construction no. 21 with 2-in glass-fiber insulation in cavity | 31 | 43 | 55 | 58 | 61 | 51 | 51 | |
| 23. 3 5/8-in steel channel studs 24 in oc with two layers 5/8-in gypsum board both sides (11 lb/ft²) | 34 | 41 | 51 | 54 | 46 | 52 | 48 | |
| 24. Construction no. 23 with 3-in mineral-fiber insulation in cavity | 38 | 52 | 59 | 60 | 56 | 62 | 57 | |
| *Exterior:* | | | | | | | | |
| 25. 4 1/2-in face brick (50 lb/ft²) | 32 | 34 | 40 | 47 | 55 | 61 | 45 | |
| 26. Two wythes of 4 1/2-in face brick, 2-in airspace with metal ties (100 lb/ft²) | 37 | 37 | 47 | 55 | 62 | 67 | 50 | |
| 27. Two wythes of plastered 4 1/2-in brick, 2-in airspace with glass-fiber insulation in cavity | 43 | 50 | 52 | 61 | 73 | 78 | 59 | |
| 28. 2 by 4 wood studs 16 in oc with 1-in stucco on metal lath on outside and 1/2-in gypsum board on inside (8 lb/ft²) | 21 | 33 | 41 | 46 | 47 | 51 | 42 | |
| 29. 6-in solid concrete with 1/2-in plaster both sides (80 lb/ft²) | 39 | 42 | 50 | 58 | 64 | 67 | 53 | |
| **Floor-Ceilings**[2,3] | | | | | | | | |
| 30. 2 by 10 wood joists 16 in oc with 1/2-in plywood subfloor under 25/32-in oak on floor side, and 5/8-in gypsum board nailed to joists on ceiling side (10 lb/ft²) | 23 | 32 | 36 | 45 | 49 | 56 | 37 | 32 |

| Building Construction | 125 Hz | 250 Hz | 500 Hz | 1000 Hz | 2000 Hz | 4000 Hz | STC Rating | IIC Rating† |
|---|---|---|---|---|---|---|---|---|
| 31. Construction no. 30 with 5/8-in gypsum board screwed to resilient channels spaced 24 in oc perpendicular to joists | 30 | 35 | 44 | 50 | 54 | 60 | 47 | 39 |
| 32. Construction no. 31 with 3-in glass-fiber insulation in cavity | 36 | 40 | 45 | 52 | 58 | 64 | 49 | 46 |
| 33. 4-in reinforced concrete slab (54 lb/ft²) | 48 | 42 | 45 | 56 | 57 | 66 | 44 | 25 |
| 34. 14-in precast concrete tees with 2-in concrete topping on 2-in slab (75 lb/ft²) | 39 | 45 | 50 | 52 | 60 | 68 | 54 | 24 |
| 35. 6-in reinforced concrete slab (75 lb/ft²) | 38 | 43 | 52 | 59 | 67 | 72 | 55 | 34 |
| 36. 6-in reinforced concrete slab with 3/4-in T&G wood flooring on 1 1/2 by 2 wooden battens floated on 1-in glass fiber (83 lb/ft²) | 38 | 44 | 52 | 55 | 60 | 65 | 55 | 57 |
| 37. 18-in steel joists 16 in oc with 1 5/8-in concrete on 5/8-in plywood under heavy carpet laid on pad, and 5/8-in gypsum board attached to joists on ceiling side (20 lb/ft²) | 27 | 37 | 45 | 54 | 60 | 65 | 47 | 62 |
| **Roofs²** | | | | | | | | |
| 38. 3 by 8 wood beams 32 in oc with 2 by 6 T&G planks, asphalt felt built-up roofing, and gravel topping | 29 | 33 | 37 | 44 | 55 | 63 | 43 | |
| 39. Construction no. 38 with 2 by 4s 16 in oc between beams, 1/2-in gypsum board supported by metal channels on ceiling side with 4-in glass-fiber insulation in cavity | 35 | 42 | 49 | 62 | 67 | 79 | 53 | |
| 40. Corrugated steel, 24 gauge with 1 3/8-in sprayed cellulose insulation on ceiling side (1.8 lb/ft²) | 17 | 22 | 26 | 30 | 35 | 41 | 30 | |
| 41. 2 1/2-in sand and gravel concrete (148 lb/ft³) on 28 gauge corrugated steel supported by 14-in-deep steel bar joists with 1/2-in gypsum plaster on metal lath attached to metal furring channels 13 1/2 in oc on ceiling side (41 lb/ft²) | 32 | 46 | 45 | 50 | 57 | 61 | 49 | |
| **Doors²** | | | | | | | | |
| 42. Louvered door, 25 to 30% open | 10 | 12 | 12 | 12 | 12 | 11 | 12 | |
| 43. 1 3/4-in hollow-core wood door, no gaskets, 1/4-in air gap at sill (1.5 lb/ft²) | 14 | 19 | 23 | 18 | 17 | 21 | 19 | |
| 44. Construction no. 43 with gaskets and drop seal | 19 | 22 | 25 | 19 | 20 | 29 | 21 | |
| 45. 1 3/4-in solid-core wood door with gaskets and drop seal (4.5 lb/ft²) | 29 | 31 | 31 | 31 | 39 | 43 | 34 | |
| 46. 1 3/4-in hollow-core 16 gauge steel door, glass-fiber filled, with gaskets and drop seal (7 lb/ft²) | 23 | 28 | 36 | 41 | 39 | 44 | 38 | |
| **Glass¹,²** | | | | | | | | |
| 47. 1/8-in monolithic float glass (1.4 lb/ft²) | 18 | 21 | 26 | 31 | 33 | 22 | 26 | |
| 48. 1/4-in monolithic float glass (2.9 lb/ft²) | 25 | 28 | 31 | 34 | 30 | 37 | 31 | |
| 49. 1/2-in insulated glass: 1/8- + 1/8-in double glass with 1/4-in airspace (3.3 lb/ft²) | 21 | 26 | 24 | 33 | 44 | 34 | 28 | |
| 50. 1/4- + 1/8-in double glass with 2-in airspace | 18 | 31 | 35 | 42 | 44 | 44 | 39 | |
| 51. Construction no. 50 with 4-in airspace | 21 | 32 | 42 | 48 | 48 | 44 | 43 | |
| 52. 1/4-in laminated glass, 30-mil plastic interlayer (3.6 lb/ft²) | 25 | 28 | 32 | 35 | 36 | 43 | 35 | |
| 53. Double glass: 1/4-in laminated + 3/16-in monolithic glass with 2-in airspace (5.9 lb/ft²) | 25 | 34 | 44 | 47 | 48 | 55 | 45 | |
| 54. Double glass: 1/4-in laminated + 3/16-in monolithic glass with 4-in airspace (5.9 lb/ft²) | 36 | 37 | 48 | 51 | 50 | 58 | 48 | |
| 55. Double glass: 1/4-in laminated + 1/4-in laminated with 1/2-in airspace (7.2 lb/ft²) | 21 | 30 | 40 | 44 | 46 | 57 | 42 | |

† IIC (*impact isolation class*) is a single-number rating of the impact sound transmission performance of a floor-ceiling construction tested over a standard frequency range. The higher the IIC, the more efficient the construction will be for reducing impact sound transmission. INR (*impact noise rating*) previously was used as the single-number rating of impact noise isolation. To convert the older INR data to IIC, add 51 to the INR number.

‡ A wide range of TL and STC performance can be achieved by gypsum wallboard constructions. Refer to ASTM E 90 laboratory report and literature from manufacturers for specific details such as type of gypsum board; gauge, width, and spacing of steel studs; glass-fiber or mineral-fiber insulation thickness and density; and complete installation recommendations.

*TL data for proprietary building construction materials should be from up-to-date full-scale tests by independent acoustical laboratories (e.g., Cedar Knolls, ETL, Riverbank) or from field tests on installed identical assemblies conducted according to current ASTM procedures. In the United States, the National Bureau of Standards (NBS) accredits testing laboratories to perform tests in the area of their established competence. A directory of National Voluntary Laboratory Accreditation Program (NVLAP) accredited laboratories is available from NBS (order from Superintendent of Documents, U.S. Government Printing Office, Washington, D C 20402).

### Test Reference

"Laboratory Measurement of Airborne Sound Transmission Loss of Building Partitions," ASTM E 90. Available from American Society for Testing and Materials (ASTM), 1916 Race Street, Philadelphia, PA 19103.

### Sources

1. "Acoustical Glazing Design Guide," Saflex Interlayer, Monsanto Co., St. Louis, Mo., 1986. (Section 1 also contains STC data for numerous exterior wall constructions.)

2. R. D. Berendt et al., "A Guide to Airborne, Impact, and Structure Borne Noise-Control in Multifamily Dwellings," U.S. Department of Housing and Urban Development, Washington, D.C., September 1967.

3. R. B. DuPree, "Catalog of STC and IIC Ratings for Wall and Floor/Ceiling Assemblies," Office of Noise Control, California Department of Health Services, Berkeley, Calif., September 1981.

4. "Noise Control Manual," Owens-Corning Fiberglas Corp., Toledo, Ohio, November 1984.

5. A. Ordubadi and R. H. Lyon, "Effect of Orthotropy on the Sound Transmission Through Plywood Panels," *Journal of the Acoustical Society of America,* January 1979.

6. H. S. Roller, "Design Data for Acousticians," United States Gypsum Co., Chicago, 1985.

7. A. C. C. Warnock, "Field Sound Transmission Loss Measurements," Building Research Note 232, National Research Council of Canada, June 1985.

**Note:** For fire-resistance ratings of building constructions, refer to current editions of "Fire Resistance Index," available from Underwriters' Laboratories (UL), 333 Pfingsten Road, Northbrook, IL 60062 and "Fire Resistance Design Manual," available from Gypsum Association, 1603 Orrington Ave., Evanston, IL 60201.

## PRINCIPLES OF ISOLATION BY COMPLEX WALLS

In the example constructions shown below, the TL performance of an 8-in-thick brick wall is increased by breaking the direct sound transmission path. Isolation can be significantly improved by dividing the wall into two separate walls of equal weight (two 4-in-thick brick layers separated by a 4-in airspace) or by resiliently supporting a 1/2-in-thick gypsum board layer with vertical furring attached to the original 8-in-thick wall.

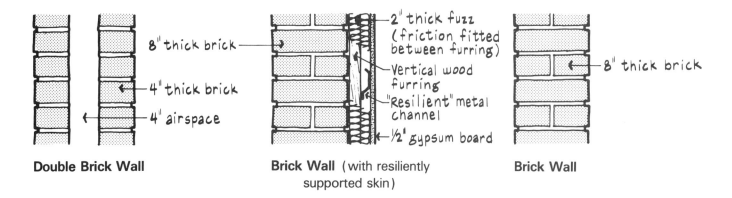

**Double Brick Wall**

**Brick Wall** (with resiliently supported skin)

**Brick Wall**

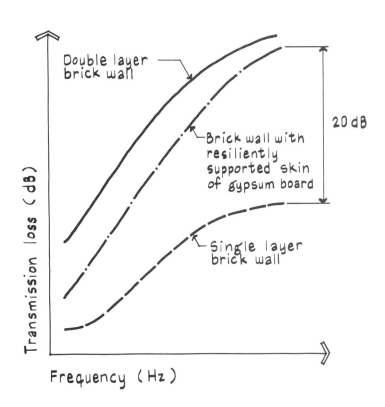

The sound-isolating effectiveness of gypsum wallboard constructions can vary over a tremendous range. The mass, stiffness, and internal damping of the board, and method of installation can all influence the result. The *heavier* the gypsum layers (usually specified as surface density in pounds per square foot), the greater the TL. Wider studs (e.g., 3 5/8-in-wide light-gauge metal instead of 2 1/2-in or 1 5/8-in) will result in greater TLs at low frequencies. If wood studs are used, staggering the studs, separating the studs (called *double-stud* construction), or adding resilient channels will improve the TL. For example, the STC can increase by more than 8 when the studs are staggered. A slight increase in STC also can result from wider spacings between wood studs (e.g., 24 in oc instead of 16 in oc).

Placing sound-absorbing blankets in cavity airspaces will improve STC and TL. Mineral-fiber insulation attached to one side of the cavity airspace can improve TL by damping the gypsum board layer. However, do *not* completely fill cavity airspaces with dense mineral-fiber insulation ($> 2$ lb/ft$^3$ density) because sound energy may bridge between the gypsum board layers through the mineral fiber. In addition, the air gap remaining between the insulation and opposite layer helps break the transmission path (or bridge) from layer to layer.

### Checklist for Achieving High TL with Gypsum Wallboard Constructions

1. Use *heavy* gypsum board constructions such as two layers of 5/8-in-thick gypsum board on each side of studs (or an unbalanced combination of two layers one side, one layer on the other) rather than one layer on each side. The heavier the construction, the higher the STC. Doubling the weight by adding a layer to both outer wall surfaces can increase STC by more than 5.

2. Break the direct sound transmission path between opposite sides of wall by using staggered wood studs, double rows of wood studs, or resilient channel supports on one side of studs. The TL of two decoupled gypsum board layers, separated by an airspace, will be far higher than a monolithic construction of identical total weight.

3. Use light-gauge metal channel studs (25 gauge or lighter) which provide higher STCs because they are less *stiff* than wood or heavy load-bearing metal studs. Wider metal channel studs also can achieve greater TLs at low frequencies.

4. Place sound-absorbing blankets, at least 2 in thick, in the cavity between studs. STC improvements can be 2 to 8 for single wood stud constructions; 4 to 8 for 25-gauge steel stud constructions. The STC increase is greater for lightweight, less stiff steel stud constructions than for heavy, stiffer steel stud constructions. Be sure blankets are installed to properly friction fit between studs or with sufficient fasteners so they do not sag. (Check also to be sure additional fibrous insulation does not adversely affect the fire resistance of an assembly.)

5. Seal *all* cracks, joints, and penetrations. For example, at base of walls, seal perimeters of bottom runners and sole plates with continuous beads of nonhardening caulking (35 durometer) at edges on each side.

## Metal-Channel-Stud Partition

**One layer gypsum board each side**  (4 lb/ft²)

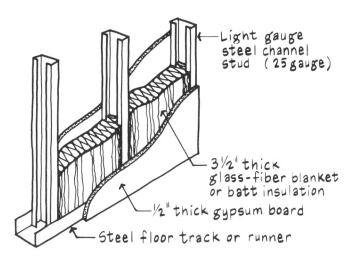

- Light gauge steel channel stud (25 gauge)
- 3½" thick glass-fiber blanket or batt insulation
- ½" thick gypsum board
- Steel floor track or runner

**Two layers gypsum board one side, one layer other side**  (6 lb/ft²)

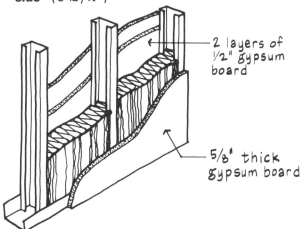

- 2 layers of ½" gypsum board
- 5/8" thick gypsum board

**Two layers gypsum board both sides**  (8 lb/ft²)

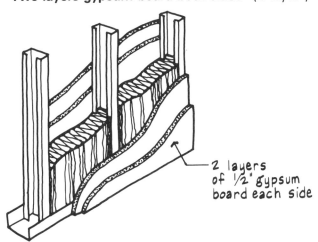

- 2 layers of ½" gypsum board each side

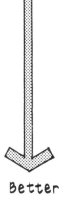

Good

Better

6. Isolate perimeters of common walls from ceilings, intersecting walls, and structural members. Fill gaps at perimeter (e.g., 1/8-in-wide clearance) with nonhardening caulking. In double-layer constructions, apply caulking to perimeter of both base and face layers.

7. Stagger electrical outlets (and telephone, intercom, TV) and switches so they will be offset by at least one stud space ($>$ 2 to 3 ft apart). Seal openings in outlet boxes (sides and back) and joints between outlets and gypsum board so they will be airtight.

8. Isolate plumbing from framing elements and gypsum board layers, which can act as sounding boards to easily transmit noise of flowing water. Use resilient pipe supports and seal all penetrations to be airtight on both sides (see Chap. 5).

### References

D. W. Green and C. W. Sherry, "Sound Transmission Loss of Gypsum Wallboard Partitions," *Journal of the Acoustical Society of America,* January 1982 and April 1982.

R. E. Jones, "How to Design Walls for Desired STC Ratings," *Sound and Vibration,* August 1978.

J. W. Kopec, "Variations in Sound Transmission on Steel Studded, Gypsum Walls," *Sound and Vibration,* June 1982.

H. S. Roller, "Research Evaluates Role of Density in Acoustical Insulation Performance," *Form & Function,* Issue 2, 1985.

## INSTALLATION OF DRYWALL

When gypsum board is attached by screws to metal studs, it will provide significantly higher TLs than when attached by adhesives. This is because the screws provide a point attachment instead of the continuous-line attachment of the adhesive, which stiffens the relatively flexible stud flanges. Shown below is an installation method to achieve widely staggered joints for multiple layers of gypsum board (cf., "Recommended Specifications for the Application and Finishing of Gypsum Board," GA-216-85, Gypsum Association, Evanston, Ill., April 1985). For wood stud partitions with multiple layers of gypsum board, attach layers together with visco-elastic adhesives rather than rigid-curing adhesives or screws.

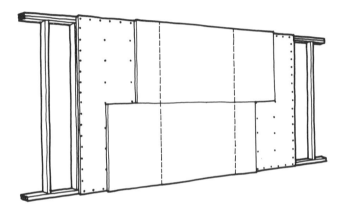

**Multilayer GWB** (with staggered panel joints)

The STC of wood stud construction can be greatly increased by adding resilient channels to one side of the studs. An example of how to attach gypsum board to resilient channels is shown below. The screws used to attach gypsum board panels to resilient channels should not contact the studs. Therefore, to maintain resiliency, use short gypsum panel screws or fasten panels only between the studs.

**Resilient Channel Supports**

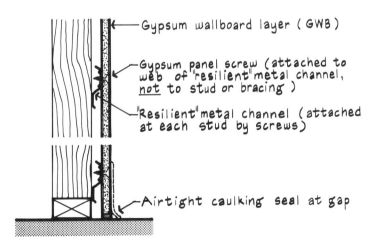

Gypsum wallboard layer ( GWB )

Gypsum panel screw (attached to web of "resilient" metal channel, not to stud or bracing )

"Resilient" metal channel (attached at each stud by screws)

Airtight caulking seal at gap

# MASONRY CONSTRUCTIONS

Shown on facing page are example concrete block constructions. For single-layer walls, the heavier the concrete block, the greater the TL. Be careful because the weight of concrete block can vary between fabricators. To increase the TL of single-layer walls, fill cells with sand or mortar (to increase *mass*) or add a heavy gypsum board layer resiliently supported by metal channels with sound-absorbing material in the wide cavity airspace (to break the direct path).

The sound-isolation performance also can be increased by using *double-wall* constructions. Place sound-absorbing blankets in the cavity airspace to reduce sound transmission through penetrations for electrical services and where shrinkage cracks may occur. The sound-absorbing material reduces noise buildup in the cavity, thereby increasing the sound-isolation performance.

It is important to note that rigid wire ties can act as direct transmission paths between layers. Therefore, where extremely high TLs are desired, use at least two independent, widely spaced layers. If the layers must be connected for structural purposes, use special sound-isolating ties which have a neoprene element to prevent bridging between layers.

## Checklist for Achieving High TL with Masonry Constructions

1. Set blocks in firm bed of mortar and be sure all joints are tightly filled and not porous.
2. Use heavy block or medium-weight block with sand- or mortar-filled cells. When cells are filled with sand or mortar, frequently tamp during installation and verify that all cells are well-compacted and completely filled.
3. For single walls, seal airtight at least one side with plaster, gypsum board supported by furring, three coats of latex block filler, or a thick application of epoxy paint.
4. To improve single walls, add a gypsum board layer resiliently supported, with low-density glass fiber or mineral fiber in the airspace (> 2 in wide) between the block and the gypsum board, or install a resilient layer without fibrous insulation on the unsealed side of the wall. (Be careful because TL at low frequencies can be reduced by resonance effects of gypsum board layers when they are installed on both sides of a wall without sound-absorbing material in the cavity airspaces.)
5. Surface mount all electrical services on sand- or mortar-filled block constructions.
6. Where especially high TLs are needed, avoid stiff wire ties, which can reduce TL of double-wall constructions by more than 7 dB.

## References

T. D. Northwood and D. W. Monk, "Sound Transmission Loss of Masonry Walls," Building Research Note 90, National Research Council of Canada, April 1974.

D. P. Walsh, "Sound Isolating Characteristics of Masonry Walls," *Masonry Industry*, April 1970.

A. C. C. Warnock and D. W. Monk, "Sound Transmission Loss of Masonry Walls," Building Research Note 217, National Research Council of Canada, June 1984.

B. G. Watters, "Transmission Loss of Some Masonry Walls," *Journal of the Acoustical Society of America*, July 1959.

| Masonry Wall | Sound-Isolating Effectiveness |
|---|---|

**Single Layer**

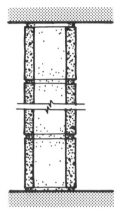

**Single Layer** (with resiliently supported skin)

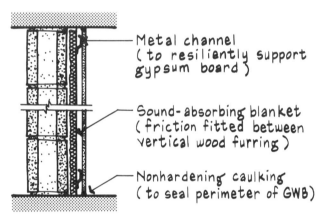

Metal channel
(to resiliently support gypsum board)

Sound-absorbing blanket
(friction fitted between vertical wood furring)

Nonhardening caulking
(to seal perimeter of GWB)

**Double Layer**

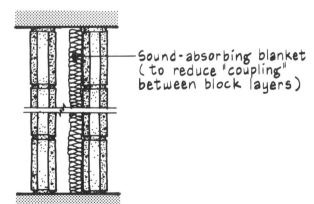

Sound-absorbing blanket
(to reduce "coupling" between block layers)

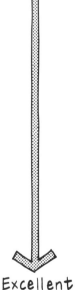

Good

Excellent

## DOUBLE-WALL TL IMPROVEMENTS FOR MASONRY CONSTRUCTIONS

The TL of a masonry wall can be greatly improved if the wall has two or more layers separated by an airspace. If the layers are widely separated, they may in effect form two independent walls, and the total TL can approach the sum of the TLs of the individual layers. For most practical situations, however, separations of less than 12 in are more common, and the TL of the double wall will be far less than the sum of the TLs of the individual layers. A narrow airspace can act like a "piston," readily transmitting sound energy between layers.

The following table can be used to estimate the TL improvement from splitting a masonry wall into two separate layers (or wythes) of equal weight and filling the airspace with fibrous blankets.

| Airspace (in) | Improvement in TL (dB) | | | | | |
| --- | --- | --- | --- | --- | --- | --- |
| | 125 Hz | 250 Hz | 500 Hz | 1000 Hz | 2000 Hz | 4000 Hz |
| 2 | 5 | 7 | 19 | 25 | 30 | 30 |
| 4 | 10 | 12 | 24 | 30 | 35 | 35 |

**Note:** To achieve maximum TL improvement from double-wall constructions, be sure airspace is sound-absorptive (fibrous blankets, porous masonry surfaces) and bridging is avoided (no rigid ties). For additional data on TL improvement, refer to R. B. Newman, "Acoustics" in J. H. Callender (ed.), *Time-Saver Standards for Architectural Design Data*, McGraw-Hill, New York, 1974, p. 709.

# EXAMPLE PROBLEM (DOUBLE-WALL TL)

Estimate the improvement in TL if a single 8-in-thick concrete block wall can be installed as two 4-in-thick concrete block layers of identical total weight, separated by a 4-in airspace, filled with glass-fiber insulation.

| Construction | Transmission Loss (dB) | | | | | |
|---|---|---|---|---|---|---|
| | 125 Hz | 250 Hz | 500 Hz | 1000 Hz | 2000 Hz | 4000 Hz |
| 8-in painted concrete block wall with sand-filled cells | 36 | 41 | 49 | 56 | 60 | 63 |
| Improvement in TL | 10 | 12 | 24 | 30 | 35 | 35 |
| 4-in concrete block + 4-in airspace + 4-in concrete block with 2-in glass fiber in airspace | 46 | 53 | 73 | 86 | 95 | 98 |

**Note:** In 1836 Professor Michael Faraday advised H.M. Commission of Prisons (England) on how to achieve high TL performance between prison cells. The most successful construction was two layers of 9-in brick (to be heavy) separated by about 6 inches (to reduce stiffness) with sound-absorbing sailcloth to "deaden" the airspace (cf., W. Allen and R. Pocock, "Sound Insulation: Some Historical Notes," *Journal of the Royal Institute of British Architects*, March 1946).

# FLOOR-CEILING CONSTRUCTIONS

The graph below shows the TL performance of wood joist and concrete floor-ceiling constructions. The higher STC ratings are achieved by the heavier concrete constructions.

To prevent "squeaking" floors in wood joist constructions, be sure nails are the proper size and properly spaced, install building paper or felt layer between subfloor and finished floor, and use only seasoned wood.

To block flanking through joist spaces, install joists parallel to party walls. In addition, cut subflooring at wall (> 1/4-in gap) to interrupt flanking path for airborne sound and vibrations. Flanking of sound energy through continuous wood frame floor constructions limits common wall STC to 40; through continuous 6-in concrete slabs to 50.

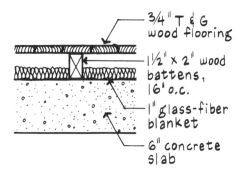

**Floated Floor**

¾" T & G wood flooring
1½" x 2" wood battens, 16' o.c.
1" glass-fiber blanket
6" concrete slab

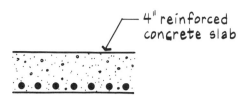

**Concrete Slab**

4" reinforced concrete slab

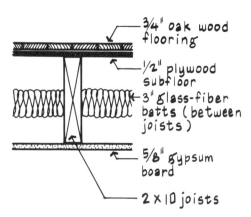

**Wood Joist Floor**

¾" oak wood flooring
½" plywood subfloor
3" glass-fiber batts (between joists)
⅝" gypsum board
2 x 10 joists

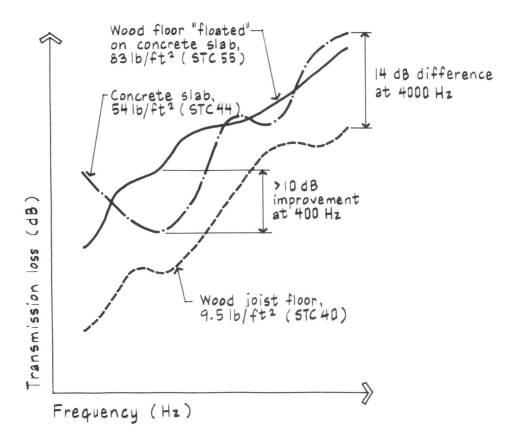

**References**

R. D. Berendt et al., "A Guide to Airborne, Impact, and Structure Borne Noise-Control in Multifamily Dwellings," U.S. Department of Housing and Urban Development, Washington, D.C., September 1967.

R. D. Berendt et al., "Quieting: A Practical Guide to Noise Control," U.S. National Bureau of Standards, NBS Handbook 119, July 1976.

P. Jensen, "How You Can Soundproof Your Home," Lexington Publishing Company, Lexington, Mass., 1974, pp. 73-75.

The ceiling must be as effective a barrier to sound transmission from room to room as the common wall. Lightweight, porous, sound-absorbing ceiling boards are relatively poor isolators. However, high-density, sound-absorbing materials backed with a nonporous laminate can provide both effective sound absorption and isolation between rooms by increasing mass and decreasing porosity. All joints and openings where the boards fit into the suspension system should be tightly sealed.

The sound-isolation performance of suspended ceiling systems can be determined by a laboratory test according to the provisions of AMA 1-II-1967, "Standard Specification for Ceiling Transmission Tests by Two-Room Method," available from Ceilings & Interior Systems Construction Association (CISCA), 104 Wilmot Road, Deerfield, IL 60015. This test measures the effectiveness of the room-to-room sound path up through the ceiling in the source room via the common overhead plenum down through the ceiling in the receiving room. The sound-isolating wall between the test rooms does not extend to the overhead slab, so there will be an uninterrupted, common plenum between the rooms. High sound-isolating wall constructions in the test facility assure that the weakest path for sound, therefore, will be the flanking path through the suspended ceiling. *Ceiling-attenuation* ratings for sound-absorbing boards (sometimes referred to as "ceiling STC") usually vary from 20 to 44, depending on the isolation properties of the ceiling materials and the quality of the installation. In the two-room laboratory test, ceiling STC is greater than 55 for 1/2-in-thick gypsum board and about 8 when no suspended ceiling of any kind is installed.

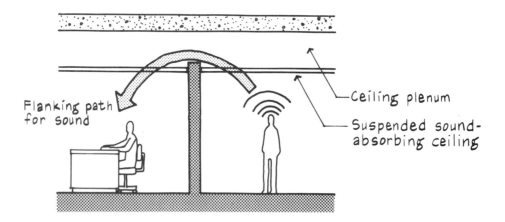

**Ceiling Flanking Path**

Prevent ceiling flanking by using sound-absorbing board with high ceiling-attenuation ratings, extending the partition to block the plenum, or installing a gypsum board ceiling. Be sure the ceiling membrane is interrupted at the top runner of the partition so that sound energy does not directly flank through the continuous surface.

# PLENUM BARRIERS

Gypsum board, lead sheet, and mineral fiber can be used as vertical barriers to prevent flanking through ceiling plenums. As shown below, these barriers can close off plenums by extending from the top of partitions to the overhead structural slab. As also shown, mineral fiber can be overlaid horizontally above suspended sound-absorbing ceilings, extending 4 ft or more on both sides of the wall-ceiling intersection. When installed this way, mineral-fiber blankets ($\geq 2.5$ lb/ft$^3$ density) can significantly reduce the transmission of flanking sound through exposed-grid panel ceilings. Ceiling-attenuation ratings can be increased more than 5. However, the amount of improvement depends on the type of sound-absorbing board, the thickness of the mineral-fiber blankets, and the configuration of the overlayment. For example, this approach is not very effective with porous, unbacked tile, such as nonfoil-back cast mineral tile or glass fiberboard.

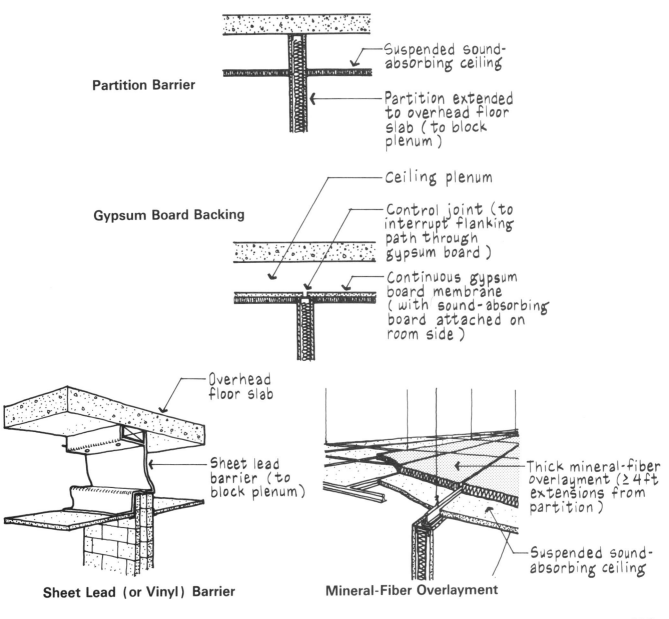

**Partition Barrier**

— Suspended sound-absorbing ceiling

— Partition extended to overhead floor slab (to block plenum)

**Gypsum Board Backing**

— Ceiling plenum

— Control joint (to interrupt flanking path through gypsum board)

— Continuous gypsum board membrane (with sound-absorbing board attached on room side)

— Overhead floor slab

— Sheet lead barrier (to block plenum)

— Thick mineral-fiber overlayment ($\geq 4$ ft extensions from partition)

— Suspended sound-absorbing ceiling

**Sheet Lead (or Vinyl) Barrier**

**Mineral-Fiber Overlayment**

The table below presents STC data for conventional wood doors and frames and proprietary metal doors and frames especially designed to achieve high TLs. To be effective as a sound barrier, a door must be heavy (high lb/ft²) and gasketed around its entire perimeter to be airtight when closed. Slightly greater than normal pressure will be required to close the door against soft, airtight seals. Doors that are louvered or undercut to allow air movement will be nearly useless as sound barriers. Ungasketed solid doors will be only slightly better, depending on how well the door fits the opening. Gasketed hollow metal doors filled with fibrous materials and dense limp materials, such as sheet lead or lead-loaded vinyl, have higher STC performance than gasketed solid wood doors of identical weight. In restoration projects, door weight can be increased by laminating a thin lead sheet to the inside of door panels so that historic finishes can be preserved.

| Door Construction | STC Rating |
|---|---|
| Louvered door (25 to 30 % open area) | 12 |
| 1 3/4-in-thick wood hollow-core door (1.5 lb/ft²), no gasketing | 17 to 19 |
| 1 3/4-in-thick wood solid-core door (4.5 lb/ft²), with gasketing | 29 to 34 |
| 1 3/4- to 2 3/4-in-thick filled-metal proprietary doors, with adjustable gasketing | 40 to 50 |

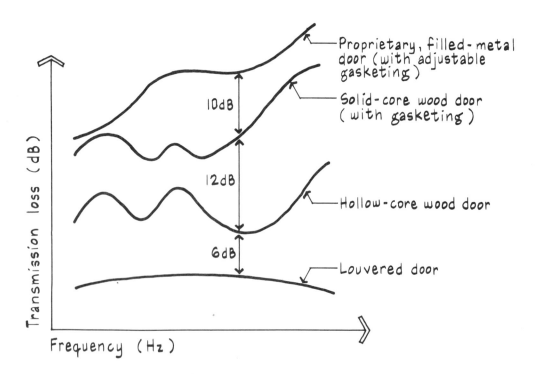

**Note:** Be sure STC rated doors are tested according to the provisions of the latest edition of ASTM E 90.

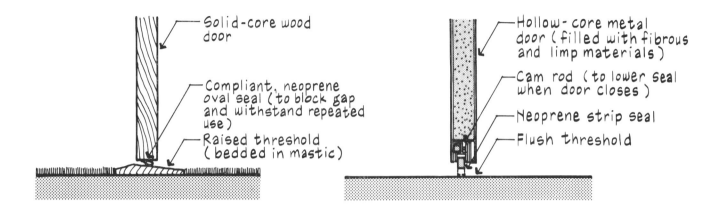

**Sections**

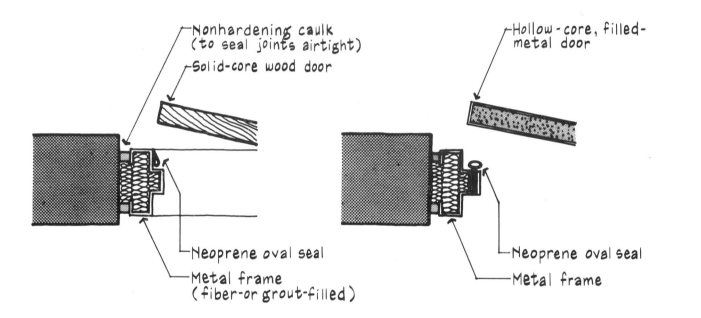

**Plans**

## Checklist on How to Improve TL of Doors

1. Do *not* use louvered or undercut doors where sound isolation is needed.

2. Use solid-core wood doors or fiber-filled, hollow-core metal doors, gasketed to be airtight when closed. Frames should be filled with grout (or packed with fibrous material) and caulked airtight at wall. For high STC requirements, use proprietary hollow metal doors that come with special frames and adjustable gasketing such as "refrigerator-type" magnetic seals.

3. Doors with raised sills usually provide better surface contact than those with flush sills and consequently can have STC ratings 3 to 6 higher. However, proprietary adjustable automatic door bottoms and cam-lift hinges are effective for use with flush thresholds.

4. Seals should be adjustable to compensate for wear, thermal movement, settlement of building structure, and other factors which cause misalignment of doors. Locate all seals in one plane to prevent sound leaks at corners due to adjacent seals that do not meet. Seals also cushion door slams.

5. Carefully adjust gasketing to attain an airtight seal and uniform closing pressure along all edges of the door. A stethoscope can be used during installation to locate leaks by detecting transmission of sound from stereo loudspeakers playing *pink noise* on the opposite side of the door. (See page 328 for sound spectrum of pink noise.) Depending on use, gasketing may require periodic adjustment, repair, or replacement.

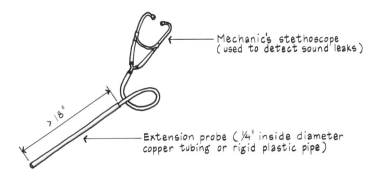

Mechanic's stethoscope (used to detect sound leaks)

Extension probe (¼" inside diameter copper tubing or rigid plastic pipe)

**Stethoscope**

6. Stagger locations of doors on opposite sides of double-loaded corridors so that noise does not pass directly from room to room across corridors.

7. Use stub corridors or vestibules as *sound locks*. Two doors in tandem, with wide spacing between, can act independently to provide TL compatible with high STC wall and floor-ceiling constructions. To be effective, surfaces of sound locks should have sound-absorbing finish treatment.

**Sound Lock**

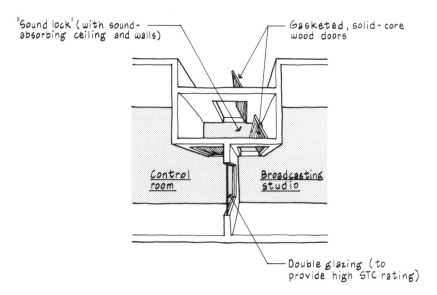

"Sound lock" (with sound-absorbing ceiling and walls)

Gasketed, solid-core wood doors

Control room

Broadcasting studio

Double glazing (to provide high STC rating)

The table below presents STC data for window constructions. The highest STC is provided by double-glass construction with wide spacing between panes of different thickness. The lowest STC is provided by double-glass construction with narrow spacing between panes of identical thickness. The narrow airspace acts as a "piston," readily transmitting sound energy from pane to pane.

| Window Construction | STC Rating |
|---|---|
| 1/8- + 1/8-in-thick double glass with 1/4-in airspace | 26 |
| 1/4-in-thick glass set in caulking | 30 |
| 1/4-in-thick laminated glass | 34 |
| 1/4- + 1/8-in-thick double glass with 2-in airspace | 39 |
| 1/4- + 1/8-in-thick double glass with 4 3/4-in airspace | 43 |

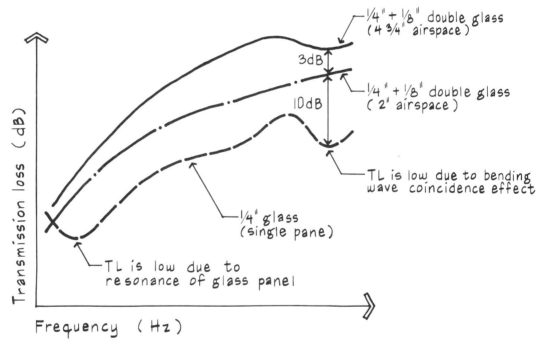

TL data for identical window constructions can vary widely from one laboratory to another. Discrepencies can be due to variations in size and shape of the panel being tested (glass dimensions affect resonant frequencies), edge support conditions (rigid support stiffens panel thereby lowering TL), and other factors. The TL of a single layer of plastic is similar to a single layer of glass of identical mass.

**Single Pane**

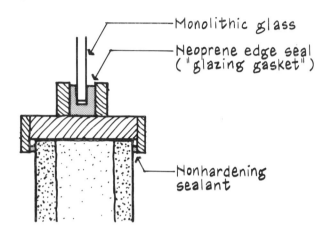

- Monolithic glass
- Neoprene edge seal ("glazing gasket")
- Nonhardening sealant

**Double Pane**

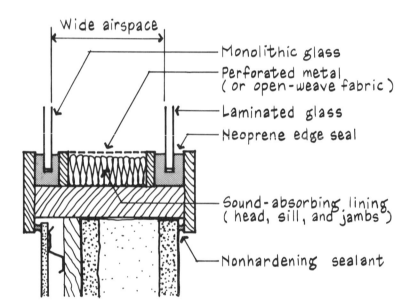

- Wide airspace
- Monolithic glass
- Perforated metal (or open-weave fabric)
- Laminated glass
- Neoprene edge seal
- Sound-absorbing lining (head, sill, and jambs)
- Nonhardening sealant

The 200-room hotel project below included adaptive reuse of the historic L&N Passenger Station at Pensacola, Fla. (Odell Associates, Inc.-Donald R. Lindsey, architects). Laminated glass was used in the guest room tower to reduce intruding noise from trains passing within 60 ft from the hotel. Train-warning sirens can exceed 100 dBA at the site.

*Gordon H. Schenck, Jr., Photographer*

**Hotel Guest Room Tower behind Historic Train Station**

**Checklist On How To Improve TL Of Glazing**

1. Increase thickness of single panes up to 1/2 in (to increase *mass*).
2. Use laminated glass, usually 30-mil-thick polyvinyl butyral interlayer sandwiched between two layers of glass (to achieve *limpness* and provide *damping*), which reduces the coincidence effect. Laminated glass can achieve STC rating 3 or more higher than monolithic glass of identical thickness. Be careful in cold climatic regions because damping provided by interlayer can be adversely affected by low temperatures thereby reducing TL of exterior glazing. In double-glass constructions, place laminated pane on warm side of window.
3. Use double-glass construction with at least 1/2-in-wide spacing between panes of different thickness (so panes will have different *resonant frequencies*). Ratio of thicknesses should be about 2:1. Tilting one pane does not affect sound transmission but may be beneficial to control reflection of light. Replacing one pane of glass with equal thickness of laminated glass increases STC by 4.

4. Increase spacing between panes up to 6 in. TL increases by about 3 dB per doubling of mean separation distance. Avoid using lightweight frames, and where especially high TL is required, use separate frames to reduce flanking of sound energy.

5. Line interior perimeter of frame with sound-absorbing treatment (to improve TL by 2 to 5 dB at high frequencies).

6. Mount panes with soft neoprene edge gaskets, which provide higher TL than putty or caulking for the same thickness of glazing.

7. Use sealed windows which usually have STC ratings 3 to 5 higher than operable windows with gasketing. Operable double windows with separate sashes can be more effective than a single sash with double glazing.

8. Do *not* evaluate glazing needed to isolate low-frequency noise based on STC ratings alone, because the STC rating does *not* include TL performance below 125 Hz. For example, single panes with STC ratings identical to double-pane constructions generally will be more effective at low-frequencies due to their greater overall weight.

### References

D. E. Bishop and P. W. Hirtle, "Notes on the Sound Transmission Loss of Residential-Type Windows and Doors," *Journal of the Acoustical Society of America,* April 1968.

J. D. Quirt, "Measurement of the Sound Transmission Loss of Windows," Building Research Note No. 172, National Research Council of Canada, April 1981.

H. J. Sabine et al., "Acoustical and Thermal Performance of Exterior Residential Walls, Doors and Windows," U.S. National Bureau of Standards, Building Science Series 77, November 1975.

G. C. Tocci, "A Comparison of STC and EWR for Rating Glazing Noise Reduction," *Sound and Vibration,* October 1987. (The *exterior wall rating* EWR is a single-number sound-isolation rating that attempts to account for the large amount of low-frequency sound energy produced by transportation noise sources such as aircraft, motorcycles, and trains.)

## OPERABLE WINDOWS

Where windows must be opened for ventilation, the noise reduction can be significantly increased if double-window combinations with offset openings are used. Shown below is a double-window design having an operable external transom and an operable inner bottom pane. When closed, the TL is comparable to that of a conventional double window, if airtight seals can be achieved. When opened, the noise reduction through the sound-absorbing lined path for ventilation air will be far greater than the 0 dB reduction if opened directly to the outdoors.

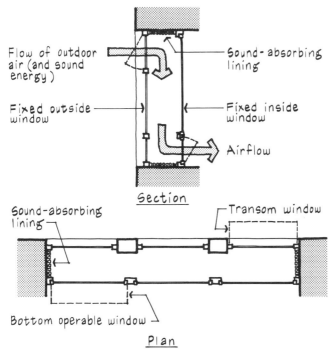

Flow of outdoor air (and sound energy)

Sound-absorbing lining

Fixed outside window

Fixed inside window

Airflow

*Section*

Sound-absorbing lining

Transom window

Bottom operable window

*Plan*

**Ventilation Window**

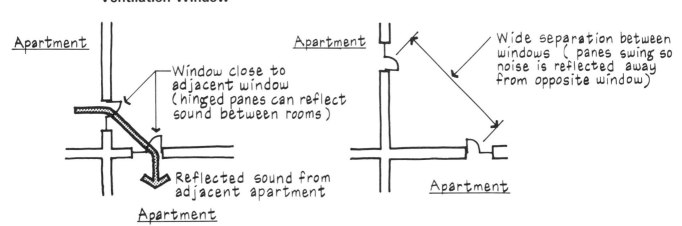

Apartment

Window close to adjacent window (hinged panes can reflect sound between rooms)

Reflected sound from adjacent apartment

Apartment

**Poor Window Layout**

Apartment

Wide separation between windows ( panes swing so noise is reflected away from opposite window)

Apartment

**Preferred Window Layout**

### References

P. G. Patil, "Flat Glass for Sound Control," *Construction Specifier*, December 1974.

K. A. Rose, *Guide to Acoustic Practice*, BBC Engineering, London, February 1980.

Where deep window recesses are used for solar shading purposes, the transmission loss of the glazing can be reduced below the performance measured according to ASTM E 90 procedures in the laboratory. This phenomenon, called the *deep-niche effect*, is due to the interreflections of sound energy in the niche and can reduce the transmission loss of the glazing. When the niche is treated with sound-absorbing materials, the noise reduction can be significantly increased. The "light shelf" shown below can be used to bounce sunlight toward ceilings and provide solar shading on the southern side of the building.

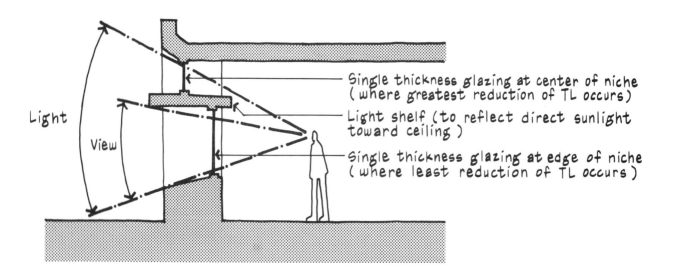

Light

View

— Single thickness glazing at center of niche (where greatest reduction of TL occurs)

— Light shelf (to reflect direct sunlight toward ceiling)

— Single thickness glazing at edge of niche (where least reduction of TL occurs)

**References**

J. C. Gilbert, "The Effect of a Deep Niche on the Laboratory Measured Sound Reduction Index," Graduate Division, University of California, Berkeley, 1979.

J. D. Quirt, "Sound Fields Near Exterior Building Surfaces," *Journal of the Acoustical Society of America*, February 1985, pp. 563-564.

# DENSITY OF CAVITY INSULATION

Controlled TL testing conducted at several laboratories shows that the *density* of fibrous cavity insulation has some effect on the STC rating of a wall. However, the thickness of the insulation may be more important, with the initial inch having the greatest effect. The table below shows typical STC ratings for metal-studded (25 gauge) gypsum board wall constructions measured in the laboratory under identical conditions with $3/4$-lb/ft$^3$-density glass fiber of 3-lb/ft$^3$-density mineral-fiber insulation in the stud cavity. For these light-gauge steel stud constructions, the more dense mineral-fiber insulation provided STC ratings slightly higher than the lighter glass-fiber insulation.

| | STC Ratings | | |
| --- | --- | --- | --- |
| Construction | No Cavity Insulation | Glass-Fiber ($3/4$ lb/ft$^3$) | Mineral-Fiber (3 lb/ft$^3$) |
| 2 1/2-in steel channel studs with one layer 1/2-in-thick gypsum board on each side | 37 | 42 | 43 |
| 3 5/8-in steel channel studs (25 gauge) with one layer 1/2-in-thick gypsum board on each side | 38 | 44 | 46 |

When low-density glass-fiber insulation ($< 2$ lb/ft$^3$) is used, it generally is best to completely fill the cavity airspace. For example, install glass-fiber insulation that is 1/2 in thicker than the stud depth. For double-row wood stud walls with 1 1/2-in-thick glass-fiber insulation, STC increases by about 2 per doubling of insulation thickness up to the full depth of the cavity.

Do *not*, however, completely fill the cavity airspace when mineral-fiber insulation ($> 2$ lb/ft$^3$) is used because the stiffer insulation tends to permit "bridging" of sound energy through the airspace. Tests also show reduced low-frequency transmission loss performance for mineral-fiber densities greater than 3 lb/ft$^3$.

### References

W. Loney, "Effect of Cavity Absorption and Multiple Layers of Wallboard on the Sound Transmission Loss of Steel-Stud Partitions," *Journal of the Acoustical Society of America*, June 1973.

"Noise Control in Residential Construction," Owens-Corning Fiberglas Corp., Toledo, Ohio, May 1981.

H. S. Roller, "Research Evaluates Role of Density in Acoustical Insulation Performance," *Form & Function*, Issue 2, 1985.

The table shows modifications to walls along with the corresponding estimated improvements in STC ratings.

| Modifications to Basic Construction | STC Improvement |
| --- | --- |
| **Drywall** | |
| 1. Sound-absorbing material (e.g., glass fiber or mineral fiber), at least 2 in thick, in cavity of wood stud gypsum board construction | 2 to 5 |
| 2. Sound-absorbing material, at least 2 in thick, in cavity of staggered wood stud construction | 3 to 7 |
| 3. Sound-absorbing material, at least 1 1/2 in thick, in cavity of double-stud construction (i.e., 2 by 4s with 1-in separation) | 6 to 12 |
| 4. Sound-absorbing material, at least 2 in thick, in cavity of 25-gauge steel stud construction | |
|    a. 2 1/2-in channel | 5 to 8 |
|    b. 3 5/8-in channel | 4 to 8 |
| **Masonry** | |
| 1. Sand- or mortar-filled cells | 2 to 5 |
| 2. Painting at least one side of lightweight hollow concrete block with latex block filler (3 coats), or 1/2-in-thick plaster sealer on one side | 2 to 4 |
| 3. Rigidly furred 1/2-in-thick gypsum board skin attached with wood furring to concrete block, sound-absorbing material installed in cavity leaving an air gap between block and modifications | 3 to 6 |
| 4. Resiliently supported 1/2-in-thick gypsum board skin attached with steel channels to unsealed side of concrete block (or with sound-absorbing material in cavity) | 5 to 8 |

*Note:* Avoid fastening cabinets, fixtures, and the like which can "short out" the resilient supports.

## EXAMPLE PROBLEM (USE OF STC TABLE)

Find the estimated improved STC for a 6-in-thick painted concrete block wall from adding a resiliently supported 1/2-in-thick gypsum board layer (or skin) to one side. Cavity airspace between block and gypsum board contains sound-absorbing material.

| Construction | STC |
|---|---|
| 6-in-thick painted concrete block (see p. 204) | 45 |
| Improvement no. 4 for masonry | + 5 |
| 6-in-thick painted concrete block with resiliently supported gypsum board skin | 50 |

**Note:** It is *always* prudent to use up-to-date TL data from laboratory tests conducted according to ASTM E 90 or reliable field measurements on a wall identical to the one being constructed. Whenever possible, use TL data that are based on measurements of current building materials and installation methods.

Background noise can contribute to sound isolation by *masking*, or covering up, intruding noise. Masking sound should be bland and steady so that it will not be noticed. Effective background masking may be provided by airflow that is carefully controlled at diffusers and registers. Fan noise and rumble from turbulence are not desirable (see Chap. 5).

The transmitted noise level should be below the normal background noise level (called *ambient sound*) in the receiving room. For example, if a noise level of 80 dB in a source room must be reduced to 5 dB below the background noise level of 20 dB in a receiving room, the required NR between the rooms will be $80 - (20 - 5) = 65$ dB. (See heavy lines on illustration.) However, by raising the background noise level in the receiving room to 35 dB, the required NR would be $80 - (35 - 5) = 50$ dB. The difference of 15 dB (i.e., $65 - 50$) is a significant diminution in the NR requirement (and required STC rating for the common barrier).

The following page introduces the concept of noise criteria which can be used as a guide to specify background noise levels in buildings.

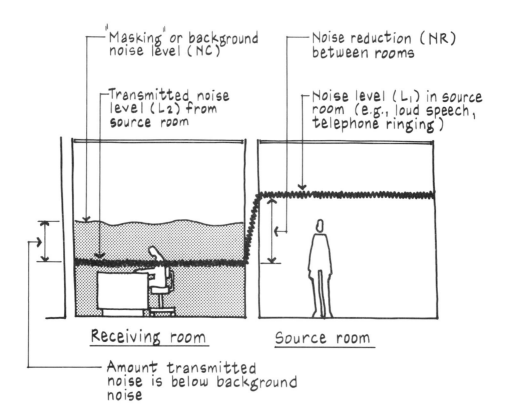

"Masking" or background noise level (NC)

Transmitted noise level (L₂) from source room

Noise reduction (NR) between rooms

Noise level (L₁) in source room (e.g., loud speech, telephone ringing)

Receiving room

Source room

Amount transmitted noise is below background noise

# NOISE CRITERIA FOR ROOMS

*Noise criteria* NC curves can be used to evaluate existing situations by measuring sound levels at the loudest locations in rooms (preferably at user ear height). They also can be used to specify the steady, or continuous, background noise levels (*not* activity noise from occupants of room) needed to help achieve satisfactory sound isolation, provided levels are 4 to 5 dB below the NC curve at both low and high frequencies. Each NC curve is defined by its sound pressure level for eight octave-band center frequencies shown by the graph on page 235. Note that the NC rating for a noise situation usually means the lowest NC curve that is *not* exceeded by any octave-band sound pressure level.

The table below presents recommended NC ranges for various indoor activity areas. For hearing-impaired persons, specify NC curves that are 5 or more below the criteria presented in the table. It is especially critical to achieve low noise levels at 63 and 125 Hz, where hearing-impaired persons have most of their residual hearing.

| Type of Space (and Listening Requirements) | Preferred Range of Noise Criteria | Equivalent dBA Level* |
|---|---|---|
| Concert halls, opera houses, broadcasting and recording studios, large auditoriums, large churches, recital halls (for excellent listening conditions) | < NC-20 | < 30 |
| Small auditoriums, theaters, music practice rooms, large meeting rooms, teleconference rooms, audiovisual facilities, large conference rooms, executive offices, small churches, courtrooms, chapels (for very good listening conditions) | NC-20 to NC-30 | 30 to 38 |
| Bedrooms, sleeping quarters, hospitals, residences, apartments, hotels, motels (for sleeping, resting, relaxing) | NC-25 to NC-35 | 34 to 42 |
| Private or semiprivate offices, small conference rooms, classrooms, libraries (for good listening conditions) | NC-30 to NC-35 | 38 to 42 |
| Large offices, reception areas, retail shops and stores, cafeterias, restaurants, gymnasiums (for moderately good listening conditions) | NC-35 to NC-40 | 42 to 47 |
| Lobbies, laboratory work spaces, drafting and engineering rooms, general secretarial areas, maintenance shops such as for electrical equipment (for fair listening conditions) | NC-40 to NC-45 | 47 to 52 |
| Kitchens, laundries, school and industrial shops, computer equipment rooms (for moderately fair listening conditions) | NC-45 to NC-55 | 52 to 61 |

*Do *not* use A-weighted sound levels (dBA) for specification purposes. Spectrum shapes and noise characteristics can vary widely for background noises with identical A-weighted sound levels (see Chap. 1).

It is good design practice for most situations to specify background noise levels which fall within a minimum-maximum NC range as suggested in the table. The minimum background noise levels are needed to help achieve sound isolation. For example, mechanical engineers can specify air-flow at diffusers and registers which, if unobtrusive and continuous, can provide sufficient background noise for effective masking in private offices. The maximum background noise levels should *not* be exceeded because higher levels can be noticeable and annoy most occupants or interfere with speech communication. Limits on intruding noise of short duration, such as noise from trains and aircraft, often can be allowed to exceed preferred NC criteria for continuous noise by 5 to 10.

## References

L. L. Beranek (ed.), *Noise and Vibration Control*, McGraw-Hill, New York, 1971, pp. 564-568 and 584-586.

S. L. Yaniv and D. R. Flynn, "Noise Criteria for Buildings: A Critical Review," U.S. National Bureau of Standards, NBS Special Publication 499, January 1978.

## NOISE CRITERIA CURVES

The numerical designation of the NC curves shown below is the arithmetic average of their respective sound pressure levels at 1000, 2000, and 4000 Hz (which are extremely important frequencies for speech perception). The NC rating for a measured noise can be found by comparing its plotted sound spectrum to the NC curves. The NC rating is the lowest NC curve *not* exceeded by the plotted sound spectrum.

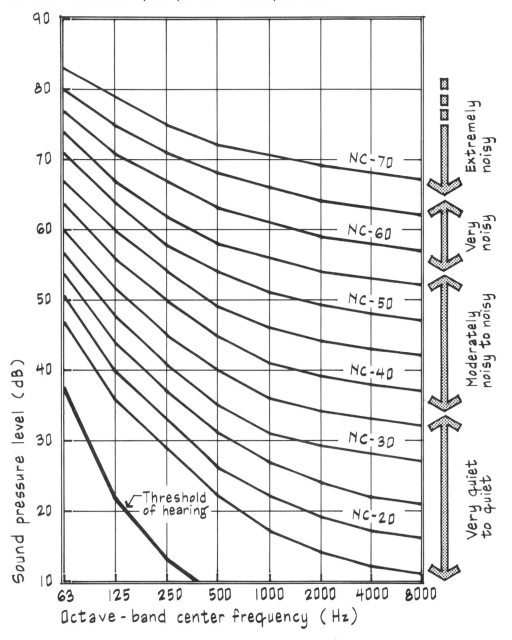

**Note:** The dark curve at the bottom of the graph indicates the threshold of hearing for continuous noise (cf., D. W. Robinson and L. S. Whittle, "The Loudness of Octave-Bands of Noise," *Acustica*, vol. 14, 1964, p. 33). The threshold of hearing for pure tones is much lower due to greater human sensitivity to such tones. Low-frequency sound levels of the NC curves are higher than high-frequency levels because humans are less sensitive to low-frequency sound energy (see Chap. 1).

Be careful because a background noise with a plotted spectrum which has the shape of an NC curve generally will *not* sound pleasant. It will be both rumbly and hissy, unless the sound levels at low frequencies ($\leq 125$ Hz) and high frequencies ($> 1000$ Hz) are reduced by 4 or 5 dB. Preferred spectra for electronic background masking systems are discussed in Chaps. 6 and 7.

NC levels can be used as design criteria to specify limits on noise generated by air diffusers and registers, fluorescent and HID lamp ballasts, and the like. For ballasts, the limit should be at least 10 below NC criteria to prevent hearing pure tones. Refer to table on page 402 for decibel values of NC curves.

### Reference

*ASHRAE Handbook (1985 Fundamentals Volume)*, American Society of Heating, Refrigerating, and Air-Conditioning Engineers, Atlanta, 1985, p. 7.9.

# ROOM CRITERIA CURVES

Room criteria (RC) curves can be used to evaluate and diagnose continuous noise from HVAC systems according to measured sound pressure level, shape of frequency spectrum, tonal content (no whining or buzzing is desired), and low-frequency forced vibrations. For example, sound levels in the shaded area A on the graph indicate high probability that noise-induced vibrations in lightweight wall and ceiling constructions will be clearly "feelable" and audible (e.g., rattling light fixtures). Levels in shaded area B indicate moderately "feelable" vibrations.

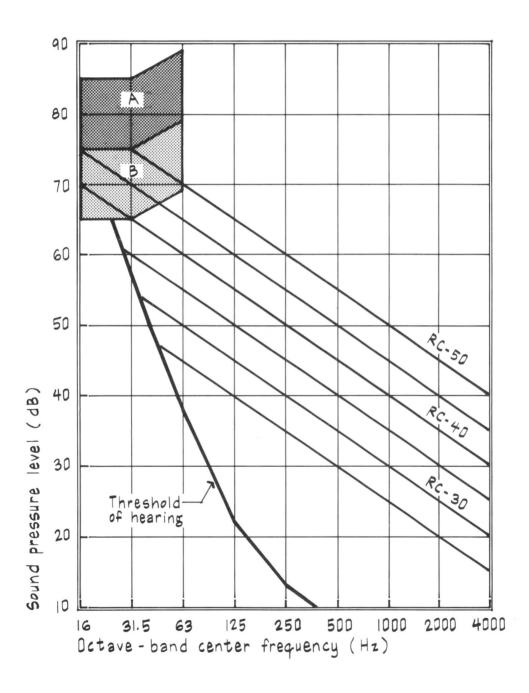

Unlike the NC rating, where different spectra can have identical ratings, the RC rating is determined by first comparing the sound spectrum, plotted at 500 to 2000 Hz, to the closest RC curve. Next, the subjective "quality" of the sound energy is assessed with respect to an ideal balanced spectrum that is neither rumbly nor hissy. A balanced spectrum would be within 2 dB above or below an RC curve at each octave-band center frequency. Rumbly sounds generally exceed an RC curve by 5 dB or more at low frequencies ($\leq$ 250 Hz); hissy sounds by 5 dB or more at high frequencies ($\geq$ 2000 Hz).

For examples of how to rate HVAC system noise by the RC method, see W. E. Blazier, "Revised Noise Criteria for Design and Rating of HVAC Systems," *ASHRAE Journal*, May 1981.

### References

L. L. Beranek et al., "Preferred Noise Criterion (PNC) Curves and Their Application to Rooms," *Journal of the Acoustical Society of America*, November 1971.

W. E. Blazier, "Revised Noise Criteria for Application in the Acoustical Design and Rating of HVAC Systems," *Noise Control Engineering Journal*, March-April 1981.

## EXAMPLE PROBLEM (TL DESIGN)

Find the TLs required to isolate an office from high noise levels in an adjacent computer equipment room. The common wall is concrete block construction. The ceiling in the office is 1 1/2-in-thick suspended sound-absorbing board, the walls are painted concrete block, and the floor is covered by heavy carpet on foam rubber underlay.

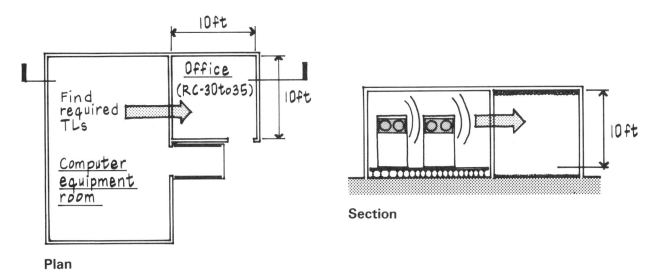

**Plan**

**Section**

First, find the absorption in the receiving room (office) by using the formula: $a_2 = \Sigma S\alpha$.

| Surface | Sound Absorption (sabins) | | | | | |
|---|---|---|---|---|---|---|
| | 125 Hz | 250 Hz | 500 Hz | 1000 Hz | 2000 Hz | 4000 Hz |
| 100-ft² ceiling, 1 1/2-in fuzz | 38 | 60 | 78 | 80 | 78 | 70 |
| 100-ft² floor, carpet | 8 | 24 | 57 | 69 | 71 | 73 |
| 400-ft² walls, concrete block | 40 | 20 | 24 | 28 | 36 | 32 |
| $a_2$ (sabins): | 86 | 104 | 159 | 177 | 185 | 175 |

Next, find the required NR by subtracting the background noise level in the receiving room (office) from the likely noise level in the source room (computer equipment room) at each frequency. To estimate the minimum masking background noise levels, use the RC-30 curve. The required TL then can be found by the formula: TL = NR − 10 log $a_2/S$.

Finally, select a wall construction from page 204 that will have a TL performance which exceeds the required TL. The table below shows the computation process at sound frequencies from 125 to 4000 Hz.

|  | 125 Hz | 250 Hz | 500 Hz | 1000 Hz | 2000 Hz | 4000 Hz |
|---|---|---|---|---|---|---|
| Likely noise in computer equipment room (see p. 34) | 75 | 73 | 78 | 80 | 78 | 74 |
| Minus background level in office, RC-30 (see p. 402) | 45 | 40 | 35 | 30 | 25 | 20 |
| Required NR (dB): | 30 | 33 | 43 | 50 | 53 | 54 |
| Minus 10 log $a_2/S$ | −1 | 0 | 2 | 3 | 3 | 3 |
| Required TL (dB): | 31 | 33 | 41 | 47 | 50 | 51 |
| Use 6-in concrete block wall, painted (34 lb/ft$^2$)    TL (dB): | 37 | 36 | 42 | 49 | 55 | 58 |

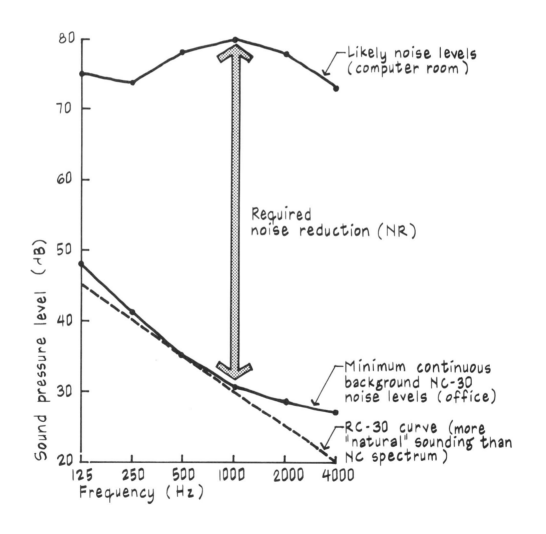

# STCs FOR SCHOOLS

Suggested STC ratings for schools can be found in the table below at the intersection of a source room row and receiving room column. For example, an STC of 50 normally would be required between a kitchen and a classroom in a school. Carefully evaluate both paths, because a receiving room also can be a source room. STC requirements which exceed 65 generally will require "floated" floors, special ceiling constructions, and careful control of all flanking paths.

**Receiving room**

| Source room | Teleconference | Classroom | Gymnasium | Kitchen | Laboratory | Library |
|---|---|---|---|---|---|---|
| Teleconference | 55 | 50 | – | 35 | 45 | 50 |
| Classroom | 45 | 40 | – | 30 | 35 | 40 |
| Gymnasium | – | – | – | 35 | – | – |
| Kitchen | 55 | 50 | 45 | – | 45 | 50 |
| Laboratory | 45 | 40 | – | 30 | 35 | 40 |
| Library | 40 | 35 | – | – | 30 | – |

**Note:** The tables of suggested STCs and NICs in this chapter are based on isolating noise levels from normal activities and on achieving the preferred NC background noise levels in the receiving room. The tables therefore may be used for preliminary planning purposes if adjustments are made for more demanding situations. For example, specific STC and TL needs should be determined only by accounting for privacy expectations of the users, size of common barrier, receiving room absorption, anticipated source room noise levels, and other factors presented in this chapter and in Chap. 6.

Recommended field-measured minimum noise isolation class NIC ratings for music rooms are presented in the table below. To achieve satisfactory isolation, the noise level of the intruding music must be reduced to be below the background noise level in the receiving room. Recommended background noise levels are 36 dBA for band rehearsal rooms, choral rehearsal rooms, and music teaching classrooms; 40 dBA for electronic music rooms and faculty teaching studios; and 44 dBA for music practice rooms (individual or ensemble). Higher background noise levels can provide a greater margin of safety for music privacy. Under no circumstances, however, should background noise levels exceed 50 dBA. In large rehearsal rooms where musicians are widely separated, background noise levels must be low ($< 40$ dBA) so that musicians can hear each other.

Convert NIC rating in the table to STC by subtracting $10 \log a_2/S$ from the table value, where $a_2$ is the absorption in the receiving room (sabins) and $S$ is the surface area (ft$^2$) of the common barrier construction separating the rooms. (Refer to ASTM E 597 for a method to verify NIC performance in the field.)

Heavyweight masonry constructions provide better low-frequency isolation than lightweight drywall constructions and therefore are normally preferred when music is to be isolated.

| | Band room | Choral room | Music classroom | Music practice room | Electronic music room | Faculty studio |
|---|---|---|---|---|---|---|
| Band room | 65 | 65 | 65 | 57 | 62 | 61 |
| Choral room | 65 | 59 | 59 | 56 | 62 | 62 |
| Music classroom | 65 | 59 | 59 | 56 | 62 | 56 |
| Music practice room | 57 | 56 | 56 | 48 | 54 | 52 |
| Electronic music room | 62 | 62 | 62 | 54 | 58 | 58 |
| Faculty studio | 61 | 62 | 56 | 52 | 58 | 52 |

**Reference**

D. L. Klepper, W. J. Cavanaugh, and L. G. Marshall, "Noise Control in Music Teaching Facilities," *Noise Control Engineering Journal*, September-October 1980, p. 75.

# LAYOUTS OF INTERIORS

Rooms often can be arranged so that less-critical spaces act as barriers or buffer zones between sensitive areas and noise sources. The storage and locker rooms in the school example shown below can be used to shield classrooms from a nearby mechanical equipment room. In the music building example, offices and individual practice rooms can be used to shield the choral room from the band room. Note that noise levels in large music practice spaces can exceed 100 dBA.

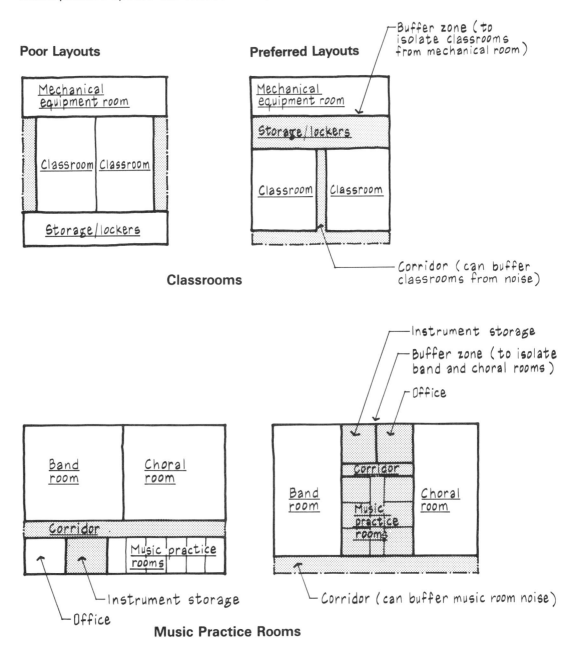

**Classrooms**

**Music Practice Rooms**

**Note:** Be sure to isolate floors in practice rooms because musical instruments such as the cello, piano, and double bass are sources of structure-borne sound (see Chap. 1).

# NICs FOR HEALTH CARE OCCUPANCIES

Recommended field-measured noise isolation class NIC ratings for health care occupancies are presented in the table below. NIC is the airborne sound isolation provided by all the construction systems separating adjacent rooms. Rooms with little absorption (e.g., exam rooms) should have construction STCs at least 5 higher than the NIC values in the table. Rooms with a relatively large amount of absorption (e.g., private offices) should have construction STCs equal to the recommended minimum NIC.

|                   | Waiting | Consult/Interview | Exam & Treatment | Private office | Laboratory | Patient room |
|-------------------|---------|-------------------|------------------|----------------|------------|--------------|
| Waiting           | 45      | 50                | 45               | 45             | 40         | 50           |
| Consult/Interview | 50      | 50                | 45               | 50             | 45         | 45           |
| Exam & Treatment  | 45      | 45                | 45               | 45             | 45         | 50           |
| Private office    | 45      | 50                | 45               | 45             | 50         | 45           |
| Laboratory        | 40      | 45                | 45               | 50             | 40         | 45           |
| Patient room      | 50      | 45                | 50               | 45             | 45         | 45           |

## STCs FOR DWELLINGS

Suggested STC ratings for dwelling units can be found in the table below at the intersection of a source room row and a receiving room column. The U.S. Federal Housing Administration (FHA) recommends STC ratings for constructions within the same dwelling based on three categories of site background noise: *quiet* (< 40 dBA), *average* (40 to 45 dBA), and *noisy* (> 45 dBA). An STC 55 is recommended for party walls at quiet sites, STC 52 at average sites, and STC 48 at noisy sites. For luxury dwellings, increase FHA recommendations by 5 to 10 or more. Constructions separating dwelling units from corridors, lobbies, or stairwells should be STC 50 or greater.

| Source room \ Receiving room | Bedroom | Living room | Kitchen | Bathroom | Family room | Corridor |
|---|---|---|---|---|---|---|
| Bedroom | 50 | 50 | 50 | 50 | 50 | 50 |
| Living room | 55 | 50 | 50 | 50 | 50 | 45 |
| Kitchen | 55 | 50 | 45 | 45 | 45 | 40 |
| Bathroom | 55 | 55 | 50 | 50 | 40 | 40 |
| Family room | 55 | 50 | 45 | 45 | 40 | 40 |
| Corridor | 50 | 45 | 40 | 45 | 35 | - |

# FUNDAMENTALS OF IMPACT NOISE ISOLATION

Typically, *impact noises* are erratic and can be caused by walking (hard heel footfall), rolling carts, dropped objects, shuffled furniture, slammed doors, and the like. Impacts on floors, as shown on the sketches below, are radiated directly downward. They also can be transmitted horizontally through the structure and be reradiated at distant locations. Therefore, it is best to prevent impact sound energy from entering the building structure.

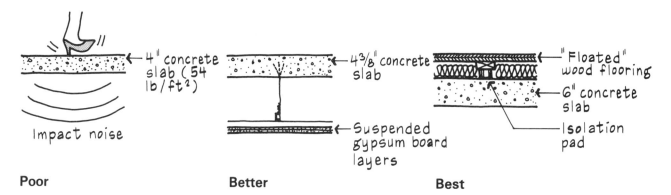

**Poor**          **Better**          **Best**

Impact isolation effectiveness for a construction element, tested over a standard frequency range, can be rated by the single-number *impact isolation class* (abbreviated IIC). Shown below are the transmitted impact noise levels from tests using a standard tapping machine on floor-ceiling constructions. The IIC ratings vary from 25 for the bare concrete slab to 57 for the "floated" floor construction. To achieve high IICs, use soft floor surfaces (carpet with soft underlay, rubber tile), ceilings suspended under slabs, floated floors, or all three of these impact control measures. Avoid hard surfaces such as bare concrete, terrazzo, vinyl tiles, and linoleum.

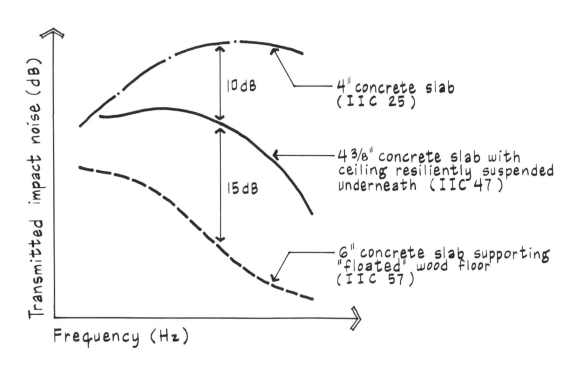

# FLOOR-CEILING CONSTRUCTIONS FOR IMPACT ISOLATION

Carpeting and resilient rubber floor tiles can be used to cushion impacts. They are most effective as isolators of mid- and high-frequency impact noises such as "clicks" from footsteps. However, low-frequency "thuds" from things being dropped still may be transmitted through constructions having these surfaces. Elaborate constructions, such as concrete slabs with suspended ceilings and floated floors, may be required to achieve high values of impact isolation over the entire frequency range.

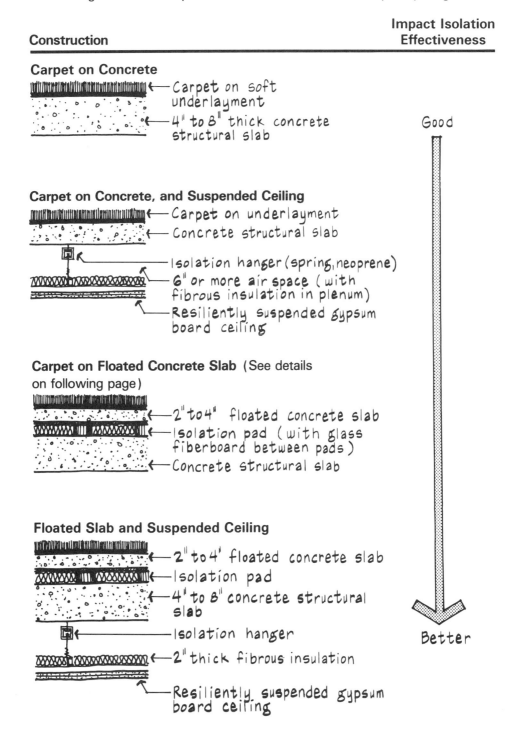

**Construction**

**Impact Isolation Effectiveness**

**Carpet on Concrete**

Carpet on soft underlayment
4" to 8" thick concrete structural slab

**Carpet on Concrete, and Suspended Ceiling**

Carpet on underlayment
Concrete structural slab
Isolation hanger (spring, neoprene)
6" or more air space (with fibrous insulation in plenum)
Resiliently suspended gypsum board ceiling

**Carpet on Floated Concrete Slab** (See details on following page)

2" to 4" floated concrete slab
Isolation pad (with glass fiberboard between pads)
Concrete structural slab

**Floated Slab and Suspended Ceiling**

2" to 4' floated concrete slab
Isolation pad
4" to 8" concrete structural slab
Isolation hanger
2" thick fibrous insulation
Resiliently suspended gypsum board ceiling

Good

Better

# FLOATED FLOORS

Floated floors are slabs (or floor assemblies) which are completely separated from the structural slab by a resilient underlayment or by resilient isolators. Partitions bordering floated floors should be designed as shown at the right. If partitions are set on a floated floor, either an overcompressed resilient isolator or a shear failure in the floated surface, as shown at the left, could provide a direct flanking path for sound energy.

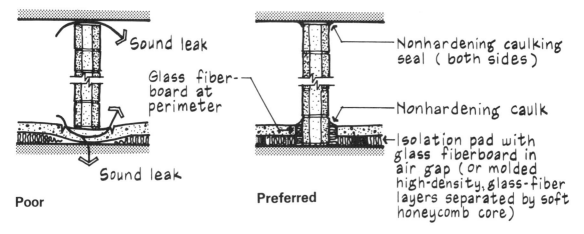

**Poor**

**Preferred**

Shown below are details of an example floated floor. Floated floors are complicated constructions requiring careful design, specification, and supervision during installation. Basic concrete floated-floor systems consist of precompressed glass-fiber or neoprene isolation pads installed under plywood forms with a moisture barrier completely covering the forms.

Where wood forms are *not* desired or permitted due to fire safety codes, *lift slab* systems can be used. In these systems, steel-reinforcing mesh is placed on the isolators and, after the concrete slab has cured, the slab is raised to its final height by jackscrews at the isolator pads (or springs). Polyethylene moisture barriers, covering the entire structural slab and perimeter of the floated slab, are used to help break the bond between concrete layers during lifting operations.

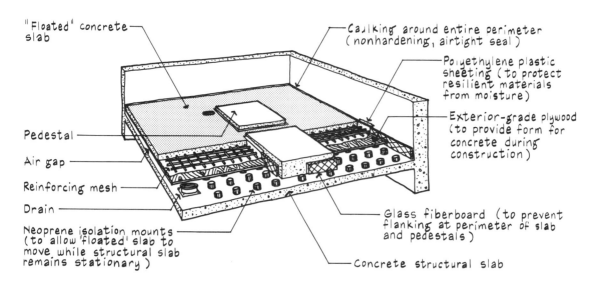

The IIC contour and standard grid shown below can be reproduced on a transparent overlay (without ordinate dB values) and then used to determine IIC ratings according to the ASTM procedures outlined on the following page. The IIC contour produces numerical ratings for impact isolation similar to the STC ratings for airborne noise isolation.

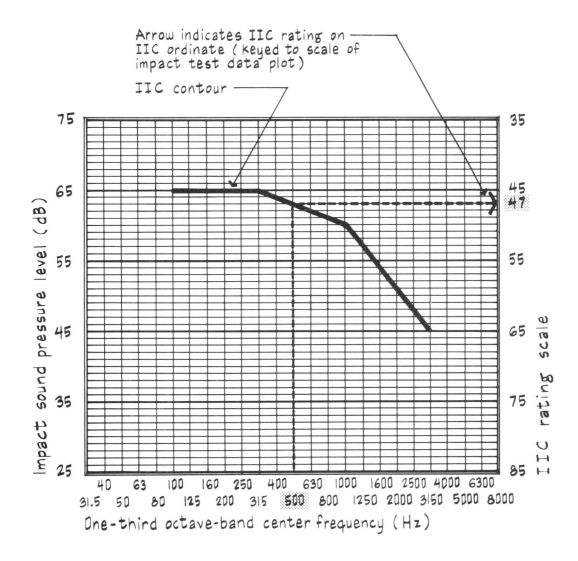

This *impact isolation class* IIC is a single-number rating of the impact sound transmission loss performance of a floor-ceiling construction measured at standard one-third octave band frequencies. The higher the IIC rating, the more efficient the construction will be in reading impact sound transmission within the frequency range of the test.

In the United States, the IIC rating method is recommended by the Federal Housing Administration (FHA) as a rating of impact sound isolation effectiveness. The IIC method is based on measurements of the absolute sound pressure levels produced in a room directly below the test floor on which the ISO standard tapping machine is operating. In this situation, lower transmitted impact sound pressure levels indicate better impact sound-isolating performance.

IIC test data are measured at 16 one-third octave bands with center frequencies from 100 to 3150 Hz. The test data, normalized to a room absorption of 108 sabins, are plotted against frequency and compared to the reference IIC contour. The IIC rating can be graphically determined by using a transparent overlay on which the IIC contour is reproduced, as shown on the preceding page. Before the overlay is used, a new vertical scale is written on the right-hand side of the test-curve graph, with values decreasing in the upward direction. The right- and left-hand scales coincide at 55 dB and have the same number of decibels per graph division. The IIC contour is shifted vertically relative to the plotted curve of test data to as low a final position as possible according to the following limited criteria:

1. The maximum deviation of the test curve above the contour at any single test frequency shall *not* exceed 8 dB.
2. The sum of the deviations above the contour at all 16 frequencies of the test curve shall *not* exceed 32 dB (an average deviation of 2 dB per frequency).

When the IIC contour is adjusted to the lowest position that meets the above criteria, the IIC rating is read from the vertical scale on the right as the decibel value corresponding to the intersection of the IIC contour and the 500-Hz ordinate (or decibel value from the vertical scale on left subtracted from 110). For example, the position of the contour shown on the preceding page would give an IIC 47 rating (the dB unit is dropped).

### References

R. D. Berendt et al., ''A Guide to Airborne, Impact, and Structure Borne Noise-Control in Multifamily Dwellings,'' U.S. Department of Housing and Urban Development, Washington, D.C., September 1967, chaps. 9 and 10.

''Field and Laboratory Measurements of Airborne and Impact Sound Transmission,'' International Organization for Standardization (ISO) Recommendation R 140.

''Laboratory Measurement of Impact Sound Transmission Through Floor-Ceiling Assemblies Using the Tapping Machine,'' ASTM E 492.

''Rating of Sound Insulation for Dwellings,'' ISO Recommendation R 717.

FHA impact noise criteria for residential urban and suburban dwelling units with *average* noise environments (called grade II) can be found in the table below at the intersection of the row for the source room (located overhead) and the column for the receiving room (located underneath). For example, an IIC 57 is required for a kitchen located on the floor directly above a living room. Be sure also that all piping and plumbing fixtures are properly vibration isolated (see Chap. 5).

This table also can be used to determine IICs for dwelling units located at suburban and peripheral suburban residential areas in *quiet* locations (called grade I) and urban areas with *noisy* environments (called grade III). For grade I, add 3 to the table values; for grade III, subtract 4.

**Receiving room (located below)**

| Source room (located above) | Bedroom | Living room | Kitchen | Bathroom | Family room | Corridor |
|---|---|---|---|---|---|---|
| Bedroom | 52 | 52 | 50 | - | 48 | - |
| Living room | 57 | 52 | 52 | - | 50 | - |
| Kitchen | 62 | 57 | 52 | - | 52 | - |
| Bathroom | - | - | 52 | 50 | - | - |
| Family room | 62 | 60 | 58 | - | - | - |
| Corridor | 62 | 57 | 52 | - | - | 48 |

A high IIC number does not necessarily mean that impact isolation will be satisfactory because the IIC method does not consider impact sound transmission below 100 Hz. Impact noise problems can arise at low frequencies, commonly occurring with lightweight steel or wood frame flooring systems. Consequently, where impact isolation is required, avoid especially long unsupported floor spans and excessive floor deflections.

# IIC AND STC IMPROVEMENTS FROM MODIFICATIONS TO FLOOR-CEILING CONSTRUCTIONS

The table shows modifications to floor-ceiling constructions along with the corresponding estimated improvements in IIC and STC ratings. Floated floors can be more effective when installed on concrete slabs than on wood-joist flooring because concrete slabs provide more rigid support.

| Modifications to Basic Construction | IIC Improvement | STC Improvement |
|---|---|---|
| **Wood Joist** | | |
| Resiliently suspended ceiling | 8 | 10 |
| Floated floor | 8 | 10 |
| Sound-absorbing material in airspace of resiliently suspended ceiling | 7 | 2 to 4 |
| **Concrete Slab** | | |
| Resiliently suspended ceiling | 8 | 10 to 12 |
| Floated floor | 15 to 20 | 10 to 12 |
| Sound-absorbing material in airspace of resiliently suspended ceiling | $> 5$ | $> 3$ |
| Wood flooring ($\geq 1/2$ in thick) set in mastic | 7 | 0 |
| **Wood Joist or Concrete-Slab** | | |
| Vinyl tile | 0 to 5 | 0 |
| Linoleum (3/32 in thick) | 3 to 5 | 0 |
| Carpet on foam rubber underlay (use higher end of IIC range for concrete slab systems) | 20 to 40 | 0 |

**Note:** It is always prudent to use up-to-date IIC data from laboratory tests in accordance with ASTM E 492 (and STC data from ASTM E 90) or reliable field measurements on a floor-ceiling identical to the one being constructed. Whenever possible, use acoustical data that are based on measurements of current building materials and installation methods.

**Reference**

L. F. Yerges, *Sound, Noise, and Vibration Control,* Van Nostrand Reinhold, New York, 1978, pp. 115-120.

# OUTDOOR BARRIERS FOR NOISE CONTROL

Outdoor barriers can be used to reduce environmental noises, especially high-frequency sound energy such as tire "whine" from cars and trucks. However, low-frequency sound energy, such as engine "roar," can readily bend over and around barriers. Noise reduction for outdoor thin-wall barriers (called *barrier attenuation*) can be estimated by the curves on page 256. Shown below are example outdoor barriers and site features that can be used to control noise.

## Poor

Thin planting of trees can provide visual, but *not* acoustical shielding!

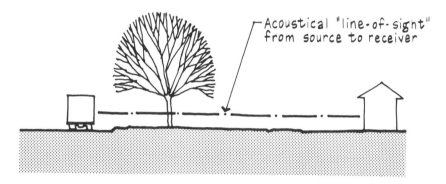

## Better

Elevated roadbed plus shielding of grass-covered earth berm and thin-wall barrier can provide useful attenuation. However, elevated highways more than 500 ft away can produce almost the same noise levels as highways at grade because the line of sight will not be blocked.

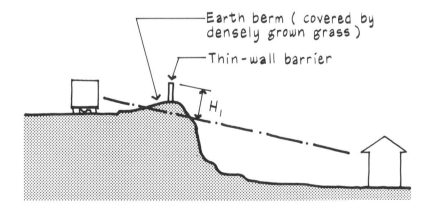

## Best

Roadbeds below grade can interrupt the direct sound path from source to receiver even further, thereby providing greater attenuation by diffraction. Roadbed depressions of 12 ft or more usually are needed to control highway noise. Note that the height $H_2$ above the acoustical line of sight for the example roadbed below grade is greater than the height $H_1$ for the example elevated roadbed.

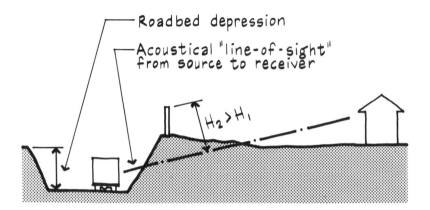

Noise from traffic can vary due to traffic volume (vehicles per hour), speed of vehicles, road surface (e.g., sealed asphalt can reduce noise by 5 dB compared to concrete), steepness of grade (especially critical for large trucks), and other factors. High-volume car and small truck traffic represents a continuous line source which radiates sound cylindrically, *not* spherically like sound from a point source. Consequently, car noise decreases by only 3 dB for each doubling of the distance from the source. Large trucks usually can be treated as point sources with 6 dB decay for each doubling of distance (from effective height of engine/exhaust at 8 ft above road surface).

**References**

G. S. Anderson et al., "Baltimore Plans Highways for Minimum Noise," *Civil Engineering*, September 1972.

D. S. Pallett et al., *Design Guide for Reducing Transportation Noise in and Around Buildings*, U.S. National Bureau of Standards, Building Science Series 84, April 1978.

H. J. Saurenman et al., *Handbook of Urban Rail Noise and Vibration Control*, U.S. Department of Transportation, Washington, D.C., October 1982.

# NOISE REDUCTION FROM OUTDOOR THIN-WALL BARRIERS

Shown below are the sound paths from source to receiver, interrupted by a thin-wall barrier. The arrows indicate the direction of travel for the direct, reflected, diffracted, and transmitted sound waves. The greater the angle of diffraction, the more effective the attenuation of the barrier.

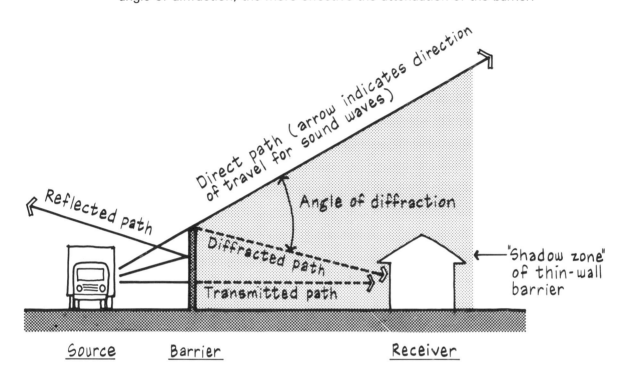

## Checklist for Effective Use of Barriers

1. Place barrier as close as possible to either the source of sound or receiver.
2. The greater the height of the barrier above the direct path from source to receiver, called the *acoustical line of sight*, the greater the attenuation.
3. Barrier should be solid ($>$ 4 lb/ft² density) and airtight. However, the TL of the construction materials used need not exceed the attenuation from diffraction effects over and around the barrier. Example barrier materials are: 1 1/2-in-thick fir, 1 1/4-in-thick plywood, 4-in-thick concrete panels or concrete block.
4. Attenuation values from the curves on the following graph represent barriers of infinite length. The diffraction of sound energy around the ends of short barriers, called *end diffraction*, will considerably reduce attenuation. Therefore, to isolate point sources provide total length of at least 4$R$, where $R$ is the shorter of the source-to-barrier and receiver-to-barrier distances.

**5.** Treat barriers that face each other (e.g., deep road cuts) with sound-absorbing materials, or tilt the barriers. For example, vertical sound-reflective barriers on opposite sides of a road can be greater than 10 dB more effective when treated with sound-absorbing materials.

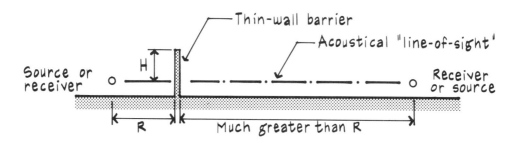

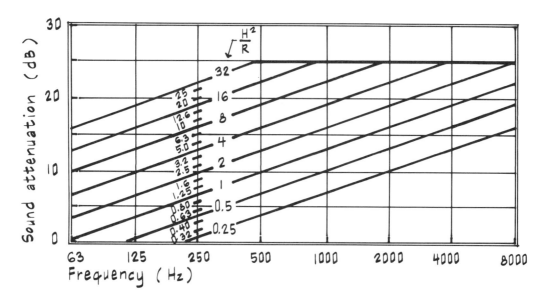

**Barrier Attenuation Graph**

**Note:** The effects of wind, temperature, and atmospheric turbulence usually can be neglected at distances of less than a few hundred feet.

## EXAMPLE PROBLEMS (THIN-WALL BARRIERS)

**1.** A source of noise is located 3 ft from a thin-wall barrier which extends 4 ft above the acoustical line of sight. Find the barrier attenuation A at 250 Hz.

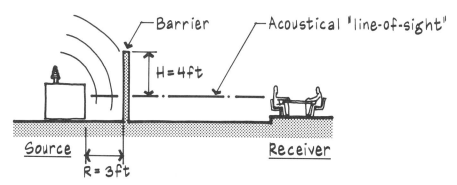

First, find $H^2/R$ ratio, which identifies curve on barrier attenuation graph (see preceding page).

$$\frac{H^2}{R} = \frac{(4)^2}{3} = \boxed{5.3}$$

Next, enter graph at 250 Hz, which gives attentuation A on ordinate scale of 14 dB.

Attenuation A, in dB, also can be found using the following formula, where f is frequency in hertz.

$$A = 10 \log \frac{H^2}{R} + 10 \log f - 17$$

$$= 10 \log (5.3) + 10 \log 250 - 17$$

$$= 10(0.7243) + 10(2.3979) - 17$$

$$A = 7 + 24 - 17 = \boxed{14\ dB} \text{ at } 250 \text{ Hz}$$

**2.** Find the barrier height H required to reduce outdoor mechanical equipment noise to 57 dB at 125 Hz. Equipment produces 67 dB at the property line as shown below. The barrier can be located 10 ft from the equipment.

First, find the required barrier attenuation A.

$$A = L_1 - L_2$$

$$A = 67 - 57 = \boxed{10\ dB} \text{ at } 125 \text{ Hz}$$

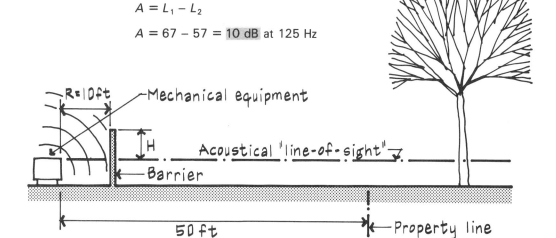

Next, find the required barrier height $H$ above the acoustical line of sight.

$$A = 10 \log \frac{H^2}{R} + 10 \log f - 17$$

$$10 = 10 \log \frac{H^2}{10} + 10 \log 125 - 17$$

$$10 = 10 \log \frac{H^2}{10} + 21 - 17$$

$$10 \log \frac{H^2}{10} = 6$$

$$\log \frac{H^2}{10} = 0.6$$

$$\frac{H^2}{10} = 3.981$$

$$H^2 = 10\,(3.981) = 39.8$$

$$H = \sqrt{39.8} = \boxed{6.3 \text{ ft.}}$$

## SELF-PROTECTING BUILDING FORMS

A *self-protecting* building has external elements which act as barrier screens by interrupting the acoustical line of sight to nearby noise sources. This feature can protect acoustically weaker elements such as windows and doors. Examples of self-protecting atriums, recessed floors, and podium bases are shown below. Be careful when designing wide podium bases because they can restrict access to upper floors for fire-fighting and rescue operations.

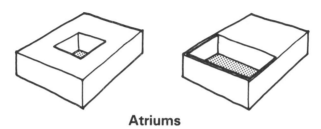

**Atriums**

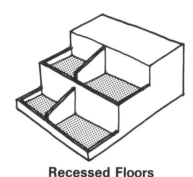

**Recessed Floors**

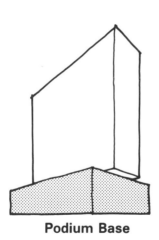

**Podium Base**

### Reference

D. J. Oldham and E. A. Mohsen, "A Technique for Predicting the Performance of Self-Protecting Buildings with Respect to Traffic Noise," *Noise Control Engineering Journal*, July-August 1980.

## BALCONIES AND OVERHANGS

Balconies and overhangs can be used to isolate buildings from surface transportation noise. Isolation can be improved if the underside of the overhang is treated with sound-absorbing material. Balconies with solid railings should be used in front of windows. Open railings should be closed with weather-treated 1/2-in-thick plywood, 1/8-in-thick molded polycarbonate, or glass. Solid balconies and overhangs with sound-absorbing treatment can reduce noise transmitted to interiors by 5 to 10 dB. Openings for ventilation should be in the shadow zone as close to the floor as possible. Barriers near the noise sources also can be effective for low-rise buildings. If there are barriers or grass-covered surfaces between the noise source and a high-rise building, sound levels at upper floors may be much higher than those at ground level. Example treatment schemes are shown below.

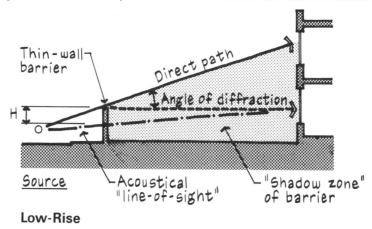

**Low-Rise**

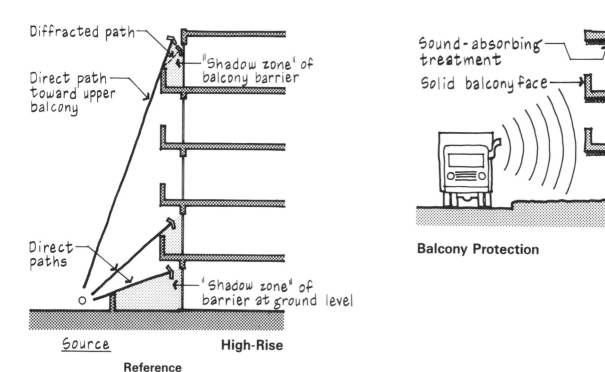

**High-Rise**

**Balcony Protection**

**Reference**

D. N. May, ''Freeway Noise and High-Rise Balconies,'' *Journal of the Acoustical Society of America*, March 1979.

## EARTH BERMS

Earth berms, completely covered by grass or other sound-absorbing plant material, can be effective isolators, reducing noise by 5 to 10 dBA. They can be as effective as reflective thin-wall barriers or lower berms which have thin-wall barriers along their tops. The effectiveness of earth berms can be reduced by reflective top surfaces (e.g., asphalt or concrete bicycle paths and walkways) and deciduous trees, which can scatter sound energy, thus reducing attenuation by 5 dB or more at frequencies greater than 250 Hz (fir trees > 4000 Hz).

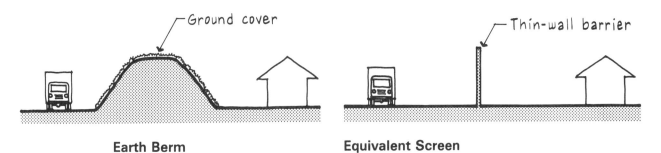

**Earth Berm**          **Equivalent Screen**

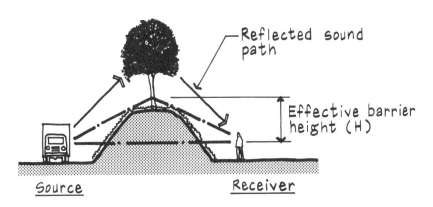

**Scattering by Trees**

### References

J. J. Hajek, "Are Earth Berms Acoustically Better Than Thin-Wall Barriers," *Noise Control Engineering Journal*, September-October 1982.

G. C. Tocci and W. H. Pickett, "Practical Applications of Outdoor Noise Control Barriers," *Sound and Vibration*, June 1979.

# CASE STUDY: THIN-WALL BARRIER AND EARTH BERM

**Moss Creek Plantation**
Hilton Head, South Carolina

  The combination earth berm and thin-wall barrier (> 3000 ft long) shown below was designed to reduce highway traffic noise at a residential development. Prior to construction, highway noise from large trucks exceeded 80 dBA at the site. The combination berm-barrier was designed to have an $H^2/R$ ratio exceeding 3 for cars and 1 for trucks. Thorny *elaeagnus pungens* rapidly grew to cover the 14-ft-high berm-barrier and to provide sound absorption on both sides of the barrier. The photos show the natural appearance of the thorny *elaeagnus* cover just two years after the berm-barrier was constructed.

*Landscape Architect:* Robert E. Marvin & Associates (Walterboro, South             Carolina)
*Acoustical Consultant:* Office of M. David Egan (Anderson, South Carolina)

**Berm-Barrier from Residential Side**  **Berm-Barrier from Highway Side**

Roger Briggs                       Roger Briggs

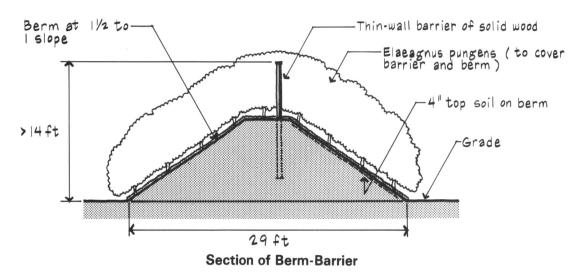

Berm at 1½ to 1 slope

Thin-wall barrier of solid wood

Elaeagnus pungens (to cover barrier and berm)

4" top soil on berm

Grade

> 14 ft

29 ft

**Section of Berm-Barrier**

# ATTENUATION FROM VEGETATION

Trees and vegetation are normally *not* effective as noise control barriers. As shown by the curve below, dense plantings of trees and shrubs at least 100 ft deep can provide 7 to 11 dB of sound attenuation from 125 to 8000 Hz. However, because attenuation from trees is mainly due to branches and leaves, sound energy near the ground will not be significantly reduced, and deciduous trees will provide almost no attenuation during the months when their leaves have fallen.

## Poor Isolation

A single row of trees has no value as an acoustical barrier! Paradoxically, when a single row of trees is added to solve an existing noise problem, the situation may seem worse because listeners tend to overestimate loudness when the view of the noise source is blocked (cf., D. E. Aylor and L. E. Marks, "Perception of Noise Transmitted Through Barriers," *Journal of the Acoustical Society of America*, February 1976).

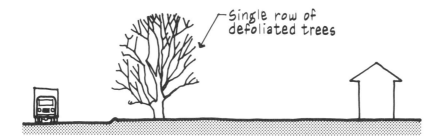

Single row of defoliated trees

## Preferred Isolation

Many rows of trees have some value as an acoustical barrier. However, the attenuation from dense plantings more than 100 ft deep will be limited by the flanking of sound energy over the top of the canopy of trees. For design estimates, use 10 dBA of attenuation for dense plantings of trees and shrubs more than 100 ft deep with a closed canopy. Mature evergreen vegetation (> 20 ft wide) may provide modest attenuation of 2 to 4 dBA if the belt is sufficiently high and long, has dense foliage extending to the ground, and can be well maintained.

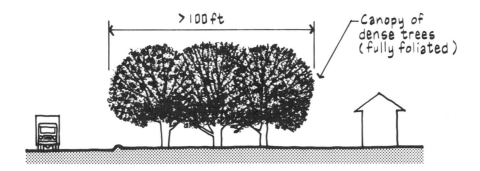

> 100 ft

Canopy of dense trees (fully foliated)

### Attenuation of Deciduous and Evergreen Woods (100 ft deep)

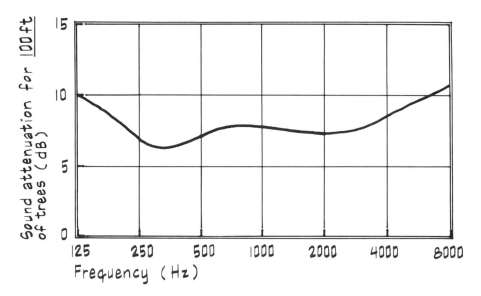

**Note:** Field measurements have shown that amplification (i.e., no mid-frequency attenuation) can occur within 50 ft of extremely loud noise sources. This phenomenon is due to resonance (or oscillation) of the branches.

### Reference

T. F. W. Embleton, "Sound Propagation in Homogeneous Deciduous and Evergreen Woods," *Journal of the Acoustical Society of America*, August 1963.

Both wind speed and temperature vary with height above ground, causing the speed of sound also to vary with height. This bends the path of sound waves from source to receiver as shown below.

### Wind

The effect of wind on sound outdoors is a complex phenomenon. Downwind from the source, sound is normally bent toward the ground increasing its sound level. Upwind, sound is bent upward causing a shadow zone where the sound level will be reduced. For example, at distances greater than 500 ft, as shown below, the upwind mid-frequency attenuation can be about 10 dB for winds of 10 mi/h. However, a reversal of wind direction can increase the sound level by about 10 dB at the same location! Consequently, do *not* rely on attenuation from the wind when designing outdoor noise control measures.

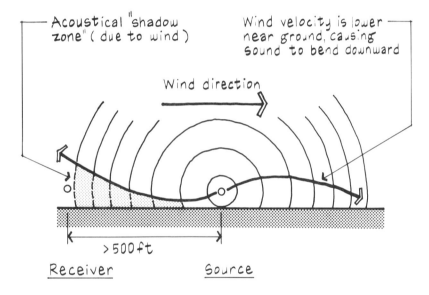

**Note:** Wind at right angles to source-receiver path has little or no effect.

### Temperature (clear, dry conditions shown by illustration)

On a clear, calm day the effect of temperature gradients (due to warmer air near the ground) can cause sound to bend upward as shown by the sketch below. Conversely, on a clear, calm night, air temperatures are inverted and sound will tend to focus and bend toward the ground. The difference in noise levels between a clear, calm summer day and night can be about 10 dB for sound sources at more than 1000 ft away.

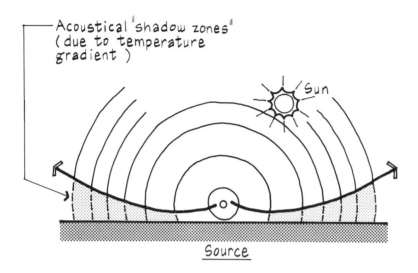

**Note:** Estimates of attenuation outdoors due to temperature and wind effects depend on complex meteorological and acoustical phenomena. In addition, attenuation varies with the wavelength or frequency of sound. For further information on sound propagation outdoors, see L. L. Beranek (ed.), *Noise and Vibration Control*, Mc-Graw-Hill, New York, 1971, pp. 164-193, and T. F. W. Embleton, "Sound Propagation Outdoors," *Noise Control Engineering Journal*, January-February 1982.

## WALK-AWAY NOISE TEST

The *walk-away test* may be used to assess the noise level acceptability of a proposed building site for low-rise buildings. [However, to evaluate compliance with noise ordinances, measurements should be made only with precision sound level meters (see Chap. 1).] Two persons with normal hearing and average voices are required to perform the walk-away test. The speaker should stand at a fixed location and read unfamiliar text material in a conversational voice level normally used indoors. The listener should back slowly away until only a scattered word or two over a period of more than 10 s is understood. Measure the distance and evaluate conditions using the table below. Test during times when noise levels are highest (e.g., during peak morning and afternoon traffic) or most annoying (e.g., after 10 p.m. when people are trying to sleep). For best results, perform the test during several visits to the site and reverse the roles of speaker and listener.

**Clearly Acceptable**

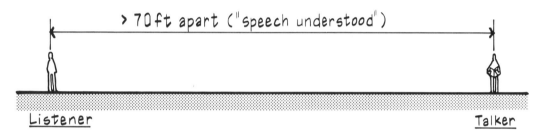

**Clearly Unacceptable**

| Distance from Which Male Speech is Understood (ft) | Noise Level Acceptability |
|:---:|:---:|
| >70 | Clearly acceptable |
| 26 to 70 | Normally acceptable |
| 7 to 25 | Normally unacceptable |
| <7 | Clearly unacceptable |

### Reference

T. J. Schultz and N. M. McMahon, *HUD Noise Assessment Guidelines*, U.S. Department of Housing and Urban Development, Washington, D.C., 1971.

Land-use planning examples to "buffer" high-noise sources are shown below.

### Aircraft Noise

In the example below, high-noise landing and takeoff operations at an airport are surrounded by industrial and commercial areas. Residential occupancies are located farther away ($> 3$ mi from major runways) because jet engine whine is extremely difficult to isolate with conventional glazing. Noise exposure forecast NEF contours are complicated, statistical metrics used to predict the response of people to commercial aircraft noise. The NEF is based on measured noise from aircraft operations, number of daily flight operations, time of operations, and other factors. In the United States, both the FAA and HUD rate locations with NEF greater than 40 as unsuited for habitation; 30 to 40, potential for complaints; and less than 25, not seriously affected by normal aircraft operations. To convert NEF to approximately equivalent sound level in dBA, add 34.

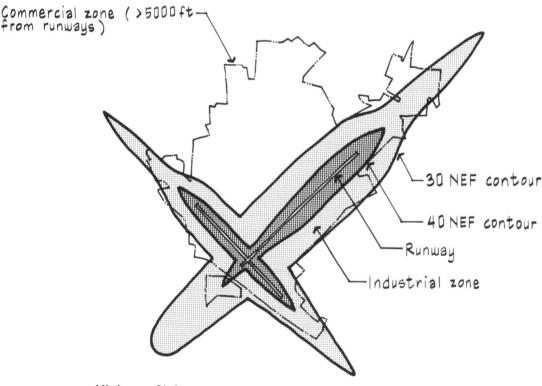

Commercial zone ( >5000 ft from runways)

30 NEF contour

40 NEF contour

Runway

Industrial zone

### Highway Noise

In the highway layout below, light industry is completely surrounded by office and research park buildings. Consequently, residential occupancies will be shielded from both the industrial noise sources and the rumbling from vehicular traffic. However, no occupancies are located within 500 ft from the highway. The noise contours connect equal dBA levels measured by precision sound level meters. Many local noise ordinances limit community noise based on "not to exceed" sound levels measured in dBA at a specific distance from the noise source. *

\* For impulsive noises such as quarry or construction blasting and sonic booms, use C-weighted sound levels (dBC) to best assess community annoyance and evaluate corrective measures because low-frequency energy produced by such sources causes building components to vibrate (cf., P. D. Schomer, "High-Energy Impulsive Noise Assessment," *Journal of the Acoustical Society of America*, January 1986, pp. 182-186).

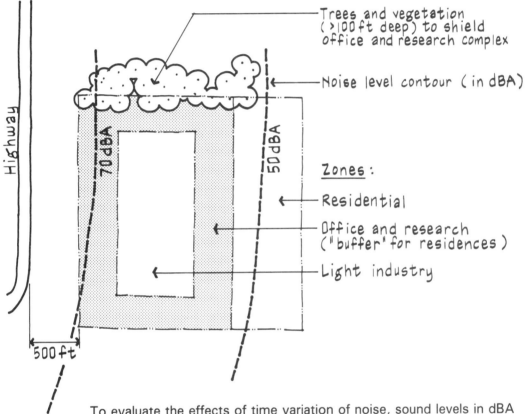

To evaluate the effects of time variation of noise, sound levels in dBA can be expressed as a percentage for which a set level is exceeded. These levels are designated $L_n$, where $n$ is the percentage which was exceeded. The most common values are $L_{10}$, $L_{50}$, and $L_{90}$, which are the levels exceeded 10, 50, and 90 percent of a measured time interval. Therefore, $L_{50}$ is the median noise level throughout the measurement period. $L_{10}$ is an indicator of the highest noise levels encountered and therefore may be used to predict annoyance.

**References**

C. J. Hemond, *Engineering Acoustics and Noise Control,* Prentice-Hall, Englewood Cliffs, N.J., 1983, pp. 145-151.

T. J. Schultz, *Community Noise Rating,* Applied Science Publishers, Barking, England, 1982, pp. 75-85 and 139-145.

# ORIENTATION OF BUILDINGS

Courtyards can be sources of considerable noise. The buildings shown below have a central courtyard enclosed by parallel walls. The hard-surfaced parallel walls cause flutter echoes which intensify the noise in the courtyard. By angling or staggering the buildings, noise buildup can be reduced.

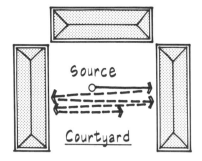

**Parallel Walls**

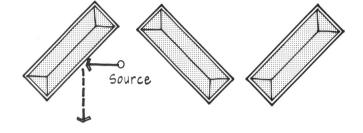

**Angle Solution**

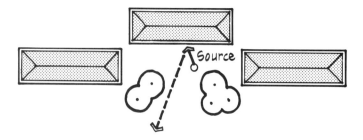

**Staggered Solution**

In the examples shown on the facing page, courtyards directly facing streets can confine vehicular noise between reflective surfaces, causing buildup of sound energy. The preferred orientations, shown on the right, locate courtyards so they will be shielded by facing away from traffic noise. Sound levels at the sides of the buildings can be 3 dB lower than at the front; sound levels at the rear can be 10 dB or more lower. Consequently, openings and sensitive areas should be located on sides which will be shielded from noise sources.

**Poor**

**Better**

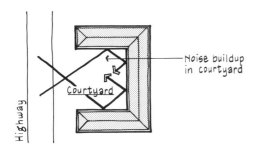

Noise buildup in courtyard

Courtyard

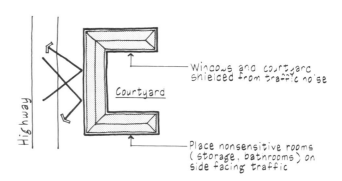

Courtyard

Windows and courtyard shielded from traffic noise

Place nonsensitive rooms (storage, bathrooms) on side facing traffic

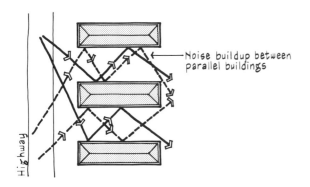

Highway

Noise buildup between parallel buildings

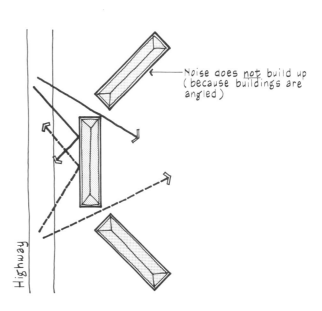

Highway

Noise does <u>not</u> build up (because buildings are angled)

Highway

# CLASSIFICATION OF ROOMS FOR NOISE CONTROL

Spaces which require quiet ambient backgrounds should be located far away from noise sources or be shielded by noncritical *buffer* spaces such as storage rooms and the like. Window openings for quiet spaces should be placed on building exposures which face away from environmental noise sources.

| Types of Space | Noise Source * | Quiet Ambient Background † |
|---|---|---|
| Auditoriums, theaters, radio/TV studios, music practice rooms, large meeting rooms, classrooms, audiovisual facilities, conference rooms | Yes | Yes |
| Residences, apartments, hotels, motels, reception areas, churches, chapels, courtrooms, large offices | Sometimes | Yes |
| Private offices, libraries, bedrooms, hospital patient rooms | No | Yes |
| Retail shops and stores, cafeterias, kitchens, laundries, school and industrial shops, computer equipment rooms, mechanical equipment rooms | Yes | No |

* When entering noisy source rooms, the high sound levels are "clearly noticeable." Example noise levels for many of the listed spaces are presented in Chap. 1.
† Recommended noise criteria NC for rooms are given on page 233.

# CHECKLIST FOR EFFECTIVE ISOLATION OF SOUND

1. Use site features such as hills or slopes, earth berms, thin-wall barriers, and nearby buildings to reduce intruding environmental noise by interrupting the direct sound path. Thin plantings of trees and vegetation (<100 ft deep) normally are *not* effective as noise control barriers.

2. Select noise criteria for all activity spaces in buildings. Intruding noise from outdoors and within buildings should be reduced to below the desired ambient background noise levels specified by NC or RC criteria. Lay out rooms so sources of noise will be located away from spaces requiring quiet or provide nonsensitive buffer zones between to reduce transmitted airborne noise. For example, mechanical rooms should be located on-grade, far away from sensitive areas (see Chap. 5).

3. Use sound-absorbing materials to reduce the buildup of noise levels in rooms and to muffle sound transmission through wall, plenum, or other cavities where sound absorption can contribute somewhat to sound isolation. Sound-absorbing materials by themselves normally provide little sound isolation!

4. Use *heavy* or double-layer constructions to achieve effective isolation, especially at low frequencies. For example, solid concrete blocks and hollow blocks with sand-filled cells are more effective than hollow blocks. Transmission loss TL of single masonry walls also can be improved by adding a resiliently supported thick gypsum board layer with sound-absorbing material in the wide cavity airspace.

5. Balance wall and ceiling constructions so that they will have nearly the same transmission losses. Balanced construction can prevent flanking of sound energy through a weaker element. For example, use plenum barriers or extend walls to overhead slab to interrupt ceiling flanking paths above sound-isolating wall constructions.

6. Seal *all* openings or cracks in building constructions because sound will travel through any opening regardless of its size. Sound leaks can greatly diminish the effectiveness of any sound-isolating construction. However, the higher the transmission loss of a construction, the more serious the sound leak.

7. Do *not* place electrical outlets or switches back-to-back or side-to-side in the same stud space, or install recessed medicine cabinets, lighting fixtures, or furniture because they can be a source of serious sound leaks. For example, in gypsum board constructions, stagger or offset electrical outlets (> 2 to 3 ft apart), seal openings in and perimeters of boxes airtight with nonhardening caulking, and pack around outlet boxes with fibrous insulation.

# Chapter 5

## Mechanical System Noise and Vibrations

# VIBRATIONS FROM MECHANICAL EQUIPMENT

The *vibrations* produced from up-and-down, side-to-side, or rocking motion by mechanical equipment in buildings can be felt ($< 20$ Hz) and heard by building occupants. When vibrations are accompanied by noise, they tend to be more annoying. Vibrations can travel in solid building elements such as columns, beams, and floor slabs (called *structure-borne* sound), and may be re-radiated as *airborne* sound great distances away from the source. Resilient mounts should be used to isolate the vibrating equipment (and anything rigidly connected to it) from the building structure. If possible, vibrating equipment should be positioned away from the center of long floor spans to locations near columns or load-bearing walls, which can provide better structural support.

## Poor Isolation

The mechanical equipment shown below is bolted to the floor slab so vibrations are transmitted directly into the structure.

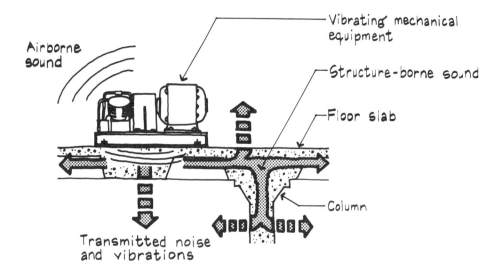

## Better Isolation

The mechanical equipment shown below is supported by resilient mounts (e.g., unhoused steel springs) and relocated close to the structural column. The equipment continues to be a source of airborne sound and vibrations, but the "feelable" vibrations in the structure and the structure-borne sound will be considerably reduced.

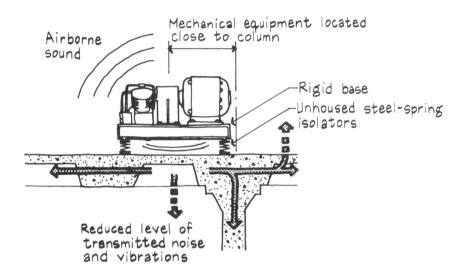

Airborne sound

Mechanical equipment located close to column

Rigid base

Unhoused steel-spring isolators

Reduced level of transmitted noise and vibrations

Vibration isolation involves installing vibrating equipment on *resilient materials* such as ribbed or waffle-shaped neoprene pads, precompressed glass-fiber pads, and steel springs. The goal is to choose an appropriate resilient material that, when loaded, will provide a system *natural frequency*, or *resonant frequency*, at least one-third of the lowest driving frequency of the equipment. This kind of support can provide the desired conditions of low transmissibility.

*Transmissibility* is the ratio of the force transmitted into the supporting structure to the vibrational force of the equipment. Driving frequency $f$ in Hz (or cycles per second) is an operational characteristic of the equipment (e.g., the lowest drive shaft rpm divided by 60) which can be obtained from the equipment specifications or the manufacturer. Natural frequency $f_n$ in Hz is the lowest frequency of vibration that occurs when a mass supported by a resilient material is deflected from its rest position and released. To calculate the natural frequency of a steel spring isolation system on a solid foundation, use the following formula:

$$f_n = 3.13 \sqrt{\frac{1}{Y}}$$

where    $f_n$ = natural frequency of isolator (Hz)

$Y$ = spring static deflection (in)

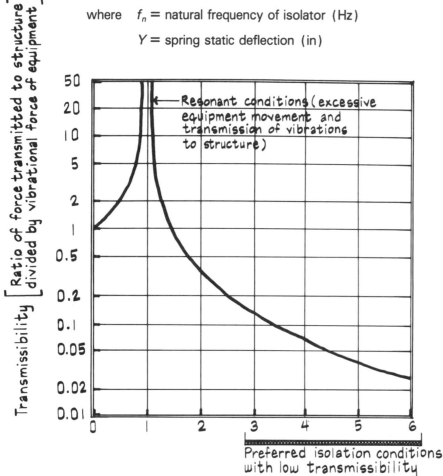

Vibration isolators are fabricated in various shapes from a variety of materials to prevent or reduce energy transfer. The curves below show the natural frequency $f_n$ when isolation is provided by free-standing coil steel springs, precompressed glass-fiber pads, rubber or neoprene, and cork. Static deflection is the distance an isolator will compress (or deflect) when the equipment weight is applied to it.

Generally springs are the most resilient of the commonly used isolators because they can provide the largest deflections and therefore can effectively isolate low-frequency vibrations. For lateral stability, the coil diameter of springs should be at least 0.8 times compressed or "working" height H. To isolate both low-frequency vibrations and high-frequency noise, use steel springs which have waffle-shaped or ribbed neoprene (< 50 durometer) attached to the bottom of their base plates. Note that cork gradually compresses under constant load and consequently loses its resilience.

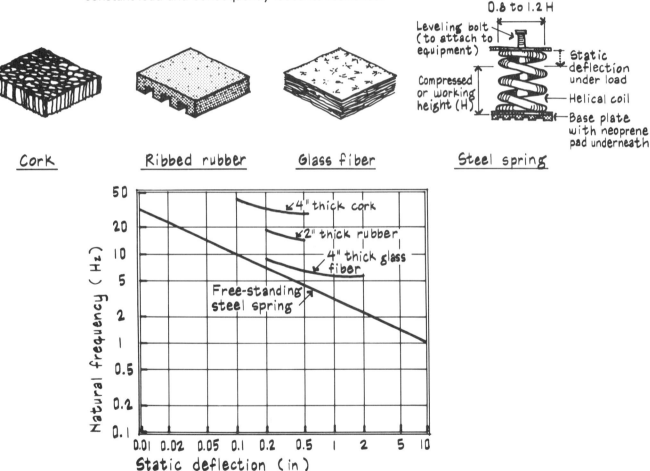

**Note:** For isolation of vibrations at extremely low frequencies (< 80 Hz), air mounts can be used as an alternative to steel springs. *Air mounts* are resiliently-reinforced neoprene chambers containing compressed air to support the applied load. A constant supply of dry air is required to compensate for normal mount leakages. Air mounts also can be used to isolate vibration-sensitive equipment, such as electron microscopes and microbalances, from the building structure. The best location for vibration-sensitive equipment is on a ground-supported slab.

# VIBRATION ISOLATION DESIGN GRAPH

The graph below can be used to find the static deflection for isolators that is required to provide a given degree of isolation from vibrating equipment. For example, in a gymnasium ("noncritical" application) an exhaust air fan operating at a driving frequency of 520 rpm will require resilient isolators which have a static deflection of at least 1 in (see dashed lines on graph).

The relationships depicted on the graph are for resilient materials supported by a rigid structural base or foundation. Nonrigid, lightweight bases (especially lightweight steel or wood frame flooring systems) used for above-grade mechanical equipment spaces require greater isolation deflections than given by the graph. Lightweight bases are less stiff and therefore require greater isolator deflections. Special care must be taken when designing vibration isolation for these situations.

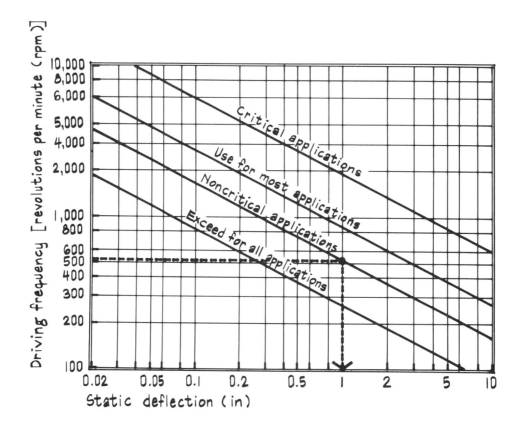

# RUBBER MOUNTS

The graph below shows the static deflection under load for examples of rubber or *neoprene-in-shear* mounts of various hardnesses as measured in durometer. Neoprene-in-shear mounts usually are shaped like truncated cones (similar to upside-down flower pots) and are bonded to top and bottom metal plates. Loads from any direction cause a shearing reaction which absorbs vibrations.

Shear occurs when the particles of a material slide relative to each other rather than push together as occurs with compression. Ribbed (or waffled) neoprene pads also provide some shearing action and absorb energy by expanding laterally into the spaces between the ribs. Pads can be stacked to obtain larger deflections, in which case stainless steel separator plates should be used between layers to help evenly distribute the load.

*Durometer*, a measure of hardness, is expressed by a scale of 0 (soft) to 100 (hard) from surface indentation measurements. Rubber mounts (usually 30 to 70 durometer) are often used to vibration-isolate mechanical equipment that is relatively small or operated at high speeds. For example, a small engine weighing 500 lb and having a driving frequency of 2000 rpm requires a static deflection of about 0.20 in for "most applications" when mounted on grade (see design graph on preceding page). If the engine is to be supported by four mounts (one at each corner), a mount with a static deflection of 0.20 in for a load of 500/4 = 125 lb will be required. Therefore, use a rubber mount which has a durometer of 30 (see intersection of dashed lines on graph below).

Install mounts so the load will be evenly distributed to the mounts, and avoid installing load bolts which are tightened to the foundation—these rigid connections eliminate the isolation effectiveness of the mounts.

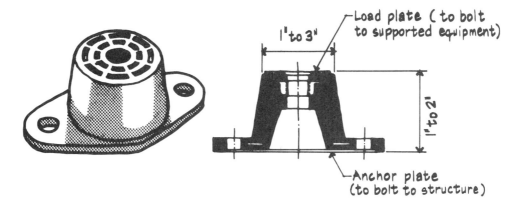

**Molded Rubber Mount Details**

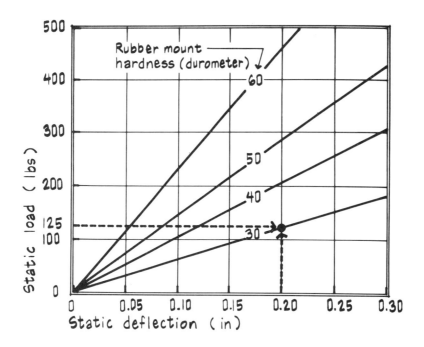

**Reference**

L. H. Bell, *Industrial Noise Control,* Marcel Dekker, *New York, 1982, p. 359.*

The preferred vibration isolation (i.e., type of isolator, static deflection of isolator, mounting support of equipment) for mechanical equipment depends on several factors. The major ones are the operating characteristics of the equipment, the location of the equipment (e.g., on-grade or on upper floors above sensitive areas), and the floor span of the structural system. Longer floor spans generally require vibration isolators with larger deflections. The sections below present basic guidelines for vibration isolation for a variety of mechanical equipment that designers may encounter in comfort systems for buildings.

### Fans

Large centrifugal fans can be a source of considerable noise and low-frequency vibration. For example, for a given fan-operating efficiency, a doubling of static pressure increases noise by 6 dB and a doubling of airflow volume increases noise by 3 dB.

To avoid misalignment, which can wear out fan belts and bearings, large fans and their motors should be mounted on a common rigid steel base which in turn should be supported by widely separated, unhoused (or open) spring isolators. The bases should have their longer dimension oriented in the direction of the airflow. For sensitive locations, install fans on an inertia block mounted on open-coil steel springs. An *inertia block* is a concrete slab base two to three times the weight of the fan assembly. It provides rigid support, maintains proper alignment between connected components of the vibrating equipment, reduces start-up motion, and evens out the load on the springs. The open-coil steel springs, sized for horizontal stability, do not bind or short-circuit like metal-housed springs. In completed installations, check to assure that springs are not totally seated and neoprene pads not underloaded. For many fan assemblies with effective soft supports, you actually should be able to rock the rigid base (see page 292 for additional isolation details).

Both supply and return air ducts should contain flexible canvas, rubber, or loaded vinyl connections ( > 3-in separation) to break the vibration path and permit start-up motion. For sensitive locations, air ducts should be resiliently supported as shown below. In addition, all pipe and conduit connections to the fan assembly should be flexible or suspended by isolation hangers.

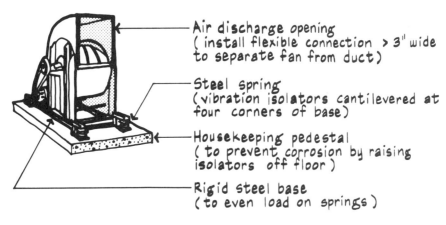

Air discharge opening
( install flexible connection > 3" wide
to separate fan from duct)

Steel spring
(vibration isolators cantilevered at
four corners of base)

Housekeeping pedestal
( to prevent corrosion by raising
isolators off floor )

Rigid steel base
(to even load on springs )

**Centrifugal Fan**

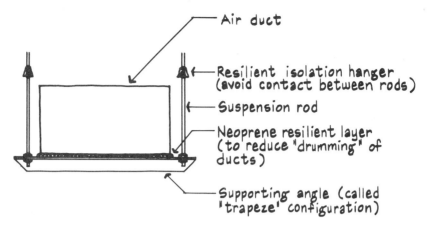

— Air duct

— Resilient isolation hanger (avoid contact between rods)

— Suspension rod

— Neoprene resilient layer (to reduce "drumming" of ducts)

— Supporting angle (called "trapeze" configuration)

**Resiliently Supported Air Duct**

## Refrigeration Compressors

Large, low-speed reciprocating compressors should be isolated by springs and inertia blocks to reduce the amplitude of the vibrations. High-speed centrifugal compressors require less isolation. They may require isolation by springs but often can be isolated properly with several layers of ribbed neoprene.

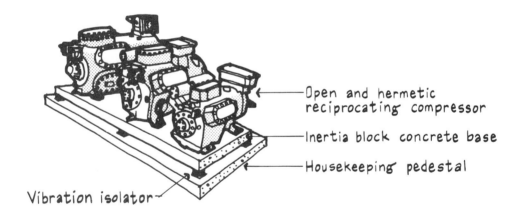

— Open and hermetic reciprocating compressor

— Inertia block concrete base

— Housekeeping pedestal

Vibration isolator

**Compressors**

**Note:** The inertia block should weigh more than twice as much as the vibrating equipment and associated pipes, ducts, and conduit when used to support fans (> 60 hp); reciprocating pumps, compressors, and engines; or centrifugal pumps and compressors (> 3 hp).

## Boilers

The combustion air blower usually is the primary source of noise and low-frequency vibration from boilers. Most airborne noise is radiated from the front face of the unit and from the air and fuel supply paths (i.e., combustion rumble). Install a flexible connection in the exhaust breeching (smoke vent) between boiler and exhaust stack. For boilers on upper floors near critical areas, use a steel mounting frame which in turn is supported by neoprene-in-shear mounts or steel springs. Gas and electrical connections should have long, "floppy" sections of braided flexible tubing and flexible armored electrical conduit.

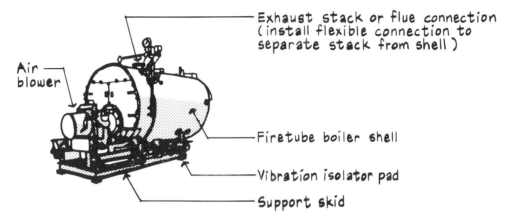

**Forced-Draft Boiler**

## Cooling Towers

Cooling tower vibration involves low-frequency vibration of the relatively slow-turning propeller-type fans as well as high-frequency impact noise from falling water. Ideally the motor, drive shaft, gear reducer, and propeller should be rigidly supported, with this support element in turn resiliently isolated from the tower. However, the more common noise control technique for roof-mounted cooling towers is to support the entire cooling tower by large-deflection steel springs and ribbed neoprene mounts.

To prevent airborne noise problems, locate ground-level cooling towers a considerable distance from buildings. Mufflers can be used to control airborne noise from cooling towers if the muffler attachments are carefully sized so that additional pressure drops will be low.

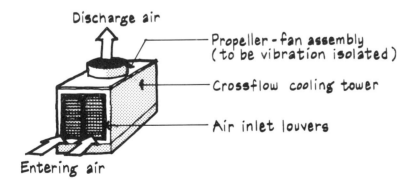

**Induced-Draft Cooling Tower**

### Transformers

In or near buildings, where structure-borne sound could be objectionable, dry-type transformers should be isolated by several layers of waffle-shaped or ribbed neoprene (40 to 50 durometer), precompressed glass fiber, or steel springs. All electrical connections should be flexible braided cable, and conduit should have a full 360° loop or manufactured flexible joints. Partial or demountable enclosures, lined with sound-absorbing materials, also can be used to help isolate annoying humming noises.

For indoor locations, use volume resonators to absorb low-frequency sound energy (about 125 Hz). Avoid upper-floor locations for dry-type transformers. These locations do not provide the rigid support that can be achieved on grade or at basement locations. To prevent noise buildup by standing waves, install the transformer so its sides are not parallel to the walls of small equipment rooms (slope >10°). Standing waves (normally heard as "booming" sound) are due to the superposition, or buildup, of low-frequency sound waves reflected between parallel wall surfaces.

For a summary of isolation techniques, see I. L. Vér et al., "Barrier-Enclosure: An Effective Way to Control the Noise Emission of Power Transformers," *Proceedings of the 1981 National Conference on Noise Control Engineering*, Noise Control Foundation, Poughkeepsie, N.Y., 1981, pp. 65-68.

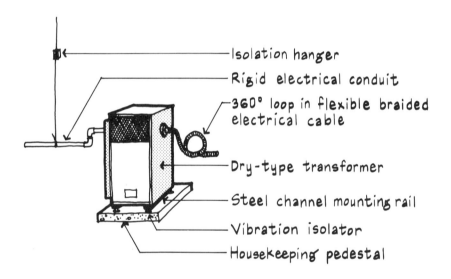

**Transformer**

### References

*ASHRAE Handbook* (*1987 HVAC Systems and Applications Volume*, Chapter 52, "Sound and Vibration Control") published periodically by the American Society of Heating, Refrigerating and Air-Conditioning Engineers, Inc. (ASHRAE), 1791 Tullie Circle, N.E., Atlanta, GA 30329.

M. D. Egan, *Concepts in Thermal Comfort*, Prentice-Hall, Englewood Cliffs, N.J., 1975.

R. E. Fischer, "Some Particular Problems of Noise Control," *Architectural Record*, September 1968.

J. B. Graham, "How to Estimate Fan Noise," *Sound and Vibration*, May 1972, pp. 24-27.

R. M. Hoover and R. H. Keith, "Mechanical Equipment Noise Control Problems in Buildings," *Proceedings of the 1980 International Conference on Noise Control Engineering*, vol. II, Noise Control Foundation, Poughkeepsie, N.Y., 1980, pp. 779-782.

R. S. Jones, *Noise and Vibration Control in Buildings*, McGraw-Hill, New York, 1984.

J. B. Moreland, "Electrical Equipment" in C. M. Harris (ed.), *Handbook of Noise Control*, McGraw-Hill, New York, 1979, pp. 25.1-25.10.

## CHARACTERISTICS OF DUCT SYSTEM NOISE

The frequency characteristics of noise from air-distribution systems are described by the graph below. Airflow noise due to *turbulence* usually occurs at mid-frequencies from 250 to 2000 Hz. Fan noise (rumble) occurs at low frequencies (< 250 Hz), and air outlet noise (hiss) occurs at high frequencies (>1000 Hz). Because fan noise increases with static pressure, air-distribution systems should be designed to have minimum resistance to airflow. Low-frequency rumble (< 63 Hz) also can be caused by air turbulence that buffets duct walls. Example equipment noise levels in dB at octave-band center frequencies from 63 to 8000 Hz are given at the end of this chapter.

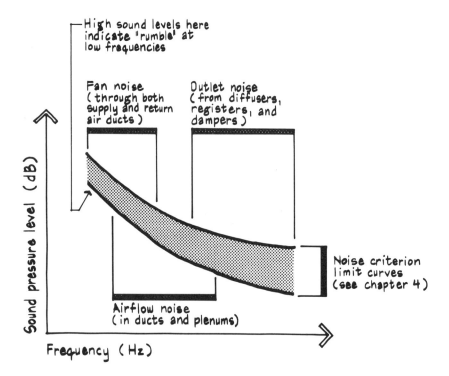

**Note:** Terminal boxes in air duct systems and fluorescent ballasts produce noise levels in the range of 125 to 1000 Hz. Noise from lighting ballasts can be amplified by the metal surfaces of luminaires and other surfaces free to vibrate with the ballasts. Consider remote mounting of ballasts for critical areas where low levels of sound are essential.

Because sound travels in ducts independently of airflow direction, the isolation of noise transmitted by mechanical air ducts (called *duct-borne noise*) must be carefully evaluated in both the supply and return air systems. Sound-attenuating mufflers and linings, sized to satisfy the requirements of the least critical spaces, can be used in the main ducts, with separate mufflers used in the branch ducts to the more critical spaces (e.g., hearing testing, music practice rooms). In buildings where critical spaces are numerous, large mufflers and linings in the main ducts can be sized to satisfy these critical demands, with the less critical spaces being overdesigned.

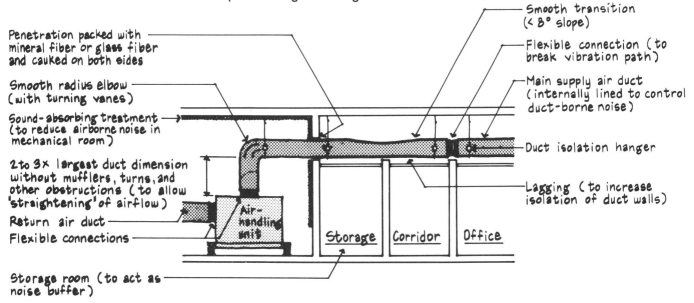

### Checklist for Duct-Borne Noise Control

1. Provide smooth duct turns and transitions (complicated duct configurations should be avoided).

2. Sound is attenuated by:
   - ☐ Distance (low-frequency duct-borne sound is reduced by transmission through rectangular duct walls)
   - ☐ Internal glass-fiber linings (≥ 1 in thick) and sound-attenuating mufflers (to reduce sound energy by absorption)
   - ☐ Turns, branches and other duct divisions, lined mixing boxes, and lined plenums (absorptive linings are much more effective at turns than in equal lengths of straight duct)
   - ☐ End reflection at openings into rooms (small openings do not efficiently radiate low-frequency sound energy)

3. Avoid high air velocities (large duct cross sections permit lower velocities for equal airflow volume).

4. Locate dampers away from air outlets (so noise generated can be attenuated before it reaches rooms).

5. Use round ducts, or rectangular ducts with low *aspect ratios* (i.e., ratio of duct depth to width), which are less rumble-prone.

6. Use several smaller air outlets rather than a few large ones.

**Note:** Refer to the latest edition of *ASHRAE Handbook (Systems Volume)* chapter on "Sound and Vibration Control" for duct-borne noise isolation computational procedures.

Fans produce less noise when the inlet air stream (e.g., ducted return air) is smooth and uniform, *not* turbulent. Consequently, in-duct obstructions and turns should not occur close to fans. At high air velocities, any abrupt change in direction (*dog-legged turn*) or cross section (*transition*) causes airflow to separate from the duct walls resulting in turbulence. This can occur over a distance of more than 5 times the duct diameter (equivalent diameter for a rectangular duct is $\sqrt{1.3A}$, where $A$ is open area of duct). Shown below are example air duct elements which can produce turbulence and noise; control measures are at the right.

## Turns

Turns should be smooth with fans and fittings located sufficient distances away so disturbed flow can dissipate. Lining turns (or elbows) with glass fiber can reduce noise. For example, a lined 90° elbow (small inside duct dimension < 36 in) can provide attenuation of 3 to 10 dB from 250 to 8000 Hz, if the lining extends 10 ft on both sides of elbow.

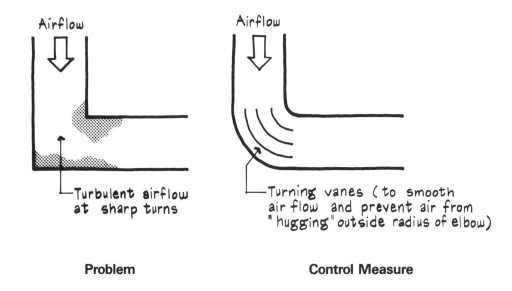

**Problem**  **Control Measure**

**Note:** Perforated, double-radius turning vanes that have a sound-absorbing core to reduce airflow noise at elbows and tees are commercially available.

## Transitions

Changes in duct sizes should be gradually tapered ($< 8°$) to reduce turbulence and noise.

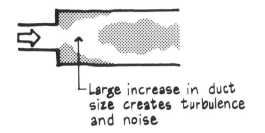

Large increase in duct size creates turbulence and noise

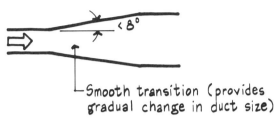

Smooth transition (provides gradual change in duct size)

**Problem**                              **Control Measure**

## Takeoffs

Branch takeoffs should be curved or chamfered because abrupt takeoffs can generate considerable noise.

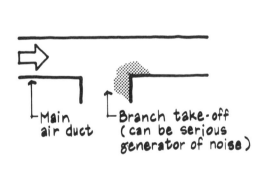

Main air duct

Branch take-off (can be serious generator of noise)

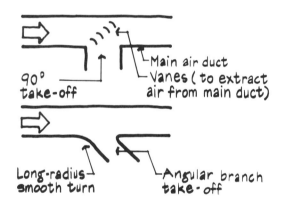

90° take-off

Main air duct

Vanes (to extract air from main duct)

Long-radius smooth turn

Angular branch take-off

**Problem**                              **Control Measures**

### Reference

C. E. Ebbing et al., "Control of Low Frequency Duct-Generated Noise in Building Air Distribution Systems," *ASHRAE Transactions*, vol. 84, part 2, 1978.

# FAN ROOM TREATMENT

Locate mechanical rooms on or below grade, far away from sensitive areas. Size mechanical rooms so they will have sufficient floor space and vertical clearance for smooth operation, inspection, and maintenance of all equipment. Do *not* place fans close to walls where sound energy can build up in the narrow space between fan and wall. Additionally, control sound buildup by treating ceiling and walls with thick, sound-absorbing materials. Often glass fiberboard or mineral fiberboard without a factory-applied finish can be used.

*Buffer zones*, such as nonsensitive corridors, storage rooms, and the like, can be used to reduce airborne noise transmission from mechanical rooms. Enclosing constructions should normally consist of heavy walls (e.g., masonry or concrete) and heavy floor-ceilings. When fan rooms are used as return air plenums, mufflers or lined elbows may be needed to reduce noise at all openings into the fan room.

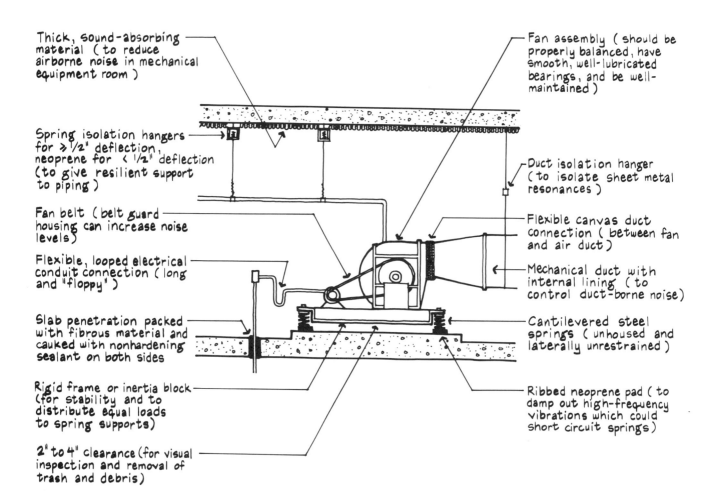

Thick, sound-absorbing material (to reduce airborne noise in mechanical equipment room)

Fan assembly (should be properly balanced, have smooth, well-lubricated bearings, and be well-maintained)

Spring isolation hangers for ≥ 1/2" deflection, neoprene for < 1/2" deflection (to give resilient support to piping)

Duct isolation hanger (to isolate sheet metal resonances)

Fan belt (belt guard housing can increase noise levels)

Flexible canvas duct connection (between fan and air duct)

Flexible, looped electrical conduit connection (long and "floppy")

Mechanical duct with internal lining (to control duct-borne noise)

Slab penetration packed with fibrous material and caulked with nonhardening sealant on both sides

Cantilevered steel springs (unhoused and laterally unrestrained)

Rigid frame or inertia block (for stability and to distribute equal loads to spring supports)

Ribbed neoprene pad (to damp out high-frequency vibrations which could short circuit springs)

2" to 4" clearance (for visual inspection and removal of trash and debris)

# CROSS TALK

*Cross talk* is unwanted sound which is transmitted from one room to another through short, common air ducts. The sound transmisson loss through common ducts should exceed, by more than 5 dB, the transmission loss of the common wall between rooms. A cross talk–prone situation is shown below.

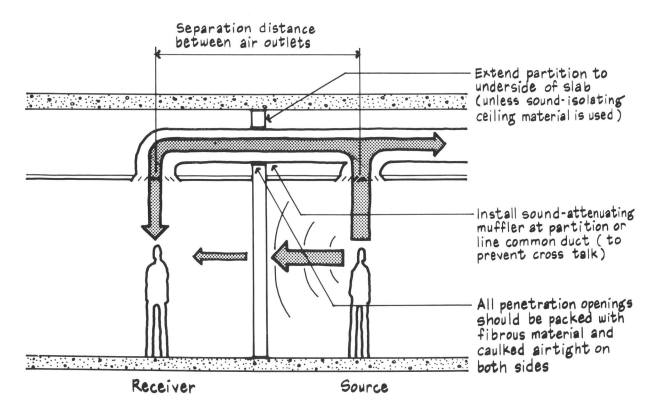

### Checklist for Cross-Talk Control

1. Provide long common ducts between room air outlets or inlets.
2. Use layouts which have turns in branch ducts or dog-legged paths between rooms.
3. Line inside surfaces of common ducts with glass fiber (e.g., on all four sides of rectangular ducts).
4. Install prefabricated, sound-attenuating mufflers in common ducts.

**Note:** Ductwork should not be rigidly connected to partitions because they may transmit mechanical system vibrations. Avoid lightweight wall and ceiling constructions where sound isolation is critical (see Chap. 4).

## AIR DUCT LAYOUT EXAMPLES

Examples of air duct layouts with reduced potential for cross talk and duct-generated noise are shown below.

### Cross Talk

To prevent cross talk between adjacent sensitive spaces (e.g., radio/TV studios, music practice rooms), use separate supply and return air branch ducts that are internally lined with fibrous insulation and/or have sound-attenuating mufflers installed in the common path. The improved duct layout shown below has far longer distances of lined duct between adjacent air outlets (or inlets). In addition, cross talk will be further reduced by two lined 90° elbows and two tee fittings within the common path through the supply air ducts serving adjacent rooms. The poor duct layout illustrates a cross talk—prone situation where straight duct runs occur above sensitive spaces. Layouts with short direct connections between rooms should be avoided.

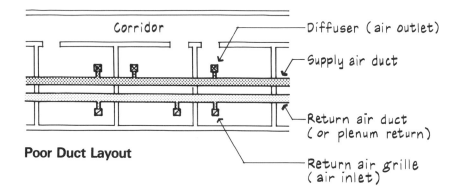

**Poor Duct Layout**

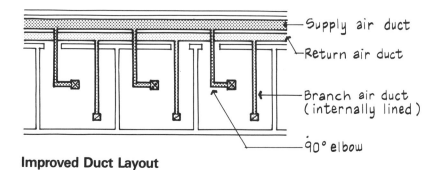

**Improved Duct Layout**

### Duct-Generated Noise

The example shown below of a supply air branch duct layout without dampers will produce considerably less noise because the volume dampers have been removed and two splitter dampers relocated farther away from the air outlets. Air turbulence also will be reduced because there are two less 90° elbows and one less transition fitting.

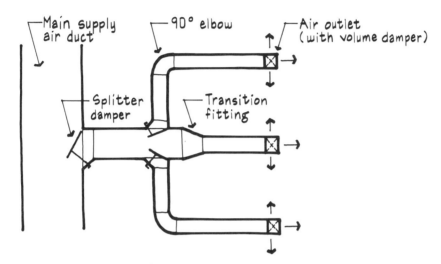

**Branch Ducts with Dampers**

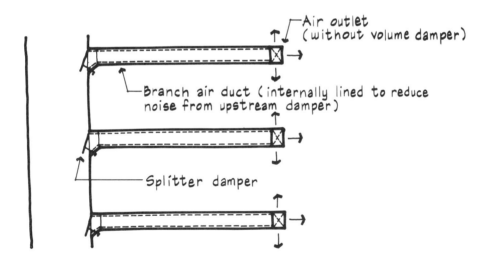

**Branch Ducts without Dampers**

### Reference

G. C. Murphy, "Practical Aspects of Ductwork Design," *ASHRAE Journal*, October 1976.

Glass-fiber *linings* are used in supply and return air ducts to prevent the propagation of noise inside the ducts and cross talk between rooms. The curves below show the sound attenuation in decibels *per foot* of duct length for internal glass-fiber linings (on all four sides of duct). The 1- and 2-in-thick lining data represent attenuation for a 16-in deep mechanical duct. Due to flanking along duct walls, maximum total attenuation (that is, dB/ft times ft of duct) is usually less than 40 dB. Actual data from independent testing laboratories should be used whenever it is available. The attenuation shown on the graph below would be less for larger ducts with linings of identical thickness.

The higher the ratio of lined-duct perimeter $[2(W + D)]$ to cross-sectional open area $(W \times D)$, the higher the attenuation of noise within the duct. Be careful because ducts with high attentuation for duct-borne noise propagation (e.g., foil-backed glass fiberboard) may provide little resistance to sound transmission through their walls. Fibrous duct linings should be coated with binders to hold surface fibers together.

As also shown on the graph, metal ducts without linings provide little attenuation with distance. However, glass-fiber wrappings used for thermal insulation can provide some damping of duct surface radiation, although attenuation with distance will still be far below that of internally lined ducts.

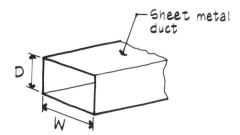

**Unlined Duct**

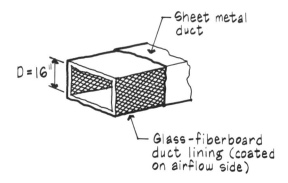

**Lined Duct**

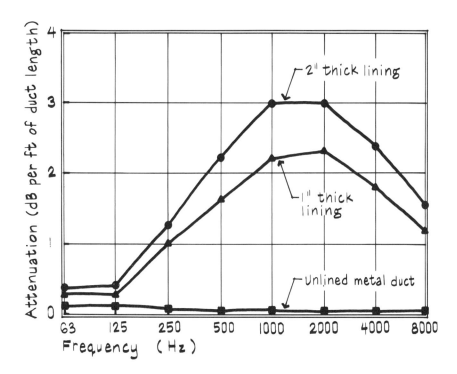

**Note:** Because ducts are usually made of thin sheet metal or lightweight, foil-backed glass fiberboard, mechanical system sound energy can easily pass through the duct wall (called *breakout*) and exterior noise can penetrate the duct wall (called *break-in*, or *pickup*). An outer cover of gypsum board or plywood may be needed to improve isolation where ducts are located above sensitive areas or where they pass through noisy spaces before reaching quiet spaces.

Sound attenuators—also called *mufflers, silencers,* or *sound traps*—are prefabricated devices designed to provide much greater sound attenuation over a wider frequency range than would be provided by an equal length of lined duct. They provide greater attenuation because the distance between absorptive layers is much smaller than in a lined duct. Mufflers are normally available in both rectangular and circular cross-sectional shapes with absorptive baffles (or splitters) as shown below.

All-metal mufflers and mufflers with "bagged" linings (i.e., polyethylene-encased fibrous material) can be used in health care and food industry occupancies where exposed fibrous linings could support organic growth of germs. The all-metal mufflers are constructed of perforated baffles with air cavities behind to provide resonant absorption (cf., *Journal of the Acoustical Society of America*, April 1981, p. 1216). The air cavities, which can be steam cleaned or vacuumed, do not contain fibrous materials to collect dirt and bacteria.

Because attenuation performance varies widely with airflow conditions, always refer to manufacturer's test data for anticipated attenuation performance at the airflow volume and pressure drop design conditions. Example sound-attenuation data for 3-ft-long rectangular mufflers with parallel baffles and staggered baffles are shown below.

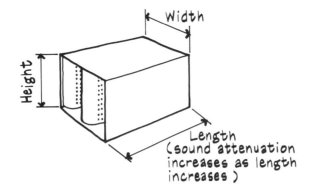

Width

Height

Length (sound attenuation increases as length increases)

**Rectangular Muffler**

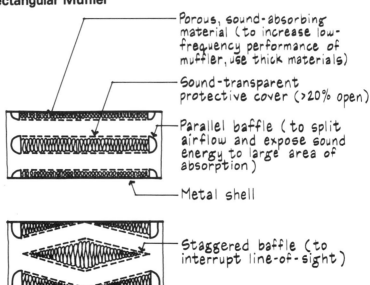

Porous, sound-absorbing material (to increase low-frequency performance of muffler, use thick materials)

Sound-transparent protective cover (>20% open)

Parallel baffle (to split airflow and expose sound energy to large area of absorption)

Metal shell

Staggered baffle (to interrupt line-of-sight)

**Section Views**

| Sound Attenuation (dB) | | | | | |
|---|---|---|---|---|---|
| 125 Hz | 250 Hz | 500 Hz | 1000 Hz | 2000 Hz | 4000 Hz |
| Parallel baffles | 15 | 20 | 25 | 30 | 30 | 35 |
| Staggered baffles | 15 | 20 | 30 | 45 | 45 | 50 |

Refer to ASTM E 477 test data for the noise generated by the muffler itself (called *self-noise*). Airflow through mufflers produces aerodynamic sound which may be unacceptable in applications where low background noise levels are essential. Therefore, when controlling fan noise, it is best to locate mufflers near or in the walls of mechanical equipment rooms, or above adjacent non-sensitive spaces (e.g., corridors, storage rooms). Be sure also to provide tapered transitions so that air ducts gradually change shape from duct to muffler. Do *not* locate mufflers too close to intake or discharge of fans or near elbows.

### References

G. J. Sanders, "Silencers: Their Design and Application," *Sound and Vibration*, February 1968.

"Testing Duct Liner Materials and Prefabricated Silencers for Acoustical and Airflow Performance," ASTM E 477.

I. L. Vér, "Prediction Scheme for the Self-Generated Noise of Silencers," *Proceedings of the 1972 National Conference on Noise Control Engineering*, Institute of Noise Control Engineering, Poughkeepsie, N.Y., 1972, pp. 294-298.

## LINED PLENUMS

Sound absorption by lined *plenums*, such as fan discharges, can provide considerable attenuation. For effective low-frequency absorption, use thick sound-absorbing materials. To isolate high frequencies, divide the plenum into small subsections so that the line of sight between duct openings is blocked. The surface area of a lined plenum should be at least 10 times greater than the inlet area. Attenuation performance increases as the ratio of cross-sectional area of plenum to cross-sectional area of inlet (or outlet) duct increases. Lined plenums can provide attenuation of more than 10 dB at low frequencies.

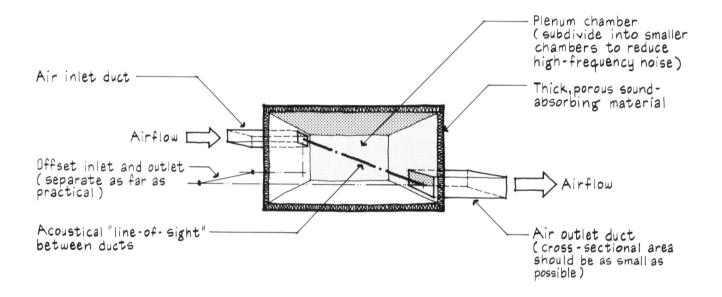

**Note:** Corridors with sound-absorbing surfaces can reduce room-to-room noise transmission by acting as lined plenums. Stagger doors on opposite sides of double-loaded corridors so openings do not allow direct cross talk between rooms.

### Reference

R. J. Wells, "Acoustical Plenum Chambers," *Noise Control*, July 1958.

# RECOMMENDED AIR VELOCITIES AT REGISTERS AND GRILLES

The table below lists supply and return air velocities in feet per minute (fpm) for airflow through unobstructed, or "free," openings and corresponding noise criteria (see Chap. 4). In auditoriums, theaters, and other critical listening spaces, the air velocities should be low so that the *signal-to-noise ratios* will be high. The values in the table apply to air ducts with internal glass-fiber linings and to registers and grilles with at least 1/2-in-wide slot openings. The values in the table should be used as rough guidelines for design purposes only when specific data on registers and grilles are unavailable for the air distribution layout, airflow volumes, and pressure drop conditions being evaluated.

| Noise Criteria | Air Velocity at Supply Register (fpm) | Air Velocity at Return Grille (fpm) |
|---|---|---|
| NC-15 to NC-20 | 250 to 300 | 300 to 360 |
| NC-20 to NC-25 | 300 to 350 | 360 to 420 |
| NC-25 to NC-30 | 350 to 425 | 420 to 510 |
| NC-30 to NC-35 | 425 to 500 | 510 to 600 |
| NC-35 to NC-40 | 500 to 575 | 600 to 690 |
| NC-40 to NC-45 | 575 to 650 | 690 to 780 |

Shown below are examples of poor and preferred air outlet conditions for "hard" and flexible ducts.

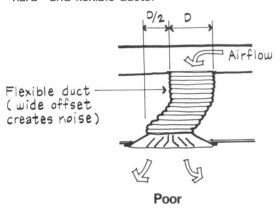

**Poor**

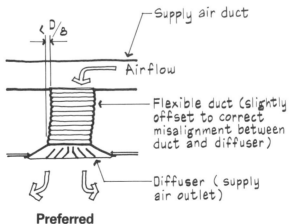

**Preferred**

Removing the dampers and grille from the hard branch duct, as shown below in the preferred example, can reduce airflow noise from turbulence by more than 10 dB at mid-frequencies and also can increase the attenuation of low-frequency sound energy due to duct end reflection. When a small duct opens into the large volume of a room, low-frequency duct-borne sound energy is reflected back into the "end" of the duct (called *end reflection*). To achieve significant attenuation of low-frequency duct-borne sound energy ( < 250 Hz) by end reflection: (1) use straight, small branch ducts greater than 3 times duct diameter **D** long; (2) suspend "deflector" (or plaque) at least 1 duct diameter beneath duct; and (3) do *not* use dampers, diffusers, or grilles.

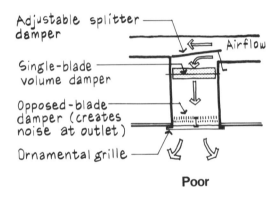

Adjustable splitter damper

Single-blade volume damper

Opposed-blade damper (creates noise at outlet)

Ornamental grille

Airflow

**Poor**

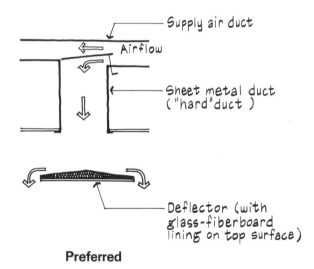

Supply air duct

Airflow

Sheet metal duct ("hard" duct)

Deflector (with glass-fiberboard lining on top surface)

**Preferred**

**Note:** Air velocities for the initial 10 ft of duct extending from supply registers or return grilles should *not* exceed the values given in the table by more than 20 percent.

**Reference**

D. L. Klepper, W. J. Cavanaugh, and L. G. Marshall, "Noise Control in Music Teaching Facilities," *Noise Control Engineering Journal*, September-October 1980, p. 75.

# WATER-PIPING SYSTEM NOISE CONTROL

### Pipe Isolation

Water pipes should be located away from acoustically sensitive areas such as auditoriums, theaters, conference rooms, and private offices. When this is not possible, the least number of turns, valves, and fittings should be used because these components can create turbulence and noise. Piping runs should be resiliently isolated by ceiling hangers or floor-mounted supports (e.g., neoprene, steel springs, or glass-fiber or neoprene-lined metal clamps, as shown below) to prevent transmission of noise and vibration into the building structure.

For domestic water-piping systems, use neoprene gaskets or "hubless" pipe (straight ends) joined by neoprene sleeves. These resilient connections can prevent direct metal-to-metal contact between sections of pipe.

Butyl rubber expansion joints can be used to allow pipes to expand and contract and to reduce the noise and vibrations transmitted along the pipe walls. The preferred location for the flexible pipe connection is parallel to the axis of the equipment rotating shaft. For high-pressure or high-temperature applications, use stainless steel braided hoses although they are not as effective isolators as flexible neoprene connections.

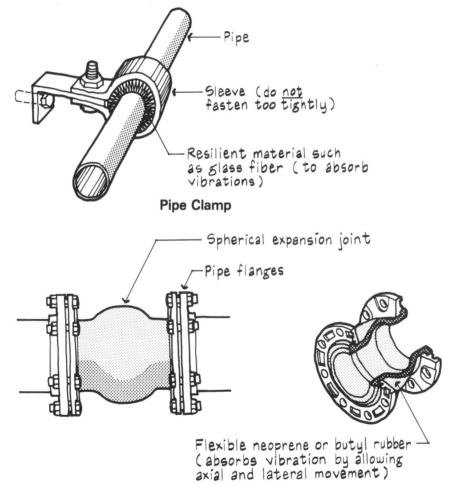

Pipe

Sleeve (do **not** fasten too **tightly**)

Resilient material such as glass fiber (to absorb vibrations)

**Pipe Clamp**

Spherical expansion joint

Pipe flanges

Flexible neoprene or butyl rubber (absorbs vibration by allowing axial and lateral movement)

**Pipe Expansion Joint**

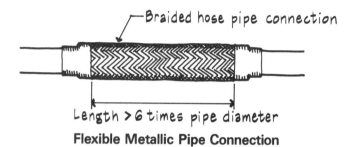

**Flexible Metallic Pipe Connection**

When piping systems penetrate the building structure, openings should be oversized for the full depth of the opening so that the pipe can be supported on both sides of the opening without contact. Pipe perimeter should be packed with fibrous materials and caulked airtight on both sides. At locations with especially large openings to be sealed, bags filled with mineral fiber can be used as packing. When commercially available pipe isolation sleeves are used in double-wall constructions, be sure each layer has an independent sleeve so that the two layers will not be tied together. Avoid solid anchorage of long vertical pipe risers to floor slabs. Use steel clamps that are in turn supported by neoprene pads or steel springs, as shown below. Noise from water flow can often be reduced by using pipes with thicker walls.

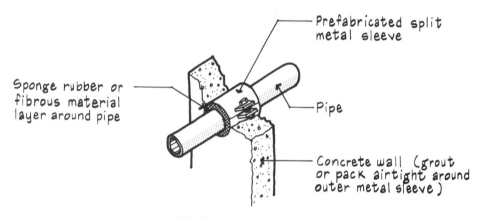

**Wall Penetration**

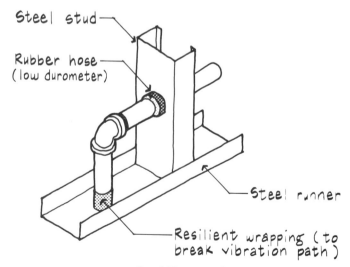

**Stud Penetration**

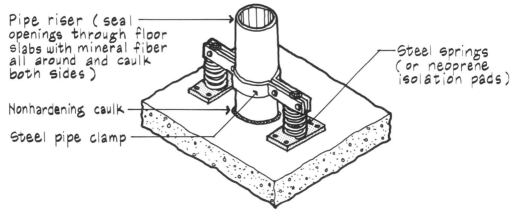

**Floor Penetration**

Pipe riser (seal openings through floor slabs with mineral fiber all around and caulk both sides)

Steel springs (or neoprene isolation pads)

Nonhardening caulk

Steel pipe clamp

## Water Flow Velocities

To prevent water flow noise generated by turbulence, velocities should be controlled by using large pipe sizes and large radius elbows, or upstream pressure-reducing devices. The table on page 307 gives the recommended maximum water flow velocities for domestic water systems.

## Water Hammer

Noise in piping systems can occur when a rapidly closed valve abruptly stops a moving column of water (e.g., quickly closing a sink faucet). The resulting forward and backward water surge within the piping produces pounding noises called *water hammer*. Water hammer noise can be prevented by using spring-operated valves to slowly close valve stems. In addition, the installation of gas-filled stainless steel bellows units can effectively absorb the surge of water at abrupt pipe turns. Compressed air chambers or accumulators also mitigate the effects of water hammer in long pipe runs.

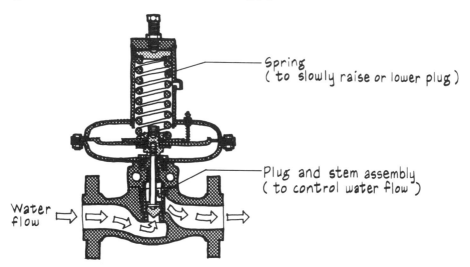

Spring (to slowly raise or lower plug)

Plug and stem assembly (to control water flow)

Water flow

**Spring-Operated Valve**

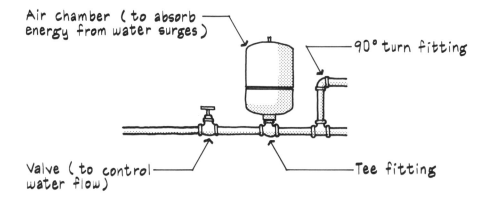

Air chamber (to absorb energy from water surges)

90° turn fitting

Valve (to control water flow)

Tee fitting

**Air Chamber**

**Note:** In areas subject to earthquakes, piping for fire suppression systems should be protected by supports at pipe joints, approved flexible connections, sway bracing, and the like.

**References**

L. H. Bell, *Fundamentals of Industrial Noise Control*, Harmony Publications, Trumbull, Conn., 1973.

M. Rettinger, *Acoustic Design and Noise Control*, Chemical Publishing Co., New York, 1973, pp. 339-345.

# SUGGESTED WATER FLOW VELOCITIES

The table below gives maximum water flow velocities in feet per second (ft/s) that should not be exceeded in water-piping systems adjacent to acoustically sensitive spaces. To avoid excessive flow velocity, use pipes with large inside diameters.

| Pipe Inside Diameter (in) | Maximum Flow Velocity (ft/s) |
|---|---|
| 1 | 3 |
| 2 | 4 |
| 3 | 6 |
| 4 | 7 |
| 6 | 8 |
| 8 and larger | 10 |

To meet stringent acoustical criteria, pipes carrying water at high flow velocities can be wrapped with a layer of glass fiber or mineral fiber inside a cover of sheet lead, dense vinyl, or sheet metal. This kind of wrapping is called *pipe lagging* (see page 310).

## Example

A 4-in riser in a shaft near an acoustically sensitive area has a water flow volume $Q$ of 250 gallons per minute (gpm). What will be the flow velocity $v$ in ft/s? Is this flow velocity satisfactory?

$$v = 0.4 \frac{Q}{d^2} = 0.4 \frac{250}{(4)^2} = \boxed{6.25 \text{ ft/s}}$$

The water flow velocity is less than 7 ft/s, so water flow noise control requirements are satisfied according to the table.

# VIBRATION ISOLATION OF PUMPS

An example vibration-isolated water pump is shown below. The pump motor assembly ( > 5 hp) is supported by a concrete inertia block sized to support more than 2 times the fluid-filled pump weight plus all filled piping to the first isolation hanger. The length and width of the inertia block should be 30 percent greater than the length and width of the supported equipment.

Isolation hangers should be used to resiliently support piping for a distance of at least 150 times the pipe diameter (or preferably the complete length of the pipeline). Butyl rubber or nylon-reinforced neoprene expansion joints can reduce noise and vibration transmission along pipe walls and absorb pressure variations by bending like an automobile tire.

Pumps ( < 5 hp) often can be supported by metal frames instead of inertia blocks, if they can be located on grade where the edges of the concrete floor slab will be entirely separated from the building structure by a continuous joint filled with resilient material (e.g., polyethylene-wrapped glass fiberboard).

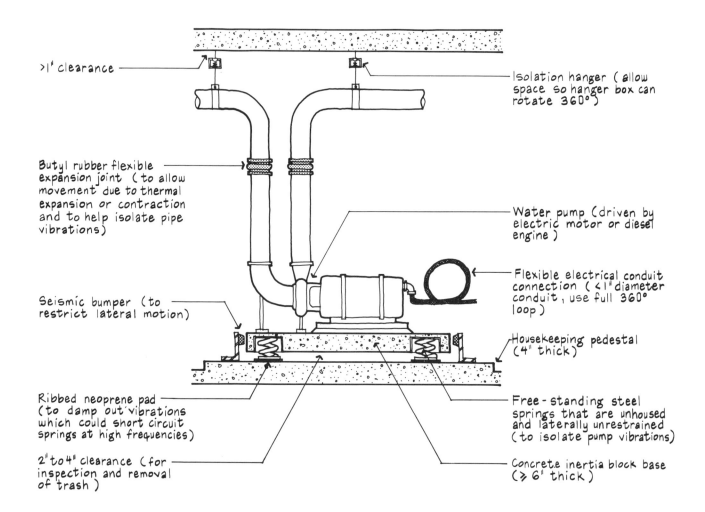

>1" clearance

Isolation hanger (allow space so hanger box can rotate 360°)

Butyl rubber flexible expansion joint (to allow movement due to thermal expansion or contraction and to help isolate pipe vibrations)

Water pump (driven by electric motor or diesel engine)

Flexible electrical conduit connection ( <1" diameter conduit, use full 360° loop)

Seismic bumper (to restrict lateral motion)

Housekeeping pedestal (4" thick)

Ribbed neoprene pad (to damp out vibrations which could short circuit springs at high frequencies)

Free-standing steel springs that are unhoused and laterally unrestrained (to isolate pump vibrations)

2" to 4" clearance (for inspection and removal of trash)

Concrete inertia block base ( ≥ 6" thick)

**Note:** Where piping systems are subject to earthquakes, piping damage due to building movement can be lessened by using flexible connections. *Snubbers*, or seismic bumpers (shown above), must allow sufficient free movement for normal operations.

## ISOLATION HANGERS

Vibration *isolation hangers* are used to support suspended pipes in equipment rooms, air ducts located below or near sensitive areas, and mechanical equipment. They are available with neoprene elements, steel springs, or a combination of the two in series as shown below. To prevent short-circuiting of vibration, hangers should be installed so that the hanger box can rotate a full 360° about the vertical axis of the hanger rods without contacting structural or other surfaces. The lower hole for the hanger rod should be oversized to permit the rod to swing within at least a 30° arc from the vertical without touching the hanger box or spring coils. Be sure also to avoid contact between upper and lower rods, and provide more than 1-in clearance between the top of the hanger box and the structure overhead to lessen the likelihood that the neoprene element will be overcompressed during installation.

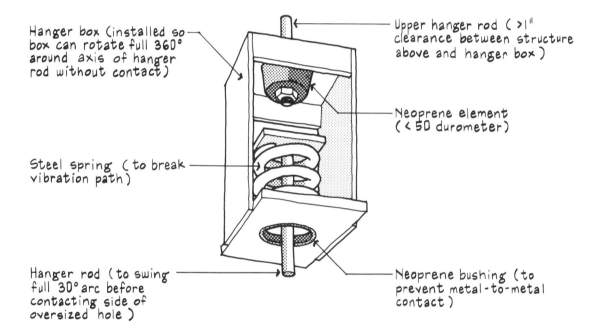

Hanger box (installed so box can rotate full 360° around axis of hanger rod without contact)

Upper hanger rod ( >1" clearance between structure above and hanger box )

Neoprene element ( < 50 durometer)

Steel spring ( to break vibration path)

Hanger rod ( to swing full 30° arc before contacting side of oversized hole )

Neoprene bushing (to prevent metal-to-metal contact )

# LAGGINGS

*Laggings* are enclosures, or wrappings, which are used to isolate noise transmitted through the walls of pipes and ducts. The lagging generally consists of a sound-absorbing layer (or blanket) wrapped on the outside by a heavy, airtight, sound-isolating membrane. The effectiveness of a lagging depends on the surface weight of the outside wrapping and the thickness and sound-absorbing efficiency of the blanket. Lightweight wrappings ( $< 1$ lb/ft$^2$) do not effectively reduce noise transmission below 500 Hz. Often reducing noise at the source will be more cost-effective than using extensive lagging treatment. For procedures on selecting laggings, see G. E. Johnson, "How to Select Effective Lagging Configurations," *Sound and Vibration*, April 1977.

## Pipe Lagging

Pipes carrying water at high velocities should be isolated from the building structure and wrapped with dense blanket materials (3 to 18 lb/ft$^3$) to isolate the water flow noise. Outer wrappings include heavy mastic, lead sheet, loaded- or leaded-vinyl, and composite metal jacket with core of laminated limp materials. An example pipe lagging is shown below. For most situations, a doubling of weight is needed to provide a significant increase in noise reduction (called *insertion loss*).

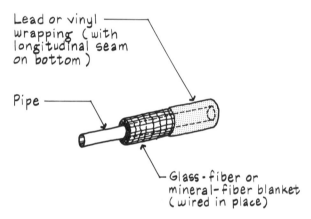

Lead or vinyl wrapping (with longitudinal seam on bottom)

Pipe

Glass-fiber or mineral-fiber blanket (wired in place)

**Pipe Lagging Details**

## Duct Lagging

Ducts in mechanical spaces and ducts which pass through noisy areas can be penetrated by the surrounding noise energy (called noise *break-in*). Enclosures of heavy-gauge sheet metal or gypsum board can be used to form a sound-isolating membrane around the ducts. As shown by the illustrations below, provide a wrapping of sound-absorbing material (e.g., glass fiber or mineral fiber) between the air duct and the sound-isolating membrane of the lagging. When duct width exceeds 36 in, support enclosures on underside with battens or other framing elements. To control the transmission of low-frequency noise ( $< 125$ Hz), use sound-isolating plenum or circular ducts instead of rectangular ducts. For example, at frequencies from 63 to 250 Hz, the transmission loss of sheet metal (without lagging) can be 30 dB or more greater for the stiffer circular ducts than for rectangular or flat oval ducts.

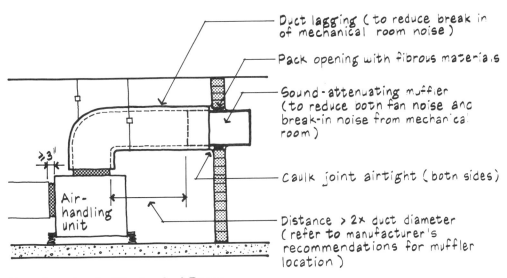

Duct lagging (to reduce break in of mechanical room noise)

Pack opening with fibrous materials

Sound-attenuating muffler (to reduce both fan noise and break-in noise from mechanical room)

Caulk joint airtight (both sides)

Distance > 2x duct diameter (refer to manufacturer's recommendations for muffler location)

≥3"

Air-handling unit

**Duct Lagging in Mechanical Room**

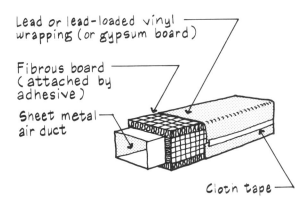

Lead or lead-loaded vinyl wrapping (or gypsum board)

Fibrous board (attached by adhesive)

Sheet metal air duct

Cloth tape

**Duct Lagging Details**

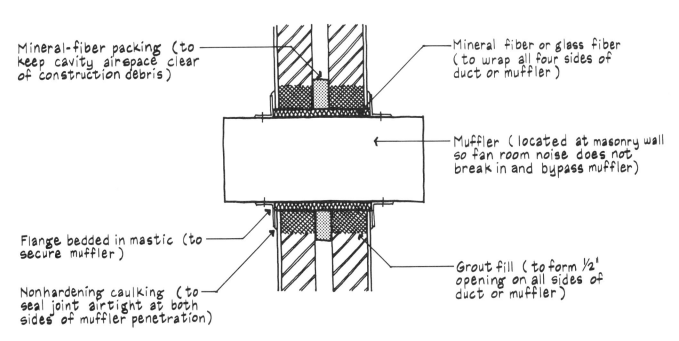

Mineral-fiber packing (to keep cavity airspace clear of construction debris)

Mineral fiber or glass fiber (to wrap all four sides of duct or muffler)

Muffler (located at masonry wall so fan room noise does not break in and bypass muffler)

Flange bedded in mastic (to secure muffler)

Nonhardening caulking (to seal joint airtight at both sides of muffler penetration)

Grout fill (to form ½" opening on all sides of duct or muffler)

**Muffler Installed at Wall of Mechanical Room**

## VIBRATION ANALYSIS GRAPH

The graph below gives typical industry standard bearing peak-to-peak *vibration displacement* in mils during normal operating conditions (1 mil is equal to 1/1000 of an inch). Much greater displacements will normally occur during start-up and shut-down operations.

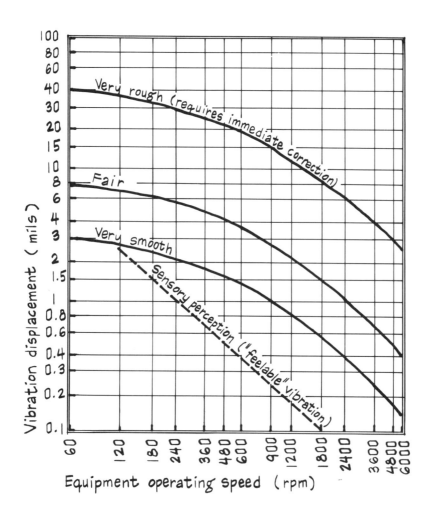

**Reference**

*ASHRAE Handbook (1987 HVAC Systems and Applications Volume)*, p. 52.28.

# WALL CONSTRUCTIONS FOR MECHANICAL EQUIPMENT ROOMS

Example concrete block wall constructions for mechanical spaces, in order of increasing sound isolation effectiveness, are shown below. The more massive a construction, the greater its resistance to airborne sound. Avoid lightweight hollow concrete block, gypsum board, and other constructions which have poor transmission loss performance at low frequencies.

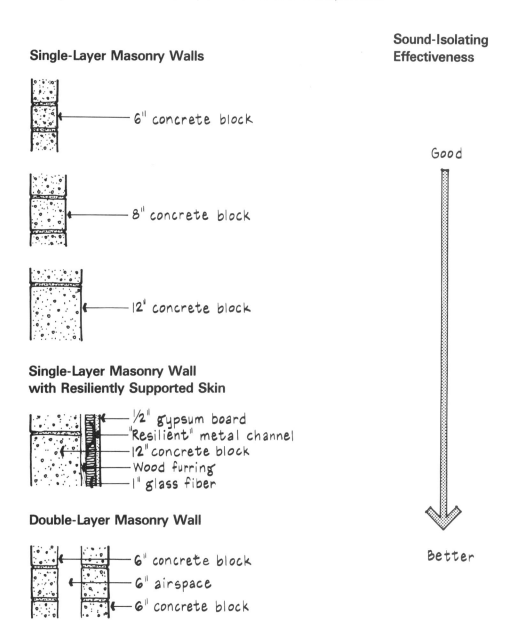

**Single-Layer Masonry Walls**

6" concrete block

8" concrete block

12" concrete block

**Single-Layer Masonry Wall
with Resiliently Supported Skin**

½" gypsum board
"Resilient" metal channel
12" concrete block
Wood furring
1" glass fiber

**Double-Layer Masonry Wall**

6" concrete block
6" airspace
6" concrete block

**Sound-Isolating Effectiveness**

Good

Better

**Note:** The heavyweight concrete block wall constructions shown above have mortar- or sand-filled cells. The installation of the mortar or sand should be frequently verified as construction progresses. Surface mount all mechanical and electrical services so the block wall will not be penetrated.

Shown below are example heavyweight constructions which can be used to contain airborne noise from mechanical equipment. Avoid metal decks with lightweight toppings because they will not provide sufficient transmission loss at low frequencies.

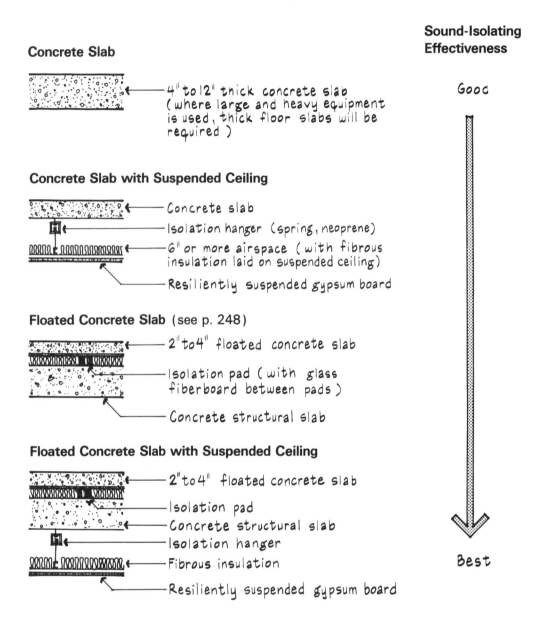

**Sound-Isolating Effectiveness**

**Concrete Slab**

4" to 12" thick concrete slab (where large and heavy equipment is used, thick floor slabs will be required)

Good

**Concrete Slab with Suspended Ceiling**

Concrete slab

Isolation hanger (spring, neoprene)

6" or more airspace (with fibrous insulation laid on suspended ceiling)

Resiliently suspended gypsum board

**Floated Concrete Slab** (see p. 248)

2" to 4" floated concrete slab

Isolation pad (with glass fiberboard between pads)

Concrete structural slab

**Floated Concrete Slab with Suspended Ceiling**

2" to 4" floated concrete slab

Isolation pad

Concrete structural slab

Isolation hanger

Fibrous insulation

Resiliently suspended gypsum board

Best

# MECHANICAL EQUIPMENT NOISE LEVEL DATA

The table below presents example octave-band sound pressure level data measured at 3 ft away from several types of mechanical equipment. In the absence of manufacturer's or field data, the values in the table may be used for preliminary design purposes if proper consideration is given to situations that may exceed these values. For example, peak values for especially large mechanical equipment can exceed the values in the table by more than 5 dB. Manufacturer's data should be used only if their test conditions are comparable to the actual installed conditions. Data from field measurements or laboratory tests conducted according to current ANSI, ASTM, or other recognized standards are always preferred and should be obtained for final design.

| Equipment | Sound Pressure Level (dB) | | | | | | | | |
|---|---|---|---|---|---|---|---|---|---|
| | 63 Hz | 125 Hz | 250 Hz | 500 Hz | 1000 Hz | 2000 Hz | 4000 Hz | 8000 Hz | dBA |
| Absorption machine | 91 | 86 | 86 | 86 | 83 | 80 | 77 | 72 | 89 |
| Axial fan | 98 | 99 | 99 | 98 | 97 | 95 | 91 | 87 | 102 |
| Boiler | 92 | 92 | 89 | 86 | 83 | 80 | 77 | 74 | 89 |
| Centrifugal fan | 86 | 95 | 89 | 90 | 87 | 82 | 76 | 77 | 92 |
| Chiller, centrifugal | 80 | 85 | 87 | 87 | 90 | 98 | 91 | 87 | 100 |
| Compressor, air | 86 | 84 | 86 | 87 | 86 | 84 | 80 | 75 | 91 |
| Condenser | 99 | 92 | 90 | 90 | 89 | 85 | 76 | 68 | 92 |
| Cooling tower | 102 | 102 | 97 | 94 | 90 | 88 | 84 | 79 | 97 |
| Fan coil unit | 57 | 55 | 53 | 50 | 48 | 42 | 38 | 32 | 53 |
| Induction unit | 57 | 58 | 56 | 54 | 45 | 40 | 35 | 33 | 54 |
| PTAC | 64 | 64 | 65 | 56 | 53 | 48 | 44 | 37 | 59 |
| Pump | 75 | 80 | 82 | 87 | 86 | 80 | 77 | 75 | 89 |
| Rooftop unit | 95 | 93 | 89 | 85 | 80 | 75 | 69 | 66 | 87 |
| Warm-air furnace | 65 | 65 | 59 | 53 | 48 | 45 | 39 | 30 | 57 |

## Reference

"Noise from Construction Equipment and Operations, Building Equipment, and Home Appliances," U.S. Environmental Protection Agency, NTID 300.1, Washington, December 1971.

# CHECKLIST FOR MECHANICAL SYSTEM NOISE CONTROL

## Mechanical Rooms and Equipment

1. Locate mechanical equipment rooms far away from sensitive rooms, use non-sensitive buffer zones between, and size equipment rooms to have sufficient space for operation, inspection, and maintenance of all equipment. When sufficient floor space and vertical clearance are provided, mechanical engineers can design air ducts and piping to have smooth turns and transitions so turbulence will be less likely to occur. Fans, chillers, and the like should not be located close to walls where sound energy can build up in the narrow space between. Noise transmission problems also can be prevented if vibration isolators, equipment bases, and all structural penetrations are accessible for routine inspection.

2. Specify the quietest equipment available based on octave-band data or size equipment to operate at low noise levels (e.g., fan coil units with low-medium-high motor speeds can be sized to operate on medium speed at the maximum thermal demand conditions).

3. Use heavyweight wall and floor-ceiling constructions with high transmission loss TL performance to enclose mechanical rooms. The mechanical rooms in large buildings can be a major source of noise, sometimes exceeding 100 dBA. In critical situations, where mechanical rooms cannot be located on grade and away from sensitive spaces, resilient isolators, floated floors, high TL-rated doors, and resiliently suspended ceilings underneath the structural floor all may be required.

4. Treat the walls and ceiling of mechanical rooms with generous amounts of thick, sound-absorbing materials to reduce the buildup of airborne sound.

5. Use soft, resilient materials (springs or pads) under the wearing surface of floors to isolate mechanical rooms from the building structure (called *floated floors*) or between the bases or supports of vibrating equipment and the structure (called *resilient isolators*) to minimize the transfer of vibrations into the structure.

6. Roof-mounted mechanical equipment subject to wind loading (e.g., cooling towers, packaged air-conditioning units) and all mechanical equipment subject to earthquake forces may require special vibration-isolation mounts. These well-anchored lateral and vertical restraints must be carefully selected and installed to avoid short-circuiting the vibration-isolation system.

## Vibration Isolation

1. Prefabricated, resilient equipment mounts and bases are commercially available and, when properly selected and installed, can provide stable support to vibrating equipment. Use *isolation mounts* such as unhoused steel springs, ribbed or waffle-shaped neoprene, or precompressed glass-fiber pads, depending on the vibration to be isolated and the support conditions.

2. Locate vibrating equipment near columns or above load-bearing walls to obtain better structural support. Long floor spans (> 20 ft) have lower natural frequencies than on-grade slabs and, therefore, require isolators with larger static deflections.

3. Use isolation hangers to isolate all pipe connections for a considerable distance from vibrating equipment (> 150 times pipe diameter).

4. Use flexible (e.g., resilient braided section) and "floppy" (e.g., full 360°
   loop) electrical conduit connections to vibrating equipment.

5. Pipes carrying water at high velocities should be isolated from the building
   structure and wrapped with dense *lagging* materials (e.g., lead sheet, vinyl-
   covered glass fiber) to reduce the transmission of water flow noise. Use reinforced flexible pipe connections to break the vibration path along the walls of
   piping.

## Air-Distribution Systems

1. Use low-velocity and low-pressure air-distribution systems to control airflow
   noise generation and conserve energy. Avoid complicated duct layouts (e.g.,
   crisscrossing of ducts, multiple dogleg turns) and abrupt changes in duct
   cross-sectional area.

2. Avoid constructions such as untreated mechanical ducts, chases and shafts,
   or rigid conduits that can act as "speaking tubes" to transmit sound from one
   area to another. To avoid cross talk through ducts, install widely separated air
   outlets, locate air inlets to plenums away from common walls, and line
   common ducts with glass fiber (at least 1 in thick), or use prefabricated,
   sound-attenuating mufflers. Where ducts pass through walls and floor-ceiling
   constructions, resiliently isolate them from the structure.

3. To effectively seal openings around mechanical penetrations through enclosing
   constructions of mechanical rooms (and through other critical barriers), use
   low-density fibrous packing to completely fill 1/2-in-perimeter ring of open
   space and use nonhardening caulking on both sides of opening to achieve an
   airtight seal.

4. To prevent low-frequency rumble from air turbulence in mechanical ducts, be
   sure to provide smooth transitions and gradual turns and takeoffs. In variable
   air volume systems, locate terminal control devices far upstream ( > 15 ft)
   from diffusers and registers so generated airflow noise can be attenuated by
   lined ducts before reaching occupied rooms.

5. Use circular ducts, or flat oval and rectangular ducts with low aspect ratios
   (ratio of side dimensions < 3:1), which are less susceptible to vibration due
   to their greater stiffness.

6. Use flexible duct connections ( > 3-in separation) to break the vibration path
   along walls of sheet metal ducts. As in most vibration isolation, the goal is to
   interrupt the transmission path by preventing metal-to-metal contact.

7. Where ducts pass through noisy spaces before reaching quiet spaces, lagging
   may be required to prevent break-in of unwanted sound energy. Use circular
   ducts or sound-isolating plenums to compensate for the poor low-frequency
   noise isolation of rectangular duct walls.

# Chapter 6
## Speech Privacy

Speech privacy in enclosed and open plans depends on the *signal-to-noise ratio* between the intruding speech level (*signal*) and the steady background sound (*noise*). The intruding speech level is largely determined by the voice effort of the speaker (how loud) and the noise reduction between enclosed rooms, or between workstations in the open plan. The background noise commonly is produced by the HVAC system (e.g., airflow noise at terminal devices), office activities, or electronic masking sound systems (see Chap. 7). The acoustical demands usually involve one or more of the following.

1. Ability to talk without having conversations understood by neighbors
2. Freedom from distracting intruding noises (usually unwanted nearby conversations)
3. Allowance for face-to-face conversations ( < 6 ft apart) and telephone conversations to be clearly understood

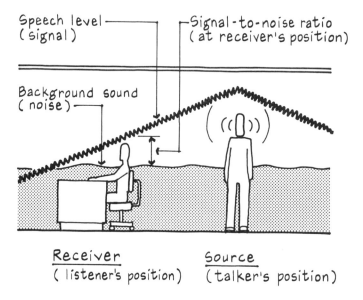

In enclosed rooms, the major paths for speech intrusion are common walls and doors, flanking such as ceiling plenums, and leaks such as cracks and holes in the intervening constructions. In open plans, the path for speech intrusion is direct, or interrupted only by partial-height barriers (called *screens*). Sound travels from speaker to listener directly; by diffraction over and around partial-height barriers; and by reflection from ceiling, partial-height barriers, walls and other vertical surfaces.

As is the situation with most acoustical problems, speech privacy can be analyzed in three parts: source, path, and receiver. The source is the speaker (talker) and the receiver is the person desiring privacy from intruding conversations. The paths are direct and flanking (for *enclosed plans*), and direct, diffracted, and reflected (for *open plans*). In open plans, the challenge to designers is considerable because raised speech levels can destroy privacy at nearby workstations.

The goal of speech privacy is to achieve unintelligible (indistinct) transmitted speech, i.e., a low speech *articulation index* AI. The AI is a measure of speech intelligibility (i.e., frequency-weighted signal-to-noise ratios) related to the percentage of a talker's words or sentences that can be understood by a listener. The index ranges from 0 (no intelligiblity and perfect privacy) to 1.0 (perfect intelligibility and no privacy). The table below presents degrees of privacy along with corresponding AI values.

| Degree of Privacy | Articulation Index (AI) |
|---|---|
| Confidential | < 0.05 |
| Normal (freedom from distraction) | 0.05 to 0.20 |
| Marginal or poor (good for eavesdroppers) | 0.20 to 0.30 |
| Poor or none | > 0.30 |

**Note:** AIs should be high ( > 0.70) where very good to excellent speech intelligibility is necessary for communication purposes in auditoriums, conference rooms, and the like (see Chap. 3).

### Sound Attenuation in Enclosed Rooms

The enclosed room shown below has hard, sound-reflecting wall and floor surfaces. Consequently, the speech levels build up to a constant level throughout most of the room. The buildup of speech levels can be reduced if additional sound-absorbing finishes are provided.

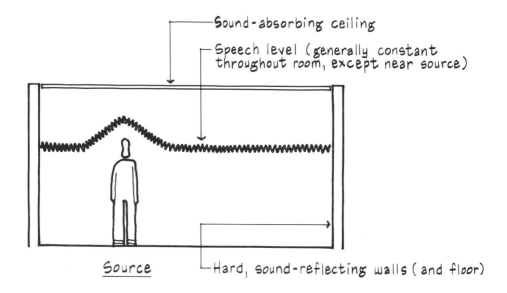

### Sound Attenuation in Open Plans

In large open plans, where the walls are a relatively insignificant part of the room, the sound attenuation can approach 6 dB per doubling of distance from the source if floors are carpeted and ceilings are sound-absorbing. The illustration below shows the attenuation of sound energy with distance.

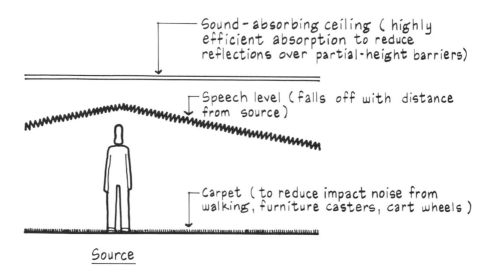

## ACOUSTICAL DEMANDS OF ENCLOSED AND OPEN PLANS

The table below shows important factors which affect speech privacy in both enclosed rooms and open plans. As indicated by the table, sound absorption controls the buildup of sound levels in enclosed rooms and also is critical in open plans where ceilings and other surfaces can reflect unwanted sound energy to nearby workstations. Background noise is important in both enclosed and open plans. However, in open plans the level of background noise should not be so high as to cause annoyance or restrict communication to within extremely short distances. This is especially important in open-plan schools or where hearing-impaired persons are present.

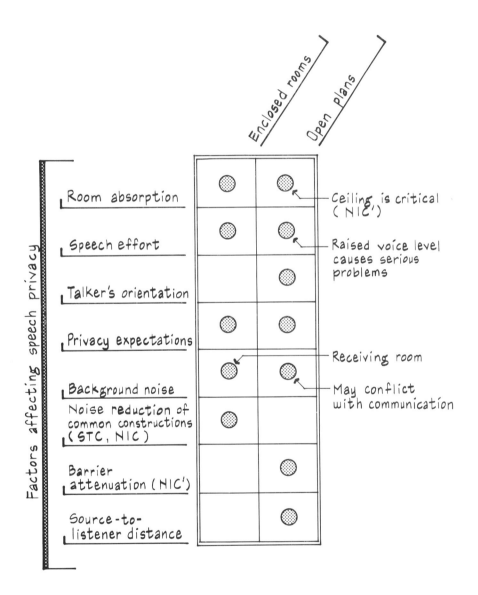

## ENCLOSED AND OPEN PLANS

The illustrations below depict many of the factors affecting speech privacy which are compared by the table on the preceding page.

### Enclosed Rooms

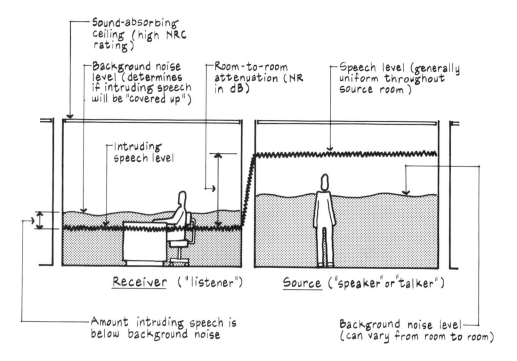

Sound-absorbing ceiling (high NRC rating)

Background noise level (determines if intruding speech will be "covered up")

Room-to-room attenuation (NR in dB)

Speech level (generally uniform throughout source room)

Intruding speech level

Receiver ("listener")

Source ("speaker" or "talker")

Amount intruding speech is below background noise

Background noise level (can vary from room to room)

### Open Plans

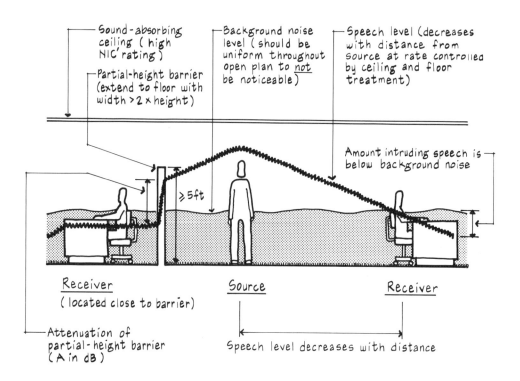

Sound-absorbing ceiling (high NIC' rating)

Partial-height barrier (extend to floor with width > 2 × height)

Background noise level (should be uniform throughout open plan to not be noticeable)

Speech level (decreases with distance from source at rate controlled by ceiling and floor treatment)

Amount intruding speech is below background noise

≥ 5ft

Receiver (located close to barrier)

Source

Receiver

Attenuation of partial-height barrier (A in dB)

Speech level decreases with distance

# SPEAKER AND LISTENER ORIENTATIONS

### Speaker

Speaker, or talker, orientation can be an important factor in open plans. As indicated in the sketch below, there is a difference of about 10 dBA in speech levels between the front and rear of a speaker (about 2 dBA per 30° of rotation away from the straight-ahead direction). Consequently, careful orientation of chairs or desks can have a beneficial effect on open-plan speech privacy conditions. In addition, average speech levels for male talkers are 2 to 5 dBA higher than for female talkers.

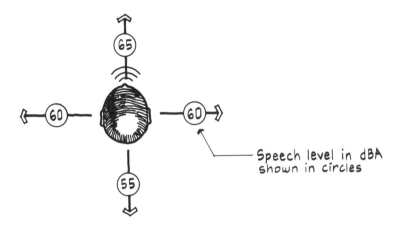

Speech level in dBA shown in circles

### Listener

Listener orientation affects the perception of source direction but *not* the decibel level, or loudness, of the source. Therefore, orientation of the listener generally is not an acoustical design consideration for speech privacy.

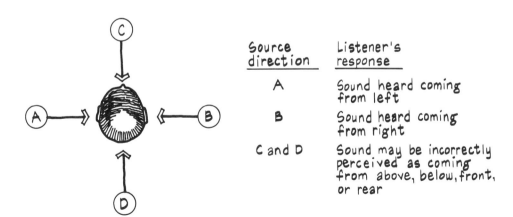

| Source direction | Listener's response |
|---|---|
| A | Sound heard coming from left |
| B | Sound heard coming from right |
| C and D | Sound may be incorrectly perceived as coming from above, below, front, or rear |

# CASE HISTORIES

The results of 37 case histories of speech privacy are depicted below. The study includes over 400 pairs of rooms in offices, hospitals, dormitories, and hotels. The encircled numbers represent the total number of case histories at a specific privacy response corresponding to a sound isolation rating, which is the average transmission loss TL of the common barrier. The scatter of the data on the graph shows that there is no clear trend relating TL to occupant satisfaction. The conclusion underlines the fact that this type of rating scheme cannot be used to predict occupant satisfaction because it does not account for other important acoustical factors such as background noise levels, sound levels of individual talkers involved, degree of privacy desired, and so on.

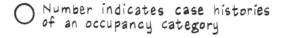

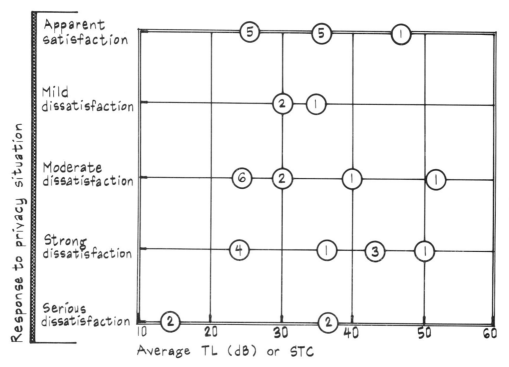

## Reference

W. J. Cavanaugh, W. R. Farrell, P. W. Hirtle, and B. G. Watters, "Speech Privacy in Buildings," *Journal of the Acoustical Society of America*, April 1962.

# ANNOYANCE, INTRUDING SPEECH, AND BACKGROUND NOISE

In speech privacy situations, *annoyance* is usually determined by the *signal-to-noise ratio* (the amount the intruding speech signal is above or below the acceptable background noise) and its consequent effect on the intelligibility of speech, rather than by the actual level of the intruding speech. On the annoyance curve shown below, the percentage of people annoyed by intruding speech varies from 0 (no one annoyed) to 100 percent (everyone annoyed). Notice that there is only a difference of 15 dB in the signal-to-noise ratios (i.e., relative change in speech level from −10 dB to about +5 dB for a given background noise level) between the extreme conditions of no one annoyed ("apparent satisfaction") and 100 percent annoyed ("serious dissatisfaction"). Background noise itself can be annoying if it is too loud or fluctuates widely (e.g., noise from typewriters, computer equipment).

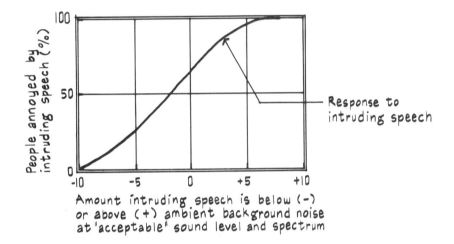

## References

L. L. Beranek (ed.), *Noise Reduction*, McGraw-Hill, New York, 1960, p. 534.

E. C. Keighley, "Acceptability Criteria for Noise in Large Offices," *Journal of Sound and Vibration*, January 1970, pp. 83-93.

# BACKGROUND NOISE SPECTRA

Occupants of rooms with extremely low background noise levels may have serious complaints about speech intrusion due to the lack of masking. An example of this condition is the "silent" spectrum shown on the graph below. The "masking noise" spectrum also shown below (at much higher sound levels than the silent spectrum) can contribute to satisfactory speech privacy by covering up intruding noises. The sound level for masking noise falls off 3 to 6 dB per octave at mid- and high frequencies and the pleasant hushing or whooshing sound produced is usually unobjectionable to most listeners. In enclosed rooms, *controlled quiet* from constant airflow at diffusers and registers of the HVAC system often can provide the minimum background noise for masking.

"Pink" noise, which has a broadband spectrum that has nearly the same sound level at all frequencies, or "white" noise, which has a rising sound level with frequency, will sound unpleasantly hissy and unnatural, or annoying. The example pink and white sound spectra shown below are for constant percent bandwidth analyses, *not* constant frequency bandwidth, which plots analogously to the pink and white color spectra for light sources.

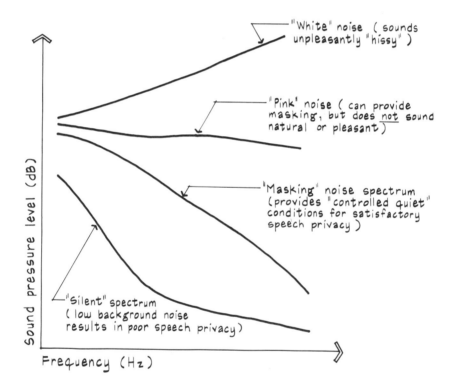

## References

R. M. Hoover, "How to Control Noise in Distribution Systems," *Heating & Air Conditioning Contractor*, March 1964.

A. P. G. Peterson and E. E. Gross, *Handbook of Noise Measurement*, General Radio, Concord, Mass., 1972, p. 132.

A. D. Pierce, *Acoustics: An Introduction to Its Physical Principles and Applications*, McGraw-Hill, New York, 1981, pp. 76-78.

# ANALYSIS SHEET (ENCLOSED PLAN)

## Analysis Sheet (Enclosed Plan)

### Anticipated response to privacy situation

Apparent satisfaction

Mild dissatisfaction

Moderate dissatisfaction

Strong dissatisfaction

Serious dissatisfaction

Speech privacy rating number

**NOTE:** Curve shows average response of people to intruding speech based on rating number figured below.

Examples

A    B    C

### Speech rating

1. **Speech effort:** how people talk in source room

   Shout    Loud    Raised    Conversational    Low

   78    72    66    60    54

2. **Source room floor area ($A_1$):** approximates effect of source room absorption

   125    250    500    1000 (sq ft)

   9    6    3    0

3. **Privacy allowance:** degree of privacy desired

   Confidential    Normal

   15    9

   ■ Speech rating total

### Isolation rating

4. **Sound transmission class (STC):** accounts for transmission loss of common barrier

5. **Noise reduction factor ($A_2/S$):** approximates effect of receiving room sound absorption and common barrier size

   1    5    10

   -2    0 2 3 5 6 7    8
          4

6. **Adjacent room background noise level (dBA):** masking sound available

   ■ Isolation rating total

### Speech privacy rating number

Find speech privacy rating number by subtracting isolation rating total from speech rating total. Then use graph at top of sheet to predict degree of satisfaction.

A _____

B _____

C _____

# GUIDELINES FOR USING THE SPEECH PRIVACY ANALYSIS SHEET (ENCLOSED PLAN)

The most important acoustical problem in many buildings is the intrusion of intelligible speech. Experience shows that most office occupants will be satisfied if they are not distracted by the intruding speech, even though it may be partially intelligible. This means the articulation index AI must be equal to or less than 0.20. For confidential work, however, the intruding speech should be unintelligible and the articulation index must be equal to or less than 0.05. The speech privacy analysis method can be used to evaluate and design offices, hotels and motels, health care facilities, dormitories, apartment buildings, and most occupancies where privacy from speech is important. However, very large rooms and spaces with electronically amplified speech or music are situations which require special study. The step-by-step procedure outlined below is keyed to the six rating factors on the speech privacy analysis sheet on the preceding page.

**Note:** Tests to determine annoyance of intruding music indicate that songs sung in the native language of the listener are more annoying than songs sung in a foreign language (cf., J.-P. Vian et al., "Assessment of Significant Acoustical Parameters for Rating Sound Insulation of Party Walls," *Journal of the Acoustical Society of America*, April 1983, p. 1242).

1. **Speech Effort (dBA):** Describes how people will talk in the source room. It is assumed that both talker and listener are located at least 2 to 3 ft away from the common barrier.

   *Conversational*: Most private offices, hotel rooms, hospital patient rooms, and so on, where face-to-face conversations between persons are within 6 ft, or words are spoken into a telephone.

   *Raised*: Boardrooms and conference rooms where people usually increase their speech effort to a raised voice level. (Seating layouts for conference rooms should be circular, oval, or lozenge-shaped so talkers and listeners will be close together.)

   *Loud*: Noisy computer equipment rooms, where operators must speak in a loud voice to communicate; psychiatrists' offices; and classrooms.

   *Shout*: Psychiatrists' treatment rooms, where patients may become excited. Under conditions of determined screaming, sound levels can be much greater than 78 dBA.

2. **Source Room Floor Area $A_1$ (ft²):** Approximates the effect of sound absorption in the source room.

   In a small room, sound reflects more frequently from the room surfaces which results in a buildup of sound energy. Conversely, in a large room sound will tend to spread out so the level of speech signals will be lower. It is assumed by the speech privacy method that at least one major surface is sound-absorbing. However, for sparsely furnished reverberant rooms, use $A_1 < 1/2$ of the actual source room floor area.

3. **Privacy Allowance:** Represents the kind of privacy that is desired.

   *Normal*: The occupant wants reasonable freedom from disturbing intruding speech. Intruding speech may be loud enough to be generally understood with careful listening but not sufficiently loud to distract occupants from work activities. For example, although engineers, accountants, and other professionals may work closely together, they routinely desire privacy from their neighbor's distracting conversations.

*Confidential*: The occupant does not want private conversations overheard in the next room. Intruding speech is reduced so that an occasional word may be recognized but comprehension of phrases and sentences is not possible. Doctors and lawyers usually require confidential privacy; likewise, such privacy is essential in courthouses between courtroom and jury room, and between courtroom and witness waiting room. Executives and supervisors also usually require this degree of privacy to be free to discuss sensitive issues with employees.

4. **Sound Transmission Class** *STC:* Accounts for sound transmission loss of common barrier.

   The STC is a single-number rating of airborne sound transmission loss performance for a barrier, measured over a standard frequency range. STC ratings are given in Chap. 4 for various building constructions. If all other speech privacy factors are known, the required STC can be determined by setting the speech privacy rating number equal to 0. A speech privacy rating number of 0 represents a condition where excessive intruding speech does not occur.

5. **Noise Reduction Factor** $A_2/S:$ Approximates the effect of sound absorption in the receiving room and the size of the common barrier.

   The receiving room size $A_2$ (floor area, ft$^2$) is important because noise buildup is greater in small rooms than in large rooms. The common barrier size $S$ (surface area, ft$^2$) is also an important factor because it will be the primary transmitter of sound energy to the receiving room. The larger the common barrier, the more sound transmitted.

6. **Adjacent Room Background Noise Level (dBA):** Represents masking sound available.

   The background noise levels in the adjacent room should be designed to cover up, or mask, the intruding speech signals. Background noise should be bland, continuous, and virtually unnoticeable to the occupants. Recommended background NC levels and corresponding RC levels are presented in Chap. 4. (Remember dBA values are about 6 to 10 greater than corresponding NC criteria.) It also is important that the source of the background noise be reliable. For example, in offices where work activity fluctuates, the noise produced by the activity also will fluctuate. Consequently, designers should always specify reliable sources of background sound such as airflow noise at air diffusers of constant-volume HVAC systems or, in special situations, neutral noise from electronic masking systems (*not* music, which contains information).

**Note:** To account for variations in building construction techniques, a margin of safety can be achieved by using speech privacy rating numbers of $-3$ to $-5$, rather than 0.

### References

W. J. Cavanaugh, W. R. Farrell, P. W. Hirtle, and B. G. Watters, "Speech Privacy in Buildings," *Journal of the Acoustical Society of America*, April 1962.

R. E. Fischer, "Acoustical Privacy in the Open-Plan Office—Updated," *Architectural Record*, June 1978, pp. 141-144.

"Speech Privacy Design Analyzer," Owens-Corning Fiberglas Corp., Toledo, Ohio, 1962.

R. W. Young, "Re-Vision of the Speech Privacy Calculation," *Journal of the Acoustical Society of America*, October 1965.

A supervisor's office and an adjacent conference room for an insurance company are described by the plan illustration below. Both rooms have carpeted floors and sound-absorbing ceilings. Occupants in the conference room can be expected to often talk in raised voices to span the distance of the conference table. In addition, both rooms will be used at times for work of a confidential nature.

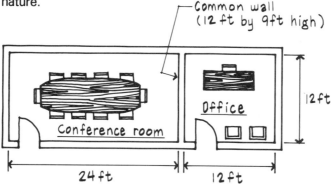

1. To evaluate rating factors 2 and 5, find the floor and common barrier surface areas. Source room (i.e., conference room) floor area $A_1$ is 24 × 12 = 288 ft². The adjacent office floor area $A_2$ is 12 × 12 = 144 ft². The common barrier size $S$ is 12 × 9 = 108 ft². The noise reduction factor $A_2/S$ for speech intrusion from the conference room to the office is 144/108 = 1.3. (Corresponding isolation rating is −2 from the scale on the analysis sheet.)

2. Minimum background levels from the HVAC system should be NC-30 (or 38 dBA) in the office and NC-25 (or 35 dBA) in the conference room. See Chap. 4 for table of recommended background levels.

3. Use the analysis sheet on the following page to find the minimum required STC for the common wall. Three example situations are evaluated using the analysis sheet.

   A. Conference room to office speech privacy conditions for a common wall construction at STC 38. (For example, 2 by 4 wood studs 16 in oc, with 5/8-in-thick layer of gypsum board on both sides, and 1/4-in-thick hardwood panel layer on one side.) According to the analysis sheet, the rating factors are: speech effort 66, source room floor area 6, and privacy allowance 15. Therefore, the speech rating total is 87 (i.e., 66 + 6 + 15). The isolation rating will be 74 (i.e., 38 − 2 + 38). The speech rating number is 13 (i.e., 87 − 74), indicating a privacy situation of "strong dissatisfaction," according to the graph at the top of the analysis sheet.

   B. Conference room to office speech privacy conditions for a common wall construction at STC 51. (For example, 2 by 4 staggered wood studs 24 in oc, with 5/8-in-thick layer of gypsum board on both sides, and 1/4-in-thick hardboard panel layer on both sides.) The speech privacy rating number is 0 (i.e., 87 − 87), indicating "apparent satisfaction."

   C. Office to conference room speech privacy conditions where source room floor area $A_1$ now is 144 ft² (i.e., supervisor's office) and $A_2/S$ becomes 288/108 = 2.7. In addition, note that conversational speech is assumed because the office is reasonably small. Background noise levels in the conference room will be 35 dBA. Using a speech privacy rating number of 0, corresponding to "apparent satisfaction" conditions, an STC 48 common barrier is required.

For satisfactory speech privacy between the office and conference room, use the STC 51 construction from example B, because the most stringent requirement always should dictate selection of common barrier constructions.

# ANALYSIS SHEET (ENCLOSED PLAN) FOR EXAMPLE PROBLEMS

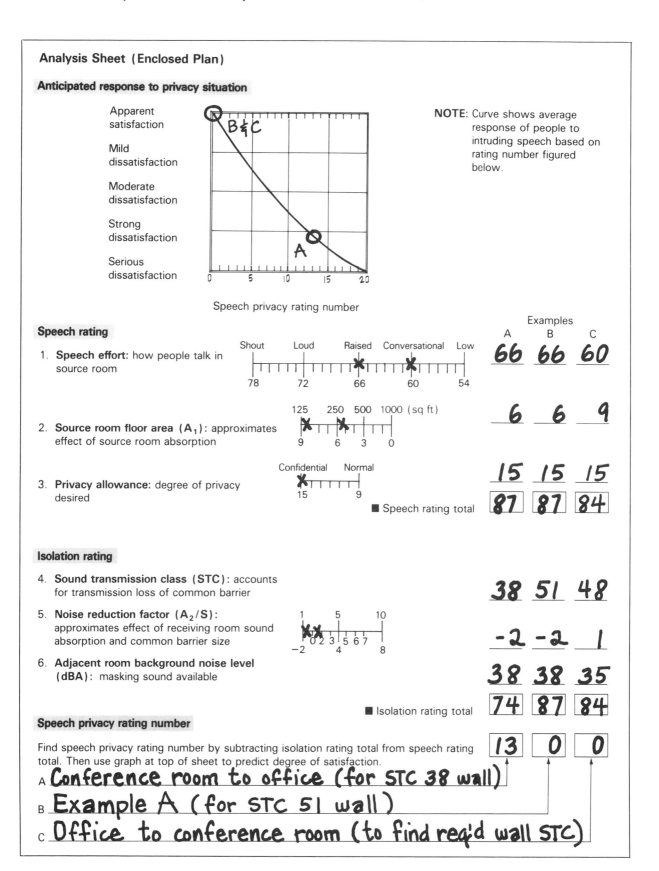

**Analysis Sheet (Enclosed Plan)**

**Anticipated response to privacy situation**

- Apparent satisfaction
- Mild dissatisfaction
- Moderate dissatisfaction
- Strong dissatisfaction
- Serious dissatisfaction

B & C

A

0    5    10    15    20

Speech privacy rating number

**NOTE:** Curve shows average response of people to intruding speech based on rating number figured below.

Examples
A    B    C

**Speech rating**

1. **Speech effort:** how people talk in source room

   Shout    Loud    Raised    Conversational    Low
   78      72      66        60                54

   66   66   60

2. **Source room floor area (A₁):** approximates effect of source room absorption

   125    250    500    1000 (sq ft)
   9      6      3      0

   6    6    9

3. **Privacy allowance:** degree of privacy desired

   Confidential    Normal
   15              9

   15   15   15

   ■ Speech rating total    **87   87   84**

**Isolation rating**

4. **Sound transmission class (STC):** accounts for transmission loss of common barrier

   38   51   48

5. **Noise reduction factor (A₂/S):** approximates effect of receiving room sound absorption and common barrier size

   1    5    10
   -2  0 2 3  5 6 7  8
        4

   -2   -2   1

6. **Adjacent room background noise level (dBA):** masking sound available

   38   38   35

   ■ Isolation rating total    **74   87   84**

**Speech privacy rating number**

Find speech privacy rating number by subtracting isolation rating total from speech rating total. Then use graph at top of sheet to predict degree of satisfaction.

**13    0    0**

A **Conference room to office (for STC 38 wall)**

B **Example A (for STC 51 wall)**

C **Office to conference room (to find req'd wall STC)**

The table below shows minimum STC ratings for common walls between enclosed spaces in conventional office and conference areas. The table is based on conversational levels of speech in the source rooms and steady background noise levels in the receiving rooms. When differing occupancies share a common wall, be sure to evaluate both as source rooms and use the higher of the two required STC values. Also, where background noise levels are below the values given in the column at the right, increase STCs by the difference in the dBA values. The table may be used for preliminary planning purposes if adjustments also are made for variations in privacy needs of users, size of common wall, and other acoustical factors presented in this chapter.

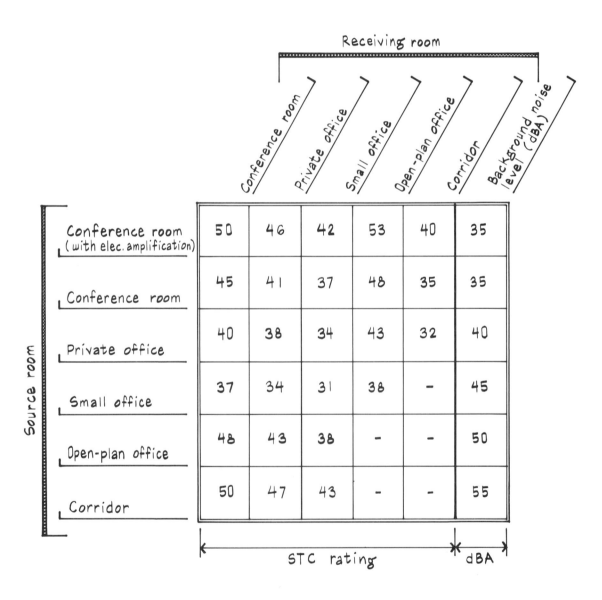

| Source room \ Receiving room | Conference room | Private office | Small office | Open-plan office | Corridor | Background noise level (dBA) |
|---|---|---|---|---|---|---|
| Conference room (with elec. amplification) | 50 | 46 | 42 | 53 | 40 | 35 |
| Conference room | 45 | 41 | 37 | 48 | 35 | 35 |
| Private office | 40 | 38 | 34 | 43 | 32 | 40 |
| Small office | 37 | 34 | 31 | 38 | – | 45 |
| Open-plan office | 48 | 43 | 38 | – | – | 50 |
| Corridor | 50 | 47 | 43 | – | – | 55 |

STC rating / dBA

Sound transmission losses for flanking paths through ceiling plenums must be compatible with the losses for the direct path through the common wall. Accordingly, extend wall to floor slab above, install plenum barrier above wall, or increase STCs in the table by 3 and use a room-to-room ceiling STC equal to the higher STC rating for the wall.

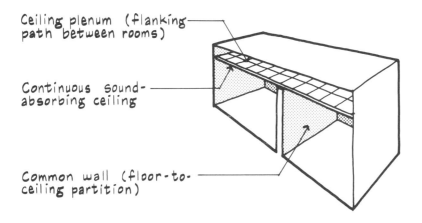

Ceiling plenum (flanking path between rooms)

Continuous sound-absorbing ceiling

Common wall (floor-to-ceiling partition)

**Open Plenum Between Offices**

**Note:** The tables of suggested STCs and NICs in this book are based on isolating speech or noise levels from "normal" activities and on achieving the preferred background noise spectrum in the receiving room (see Chap. 4).

**Reference**

A. C. C. Warnock, "Office Partitions: Acoustical Requirements for Design and Construction," Division of Building Research, National Research Council of Canada, CBD 186, May 1977.

*Open plans* (i.e., large rooms where length and width are much greater than height, and full-height barriers are not used) are believed by many building owners to provide flexibility in layout and ease in arranging and rearranging workstations in offices. In addition, open plans often permit the use of simple, efficient HVAC systems to serve all workstations. As everyone is in the same room, there is no need to provide the complex ductwork and multiple temperature controls required by enclosed offices. Without walls from floor to ceiling, less light energy will be absorbed and adjacent workstations can share light. Consequently, the same overall lighting levels can be provided by a reduced number of overhead lighting fixtures. *Task-ambient lighting* also can be used in open plans. For example, furniture-integrated light sources can provide direct light on the work surface (*task*) and uplight on the ceiling so reflected light softens brightness ratios throughout the room (*ambient light*).

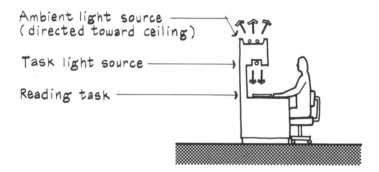

**Task-Ambient Lighting**

In offices, worker job satisfaction and productivity may be enhanced by freedom from noise and the distraction of intruding speech. To achieve acoustical privacy in open plans, the following must be provided:

1. Partial-height barriers, called *screens*, ( $\geq$ 5 ft high) between workstations
2. Electronic background masking (40 to 50 dBA)
3. Efficient, sound-absorbing finishes on ceiling, walls, and other surfaces

Unfortunately, these measures to control speech privacy present barriers to handicapped persons. For example, sight-impaired persons use the reflection of sound off vertical surfaces to locate walls and other obstructions to their movement (called *echo location*). Hearing-impaired persons require background levels less than 30 dBA to avoid unwanted covering up of desired speech signals. Therefore, in open plans essential masking noise and efficient sound absorption will be acoustical barriers to use by hearing- and sight-impaired persons unless these conflicts are recognized and resolved.

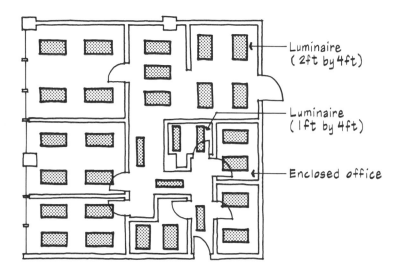

**Enclosed Plan**

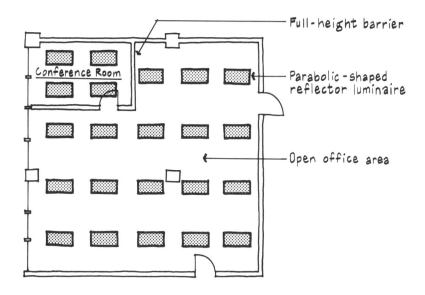

**Open Plan**

# SCREENS

Screens can contribute to achieving satisfactory speech privacy in open plans by interrupting the direct path of sound between workstations (when talker and listener are > 6 ft apart). Screens usually are open-weave, fabric-covered panels consisting of two layers of sound-absorbing material (NRC > 0.80) installed on opposite sides of an airtight hardboard or aluminum foil core (called a *septum*). The STC of the screen construction normally need not exceed 25 because its overall effectiveness is limited by diffraction of sound energy over the top and around the sides. The larger the screen (height and width dimensions) and the closer its location to the talker or listener, the better its attenuation of sound. Effective screens are 2 times wider than their height and extend to the floor avoiding gaps at the base. Gaps should not exceed 1 in and floor surface should be carpeted to help prevent flanking at the base.

The *noise isolation class prime* NIC' of a screen can be increased by 3 or more when the *overall screen height H* is increased from 4 to 5 ft, and by 1 or more when *H* is increased from 5 to 6 ft. Screens less than 4 ft high are normally not effective barriers in the open plan. See following page for procedures on how to determine NIC' ratings.

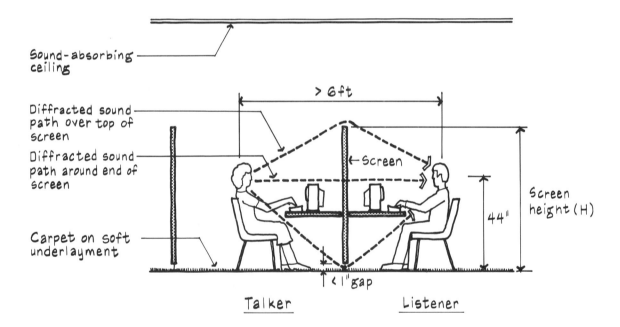

## References

R. K. Herbert, "Use of the Articulation Index to Evaluate Acoustical Privacy in the Open Office," *Noise Control Engineering Journal*, September-October 1978.

J. B. Moreland, "Role of the Screen on Speech Privacy in Open Plan Offices," *Proceedings of the 1986 International Conference on Noise Control Engineering*, vol. I, Noise Control Foundation, Poughkeepsie, N.Y., 1986, pp. 513-518.

Laboratory and field tests can be used to rate the isolation effectiveness of ceiling systems in open plans. The *noise isolation class prime* (abbreviated NIC') is a single-number rating of the speech-isolating performance of screen/ceiling combinations. It can be determined by using a standard partial-height barrier (screen) and standard locations for measurement of sound levels between workstations (see illustration of test setup below). Readings of transmitted sound levels from a standard source of "random" noise are taken at 1-ft intervals along a survey path on the opposite side of the screen. The attenuation is measured in decibels at one-third octave bands with center frequencies from 400 to 2000 Hz. To determine the NIC', the measured attenuation values are plotted against frequency and compared to a standard contour according to a procedure that is similar to the STC rating method described in Chap. 4.

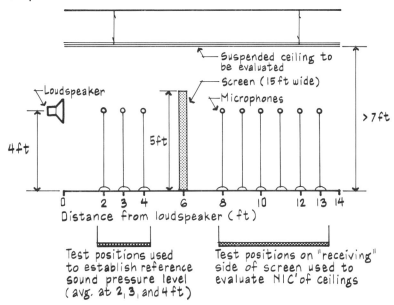

**NIC' Ceiling Test**

The table below shows examples of NIC' values for a variety of ceilings.

| NIC' | Overhead Surface |
| --- | --- |
| 23 | Open sky (i.e., perfect absorption which can be simulated by evaluating NIC' outdoors with sky overhead) |
| 20 to 16 | Commercially available sound-absorbing ceiling boards |
| 11 | Gypsum board, plaster, concrete |

According to criteria published by the U.S. General Services Administration (GSA), speech privacy potential SPP, where SPP = NIC' + $NC_{40}$, should be greater than 60 for open-plan offices. The GSA computation roughly corresponds to the open-plan speech privacy analysis procedure in this chapter. NIC' is similar to isolation rating numbers 3 and 4 from the analysis sheet, and NC is isolation rating number 5.

Sound energy can be reflected by ceiling surfaces over partial-height barriers toward adjacent workstations. As a consequence, for speech privacy, absorption efficiency of ceiling surfaces ideally should be highest at incident angles of 40 to 60° from the normal to flat ceilings and at the sound frequencies which contribute most to speech intelligibility (i.e., 1000, 2000, and 4000 Hz).

If NIC' values have not been measured, ceiling materials can be be evaluated by a speech absorption coefficient SAC computed from random incidence sound absorption coefficients measured in reverberation rooms according to the provisions of ASTM C 423. The speech absorption coefficient can be found as follows:

$$SAC = \Sigma \ (0.06\alpha_{250} + 0.15\alpha_{500} + 0.24\alpha_{1000} + 0.32\alpha_{2000} + 0.23\alpha_{4000})$$

Examples of sound-absorbing treatment schemes to reduce ceiling reflections are shown below.

**Flat**

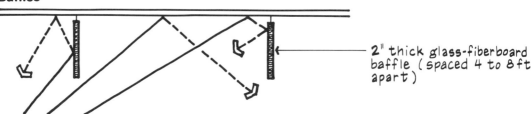

Thick sound-absorbing board (with high NIC' rating)

**Baffles**

2" thick glass-fiberboard baffle (spaced 4 to 8 ft apart)

**Coffers**

Thick glass-fiberboard recessed panel

**Reference**

R. Pirn, "Speech Absorption Coefficient," *Journal of the Acoustical Society of America*, vol. 48, no. 84(A), 1970.

# LUMINAIRES

Sound energy can be reflected between workstations by hard-surfaced ceiling lighting fixtures (also called *luminaires*), reducing the level of speech privacy. Flat-lens luminaires can reduce isolation between workstations (located 8 to 10 ft apart) by as much as 10 dB at the higher sound frequencies. The graph below shows the reduction in attenuation between workstations when continuous rows of flat-lens luminaires are located in ceilings at positions directly over and 90° to the orientation of partial-height barriers. To maintain efficient ceiling absorption, the preferred size for luminaires is small (e.g., 1 by 4 ft and 2 by 2 ft are better than 2 by 4 ft) and the preferred layout would be an ashlar or random-staggered pattern which avoids positions above barriers. Task-ambient lighting systems eliminate all ceiling fixtures by using furniture-integrated lighting to provide indirect ambient light reflected off the ceiling. Parabolic-shaped reflectors and recessed V-lens fixtures do not reflect sound to adjacent workstations as readily as the flat or prismatic-lens luminaires. For a discussion of fixture glare control and lenses, see M. D. Egan, *Concepts in Architectural Lighting*, McGraw-Hill, New York, 1983.

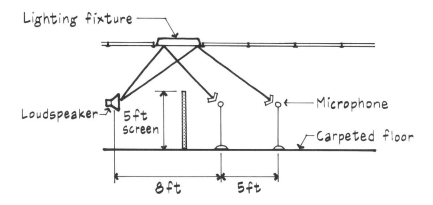

**Attenuation Test for Lighting Fixtures**

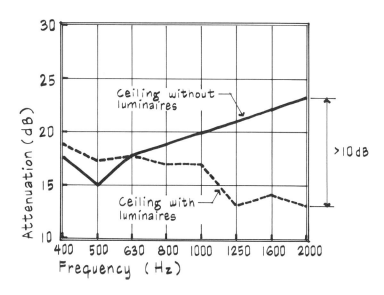

When workstations are less than 20 ft from walls, sound energy can be reflected around the ends of partial-height barriers as depicted by the sketch below. Large columns ( > 2 ft diameter) and metal cabinets can create similar flanking problems and should be treated with efficient sound-absorbing materials.

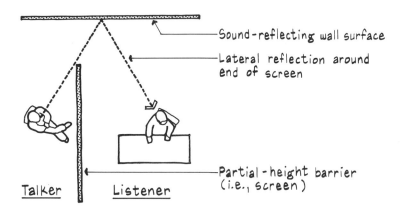

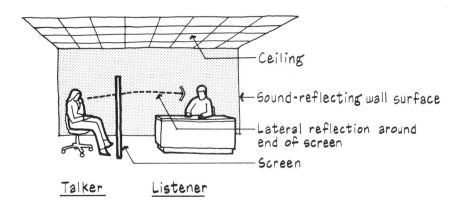

**Overhead and End Views of Workstations**

Example wall treatments to minimize reflections in open plans include:

1. Sound-absorbing wall panels extending from 2 to 6 ft above the floor
2. Thick, sound-absorbing curtains ( > 8 oz/yd²) hung 100 percent full, at least 3 in from wall (however, acoustical privacy will be lost when curtains are opened to permit view of outdoors!)
3. Wide slat, perforated vertical blinds ( > 3 in wide) with sound-absorbing cores
4. Sound-absorbing window wall baffles (see below)

**5.** Closure panels that extend partial-height barriers to walls (see below)

**6.** Tilted or sloped wall surfaces

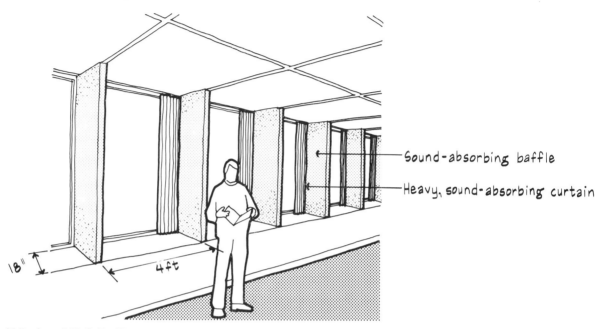

Sound-absorbing baffle

Heavy, sound-absorbing curtain

18"

4 ft

**Window Wall Baffles**

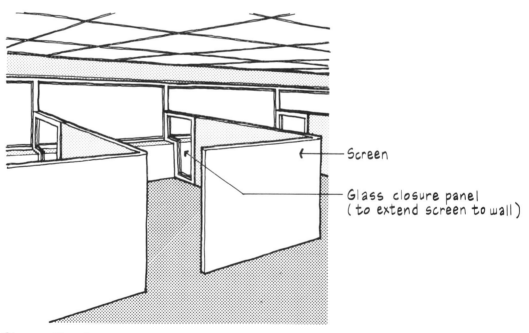

Screen

Glass closure panel
(to extend screen to wall)

**Closure Panels**

**Reference**

D. A. Harris et al., *Planning and Designing the Office Environment*, Van Nostrand Reinhold, New York, 1981, pp. 46-82.

# ANALYSIS SHEET (OPEN PLAN)

## Analysis Sheet (Open Plan)

### Open-plan dimensions

### Speech rating

Examples

| | A | B | C |

1. **Speech effort**: how people talk in room

Loud    Raised    Conversational    Low

72    66    60    54

2. **Privacy allowance**: degree of privacy desired

Confidential    Normal

15    9

■ Speech rating total

### Isolation rating

3. **Distance from source to listener**: table approximates effect of room sound absorption and sound level falloff with distance D from source to listener

| Room finishes | | Distance D (ft) | | | | |
|---|---|---|---|---|---|---|
| Ceiling | Floor | 3 | 6 | 12 | 24 | 48 |
| Reflecting | Reflecting | 0 | 3 | 6 | 9 | 12 |
| Reflecting | Absorbing | 0 | 4 | 8 | 12 | 16 |
| Absorbing | Reflecting | 0 | 5 | 10 | 15 | 20 |
| Absorbing | Absorbing | 0 | 6 | 12 | 18 | 24 |

4. **Partial-height barrier**: table accounts for attenuation from barrier with ceiling absorption at NRC of 0.80. (Barrier width should be at least twice its total height.)

| Barrier height H (ft) | Distance D (ft) | | | | |
|---|---|---|---|---|---|
| | 3 | 6 | 12 | 24 | 48 |
| 1 | 11 | 7 | 4 | 2 | 0 |
| 2 | 14 | 10 | 7 | 4 | 3 |
| 3 | 15 | 11 | 8 | 5 | 4 |
| 4 | 16 | 12 | 9 | 6 | 5 |

5. **Room background noise level (dBA)**: masking sound available

■ Isolation rating total

### Speech privacy rating number

Find speech privacy rating number by subtracting isolation total from speech rating total. Then use graph at top of p. 329 to assess degree of satisfaction. Satisfactory conditions are anticipated when speech privacy rating number is 0 or less.

A _____

B _____

C _____

# GUIDELINES FOR USING THE SPEECH PRIVACY ANALYSIS SHEET (OPEN PLAN)

In the open plan, one of the most important design problems is to provide the occupants with acoustical privacy from speech transmitted between workstations. The speech privacy analysis method can be used to evaluate and design offices, schools, banks, and similar occupancies. The method assumes that the length and width of the open plan are large compared to the ceiling height. However, open plans with subareas largely enclosed by hard-surfaced partial-height barriers may have the acoustical characteristics of small rooms and therefore fall outside the scope of the method. The step-by-step procedure outlined below is keyed to the five rating factors on the open-plan speech privacy analysis sheet on the preceding page.

1. **Speech Effort (dBA):** Describes how people will talk in the room.

   *Low:* The situation in most open-plan spaces when an occupant does not want speech to be overheard. (A whispering voice, for example, would fall below the low voice level.)

   *Conversational:* Persons in the open plan within close proximity to each other ( < 6 ft apart) usually speak in a conversational voice level (or lower) so they will not disturb their neighbors.

   *Raised:* People in conference situations can be expected to talk in a raised voice level to span the distance of conference tables.

   *Loud:* Workers in spaces with noisy machines must speak in a loud voice to communicate.

2. **Privacy Allowance:** Deals with the kind of privacy that is desired.

   *Normal:* The occupant wants reasonable freedom from disturbing intruding speech. That is, occupants sitting in a workstation may hear speech from the adjacent workstation but will not be able to understand conversations without concentration. Generally, select normal privacy in designing most open-plan privacy situations.

   *Confidential:* The occupant does not want private conversations overheard. Spaces in financial institutions, criminal justice centers, embassies, and some health care occupancies usually require confidential privacy. Executives, supervisors, and counselors also may need this degree of privacy to be able to discuss employee relations, costs and fees, and so on. Confidential privacy is difficult to achieve in open plans and can best be achieved by enclosed rooms.

3. **Distance from Source to Listener *D*:** Accounts for the attenuation of voice levels with distance.

   The distance *D* (ft) from the position of the nearest listener is important because the voice level of the source is attenuated by distance. Use the smallest value of *D* measured between occupants who want privacy from each other. Conditions may vary from a room with a hard, sound-reflecting ceiling and floor to one with a sound-absorbing ceiling and deep-carpeted floor. Consequently, attenuation varies from 3 to 6 dB per doubling of distance as shown by the values in the table on the analysis sheet (isolation rating 3).

4. **Partial-Height Barrier:** Accounts for attenuation provided by partial-height barrier.

   *H* (ft) is the portion of the barrier above the acoustical line of sight between the source and listener. It is assumed that the ceiling is covered with an efficient sound-absorbing material and that the barrier is located midway between the source (talker) and receiver (listener)—the least effective location. Partial-height barriers should have an overall height of 5 to 6 ft, extend to the floor to prevent flanking of speech under bottom edge, and have airtight joints between sections of panels. High barriers can create the illusion of an enclosed space causing occupants to raise their voice levels. Barrier width should be at least twice the overall height to prevent flanking around the ends. Barriers should have a solid septum (e.g., mass of at least $3/4$ lb/ft$^2$) and both sides should be treated with sound-absorbing materials to control sound reflections at workstations.

5. **Room Background Noise Level (dBA):** Represents masking sound available.

The background noise levels throughout the open plan should be designed to mask, or cover up, the intruding speech signals at workstations. Background noise should be bland, continuous, and uniform over the entire open-plan area to be barely noticeable. Recommended ranges for background NC levels are presented in Chap. 4. (Remember dBA values are about 6 to 10 greater than corresponding NC criteria.) Where background noise levels exceed 50 dBA, occupants are likely to be annoyed and may raise their voice levels to be heard, thus defeating the intended masking effects.

Sound energy produced by air distribution systems rarely provides the spatial uniformity, smooth frequency spectra, and proper decibel level needed to achieve successful speech privacy in open plans. A reliable method of producing background noise in the open-plan space is to provide an electronic masking system with loudspeakers distributed above the sound-absorbing panels of a suspended ceiling (see Chap. 7). Coverage should include adjacent circulation and enclosed spaces so occupants moving between enclosed and open areas do not notice the masking due to a dramatic change in background noise levels.

### References

ASTM Task Group E 33.04 C, "Acoustical Environment in the Open-Plan Office," *ASTM Standardization News*, August 1976, pp. 8-16.

L. L. Beranek (ed.), *Noise and Vibration Control*, McGraw-Hill, New York, 1971, pp. 588-594.

P. W. Hirtle, B. G. Watters, and W. J. Cavanaugh, "Acoustics of Open Plan Spaces—Some Case Histories," *Journal of the Acoustical Society of America*, vol. 46, no. 91(A), 1969.

R. Pirn, "Acoustical Variables in Open Planning," *Journal of the Acoustical Society of America*, May 1971.

K. W. Walker, "Open-Plan Acoustics," *The Construction Specifier*, February and March 1979.

## EXAMPLE PROBLEMS (OPEN PLAN)

An open-plan office for an engineering firm has desks arranged 12 ft apart as shown on the layout plan sketch below. The office has an electronic background masking system designed to provide an evenly distributed 50 dBA throughout the room.

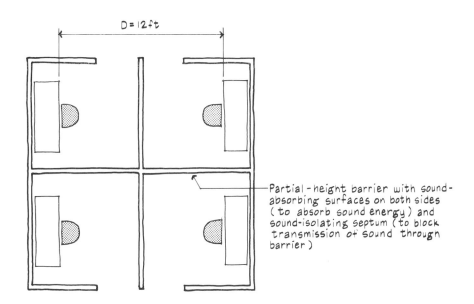

1. Find the speech rating for conversational voice levels and normal speech privacy. According to the analysis sheet on the following page, speech effort is 60 and privacy allowance is 9. Therefore, the speech rating total is 69.

2. For conditions of sound-absorbing ceiling, hard-surfaced sound-reflecting floor, and barrier height $H$ of 1 ft above the acoustical line of sight, the isolation rating will be 64 (i.e., $10 + 4 + 50$). The speech privacy rating number is 5 (i.e., $69 - 64$), indicating a privacy situation between "mild dissatisfaction" and "moderate dissatisfaction" (see graph on page 329).

3. For conditions of sound-absorbing ceiling, carpeted floor, and increased barrier height $H$ of 2 ft above the acoustical line of sight, the isolation rating will be 69 (i.e., $12 + 7 + 50$). The speech privacy rating number is 0, indicating "apparent satisfaction."

4. If management desires confidential privacy with a speech rating total of 75, satisfactory speech privacy cannot be achieved for 12-ft spacing between workstations even with sound-absorbing ceiling, carpeted floor, and barrier height $H$ of 2 ft above the acoustical line of sight. For these conditions, the speech privacy rating number is 6, indicating "moderate dissatisfaction."

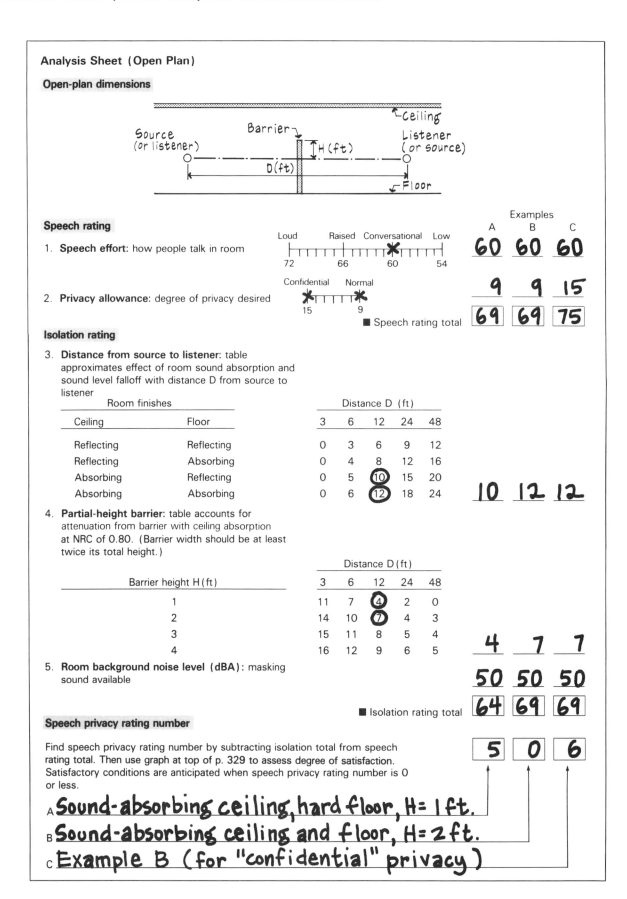

## Analysis Sheet (Open Plan)

### Open-plan dimensions

### Speech rating

|  | | Examples |
|---|---|---|
|  | | A   B   C |

1. **Speech effort:** how people talk in room — Loud 72, Raised 66, Conversational 60, Low 54 — **60  60  60**

2. **Privacy allowance:** degree of privacy desired — Confidential 15, Normal 9 — **9  9  15**

■ Speech rating total — **69  69  75**

### Isolation rating

3. **Distance from source to listener:** table approximates effect of room sound absorption and sound level falloff with distance D from source to listener

| Room finishes | | Distance D (ft) | | | | |
|---|---|---|---|---|---|---|
| Ceiling | Floor | 3 | 6 | 12 | 24 | 48 |
| Reflecting | Reflecting | 0 | 3 | 6 | 9 | 12 |
| Reflecting | Absorbing | 0 | 4 | 8 | 12 | 16 |
| Absorbing | Reflecting | 0 | 5 | (10) | 15 | 20 |
| Absorbing | Absorbing | 0 | 6 | (12) | 18 | 24 |

**10  12  12**

4. **Partial-height barrier:** table accounts for attenuation from barrier with ceiling absorption at NRC of 0.80. (Barrier width should be at least twice its total height.)

| Barrier height H (ft) | Distance D (ft) | | | | |
|---|---|---|---|---|---|
|  | 3 | 6 | 12 | 24 | 48 |
| 1 | 11 | 7 | (4) | 2 | 0 |
| 2 | 14 | 10 | (7) | 4 | 3 |
| 3 | 15 | 11 | 8 | 5 | 4 |
| 4 | 16 | 12 | 9 | 6 | 5 |

**4  7  7**

5. **Room background noise level (dBA):** masking sound available — **50  50  50**

■ Isolation rating total — **64  69  69**

### Speech privacy rating number

Find speech privacy rating number by subtracting isolation total from speech rating total. Then use graph at top of p. 329 to assess degree of satisfaction. Satisfactory conditions are anticipated when speech privacy rating number is 0 or less.

**5  0  6**

A Sound-absorbing ceiling, hard floor, H = 1 ft.
B Sound-absorbing ceiling and floor, H = 2 ft.
C Example B (for "confidential" privacy)

## WORKSTATION FURNITURE LAYOUTS IN OPEN PLANS

The greater the distance from talker to listener *D*, the higher the degree of privacy in open plans. Where workers are only 6 ft apart, speech can be overheard by adjacent workers and consequently there will be unsatisfactory speech privacy. In arranging desks within workstations, the important goal is to increase occupant head-to-head separation distance, rather than distance between workstation centers. Shown below are example furniture layouts presented in order of increasing potential to achieve satisfactory speech privacy.

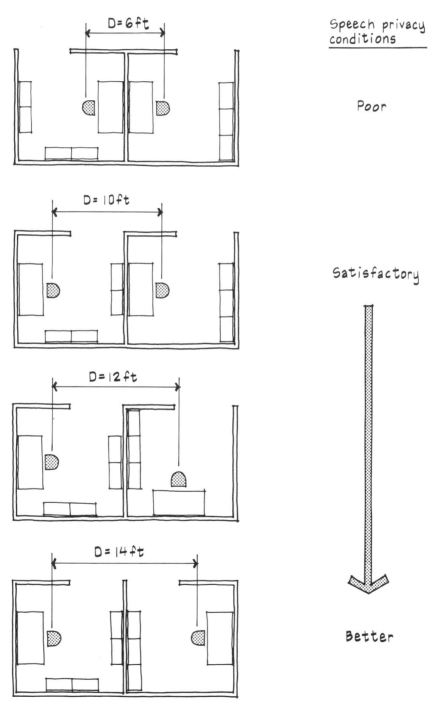

## WORKSTATION CONFIGURATIONS

The worker's primary orientation should be away from the entrance to the workstation. Shown below are adjacent pairs of workstations with desks and entrances rearranged so privacy will be improved. Speech levels within workstations normally will be low if conversation distance is less than 6 ft. Locate telephones so users face sound-absorbing screens. Select telephone and other office equipment for quiet operation.

**Poor Layouts**                    **Improved Layouts**

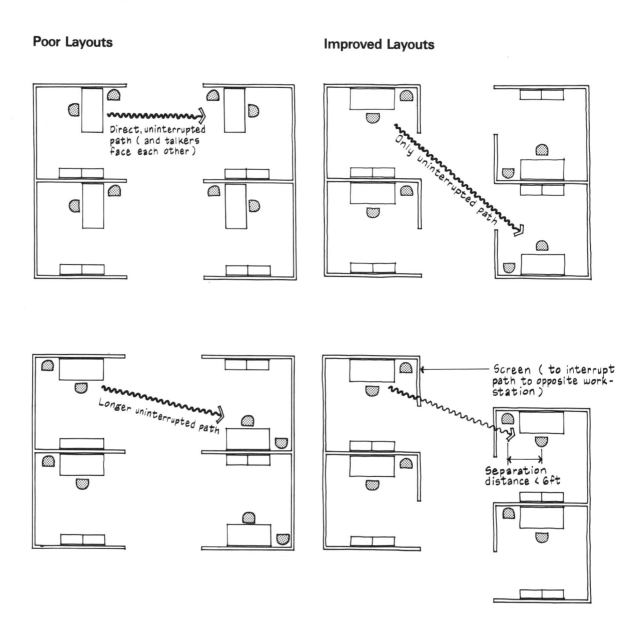

### Reference

V. V. Cerami, "Sound Control in the Open Office: A Guide to Speech Privacy," Shaw-Walker Company, Muskegon, Mich., 1979.

# COMMUNICATION IN THE OPEN PLAN

   Background noise levels in the open plan must be high enough to provide satisfactory speech privacy conditions and may therefore interfere with speech communication. The graph below can be used to estimate the maximum distance people may be separated and still converse satisfactorily at a given voice level. (In general, talker-to-listener distances more than 5 ft are intended for conversations that other persons can overhear; those less than 5 ft, however, are intended for personal or confidential exchanges.) For example, in an open plan which has a background level of 55 dBA, two people can converse with normal speech effort up to a distance of only 9 1/2 ft (see dashed lines on graph). However, in most situations where background noise exceeds 50 dBA in open plans, speakers tend to raise their voices, thus defeating any anticipated increased privacy benefits from the masking. If conversations or lectures to large groups cannot be restricted to the distance given by the graph, they must be held in enclosed rooms to avoid loss of speech privacy for other occupants of the open plan. Note that speech effort increases by about 6 dBA per 10 dBA increase in background noise up to 70 dBA, a condition where occupants must resort to gathering close together to communicate.

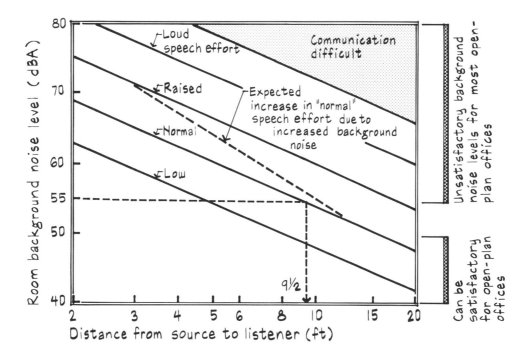

**Note:** The graph is based on tests of average male voices with talker and listener facing each other, using unexpected word material. For privacy between open-plan classrooms, avoid layouts where teachers face each other, encourage small class sizes to restrict the distance from source to listeners, and use solid panel bookcases and other furnishings to provide barrier attenuation between classes.

## References

L. L. Beranek, *Acoustics*, McGraw-Hill, New York, 1954, p. 420.

J. C. Webster, "SIL-Past, Present, and Future," *Sound and Vibration*, August 1969.

# LAYOUTS FOR COMMUNICATION IN OPEN PLANS

Effective communication in small groups (or classes) can be achieved in the open plan if talker-to-listener distances are less than 20 ft, ceilings are highly absorptive (NRC > 0.80), and speech privacy is maintained between nearby groups. Be careful—masking sound levels should *not* exceed 50 dBA.

Example circular and semicircular layouts are shown below for groups where listeners and talker are close together. Acoustical separation (or noise reduction) between groups must be at least 15 dBA to achieve a reasonable degree of privacy. For example, in open-plan schools teachers should not face each other at their normal teaching locations, and layouts should be avoided where the last row of students in one class is closer to the adjacent teacher than to their own teacher (see poor layout of adjacent classes example below).

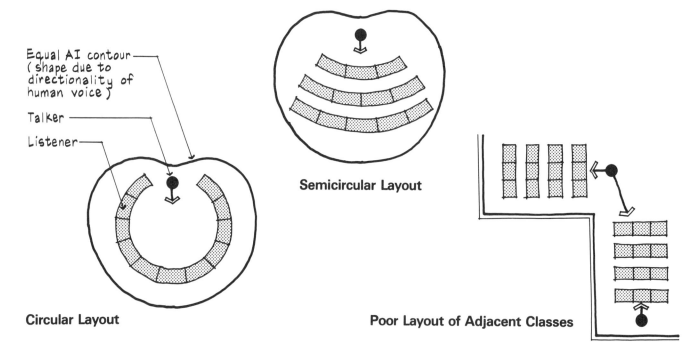

Equal AI contour (shape due to directionality of human voice)

Talker

Listener

**Circular Layout**

**Semicircular Layout**

**Poor Layout of Adjacent Classes**

**Note:** Activities which are not compatible with open plans include loud audiovisual presentations, any music, shop activities, and speech therapy classes. These spaces should be located in separate rooms which are completely enclosed by heavy sound-isolating constructions (see Chap. 4).

### References

D. P. Walsh, "Noise Levels and Annoyance in Open Plan Educational Facilities," *Journal of Architectural Research*, August 1975.

J. F. Yerges and J. G. Bollinger, "Development and Utilization of Open-Plan Educational Facilities," *Sound and Vibration*, June 1972.

L. F. Yerges, "The Open-Plan School Revisited," *Noise Control Engineering Journal*, January-February 1976.

## CHECKLIST FOR SPEECH PRIVACY IN OPEN PLANS

1. Use partial-height barriers between workstations. Barriers that are properly sized (height and width), extend to the floor, have airtight joints between sections, and are located close to talker or listener will achieve the greatest noise reduction by diffraction. Barriers should have a solid core, should be sound-absorbing on both sides, and should not be too low (e.g., sound energy readily diffracts over the top of low barriers < 5 ft high) or too high (e.g., occupants may raise voice levels due to the illusion of enclosed private space).

2. Avoid workstations that are close together, and arrange entrances to be offset so that direct line of sight situations do not occur between opposite workstations.

3. Use efficient, sound-absorbing ceilings which absorb considerable sound energy at near-grazing angles of incidence. The goal is to approach open-sky conditions as closely as possible. High noise isolation class prime NIC' values are essential for open-plan speech privacy.

4. Use ceiling materials that provide both efficient absorption for open-plan privacy and sufficient isolation for room-to-room privacy. This kind of ceiling system allows flexibility in arranging both partial-height barriers and demountable partitions.

5. Provide sound-absorbing floor and wall surfaces (especially critical at perimeter workstations). Carpeted floors (e.g., 1/4-in pile height, > 24 oz/yd² density) can eliminate impact noises from walking, furniture casters, and cart wheels. Sound-absorbing treatment on walls, windows, and columns can prevent flanking of sound energy by reflection around the ends of partial-height barriers.

6. Install controlled electronic background masking sound. Masking sound must be unobtrusive, uniformly distributed throughout the space, and not too loud (< 50 dBA). Where communication also is important in open plans, be sure that background levels are no higher than absolutely necessary for satisfactory speech privacy conditions.

7. Be sure to consider the consequences of speech privacy decisions on the usability of open plans by hearing- and sight-impaired persons. When noise levels exceed 30 dBA, speech intelligibility will be much lower for hearing-impaired persons than for normal-hearing persons.

# Chapter 7
## Electronic Sound Systems

## BASIC ELEMENTS

The goal of an electronic sound-reinforcing system is to provide all listeners with good hearing conditions where the unamplified sound would not be sufficient. For good speech intelligibility, the direct signal from the loudspeaker to the listener's ears must be louder than any competing sound (satisfactory *signal-to-noise ratio*) and be free from distortion (*not* "tinny" or "boomy" sound). Competing sounds include intruding noise from outdoors or within the building, mechanical system noise (see Chap. 5), noise from the audience, or reverberant sound energy. In highly reverberant rooms, the sound-reinforcing system must increase the direct sound field more than it increases the reverberant sound field. In addition, a successful system must be free from *feedback* ("squealing" or "howling" sound regenerated between microphones and loudspeakers) at the required operating sound level. The basic types of sound-reinforcing systems are:

1. *Central* (cluster of loudspeakers located above the actual source of sound)
2. *Distributed* (array of loudspeakers located over the listeners)
3. *Seat-integrated* (loudspeakers located in backs of seats or pews)
4. *Combination* of these systems tailored to the needs of users and natural acoustics of the room or environment

The three basic elements of a sound-reinforcing system—microphones, electronic controls, and loudspeakers—are shown below.

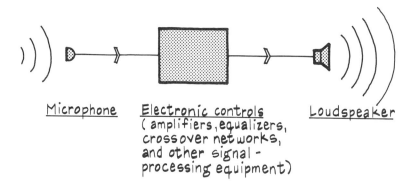

Microphone    Electronic controls
(amplifiers, equalizers,
crossover networks,
and other signal-
processing equipment)    Loudspeaker

### Microphones

Microphones convert sound energy in air into electric energy. To avoid feedback, they normally should be located out of the loudspeaker coverage, and their frequency response should be as smooth as possible. Three common types of microphones are:

1. *Dynamic moving coil* (thin diaphragm, set into vibration by sound waves, moves coil of wire between two magnetic poles, generating electric potential)
2. *Ribbon* (variation of moving coil, where aluminum composite ribbon acts as diaphragm and one-turn coil)
3. *Condenser* (polarized movable thin diaphragm vibrates in front of fixed plate, changing capacitance to vary an electric signal; requires an outside source of power)

Microphones are also identified by their directional sensitivity. Common directional patterns are *omnidirectional* (equal response at all directions) and *unidirectional* or *cardioid* (greatest response at front or head). If multiple microphones are used, their signals must be electronically mixed. Only the microphones actually being used at the moment should be included in the mixed sound. Additional input to a sound-reinforcing system may include recordings and telephone interconnection to remote locations.

## Electronic Controls

Electronic controls are used to increase the magnitude of the electric signal (*amplifiers*); to distribute electric energy to high-frequency and low-frequency loudspeakers at the proper level and frequency (*crossover networks*); to control feeds from microphones in large multimicrophone systems (*mixers*); and to allow tone control for signal shaping (*equalizers*) in order to match the system output with the acoustical properties of the room and to compensate for frequency-dependent characteristics of loudspeakers.

It is extremely important to locate the control console where the operator can hear the mixture of natural sound (called *live sound*) and reinforced sound as the audience hears it. The best location would be a slightly off-center location at the rear-third point of the seating area on the main floor or at front of balcony (e.g., DAR Constitution Hall, Washington, D.C., and Grand Concert Hall in the UT Performing Arts Center, Austin, Texas). Control consoles can require more than 50 ft² of floor area. For performance recording functions, headphones should be used to monitor what is being taped from the microphones. For some basic reinforcement systems, automatic microphone mixers may be used. Automatic mixers sense the presence of acoustical input and turn microphones on and off as needed. Even where automatic mixers are used, they normally must be supplemented by an overall system volume control located in the listening area.

## Loudspeakers

Loudspeakers convert electric energy into airborne sound. They should be positioned so their direct sound will be evenly distributed at the proper sound level to all listeners in the room. For rooms with a reverberation time of less than 2 s, the maximum loudspeaker-to-listener distance $d$ can be found by:

$$d \simeq 0.1\sqrt{\frac{QV}{T}}$$

where   $d$ = maximum loudspeaker-to-listener distance (ft)
   $Q$ = loudspeaker directivity (no units)
   $V$ = room volume (ft³)
   $T$ = reverberation time (s)

The distance between a loudspeaker and its most distant listener can be longer for spaces which have low reverberation times and use highly directional loudspeakers. Directivity $Q$ for loudspeakers varies from 2 to 15, depending on the beam spread angle and other characteristics of the loudspeaker. The directivity of the human voice is about 2 at 500 Hz, but this figure can be raised considerably by cupping hands around the mouth or by using a megaphone.

# FUNCTIONAL DIAGRAMS AND LOUDSPEAKERS

### Central Loudspeaker System Functional Diagram

The *functional diagram* below shows the interrelationship of the major elements of a central loudspeaker-type system. The crossover network contains electronic filters which pass sound signals above a selected frequency (*crossover frequency*) to the high-frequency horns and sound signals below this frequency to the low-frequency loudspeakers. In more complex systems, supertweeters may be used to augment the high-frequency response and subwoofers to augment low-frequency response.

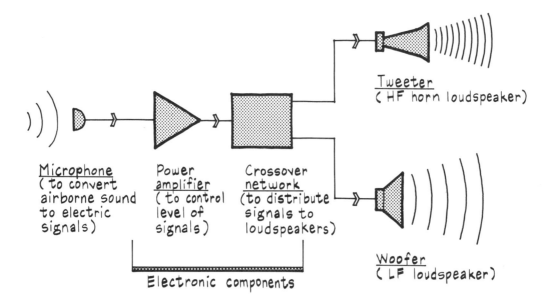

Microphone
(to convert
airborne sound
to electric
signals)

Power
amplifier
(to control
level of
signals)

Crossover
network
(to distribute
signals to
loudspeakers)

Electronic components

Tweeter
(HF horn loudspeaker)

Woofer
(LF loudspeaker)

**Note:** In "highly powered" systems, which operate close to the power limit of the loudspeakers, it is good practice to use *multiamplification*. This is a system in which the crossover network precedes the power amplifiers, and separate power amplifiers are used for each frequency range.

### High-Frequency Horn Loudspeaker (Tweeter)

The flared shape of the horn gives direction to the shorter wavelengths of high-frequency sound energy and couples the small high-frequency diaphragm to the air. Low frequencies must be filtered out of the signal to the tweeter because the large cone displacements which they produce could damage the driver.

### Low-Frequency Loudspeaker and Enclosure (Woofer)

A large loudspeaker (15 to 18 in diameter) in a large cabinet enclosure ($> 10$ ft$^3$) incorporating a flared horn is required to efficiently generate low-frequency sound energy, which has longer wavelengths and requires greater cone movement than high-frequency sound energy.

Smaller, *critically tuned* enclosures without horns also can reproduce low-frequency sound energy. They demand greater power input for equivalent sound output, but can be used to produce lower frequencies than horn-coupled enclosures of moderate size.

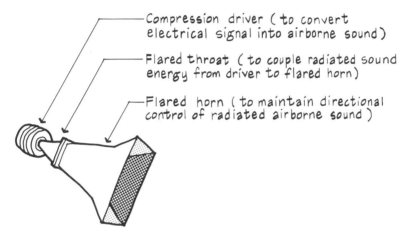

Compression driver (to convert electrical signal into airborne sound)

Flared throat (to couple radiated sound energy from driver to flared horn)

Flared horn (to maintain directional control of radiated airborne sound)

**Biradial Horn**

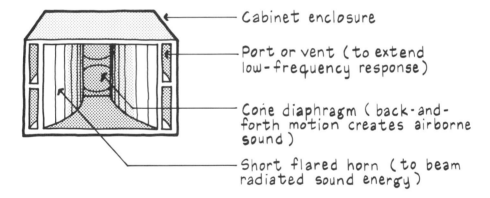

Cabinet enclosure

Port or vent (to extend low-frequency response)

Cone diaphragm (back-and-forth motion creates airborne sound)

Short flared horn (to beam radiated sound energy)

**Horn-Loaded Low-Frequency Enclosure** (Bass horn)

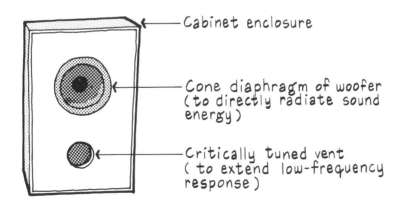

Cabinet enclosure

Cone diaphragm of woofer (to directly radiate sound energy)

Critically tuned vent (to extend low-frequency response)

**Tuned Low-Frequency Enclosure** (Direct radiator)

## CENTRAL LOUDSPEAKER SYSTEM

The *central* loudspeaker system usually locates the loudspeaker, or cluster of loudspeakers, 20 to 40 ft above and slightly in front of the actual source of sound. The cluster can be exposed or hidden behind a sound-transparent grille cloth. This system can provide maximum realism because the listener will hear the amplified sound from the direction of the live source location. This is because human ears differentiate sounds better in the horizontal plane (where ears are located) than in the vertical plane. Therefore, amplified sound from a properly designed central system should not be noticeable. Central loudspeaker clusters should use directional loudspeakers aimed to concentrate amplified sound energy on the audience, which absorbs sound, *not* on sound-reflecting floor, wall, and ceiling surfaces. In this way, reinforcement systems can provide high intelligibility by increasing the level of sound energy from the location of the talker more than they increase the reverberant sound energy.

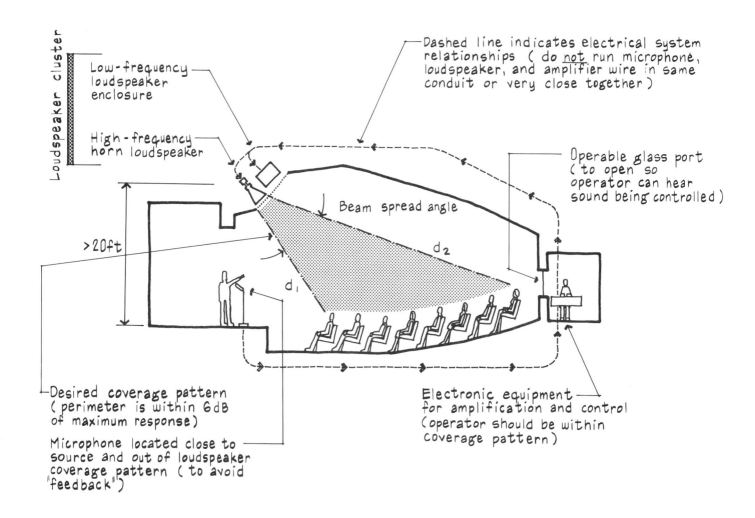

## Checklist for Central Systems

1. Audience should have unobstructed line of sight to loudspeaker cluster because high-frequency sound is very directional.

2. In general, the distance from any high-frequency horn in a central cluster to the farthest listener covered by that horn $d_2$ should be less than twice the distance from the horn to the nearest listener $d_1$. That is, the ratio of coverage distances $d_2/d_1$ for an individual horn should be less than 2.

3. High-frequency horns should be aimed directly at the audience so that sound is not reflected by room surfaces. Audience or unoccupied upholstered seats should absorb most of the amplified sound before it can be reflected and contribute to reverberation.

4. System operator should be located within the coverage pattern of the loudspeakers so that operator can hear the same mix of live and reinforced sound the audience hears. If control consoles must be located in a control room at the rear of the auditorium, provide an operable float-glass observation port which can be opened to the main space ($>$ 24 ft$^2$ open area) and orient console so operator will be seated adjacent to the opening.

## References

D. H. Kaye, "The Sound Amplification System for Mechanics Hall," *Technology & Conservation*, Fall 1980.

D. H. Kaye and D. L. Klepper, "Sound System Specifications," *Journal of the Audio Engineering Society*, April 1962.

A loudspeaker system *cluster* takes up a great deal of space and, as shown below, the area in front must be completely open or be hidden behind a grille that is transparent to sound (called *transondent*; see Chap. 2).

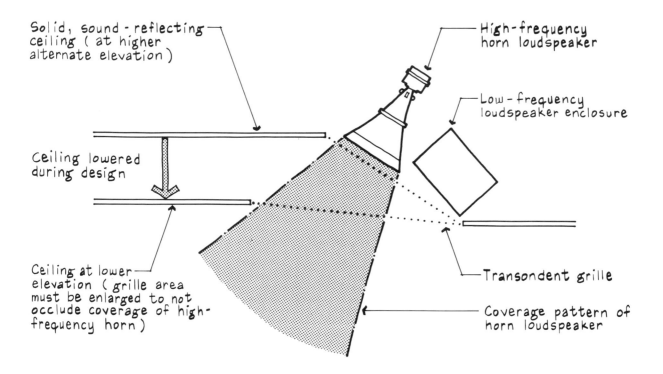

**Central Loudspeaker Cluster**

### Checklist for Loudspeaker Clusters

1. Extent of required open area in front of loudspeakers is determined by coverage patterns of the loudspeakers.
2. Suitable transondent grille materials include loudspeaker grille cloth, most open-weave fabric, and some perforated and expanded metals (if sufficiently open).
3. Any solid framing members must be small ($< 1/2$ in width and at right angle to centerline of loudspeakers) and have wide, irregular spacings so they will not occlude the coverage patterns of the loudspeakers.
4. Install high-frequency horns using supports which allow reorientation of at least 5° in any direction and which can be secured into precise orientation, determined by performance evaluation in the completed space.
5. Where fire-rated constructions are required, the fire resistance integrity of the ceiling should be maintained. (See Underwriters' Laboratories *Fire Resistance Index*, current edition, or M. D. Egan, *Concepts in Building Firesafety*, Wiley-Interscience, New York, 1978, pp. 63-109.)

# DIRECTIONAL PATTERNS FOR HIGH-FREQUENCY HORNS

The dispersion of sound energy (called *beam spread*) from a loudspeaker can be plotted on polar coordinate graphs. 0° is the *on-axis direction*, meaning straight ahead as projected from the front of the loudspeaker. 180° is the direction to the rear or from behind the driver of the loudspeaker. Measurements in decibels (dB) are usually made in both the horizontal and vertical planes with the results given for several octave-frequency bands.

Equal-level contours are plots of relative sound levels from a horn loudspeaker. These contours can provide useful aiming information to assist in cluster design of modern biradial high-frequency horns, which have relatively constant directivity over a wide frequency range.

Shown below are examples of directional response patterns for radial and biradial horns and example equal-level contours.

**Radial Horn** (or "sectoral" horn, because shape in plan view is similar to piece of pie)

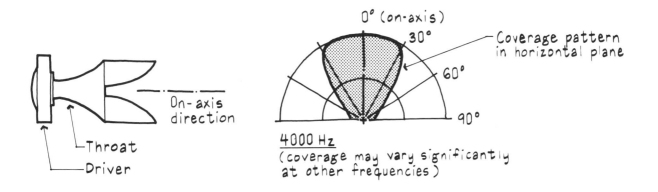

**Biradial Horn** (or "constant-directivity" horn)

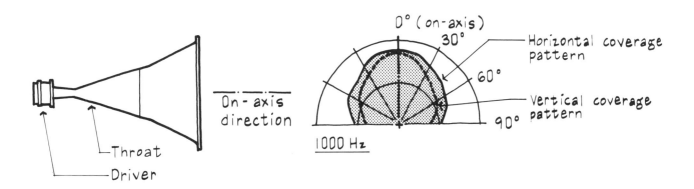

**Equal-Level Contours** (for biradial horn)

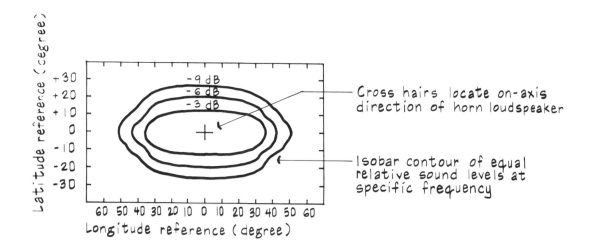

**Reference**

T. Uzzle, "Loudspeaker Coverage by Architectural Mapping," *Journal of the Audio Engineering Society*, June 1982.

## DISTRIBUTED LOUDSPEAKER SYSTEM

The *distributed* loudspeaker system consists of an array of loudspeakers usually located in the ceiling or suspended overhead. Each loudspeaker supplies low-level amplified sound to a small area. The system is used when the ceiling height is inadequate for a central system, when all listeners cannot have line of sight to a central cluster position (e.g., deep underbalcony seating, subdivided rooms), when directional realism is not important (e.g., announcements in air-port concourses, offices), or when the sound source location may vary (e.g., hotel function rooms, church fellowship halls).

Distributed systems work best when the ceiling or floor or both are sound-absorbing. For uniform coverage, spacing between wide-dispersion loudspeakers should be 1.4 (*H* – 4) or less for seated audience, where *H* is room height in feet and 4 ft is the average seated ear height. Closer spacings may be needed in reverberant rooms or where room heights are greater than 12 ft.

Wide-dispersion loudspeakers used in distributed loudspeaker systems are usually 8-in-diameter (or larger where better bass response is desired for music) coaxial loudspeakers with 3-in-diameter (or less) tweeters, or 4-in-diameter full-range loudspeakers. "Whizzer" loudspeakers or plain-cone loud-speakers larger than 4 in diameter have narrower dispersion within the frequency range which is necessary for high intelligibility of speech and, therefore, require closer spacing.

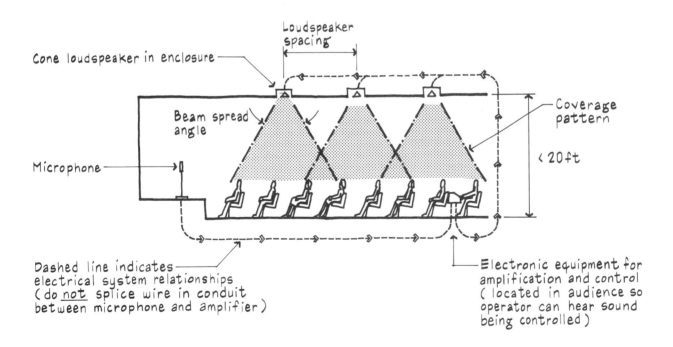

## Checklist for Distributed Systems

1. Ceiling height $H$ should not exceed 20 ft, which is about the minimum height for the preferred central system. In reverberant rooms, $H$ should not exceed 12 ft unless dense loudspeaker coverage can be achieved.

2. Loudspeakers should be distributed in an array so each listener will receive direct sound from the closest loudspeaker and, after a short delay, sound from nearby loudspeakers ($< 20$ ft away). However, sound from the more distant loudspeakers will be greatly attenuated by distance and because listeners will be located well off-axis of the loudspeakers.

3. Signal-delay features (see p. 374) may be required to avoid *artificial echo*, which occurs when the path difference (loudspeaker-to-listener distance compared to the natural source-to-listener distance) is greater than about 30 ft and the level of the natural source is within 5 to 10 dB of the amplified level.

4. Distributed systems with signal-delay features should be used for loud live sources in long rooms or to complement central sound systems at underbalcony locations.

5. A "localizer" loudspeaker, aimed at the audience and located in the podium or on the lecture platform, can be used with distributed systems. Use of these loudspeakers may enhance the illusion that sound is coming from the person who is talking rather than from the signal-delayed loudspeakers located overhead.

## LOUDSPEAKER SPACING FOR DISTRIBUTED SYSTEMS

Distributed loudspeaker systems should be arranged so the coverage patterns of the loudspeakers will sufficiently overlap. Practical spacing $S$ for uniform coverage with wide-dispersion cone loudspeakers can be found by the following formulas:

$$S = 1.4(H - 4) \quad \text{for seated audience}$$
$$S = 1.4(H - 6) \quad \text{for standing (e.g., airport concourse)}$$

where $S$ = spacing between loudspeakers (ft)
$H$ = floor-to-ceiling height (ft)

**Loudspeaker Spacing** (section view)

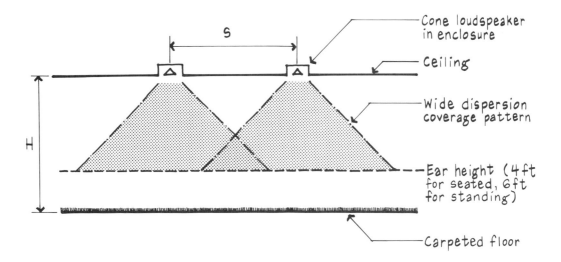

### Coverage Patterns at Ear Height

Example cone loudspeaker placement patterns are shown in plan view below. Cone loudspeakers distribute sound over a beam spread angle which narrows as frequency increases. The coverage pattern shown represents the position at ear height where the loudspeaker sound level at 4000 Hz drops off 6 dB from the level directly underneath (on-axis orientation). Uniformity of coverage at 4000 Hz is important because, if the sound level up to this frequency is well distributed, the consonants which determine speech intelligibility can be clearly heard.

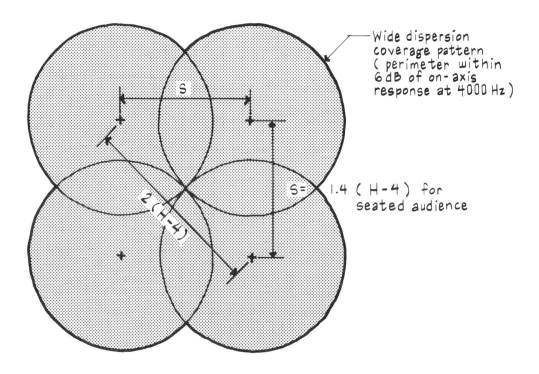

Wide dispersion coverage pattern (perimeter within 6 dB of on-axis response at 4000 Hz)

S = 1.4 (H-4) for seated audience

**Reference**

R. Sinclair, "The Design of Distributed Sound Systems from Uniformity of Coverage and Other Sound-Field Considerations," *Journal of the Audio Engineering Society*, December 1982.

## SEAT-INTEGRATED LOUDSPEAKER SYSTEM

The *seat-integrated* loudspeaker system consists of a number of loud-speakers (spaced 5 to 8 ft apart) which are located in the backs of seats or pews. Each loudspeaker is a short distance from the nearest listener and there-fore supplies low-level amplified sound to a small area (e.g., one loudspeaker for every two to four listeners). This system can be used in rooms where re-verberation times are extremely long (2 to 5s at mid-frequencies) or where the audience is seated behind the performing area. Signal-delay features can be used to improve intelligibility and realism. To synchronize amplified sound with live sound, signal-delay zones should be less than about 28 ft in length.

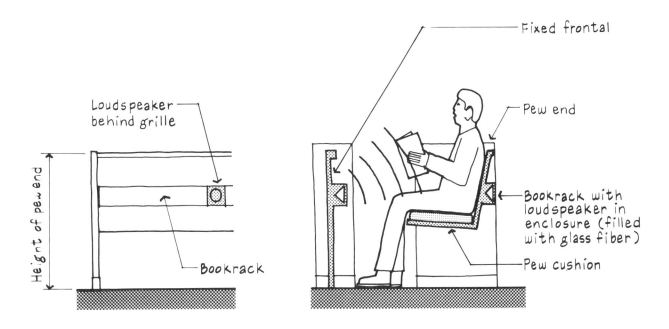

**Pew Seating**

## COLUMN LOUDSPEAKER SYSTEM

A *column loudspeaker* consists of a linear array of cone loudspeakers (usually vertical with one above the other) to concentrate sound into a narrow vertical beam. In the vertical plane, the cone loudspeakers reinforce each other creating high directionality. In the horizontal plane, the directional pattern is similar to that of a single-cone loudspeaker. The dispersion or beam spread usually narrows at higher frequencies and may deviate from the smooth patterns shown below.

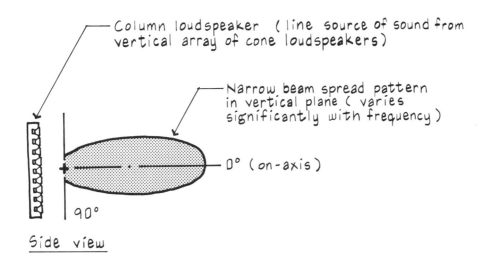

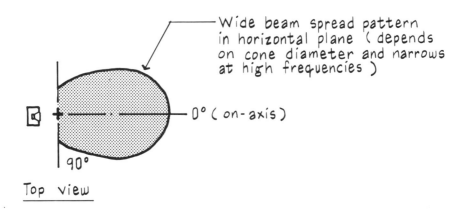

**Directional Response Patterns**

Column loudspeakers can be used along the walls of long, reverberant spaces (or mounted on or within structural columns in churches) to direct amplified speech evenly throughout the audience. The spacing between column loudspeakers should be less than 25 ft so that the direct sound field will be increased more than the reverberant sound. For example, satisfactory intelligibility can be achieved in narrow churches (< 45 ft wide) if column loudspeakers are properly spaced and aimed (e.g., tilted toward the nearby congregation) and the throw distances are short. All column loudspeakers should be aimed toward the rear of a church, *not* side-to-side. Signal-delay features will be required to synchronize column loudspeakers with each other and with the live sound from the front of the room (e.g., St. Paul's Cathedral, London).

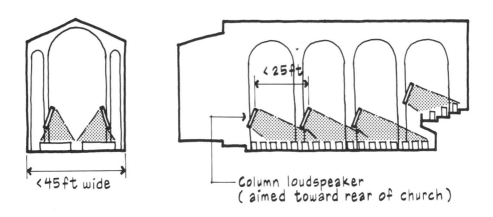

**Column Loudspeakers in Church Sanctuary**

**Note:** To help the congregation localize on live source of sound, a loudspeaker (or small cluster of loudspeakers) can be installed near or in the ceiling above the pulpit location.

# MICROPHONE PLACEMENT EXAMPLES

### Microphone Placement

The condenser microphone is usually preferred for reinforcement of choirs. To estimate the number of microphones needed, use the 3-to-1 rule, which means the distance $d_2$ between adjacent microphones must be at least 3 times the distance $d_1$ each microphone is from its nearest source. Shown below is an example microphone layout for a conventional choir, three rows deep. Avoid microphone positions too close to the singer. *Cardioid microphones* (so called due to heart-shaped pickup response pattern, which is relatively low at sides and rear) can be spaced closer together if the heads of adjacent microphones are angled away from each other. When two microphones are used close together ($<$ 18 in apart), avoid frequency-response interference by placing the heads directly together.

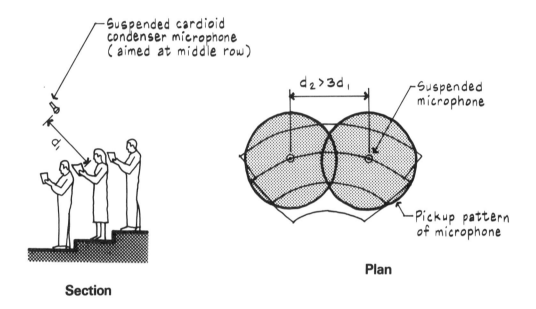

Section

Plan

### Working Distances

One cardioid microphone can cover an entire pulpit or lectern area. Shown below are example working distances for cardioid and omnidirectional microphones. *Omnidirectional microphones* pick up sound equally from all directions. Cardioid microphones can be located up to 1.7 times farther away from the source than omnidirectional microphones. However, when cardioid microphones are placed too close to users (e.g., at "lips-touching" distances), low frequencies, which do not contribute to the intelligibility of consonants, can be seriously overemphasized. Some manufacturers carry models which have no "proximity effect"; information on this feature would usually be provided in their technical literature.

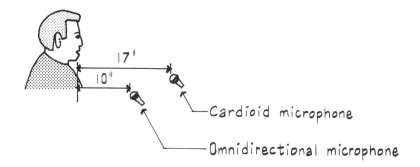

Cardioid microphone

Omnidirectional microphone

**References**

L. R. Burroughs, *Microphones: Design and Application*, Sagamore Publishing, Plainview, N.Y., 1974.

T. Ludwig, "A General Microphone Primer," *Sound & Video Contractor*, Part 2, October 1983.

## SIGNAL DELAY FOR LOUDSPEAKER SYSTEMS

Signal-delay devices can be used in sound-reinforcing systems to avoid *artificial echo* ("muddying" or "garbling" effects) caused when the natural sound is heard later than the amplified sound. This occurs because sound in air travels at 1130 ft/s, whereas the electric signal to loudspeakers travels almost instantaneously, at the speed of light. Therefore, signal-delay devices are used to delay the electric signal to distant loudspeakers so that the amplified sound will arrive at the listener's ears within 25 ms before or after the natural sound (e.g., sound from a central cluster in large rooms with overhead cone loudspeakers covering underbalcony seating).

For an initial check on signal-delay requirements, measure the distances from the live source of sound and the central cluster to both nearest and farthest listeners. Convert to signal delays by dividing distance differences by 1130. Delays should be less than 25 ms. For the example shown below, listeners located 80 ft from a loudspeaker at the front of an auditorium and 8 ft directly beneath a cone loudspeaker, without signal-delay features, will perceive an artificial echo due to a delay of 64 ms. That is,

Signal delay = distance ÷ velocity = (80 – 8) ÷ 1130 = 64ms

Signal delay should be used to avoid artificial echo, and to permit listeners to hear intelligible sound and to localize on the actual source of sound. If the delayed sound which reaches the listeners' ears is less than 10 dB louder than the natural sound and arrives less than 25 ms before or after the natural sound, it will be synchronized with and perceived as coming from the original source, not the loudspeaker with signal delay (a phenomenon called the *precedence*, or *Haas, effect*).

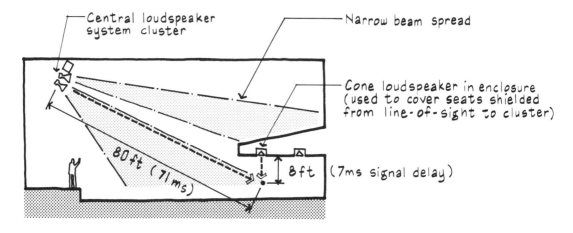

**Section View of Auditorium**

Signal delay can be used for the following loudspeaker system applications.

1. Distributed loudspeakers for loud live sources, such as bands, in long rooms with low ceiling heights.
2. Seat-integrated loudspeaker systems (usually signal-delay zones change about every third or fourth row).
3. Central system with distributed loudspeakers covering seating areas under deep balcony overhangs or transepts in a church.
4. Central loudspeaker system clusters located far in front of stage.
5. Distributed loudspeaker clusters for outdoor concerts or for large sports arenas.

Sound systems may excite undesirable system resonances causing "squealing" or "howling" feedback and uneven distribution of sound, particularly in highly reverberant spaces. "Ringing" occurs when a specific frequency is regenerated through the sound system. Feedback frequencies are dependent on the physical dimensions of the room, the sound-absorbing treatment present, the frequency-response characteristics of the microphones and loudspeakers (e.g., lack of smoothness of response), and the distance from microphone to loudspeaker. In theaters for drama, feedback is best avoided by locating the microphone near the sound source and using as few open microphones as possible.

Adjustable electronic filters can be used to smooth out the frequency response of a sound system and reduce its tendency to ring. Filters with center frequencies spaced one-third of an octave apart are usually used. This procedure is highly specialized and should be performed only by qualified sound system engineers after the system has been installed in the finished space.

**References**

C. R. Cable, "Time-Delay Spectrometry Investigation of Regenerative Sound Systems," *Journal of the Audio Engineering Society*, March 1978.

D. B. Davis and C. Davis, *Sound System Engineering*, Howard W. Sams, New York, 1987.

T. Uzzle, "The Effect of Reinforcement System Regeneration on Gain and Reverberative Decay," Audio Engineering Society Preprint #2019, October 1983.

## LOUDSPEAKER LAYOUTS TO BE AVOIDED

A poor loudspeaker layout or placement can mean ineffective sound reinforcement. In the auditorium example shown below, where loudspeakers are located at both sides of the proscenium opening (called *split-stack* layout by rock performers), the intelligibility can actually be improved by shutting off one loudspeaker! As indicated on the illustration, coverage will be poor, with both interference for listeners near the center of the room and lack of directional realism.

Both example loudspeaker layouts shown below can produce unpleasant effects because they create areas of interference where their coverage patterns overlap (i.e., cancellation of certain frequencies).

### Loudspeakers at Both Sides of Wide Proscenium

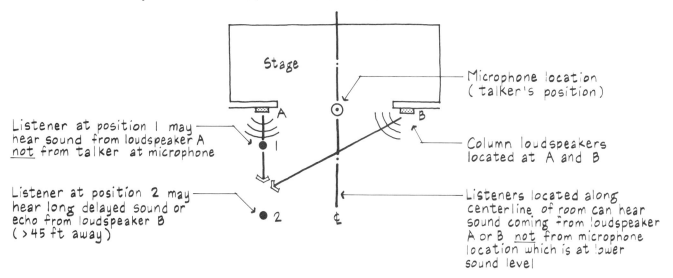

### Loudspeakers Aimed along Circulation Space

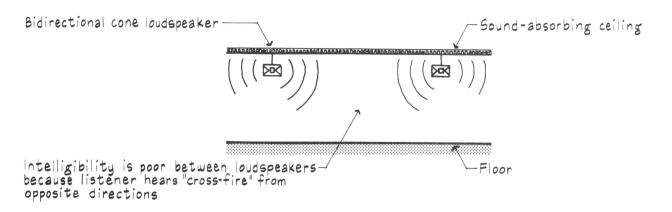

### Reference

R. B. Newman and W. J. Cavanaugh, "Sound Systems," *Architectural Record*, December 1961 and January 1962.

# COMPARISON OF BASIC SOUND-REINFORCING SYSTEMS

Design, installation, and relative equipment cost characteristics of the basic sound-reinforcing systems are shown below. It should be noted that the specific application and room design (shape, height, seating layout) may override decisions based on auditory directional realism or on cost alone. For example, in a large church with volume greater than 250 ft³ per person, the congregation may, for visual reasons, object to the preferred central cluster of highly directional horns suspended 30 ft above the pulpit location. Unless the conflict can be resolved, auditory realism will suffer. In this wide church, the best alternative to the central system would be the seat-integrated system. Unfortunately, even a well-designed pew-back system may not be able to achieve everywhere the illusion of sound coming from the pulpit location.

| System | Operational and Installation Characteristics | | | |
| --- | --- | --- | --- | --- |
| | Auditory Directional Realism | Visibility of Loudspeakers | Electronic Signal Delay | Relative Equipment Cost |
| Central cluster | Excellent | High (or medium if recessed) | No | Low |
| Split cluster* | Good | Can be medium | No | Moderate |
| Distributed (overhead) | Poor | Low (if recessed) Medium or high (if suspended) | Sometimes | Low to moderate |
| Column (distributed along length of room) | Fair | Can be medium | Yes | Moderate to high |
| Seat-integrated | Poor | Low | Yes | High |
| Combinations | (depends on room and systems design) | | | |

*Split cluster* can be used in rooms with two main speaking positions (e.g., church with lectern and pulpit, separated at left and right). The system works best when the cluster amplifies speech from the closest source position only, thereby working like two independent clusters. Another variation, used in drama theaters, locates three to five clusters above and across the width of the proscenium opening. Microphone inputs can be designed so the apparent direction of sound moves with its source.

## ELECTRONIC BACKGROUND MASKING SYSTEM

Electronic background *masking systems* can be used to cover up unwanted intruding sound in enclosed and open-plan offices. To be effective, the sound level of the masking system should be neither too loud nor too low, and the spectrum should roll off at the high end of the frequency range.

In open plans, loudspeakers usually can be hidden in plenums above suspended sound-absorbing ceilings. This strategy can achieve uniform masking sound throughout the room. Be careful when designing this kind of installation because openings for return or supply air in ceilings and luminaires can be noticeable sound leaks, which make it difficult to achieve a uniform masking sound. In addition, to avoid obvious nonuniform sound conditions within rooms the masking system should use at least two noise generators feeding alternate loudspeakers (called *channels*).

For preliminary planning, loudspeaker spacing $S$ can be found by:

$$S \cong 1.4 \ (2D + H - 4)$$

where   $S$ = spacing between loudspeakers (ft)
$D$ = plenum depth (ft)
$H$ = floor-to-ceiling height (ft)

Closer spacings may be required when spray-on, sound-absorbing fire protection is applied to the underside of structural decks, or when complicated air duct layouts or deep structural members (e.g., baffles, coffers) obstruct plenums.

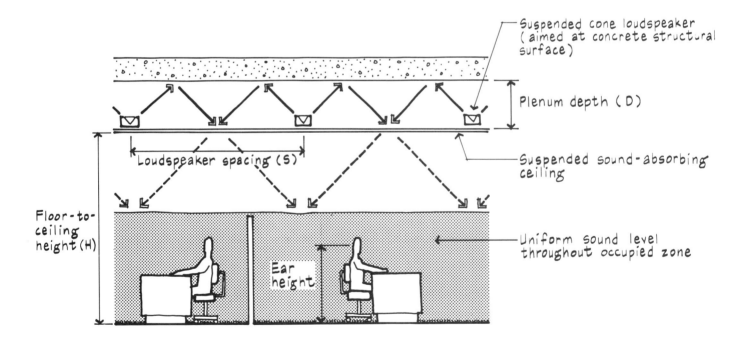

## Checklist for Masking Systems for Open Plans

1. Loudspeakers should be in enclosures located just above suspended ceilings, aimed upward toward hard plenum surfaces, or be unenclosed loudspeakers on sheet metal baffles hung vertically in the plenum space.

2. Plenums should have uncomplicated air duct layouts and smooth sound-reflecting structural surfaces to allow wider spacings between loudspeakers.

3. Coverage should include adjacent areas (or zones) so occupants moving about the building will *not* notice the masking system.

4. Masking should not exceed a sound level of 45 to 50 dBA because occupants tend to raise their voices to compensate, thus defeating the intended masking effects. Occupants may also begin to complain about the sound level when it exceeds 50 dBA.

5. To reduce the likelihood that occupants will notice background masking, consider installation procedures that initially operate the system at low sound levels. Then gradually increase the level by about 1 dB each day until the desired masking level is reached in a week to ten days or longer.

6. A well-designed masking system deliberately garbles the sound it produces and therefore should not be used for paging and routine announcement functions.

7. Provisions can be made to reduce masking noise levels during off-hours to enhance the ability of security personnel to hear unusual sounds.

8. Be sure to consider the consequences of background masking on the usability of open plans by hearing-impaired persons. For example, when background noise levels exceed 30 dBA, hearing-impaired persons (even when using hearing aids) have far more difficulty understanding speech than do normal-hearing persons.

# SOUND SPECTRA FOR MASKING SYSTEMS

In addition to avoiding excessive sound levels, background noise from electronic masking systems in open-plan offices should have a *neutral* tonal quality. This may be facilitated by designing the system to simulate familiar building sounds, such as the airflow at diffusers and registers of HVAC systems. Shown below is a range of background masking spectra at octave-band frequencies from 250 to 8000 Hz. (The spectra are similar to RC noise spectra where sound levels drop off by 5 dB per octave.) These spectra can provide a pleasant acoustical background after they have been adjusted by filters so that the electronically produced sound levels in the finished room are no higher than necessary to mask unwanted intruding speech and so that pronounced hisses are avoided. Again, preferred background masking sound levels generally should *not* exceed 45 to 50 dBA.

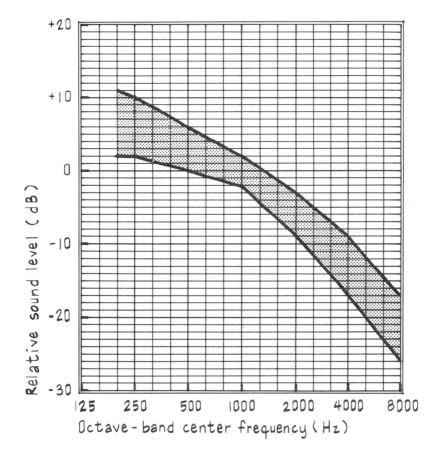

## References

L. L. Beranek, W. E. Blazier, and J. J. Figwer, "Preferred Noise Criterion (PNC) Curves and Their Application to Rooms," *Journal of the Acoustical Society of America,* November 1971.

W. E. Blazier, "Revised Noise Criteria for Application in the Acoustical Design and Rating of HVAC Systems," *Noise Control Engineering Journal,* March-April 1981.

# CASE STUDY 1: OPEN-PLAN OFFICE

## South Central Bell Telephone Company
Birmingham, Alabama

The 450,000-ft² earth-covered corporate office building opened in 1981. The open-plan office spaces have satisfactory speech privacy due to careful layout of workstations, strategically placed partial-height barriers, and installation of a designed electronic background masking system. The loudspeakers used for masking are distributed above the suspended sound-absorbing ceiling and are aimed upward at the overhead metal deck (shown in isometric section below). The masking system uses 4-in cone loudspeakers in protective metal enclosures installed at a density of 125 ft² per loudspeaker. Background masking sound levels are adjusted not to exceed 48 dBA throughout the open-plan office and adjacent areas.

*Architect:* Giattina Fisher & Company (Birmingham, Alabama)
*Acoustical Consultant:* Office of M. David Egan (Anderson, South Carolina)
*Sound System Designer:* David H. Kaye (Boston, Massachusetts)

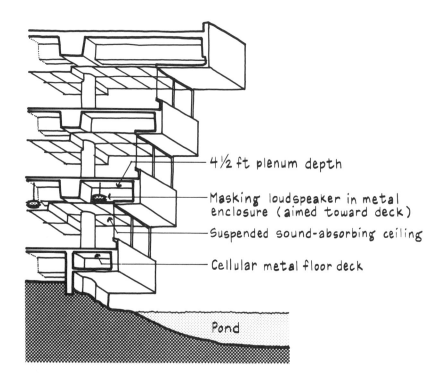

4½ ft plenum depth

Masking loudspeaker in metal enclosure (aimed toward deck)

Suspended sound-absorbing ceiling

Cellular metal floor deck

Pond

**Isometric Section**

## Reference

J. Murphy, "Southern Bell," *Progressive Architecture*, April 1982, pp. 162-166.

© Paul C. Beswick

**Cantilevered Floors over Pond**

**Typical Open-Office Workstations**

© Wolfgang Hoyt/ESTO

# CASE STUDY 2: CHURCH

## First Baptist Church
### Greenville, South Carolina

The 400,000-ft³ sanctuary of the First Baptist Church has a seating capacity of 1350 persons. Volume-to-audience-area ratio is 46. The sanctuary, completed in 1984, was designed to enhance sound from a large pipe organ and support an active music program. Because mid-frequency reverberation time is longer than 2.2 s, it was essential that the *central* sound-reinforcing system be carefully incorporated into the "tree of life" ribbed elements located behind the altar. The loudspeaker cluster includes four directional high-frequency horns ( > 500 Hz) and two custom mid-frequency enclosures (150 to 500 Hz), supplemented by two subwoofer loudspeakers ( < 150 Hz) at the platform level.

*Architect:* CRS Sirrine (Greenville, South Carolina)
*Acoustical Consultant:* Office of M. David Egan (Anderson, South Carolina)
*Sound System Designer:* David H. Kaye (Boston, Massachusetts)

Toy L. Belcher, CRS Sirrine, Inc.

**Sanctuary from the Underbalcony**

**View of Steeple and Church**

*Courtesy of CRS Sirrine, Inc.*

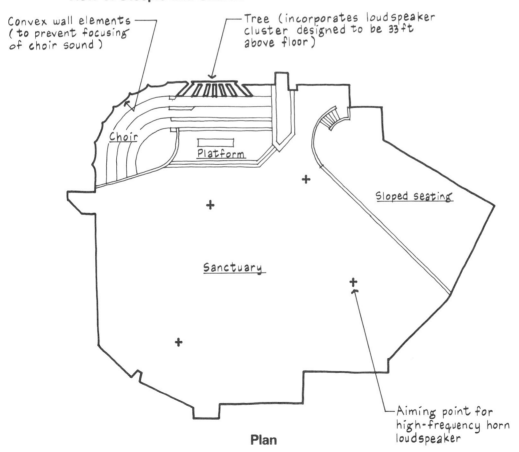

Convex wall elements (to prevent focusing of choir sound)

Tree (incorporates loudspeaker cluster designed to be 33 ft above floor)

Choir

Platform

Sloped seating

Sanctuary

Aiming point for high-frequency horn loudspeaker

**Plan**

# CHECKLIST FOR EFFECTIVE USE OF ELECTRONIC SOUND SYSTEMS

1. A well-designed sound-reinforcing system should augment the natural transmission of sound from source to listener. It should be properly integrated with the room acoustics design to provide adequate loudness and good distribution of sound. It should never, however, be considered as an alternative to good room acoustics design, because it will rarely overcome or correct serious deficiencies and could indeed exaggerate them.

2. If used by experienced talkers, spaces with good room acoustics seating fewer than 500 will seldom need a sound-reinforcing system; spaces seating 500 to 1000 may need a sound system, depending on the space use; and spaces seating more than 1000 will probably need a sound system, although it may not be used all the time. Courtrooms, governmental council chambers, and the like, regardless of their size, almost always require sound-reinforcing systems because they are used by inexperienced talkers.

3. The preferred type of sound-reinforcing system is *always* the *central* system, in which a loudspeaker (or cluster of loudspeakers) is located directly above the source of sound to provide sound of high intelligibility. The central system also is the most natural sounding system.

4. The other principal type of sound-reinforcing system is the *distributed* system, in which a large number of loudspeakers, each supplying low-level amplified sound to a small area, are located in close proximity overhead. The distributed system should be used in auditoriums when the ceiling height is inadequate to use a central system, when all listeners do not have line of sight to a central loudspeaker cluster, or when the source of live sound is not at a fixed location. The distributed system also can be used for paging and announcements, where directional realism is not important.

5. Locate microphones out of the coverage pattern of loudspeakers to avoid feedback, unless it is certain that talkers always will be close to microphones of sound systems that are properly equalized. Feedback is the regeneration of a signal between loudspeaker and microphone which is heard as howling or screeching.

6. Use equipment designs (e.g., consoles and racks) which can be prefabricated in the shop or factory, thereby avoiding potential damage and dirt accumulation from building construction operations.

7. Background masking sound systems should provide sound energy at levels and frequency content that are not noticeable to room occupants. Ideally, masking sound spectra should provide privacy by simulating familiar sounds, such as pleasant hushes from the gentle flow of air at room diffusers and registers. In open plans, the sound energy should be uniformly distributed throughout the room and *not* be too loud, causing occupants to raise their voices to be heard.

8. Design and specifications documents for a sound system should include performance criteria, functional diagrams, loudspeaker layout drawings, identification of alternate equipment by major manufacturers (to facilitate competitive bidding), and provisions for qualified supervision of acceptance testing and final adjustment of the installed system. For example, the acceptability of masking sound at the levels required for speech privacy in open plans depends upon the skillful adjustment of the sound spectrum.

# Selected References on Architectural Acoustics and Noise Control

L. L. Beranek, *Music, Acoustics and Architecture*, Wiley, New York, 1962.

L. L. Beranek (ed.), *Noise and Vibration Control*, McGraw-Hill, New York, 1971.

R. D. Berendt et al., *Quieting: A Practical Guide to Noise Control*, U.S. National Bureau of Standards, NBS Handbook 119, July 1976.

L. Cremer and H. A. Müller, *Principles and Applications of Room Acoustics*, vol. 1, Applied Science Publishers, Barking, England, 1978. (English translation by T. J. Schultz.)

D. J. Croome, *Noise, Buildings and People*, Pergamon Press, Oxford, England, 1977.

B. F. Day et al., *Building Acoustics*, Elsevier Publishing, Barking, England, 1969.

L. L. Doelle, *Environmental Acoustics*, McGraw-Hill, New York, 1972.

M. D. Egan, *Concepts in Architectural Acoustics*, McGraw-Hill, New York, 1972.

W. Furrer, *Room and Building Acoustics and Noise Abatement*, Butterworths, Washington, D.C.,1964. (English translation by E. R. Robinson and P. Lord.)

C. J. Hemond, *Engineering Acoustics and Noise Control*, Prentice-Hall, Englewood Cliffs, N.J., 1983.

R. S. Jones, *Noise and Vibration Control in Buildings*, McGraw-Hill, New York, 1984.

V. O. Knudsen and C. M. Harris, *Acoustical Designing in Architecture*, Wiley, New York, 1950. (Softcover reprint edition available from Acoustical Society of America, 500 Sunnyside Blvd., Woodbury, NY 11797.)

H. Kuttruff, *Room Acoustics*, Applied Science Publishers, Barking, England, 1979.

A. B. Lawrence, *Architectural Acoustics*, Elsevier Publishing, Barking, England, 1970.

J. E. Moore, *Design for Good Acoustics and Noise Control*, Macmillan Press, London, 1978.

R. B. Newman, "Acoustics" in J. H. Callender (ed.), *Time-Saver Standards for Architectural Design Data*, McGraw-Hill, New York, 1974.

T. D. Northwood (ed.), *Architectural Acoustics*, Dowden, Hutchinson, and Ross, Stroudsburg, Pa., 1977.

P. H. Parkin et al., *Acoustics, Noise and Buildings*, Faber and Faber, London, 1979.

D. D. Reynolds, *Engineering Principles of Acoustics*, Allyn and Bacon, Boston, 1981.

W. C. Sabine, *Collected Papers on Acoustics*, Dover, New York, 1964. (Softcover reprint edition of papers by Prof. Sabine published during period of 1900 to 1915.)

H. E. White and D. H. White, *Physics and Music*, Holt, Rinehart and Winston, New York, 1980.

L. F. Yerges, *Sound, Noise, and Vibration Control*, Van Nostrand Reinhold, New York, 1978.

# Appendix A
# Summary of Useful Formulas

**General**

*Character:*

$$T_p = \frac{1}{f} \qquad (1)$$

where    $T_p$ = period of one complete vibration (s)

      $f$ = frequency (Hz)

$$\lambda = \frac{c}{f} \qquad (2)$$

where    $\lambda$ = wavelength (ft)

      $c$ = speed of sound in air (ft/s)

      $f$ = frequency (Hz)

*Magnitude:*

$$L_I = 10 \log \frac{I}{I_0} \qquad (3)$$

where    $L_I$ = sound intensity level (decibels, abbreviated dB)    .

      $I$ = sound intensity (watts/meter squared, abbreviated $W/m^2$)

      $I_0$ = reference sound intensity ($W/m^2$, usually taken as $10^{-12}$ $W/m^2$ or the equivalent $10^{-16}$ $W/cm^2$)

$$L_P = 20 \log \frac{P}{P_0} \qquad (4)$$

where    $L_P$ = sound pressure level (dB)

      $P$ = sound pressure (newtons/meter squared, abbreviated $N/m^2$, or pascals, abbreviated Pa)

      $P_0$ = reference sound pressure ($N/m^2$, always taken as 0.00002 $N/m^2$)

**Note:** $L_P$ may be considered equal to $L_I$ in most architectural acoustics situations.

$$L_W = 10 \log \frac{W}{W_0} \tag{5}$$

where   $L_W$ = sound power level (dB)

$W$ = sound power (W)

$W_0$ = reference sound power (W, usually taken as $10^{-12}$ W)

**Note:** $L_W$ is used by testing laboratories to rate a sound source independently of its environment.

*Noise Reduction:*

$$NR = L_1 - L_2 \tag{6}$$

where   NR = noise reduction, or the difference in sound levels between two conditions (dB)

$L_1$ = sound level under one condition, usually taken as the higher value (dB)

$L_2$ = sound level under another condition (dB)

$$NR = 10 \log \frac{I_1}{I_2} \tag{7}$$

where   NR = [see formula (6)]

$I_1$ = sound intensity under one condition (W/m²)

$I_2$ = sound intensity under another condition (W/m²)

## Sound Source Under Free Field Conditions: Outdoors

$$I = \frac{W}{4\pi d^2} \tag{8}$$

where   $I$ = sound intensity (W/m²)

$W$ = sound power (W)

$\pi$ = 3.14

$d$ = distance from sound source (m)

If distance is given in feet, use $I = W/4\pi d^2 \times 10.76$

*Inverse-Square Law:*

$$\frac{I_1}{I_2} = \left(\frac{d_2}{d_1}\right)^2 \tag{9}$$

where  $I_1$ = sound intensity at distance $d_1$ (W/m²)

$I_2$ = sound intensity at distance $d_2$ (W/m²)

$d$ = [see formula (8)]

$$NR = 20 \log \frac{d_2}{d_1} \qquad (10)$$

where  NR = noise reduction (dB)

$d_2$ = distance from sound source at one location (ft or m)

$d_1$ = distance from sound source at another location (ft or m)

**Note:** The sound level is decreased outdoors by 6 dB for each doubling of distance from a point source because 20 log (2) = 20(0.3) = 6 dB. For line sources, use 10 log in formula.

### Sound Source in Reverberant Field: Indoors

$$a = \Sigma \, S \, \alpha \qquad (11)$$

$$\text{or } a = S_1\alpha_1 + S_2\alpha_2 + \cdots + S_n\alpha_n$$

where  $a$ = total room absorption at given frequency (sabins)

$S$ = surface area (ft²)

$\alpha$ = sound absorption coefficient at given frequency (decimal percent)

$$I = \frac{W}{a} \times 10.76 \qquad (12)$$

where  $I$ = sound intensity in reverberant field (W/m²)

$W$ = sound power (W)

$a$ = total room absorption (sabins)

If absorption is calculated in m², use $I = W/a$.

$$\frac{I_1}{I_2} = \frac{a_2}{a_1} \qquad (13)$$

where  $I_1$ = sound intensity in reverberant field at total room absorption $a_1$ (W/m²)

$I_2$ = sound intensity in reverberant field at total room absorption $a_2$ (W/m²)

$a$ = [see formula (11)]

$$NR = 10 \log \frac{a_2}{a_1} \qquad (14)$$

where   NR = room noise reduction in reverberant field (dB)

$a_2$ = total room absorption after treatment (sabins)

$a_1$ = total room absorption before treatment (sabins)

$$L_P = L_W - 10 \log a + 16 \qquad (15)$$

where   $L_P$ = sound pressure level (dB)

$L_W$ = sound power level (dB)

$a$ = [see formula (11)]

*Sabine Formula:*

$$T = 0.05 \frac{V}{a} \qquad (16)$$

where   $T$ = reverberation time, or time required for sound to decay 60 dB after source has stopped (s)

$V$ = room volume (ft$^3$)

$a$ = [see formula (11)]

*Eyring Formula:*

$$T = 0.05 \frac{V}{-S \times 2.3 \log (1-\bar{\alpha})} \qquad (17)$$

where   $T$ = reverberation time (s)

$V$ = room volume (ft$^3$)

$S$ = total surface area (ft$^2$)

$\bar{\alpha} = \dfrac{\Sigma S\alpha}{\Sigma S} = \dfrac{S_1\alpha_1 + S_2\alpha_2 + \cdots + S_n\alpha_n}{S_1 + S_2 + \cdots + S_n}$ = mean sound absorption coefficient (decimal percent)

**Note:** Use the constant 0.16 instead of 0.05 where absorption is calculated in *metric sabins* (surface areas in m$^2$). In large rooms, add air absorption to denominator of *T* formulas.

*Noise Reduction Coefficient:*

$$\text{NRC} = \frac{\alpha_{250} + \alpha_{500} + \alpha_{1000} + \alpha_{2000}}{4} \qquad \text{with result rounded to nearest} \qquad (18)$$
$$\text{0.05 increment}$$

where   NRC = noise reduction coefficient (decimal percent)

$\alpha$ = sound absorption coefficient (decimal percent)

## Sound Transmission Through Common Barrier

$$TL = L_1 - L_2 \qquad (19)$$

where   TL = sound transmission loss (dB)

$L_1$ = sound level in laboratory source room (dB)

$L_2$ = sound level in laboratory receiving room (dB)

$$TL = 10 \log \frac{1}{\tau} \qquad (20)$$

where   TL = sound transmission loss (dB)

$\tau$ = sound transmission coefficient (no units)

*Composite TL:*

$$TL = 10 \log \frac{\Sigma S}{\Sigma \tau S} \qquad (21)$$

where      TL = sound transmission loss of composite barrier (dB)

$\Sigma S = S_1 + S_2 + \cdots + S_n$
= total surface area of barrier (ft$^2$)

$\Sigma \tau S = \tau_1 S_1 + \tau_2 S_2 + \cdots + \tau_n S_n$
= sum of sound transmission coefficients of each part of barrier
times the respective areas (ft$^2$)

*Homogeneous Materials:*

$$TL = 20 + 20 \log G \qquad (22)$$

where   TL = sound transmission loss at 500 Hz (dB)

$G$ = surface density (lb/ft$^2$)

$$NR = TL + 10 \log \frac{a_2}{S} \qquad (23)$$

where   NR = $L_1 - L_2$ = noise reduction, or difference in sound levels,
between rooms (dB)

TL = sound transmission loss of common barrier (dB)

$a_2$ = absorption in receiving room (sabins)

$S$ = surface area of common barrier (ft$^2$)

## Mechanical System Noise and Vibrations

*Vibration Isolation:*

$$f_n = 3.13 \sqrt{\frac{1}{y}} \tag{24}$$

where $f_n$ = natural or resonant frequency of isolator (Hz)

$y$ = spring static deflection (in)

*Lined Duct:*

$$A = 12\, \alpha^{1.4} \left(\frac{P}{S}\right) \tag{25}$$

where $A$ = attenuation for lined duct (dB/ft)

$\alpha$ = sound absorption coefficient of duct liner (decimal percent)

$P$ = perimeter of rectangular duct (in)

$S$ = cross-sectional open area of duct (in²)

## Sound Systems

*Loudspeaker-to-Listener Distance:*

$$d \simeq 0.1 \sqrt{\frac{QV}{T}} \tag{26}$$

where $d$ = maximum loudspeaker-to-listener distance (ft)

$Q$ = loudspeaker directivity (no units)

$V$ = room volume (ft³)

$T$ = reverberation time (s)

*Distributed Loudspeakers for Seated Audience:*

$$S = 1.4\,(H - 4) \tag{27}$$

where $S$ = spacing between loudspeakers (ft)

$H$ = floor-to-ceiling height (ft)

*Background Masking:*

$$S \simeq 1.4\,(2D + H - 4) \tag{28}$$

where   $S$ = spacing between loudspeakers (ft)

   $D$ = plenum depth (ft)

   $H$ = floor-to-ceiling height (ft)

## Miscellaneous

*Vibrating Panels:*

$$f_r = \frac{170}{\sqrt{wd}} \qquad (29)$$

where   $f_r$ = resonant frequency (Hz)

   $w$ = surface weight of panel (lb/ft²)

   $d$ = depth of airspace behind panel (in)

*Perforated Facings:*

$$f_c \simeq \frac{40P}{D} \qquad (30)$$

where   $f_c$ = critical frequency (Hz)

   $P$ = open area (percent)

   $D$ = hole diameter (in)

*Double Walls:*

$$f_0 = \frac{170}{\sqrt{\left(\dfrac{G_1 \times G_2}{G_1 + G_2}\right)d}} \qquad (31)$$

where   $f_0$ = mass-air-mass resonant frequency (Hz)

   $G_1$ = weight of panel layers on one side (lb/ft²)

   $G_2$ = weight of panel layers on opposite side (lb/ft²)

   $d$ = thickness of cavity insulation times $\sqrt{2}$ plus cavity depth not containing insulation (in)

*Outdoor Barriers:*

$$A = 10 \log \frac{H^2}{R} + 10 \log f - 17 \qquad (32)$$

where   $A$ = attenuation for thin-wall barrier (dB)

$H$ = height of barrier above line of sight between source and receiver (ft)

$R$ = distance from source (or receiver) to barrier (ft) *Note:* Use smaller of the two distances.

$f$ = frequency (Hz)

*Ceiling Height for Auditoriums:*

$$H \simeq 20T \qquad (33)$$

where   $H$ = average ceiling height for auditorium with upholstered seats and absorptive rear wall (ft)

$T$ = mid-frequency reverberation time (s)

# Appendix B
# Conversion Factors

The table below presents conversion factors for common acoustical units to corresponding metric system units, often referred to as *le Système Internationale d'Unités* (SI units). The basic SI units are expressed as follows: length by meter (abbreviated m), mass by kilogram (kg), time by second (s), and temperature by degree kelvin (K). For a comprehensive presentation of metric system units, refer to "Standard for Metric Practice," ASTM E 380. This publication is available from the American Society for Testing and Materials (ASTM), 1916 Race Street, Philadelphia, PA 19103.

| To convert | Into | Multiply by* | Conversely, Multiply by* |
|---|---|---|---|
| atmosphere (atm) | lb/in$^2$ (psi) | 14.7 | $6.8 \times 10^{-2}$ |
| | newtons (N)/m$^2$ | $1.0132 \times 10^5$ | $9.872 \times 10^{-6}$ |
| °C | °F | (°C $\times$ 9/5) + 32 | (°F $-$ 32) $\times$ 5/9 |
| | K | °C + 273 | K $-$ 273 |
| cm | in | 0.3937 | 2.54 |
| | ft | $3.281 \times 10^{-2}$ | 30.48 |
| | mm | 10 | $10^{-1}$ |
| | m | $10^{-2}$ | $10^2$ |
| deg (angle) | radians | $1.745 \times 10^{-2}$ | 57.3 |
| dynes/cm$^2$ (microbars) | lb/ft$^2$ (force) | $2.09 \times 10^{-3}$ | 478.5 |
| | N/m$^2$ | $10^{-1}$ | 10 |
| °F | °C | (°F $-$ 32) $\times$ 5/9 | (°C $\times$ 9/5) + 32 |
| | K | (°F + 460) $\times$ 5/9 | 1.8 K $-$ 460 |
| ft | in | 12 | 0.0833 |
| | mm | 304.8 | $3.281 \times 10^{-3}$ |
| | cm | 30.48 | $3.281 \times 10^{-2}$ |
| | m | 0.3048 | 3.281 |
| ft$^2$ | in$^2$ | 144 | $6.944 \times 10^{-3}$ |
| | cm$^2$ | $9.29 \times 10^2$ | 0.01076 |
| | m$^2$ | $9.29 \times 10^{-2}$ | 10.76 |
| ft$^3$ | in$^3$ | 1728 | $5.787 \times 10^{-4}$ |
| | cm$^3$ | $2.832 \times 10^4$ | $3.531 \times 10^{-5}$ |
| | m$^3$ | $2.832 \times 10^{-2}$ | 35.31 |
| gal (liquid US) | liters (L) | 3.785 | 0.2642 |
| | m$^3$ | $3.785 \times 10^{-3}$ | 264.2 |
| gal/min (gpm) | m$^3$/sec | $6.309 \times 10^{-5}$ | $1.585 \times 10^4$ |
| hp | watts (W) | 745.7 | $1.341 \times 10^{-3}$ |
| | kW | 0.7457 | 1.341 |
| in | ft | 0.0833 | 12 |

| To convert | Into | Multiply by* | Conversely, Multiply by* |
|---|---|---|---|
| | mm | 25.4 | 0.03937 |
| | cm | 2.54 | 0.3937 |
| | m | 0.0254 | 39.37 |
| in$^2$ | ft$^2$ | 0.006944 | 144 |
| | cm$^2$ | 6.452 | 0.155 |
| | m$^2$ | $6.452 \times 10^{-4}$ | 1550 |
| in$^3$ | ft$^3$ | $5.787 \times 10^{-4}$ | $1.728 \times 10^3$ |
| | cm$^3$ | 16.388 | $6.102 \times 10^{-2}$ |
| | m$^3$ | $1.639 \times 10^{-5}$ | $6.102 \times 10^4$ |
| in ($H_2O$) | pascals (Pa) | $2.488 \times 10^2$ | $4.02 \times 10^{-3}$ |
| K | °C | K − 273 | °C + 273 |
| | °F | 1.8 K − 460 | (°F + 460) × 5/9 |
| | °R (Rankine) | 1.8 K | °R × 5/9 |
| kg | lb (weight) | 2.2046 | 0.4536 |
| | grams (g) | $10^3$ | $10^{-3}$ |
| kg/m$^3$ | lb/ft$^3$ (weight) | $6.243 \times 10^{-2}$ | 16.02 |
| lb (weight) | kg | 0.4536 | 2.2046 |
| lb/ft$^2$ (weight) | lb/in$^2$ | $6.945 \times 10^{-3}$ | 144 |
| | kg/m$^2$ | 4.882 | 0.2048 |
| lb/in$^2$ (psi) | Pa | $6.895 \times 10^{-3}$ | $1.45 \times 10^{-4}$ |
| m | in | 39.37 | 0.0254 |
| | ft | 3.281 | 0.3048 |
| | yd | 1.0936 | 0.9144 |
| | mm | $10^3$ | $10^{-3}$ |
| | cm | $10^2$ | $10^{-2}$ |
| m$^2$ | in$^2$ | 1550 | $6.452 \times 10^{-4}$ |
| | ft$^2$ | 10.76 | $9.29 \times 10^{-2}$ |
| m$^3$ | ft$^3$ | 35.31 | $2.832 \times 10^{-2}$ |
| mil | in | $10^{-3}$ | $10^3$ |
| miles | ft | 5280 | $1.894 \times 10^{-4}$ |
| | km | 1.6093 | 0.6214 |
| mph (mi/h) | ft/min | 88 | $1.136 \times 10^{-2}$ |
| | km/h | 1.6093 | 0.6214 |
| oz | kg | $2.835 \times 10^{-2}$ | 35.27 |
| W | hp | $1.341 \times 10^{-3}$ | 745.7 |

*Round converted quantity to proper number of significant digits commensurate with the intended precision.

# Appendix C

# Use of Sound Power Level Data

Sound power level $L_W$ expresses the amount of sound energy that is radiated by a given source, regardless of the space into which the source is placed. The sound pressure level $L_P$ can be estimated if the absorption and volume of the room are known.

For example, a 30-hp electric motor is placed in a mechanical equipment room finished entirely in painted concrete. This bare reverberant cubical room is 10 by 10 by 10 ft. The sound power levels $L_W$ listed in the table below were obtained by the manufacturer from laboratory tests conducted according to the provisions of ANSI S1.35.

|  | 125 Hz | 250 Hz | 500 Hz | 1000 Hz | 2000 Hz | 4000 Hz |
|---|---|---|---|---|---|---|
| $L_W$ (dB re: $10^{-12}$ W)* for 30-hp electric motor at 3600 rpm | 88 | 92 | 93 | 93 | 92 | 86 |

To find the reverberant sound pressure levels $L_P$ from this motor in the mechanical room, first calculate the room absorption and reverberation time at octave-band center frequencies from 125 to 4000 Hz. Next, estimate the $L_P - L_W$ difference at 1000 ft³ from the graph on the following page. Finally, the reverberant $L_P$ equals $L_W$ plus the $L_P - L_W$ difference.

|  | 125 Hz | 250 Hz | 500 Hz | 1000 Hz | 2000 Hz | 4000 Hz |
|---|---|---|---|---|---|---|
| Room absorption (sabins) | 60 | 30 | 36 | 42 | 54 | 48 |
| Reverberation time (s) | 0.8 | 1.7 | 1.4 | 1.2 | 0.9 | 1.0 |
| $L_W$ (dB re: $10^{-12}$ W)* | 88 | 92 | 93 | 93 | 92 | 86 |
| $L_P - L_W$ | −1 | 2 | 1 | 0 | −1 | 0 |
| Reverberant $L_P$ (dB) | 87 | 94 | 94 | 93 | 91 | 86 |

Find the reduced sound level if the walls and ceiling are treated with 2-in-thick sound-absorbing materials. First, find the new room absorption and reverberation time at 125 to 4000 Hz.

| Room surface: | | | | | | |
|---|---|---|---|---|---|---|
| Floor | 10 | 5 | 6 | 7 | 9 | 8 |
| Walls and ceiling | 190 | 300 | 390 | 400 | 390 | 350 |
| Room absorption (sabins) | 200 | 305 | 396 | 407 | 399 | 358 |
| Reverberation time (s) | 0.25 | 0.16 | 0.13 | 0.12 | 0.13 | 0.14 |
| $L_W$ (dB re: $10^{-12}$ W)* | 88 | 92 | 93 | 93 | 92 | 86 |
| $L_P - L_W$ | −6 | −8 | −9 | −9 | −9 | −9 |
| Reverberant $L_P$ (dB) | 82 | 84 | 84 | 84 | 83 | 77 |

\* It is extremely important to know the reference power because manufacturers, until recent years, presented data with $10^{-13}$ W as the reference value. Note that a 10 dB error easily could result if the manufacturer's reference were unknown.

## REVERBERANT $L_P - L_W$ GRAPH

A 1000-ft³ room has a reverberation time $T$ of 1.4 s at 500 Hz. To find the $L_P$ of a 30-hp electric motor with a $L_W$ of 93 dB at 500 Hz, enter graph at 1000 ft³ and read opposite $T = 1.4$ s curve to 1 dB. Therefore, $L_P - L_W = 1$ dB and $L_P = 93 + 1 = 94$ dB at 500 Hz.

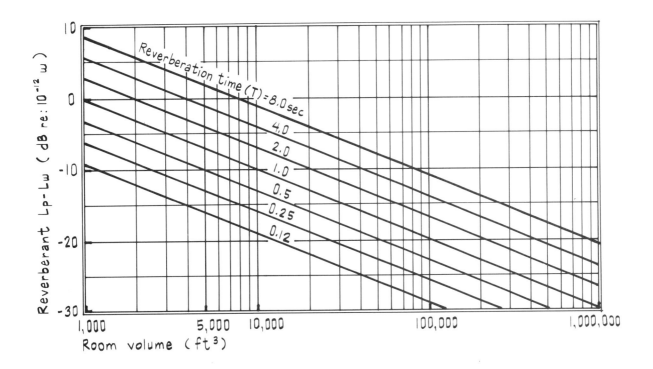

# Appendix D

# Word Lists for Articulation Testing

The *R lists* were developed to evaluate electronic communication systems by Professors J. P. Egan and S. S. Stevens during the 1940s at the Psycho-Acoustic Laboratory, Harvard University. Lists of sentences, words, or syllables can be used to measure the intelligibility of speech by determining the percentage correctly recognized by a listener (called an *articulation test*). For example, the lists can be used by talkers and normal-hearing listeners to evaluate the effect of ambient noise, long-delayed reflections and echoes, and other room acoustics faults on listening conditions in churches, small auditoriums, classrooms, and the like. The talker should stand at the lectern or podium and read from the lists in a normal speaking voice. Because the test is designed to assess hearing, not memory, the lists should be read in altered sequence when several locations are to be evaluated in the same room. In addition, test results should be scored for correct hearing, not spelling. Convert score of percent understood to an articulation index (AI) by using the graph on page 400. For very good speech listening conditions in rooms, the AI should be greater than 0.7.

## Egan's R List 1

| | | | | |
|---|---|---|---|---|
| 1. aisle | 21. dame | 41. jack | 61. rack | 81. still |
| 2. barb | 22. done | 42. jam | 62. ram | 82. tale |
| 3. barge | 23. dub | 43. law | 63. ring | 83. tame |
| 4. bark | 24. feed | 44. lawn | 64. rip | 84. toil |
| 5. baste | 25. feet | 45. lisle | 65. rub | 85. ton |
| 6. bead | 26. file | 46. live | 66. run | 86. trill |
| 7. beet | 27. five | 47. loon | 67. sale | 87. tub |
| 8. beige | 28. foil | 48. loop | 68. same | 88. vouch |
| 9. boil | 29. fume | 49. mess | 69. shod | 89. vow |
| 10. choke | 30. fuse | 50. met | 70. shop | 90. whack |
| 11. chore | 31. get | 51. neat | 71. should | 91. wham |
| 12. cod | 32. good | 52. need | 72. shrill | 92. woe |
| 13. coil | 33. guess | 53. oil | 73. sing | 93. woke |
| 14. coon | 34. hews | 54. ouch | 74. sip | 94. would |
| 15. coop | 35. hive | 55. paw | 75. skill | 95. yaw |
| 16. cop | 36. hod | 56. pawn | 76. soil | 96. yawn |
| 17. couch | 37. hood | 57. pews | 77. soon | 97. yes |
| 18. could | 38. hop | 58. poke | 78. soot | 98. yet |
| 19. cow | 39. how | 59. pour | 79. soup | 99. zing |
| 20. dale | 40. huge | 60. pure | 80. spill | 100. zip |

**Egan's R List 2**

| | | | | |
|---|---|---|---|---|
| 1. ball | 21. dial | 41. hen | 61. peep | 81. tap |
| 2. bar | 22. dig | 42. huff | 62. peeve | 82. them |
| 3. bob | 23. dine | 43. hush | 63. phase | 83. then |
| 4. bong | 24. ditch | 44. jar | 64. pull | 84. title |
| 5. book | 25. doubt | 45. job | 65. put | 85. tine |
| 6. boot | 26. dowel | 46. joy | 66. raid | 86. tong |
| 7. booth | 27. drain | 47. joys | 67. raze | 87. toot |
| 8. bout | 28. em | 48. kirk | 68. rich | 88. tooth |
| 9. bowel | 29. en | 49. leap | 69. rig | 89. tout |
| 10. boy | 30. fade | 50. leave | 70. ream | 90. towel |
| 11. boys | 31. far | 51. made | 71. roe | 91. toy |
| 12. brain | 32. foam | 52. maize | 72. root | 92. toys |
| 13. bull | 33. fob | 53. mew | 73. rough | 93. weave |
| 14. crane | 34. foe | 54. muff | 74. rush | 94. weep |
| 15. cue | 35. foot | 55. mush | 75. ruth | 95. while |
| 16. curb | 36. full | 56. mute | 76. sack | 96. whine |
| 17. curd | 37. gall | 57. new | 77. sap | 97. wig |
| 18. curse | 38. gong | 58. newt | 78. slain | 98. witch |
| 19. curt | 39. grain | 59. oh | 79. tack | 99. yak |
| 20. cute | 40. hem | 60. ohm | 80. tall | 100. yap |

**Reference**

L. L. Beranek, *Acoustic Measurements,* Wiley, New York, 1949, p. 792.

# Appendix E

# Numerical Values for NC and RC Curves

For convenience when performing computations with noise criteria or room criteria data, the following tables list sound pressure levels in dB at 125 to 4000 Hz for both NC and RC curves from Chap. 4.

## NC Table

| Curve | Sound Pressure Level (dB) | | | | | |
|---|---|---|---|---|---|---|
| | 125 Hz | 250 Hz | 500 Hz | 1000 Hz | 2000 Hz | 4000 Hz |
| NC-65 | 75 | 71 | 68 | 66 | 64 | 63 |
| NC-60 | 71 | 67 | 63 | 61 | 59 | 58 |
| NC-55 | 67 | 62 | 58 | 56 | 54 | 53 |
| NC-50 | 64 | 58 | 54 | 51 | 49 | 48 |
| NC-45 | 60 | 54 | 49 | 46 | 44 | 43 |
| NC-40 | 56 | 50 | 45 | 41 | 39 | 38 |
| NC-35 | 52 | 45 | 40 | 36 | 34 | 33 |
| NC-30 | 48 | 41 | 35 | 31 | 29 | 28 |
| NC-25 | 44 | 37 | 31 | 27 | 24 | 22 |
| NC-20 | 40 | 33 | 26 | 22 | 19 | 17 |
| NC-15 | 36 | 29 | 22 | 17 | 14 | 12 |
| Threshold* | 22 | 13 | 8 | 5 | 3 | .. |

## RC Table

| Curve | Sound Pressure Level (dB) | | | | | |
|---|---|---|---|---|---|---|
| | 125 Hz | 250 Hz | 500 Hz | 1000 Hz | 2000 Hz | 4000 Hz |
| RC-50 | 65 | 60 | 55 | 50 | 45 | 40 |
| RC-45 | 60 | 55 | 50 | 45 | 40 | 35 |
| RC-40 | 55 | 50 | 45 | 40 | 35 | 30 |
| RC-35 | 50 | 45 | 40 | 35 | 30 | 25 |
| RC-30 | 45 | 40 | 35 | 30 | 25 | 20 |
| RC-25 | 40 | 35 | 30 | 25 | 20 | 15 |
| Threshold* | 22 | 13 | 8 | 5 | 3 | .. |

*Approximate threshold of hearing for continuous noise by listeners with normal hearing.

# Indexes

Yaniv, S. L., 234
Yee, R., 162
Yerges, J. F., 352
Yerges, L. F., 252, 352, 387
Young, R. W., 331

## SUBJECT INDEX*

*For easy reference, *case studies, checklists, example problems, tables,* and *worksheets* are listed on pages 410 and 411.